HANDBOOK ON RISK AND INEQUALITY

ELGAR HANDBOOKS IN INEQUALITY

Original and comprehensive, this *Handbook* series offers a unique overview of the state-of-the-art of research in inequality. Each *Handbook* will consist of original contributions by preeminent authors, selected by an esteemed editor internationally recognised as a leading scholar within the field. The *Handbooks* provide new perspectives on established and more recent research areas, expand current debates, and signpost how research may advance in the future. Equally useful as reference tools or high-level introductions to specific topics, issues and methods, these *Handbooks* make an invaluable contribution to the field.

Titles in the series include:

Handbook on Digital Inequality
Edited by Eszter Hargittai

Handbook on Risk and Inequality
Edited by Dean Curran

Handbook on Risk and Inequality

Edited by

Dean Curran

Associate Professor of Sociology, Department of Sociology, University of Calgary, Canada

ELGAR HANDBOOKS ON INEQUALITY

 Edward **Elgar**
PUBLISHING

Cheltenham, UK • Northampton, MA, USA

Published by
Edward Elgar Publishing Limited
The Lypiatts
15 Lansdown Road
Cheltenham
Glos GL50 2JA
UK

Edward Elgar Publishing, Inc.
William Pratt House
9 Dewey Court
Northampton
Massachusetts 01060
USA

Paperback edition 2024

A catalogue record for this book
is available from the British Library

Library of Congress Control Number: 2022941197

This book is available electronically in the **Elgar**online
Sociology, Social Policy and Education subject collection
http://dx.doi.org/10.4337/9781788972260

MIX
Paper | Supporting
responsible forestry
FSC
www.fsc.org   FSC® C013604

ISBN 978 1 78897 225 3 (cased)
ISBN 978 1 78897 226 0 (eBook)
ISBN 978 1 0353 4443 7 (paperback)

Printed and bound by CPI Group (UK) Ltd, Croydon, CR0 4YY

Contents

Figures

Tables

Contributors

Steven Bittle is an Associate Professor of Criminology at the University of Ottawa. His research and teaching interests include crimes of the powerful, corporate crime and the sociology of law. He is the co-editor (with L. Snider, S. Tombs and D. Whyte) of *Revisiting Crimes of the Powerful: Marxism, Crime and Deviance* (Routledge 2018). His recent publications appear in *The Journal of White-Collar and Corporate Crime*, *The Howard Journal of Crime and Justice*, *Capital and Class*, *Critical Criminology*, *Labour/Le Travail*, *Social Justice* and *Studies in Political Economy* (forthcoming). His current research (with J. Frauley, L. Snider and J. Quaid), funded by the Social Sciences and Humanities Research Council of Canada, examines corporate corruption in Canada.

Elizabeth Cameron plans to pursue graduate studies in sociology after completing a Bachelor of Arts in Sociology at the University of Calgary, where she works as a research assistant. Her interests are focused on the intersection of the socially located body, digital society and visual sociology. She is a writer, photographer and video creator who previously worked as a multimedia journalist covering health topics in Alberta, Canada.

David Champagne is a Vanier Scholar and PhD candidate in Sociology at the University of British Columbia. His doctoral research investigates the equity of sustainability policies in North America. His research questions the historical roots of contemporary urban inequality and the dynamics constituting community and place in the face of climate hazards. In so doing, he explores how climate change transforms the political economy of the city.

Dean Curran is an Associate Professor of Sociology at the University of Calgary. He has previous degrees in economics and the philosophy of the social sciences, and a PhD in sociology. His research areas include risk, economic sociology, social theory and inequalities. He has publications in the *British Journal of Sociology*, *Economy and Society*, *Antipode*, *Theory, Culture, and Society*, *Urban Studies*, *European Journal of Social Theory* and a book with Palgrave Macmillan, *Risk, Power and Inequality in the 21st Century* (2016).

Thibault Darcillon is an Associate Professor of Economics at the University of Paris 8 (LED), France. His main research focuses on political economy, financial macroeconomics and labor economics in the OECD countries. His main research interests lie in understanding the determinants and consequences of financial mutations adopting a political economy approach. More recent research tends to focus on the role of growing inequality on political cleavages as well as on the determinants of labor restructuring at the firm level.

Md Saidul Islam (PhD, York, Canada) is Associate Professor of Sociology at Nanyang Technological University, Singapore. He's a former Visiting Scholar of MIT, and the past Chair of the Sociology of Development Cluster, Canadian Sociological Association. On his areas—international development and environmental sociology focusing on the global agro-food system—he has published seven books and over four dozen articles and book chapters. He also taught at York University in Canada, the College of William and Mary in the United States, and Nankai University in China.

Katarina Giritli Nygren is a professor in sociology whose research addresses different forms of governance relationships with a focus on processes of inclusion and exclusion in terms of gender, class and ethnicity in different contexts. In her most recent research, she argues for feminist and intersectional analyses of the shifting governmentalities of neoliberal welfare states.

Susanna Öhman is a professor in sociology and director of the Risk and Crisis Research Centre at Mid Sweden University. She conducts research on risk and people's perceptions and experiences of risk in society. In her research, she is interested in risk and stratification in terms of gender, sexuality, class and ethnicity in different contexts.

Anna Olofsson is a professor in sociology and has been studying risk for many years, initially risk perception and communication, and later on from a critical, gender and intersectional perceptive. Her most recent work includes empirical studies of Covid-19 in the Swedish public debate, as well as theoretical work such as the monography *A Framework for Intersectional Risk Theory in an Ambivalent World* written with Katarina Giritli Nygren and Susanna Öhman, and published by Palgrave in 2020.

David N. Pellow is the Dehlsen Chair and Professor of Environmental Studies and Director of the Global Environmental Justice Project at the University of California, Santa Barbara. His teaching, research and activism focus on environmental justice in the US and globally. His books include *What is Critical Environmental Justice?* and *Garbage Wars: The Struggle for Environmental Justice in Chicago*. He has served on the Board of Directors of Greenpeace USA and International Rivers.

Klaus Rasborg, PhD and MA, is Associate Professor of Social Dynamics and Change at the Department of Social Sciences and Business, Roskilde University. His key research interests include classical and modern sociology, social differentiation, inequality, individualisation, reflexive modernity, world risk society and cosmopolitanism. He has published on these topics in journals such as *Thesis Eleven, Theory, Culture & Society* and *Irish Journal of Sociology*. His most recent book is *Ulrich Beck: Theorising World Risk Society and Cosmopolitanism* (Palgrave Macmillan, 2021). He is the Danish translator of Ulrich Beck's most influential work, *Risikogesellschaft* (1986), which was published in Danish in 1997. He spent time in 1984/85 at the Department of Philosophy, Johann Wolfgang Goethe University, Frankfurt am Main and followed lectures by, among others, Jürgen Habermas and Axel Honneth.

Philipp Rehm (PhD, Duke University) is Associate Professor of Political Science at Ohio State University. His work is located at the intersection of political economy and political behavior with a particular interest in the politics of risk. He recently published his second book on the topic, *Big Data and the Welfare State: How the Information Revolution Threatens Social Solidarity* (with Torben Iversen), at Cambridge University Press.

Aleena Shafique explores the intersection of gender, inequality and development. She has an undergraduate degree in Anthropology and Sociology from the Lahore University of Management Sciences (LUMS), and is currently pursuing an Erasmus Mundus Master's in Education Policy for Global Development (GLOBED). Her work focuses on the lived experiences of marginalised groups and the strategies they employ to cope with structural inequalities.

Laureen Snider is an Emeritus Professor of Sociology at Queen's University, Kingston, Ontario. She has written extensively on corporate crime, crimes of the powerful, surveillance/ technology, punishment and the criminalization of women. Recent publications include *Revisiting Crimes of the Powerful: Marxism, Crime and Deviance* (ed., with S. Bittle, S. Tombs and D. Whyte, 2018); "Beyond Trump: Neoliberal Capitalism and the Abolition of Corporate Crime", *Journal of White Collar and Corporate Crime* (2020); "How Employers Steal from Employees: The Untold Story" (with Steve Bittle), *Social Justice: A Journal of Crime, Conflict, and World Order* (2019); and "Enabling Exploitation: Law in the Gig Economy", *Critical Criminology* (2018). She is presently doing research on tax evasion as part of an SSHRC-funded study on *Corruption in Canada* with S. Bittle, (the PI), Jon Frauley and Jennifer Quaid.

David Tyfield is Professor in Sustainable Transitions and Political Economy at the Lancaster Environment Centre (LEC), Lancaster University and Associate Director of Lancaster's Centre for Mobilities Research (CeMoRe). His research focuses on sustainable transition, especially urban e-mobility and associated infrastructures, focusing on "ecological civilisation" in China, which he has been studying since 2007. His latest book is *Liberalism 2.0 and the Rise of China: Global Crisis, Innovation and Urban Mobility* (Routledge, 2018) and he is a co-editor of *Mobilities* journal.

Philip Walsh is Associate Professor of Sociology at York University in Toronto. His research has focused mostly on the theoretical foundations of the social sciences. His books include *Skepticism, Modernity and Critical Theory* (Palgrave, 2008), *Arendt Contra Sociology* (Routledge, 2015) and, edited with Peter Baehr, *The Anthem Companion to Hannah Arendt* (Anthem, 2017). His current research explores the significance of critical realism in the fields of the sociology of knowledge and of emotions.

Patrick G. Watson is an assistant professor of Criminology at Wilfrid Laurier University. He studies the use of evidence in government meetings, military inquiries and courts of law, from an ethnomethodological perspective. He has recently published a number of book chapters and articles on police, courts, and how video evidence is used in criminal trials for police officers accused of on-duty shootings. He is the principal investigator of two Social Science and Humanities Research Council of Canada grants examining police oversight practice.

Dr Joy Y. Zhang is a British sociologist with a first degree in medicine. She is the Founding Director of the Centre of Global Science and Epistemic Justice at the University of Kent. Her work contributes to sociological theories of risk, cosmopolitanism, decolonisation and subaltern politics through empirical studies on emerging life sciences and environmental movements. She is the author of *The Cosmopolitanization of Science*, *Green Politics in China* and *The Elephant and the Dragon in Contemporary Life Sciences*.

Ghazal Mir Zulfiqar is Associate Professor at the Lahore University of Management Sciences (LUMS). Her research focuses on the political economy of transnational advocacy networks, financialisation, and the informal economy from a gender and class perspective. She has a PhD in Public Policy from the University of Massachusetts, Boston and an MSc in Development Finance from the School of Oriental and African Studies (SOAS), London. She is Associate Editor of the journals *Organization* and *Gender, Work & Organization*, and is on the editorial board of *Human Relations*.

Preface

This book project has been a long time coming. COVID-19 created a series of challenges, with several authors needing to withdraw in the last two years. Nevertheless, as the Handbook comes to fruition its preparation has proved a valuable task. Ultimately, it is filled with different, fresh and exciting approaches to a relatively novel area of study: risk and inequality. Rather than comprising an overview, or an idiosyncratic map of the existing state of the literature, this book is in many ways a statement of potential paths of research, as much as a description of the literature. I would like to thank all the authors for their hard work on their contributions.

I would also like to thank my family for their continued support and good cheer throughout the process of completing this Handbook. As always, it is greatly appreciated.

1. Introduction to the *Handbook on Risk and Inequality*

Dean Curran

Inequality is one of the dominant challenges of the current age. With the increasing decline of the Keynesian National Welfare State (Jessop 2002) beginning in the 1970s, economies around the world saw incomes at the top skyrocketing alongside stagnating incomes for those in the bottom half of the income distribution. By the early 2000s these events had begun to gain increasing notice. Inequality studies, initially in economics, began to chart these massive inequalities (Piketty and Saez 2003; Atkinson, Piketty, and Saez 2011; Saez 2012; Piketty 2014).[1] With the financial crisis further demonstrating the gap in fates between the top 1% and the 99% (Saez 2012; Volscho and Kell 2012), the political and academic salience of inequalities have continued to grow. Likewise, studies of other forms of inequality, including racial and gender, have increased in prominence in academic treatments of society (Collins and Bilge 2016). In response to the extension of global right-wing populism and nativism into the United States and the election of Trump in 2016, analyses of other intersectional inequalities beyond class have grown rapidly (Roth 2018). The emergence of COVID-19 and the inequalities in deaths from the pandemic have similarly led to further focus and analysis on the fundamental importance of inequalities to lives and to deaths (Ahmed et al. 2020; Abedi et al. 2021).

Furthermore, as inequalities and the focus on them have been growing since the late 1970s and early 1980s, we have seen a corresponding 'risk turn'. While hazards and harms have always been a factor in human life and the concept of risk has been available since the late Middle Ages (Giddens 1990), we have seen a major shift in the prominence of risk in societies across the world in the last four decades.

For some scholars, the primary shift in the role of risk is in terms of culture and orientation to risks – we have become more oriented to risks and more likely to fear our own societies and its products (Douglas and Wildavsky 1982; Furedi 1997). Yet, alongside this acknowledgement that our politics and society is more oriented to risk, there are an increasing number of analyses that highlight how we are either facing greater risks or are at least, as a society, generating greater risks than we were before (Giddens 1990; Beck 1992 [1986]). From the catastrophic environmental effects of DDT (Carson 2002 [1962]) to air pollution and pesticides more generally (Beck 1992 [1986]) to the effects of Chernobyl across much of Europe (Beck 1987) to 9/11 (Beck 2002) to the financial crisis of 2008 (Engelen et al. 2011) to ceaseless cyber-insecurity (Schneier 2018) and climate change, an increasing number of the challenges we face are socially generated risks. With the emergence of COVID-19 and a global pandemic and quarantine, the sense that we live within a 'risk society' is much greater than it was even when Beck originally developed his theory of risk society in the 1980s, alongside the foreshadowing of Chernobyl.

Despite the centrality of both inequalities and risks to contemporary societies and to academic understandings of these societies, work on the intersection of risks and inequalities tend to still be quite siloed. Undoubtedly, there have been important studies of inequalities in specific risks, especially in the areas of health (Wilkinson and Pickett 2010) and environmental risks (Bullard 1990; Walker 2012). Nevertheless, there has been much less research that has moved beyond these siloes to look across different domains of risk to see what kind of systemic effect the growth of socially produced risks is having across society. While there has been some work that has sought to address this lacuna, this handbook is motivated by an attempt to better address these limitations and to articulate novel approaches to the study of risk and inequality. Before outlining many of the key points that the contributors have made, this introduction attempts to identify some of the theoretical and empirical issues related to the study of risk and inequality and some possible paths forward in meeting these challenges.

1.   THEORIZING RISK AND INEQUALITY

As mentioned above, there have been many important studies that looked at the distributional outcomes of several negative factors in life, including environmental damage (Redefining Progress 2004; Ibarrán and Ruth 2009) and health problems and higher mortality rates (Wilkinson and Pickett 2010; Case and Deaton 2020). Nevertheless, there has been much less research that more generally examines how increasing social production of risk is impacting inequalities across different aspects of society. One of the reasons for this lacuna is the academic division of labour: while there are huge communities of scholars looking at health or environmental risk or crime, there is a much smaller group of scholars who are looking at risks more generally, or across different domains. As in other aspects of life, siloes of knowledge can often be a challenge to bringing together mutually relevant pieces of information, which are held by different groups (Tett 2009, 2015). Nevertheless, this is true of any interdisciplinary research and there are many examples of excellent interdisciplinary research currently being pursued, so while the siloed feature of much of academia is a factor, it cannot be the sole or primary reason. There are a couple of other factors that are also of relevance in thinking about these challenges. The first may be described as the risk society universalization thesis. The second is the incommensurability of risks problem. Both are discussed below.

1.1   The Risk Society Universalization Thesis

While the research paradigm of examining the relationship between risk and inequality is still emerging, the debate regarding what type of systematic relationship is manifested between risks and inequalities was first dealt with, at some length, over thirty years ago. In fact, Beck, in his *Risk Society* (1992 [1986]) devoted a significant amount of effort towards theorizing some of the key threads of the relationship between socially produced risks and inequalities. For Beck, we are entering a second modernity, in which the greater control over society and nature characteristic of 'first modernity' is being overrun by the growing side-effects from these processes that seek to exercise greater control. As Beck indicates, '*Along with the growing capacity of technical options grows the incalculability of their consequences*' (Beck 1992: 22, original italics). While this earlier form of modernity was dominated by the growing production of goods and conflicts around the distribution of goods, for Beck we are increasingly shifting from the dominance of the logic of the distribution of goods towards the dominance of the logic of the distribution of risks (Beck 1999: 8). From early in his writing on risk, Beck sought to highlight the fundamental importance of the relationship of risk, inequality, and power (Beck 1992 [1986], 1999). As Beck indicates, 'Risks like wealth are the object of distributions, and both constitute positions – risk positions and class positions respectively' (Beck 1992: 26). In this way, Beck, early in his work made the key conceptual innovation in identifying risks as objects of distribution that can have systematic impacts on life chances.

Nevertheless, despite having identified the core problem situation – that as we systematically increase the production of risks, the differential impacts of these processes need to be integrated into analyses of society and inequalities – Beck then proceeded to limit the potential of this framework to illuminate the evolving nexus between risk and inequality. He acted to do so by arguing that, while conventional logics of the distribution of goods were unequal, the logic of the distribution of risks tended towards greater and greater equality. As Beck stated, 'With the expansion of modernization risks – with the endangering of nature, health, nutrition, and so on – the social differences and limits are relativized' such that 'risks display an *equalizing* effect within their scope and among those affected by them' (Beck 1992 [1986]: 36, original italics). These considerations led Beck to conclude, in one of his best-known (and most critiqued) turns of phrase, '*poverty is hierarchic, smog is democratic*' (Beck 1992 [1986]: 36, original italics). As such, while providing a potential framework to explore the relations of risk and inequality, Beck denied its relevance as he argued that risks would undermine inequalities in the emerging risk society.

Despite the massive influence of Beck's theory of risk society more generally (cf. Giddens 1990, 1994; Lash 1994, 2000; Wynne 1996; Bauman 2000; Furlong and Cartmel 2007 [1997]; Outhwaite 2009), quite early on, Beck's claims about the relationship between risk and class inequalities were subject to a series of important critiques. Of all Beck's bold claims made in the *Risk Society* (1992), the dictum that 'smog is democratic' stands out as a claim that has received a significant amount of sustained critical attention. There are two key arguments that have been made against Beck's claim that the equalizing effect of the distribution of risks undermines the importance of class relations. The first is that, contrary to Beck's claims, the distribution of the kinds of risks that are characteristic of the risk society continues to be heavily shaped by class (Mythen 2005a, 2005b, 2007). The second focuses its rejection of Beck's claims on the fact that, *contra* Beck, the distribution of *goods* continues to be fundamentally important to life chances and, therefore, the distribution of risk cannot simply replace the importance of the distribution of *goods* (McMylor 1996; Goldthorpe 2002; Scott 2002; Mythen 2005b).

As some scholars argued, one of Beck's key claims – that the shift from the first modernity to the risk society is a shift from 'scarcity' to a risk society in which scarcity no longer plays a key role – is based upon the assumption that the 'worst imaginable accidents are the paradigmatic form of contemporary risk' (Mythen 2005b: 4.2). Responding in particular to Beck's bifurcation of earlier periods of unequal distribution of goods and the risk society's 'democratic' nature of risk distribution, Scott argued that by highlighting the key continuities in risk distribution: the 'wealthy were protected from scarcity and remain protected from risk[,] "protection" here being understood as "relative protection". Smog is just as hierarchical as poverty so long as some places are less smoggy than others' (Scott 2000: 35). Summarizing the important and continued connection between economic inequality and inequality of risks, Mythen declared that 'risks invariably track the tramlines of poverty and disadvantage' (Mythen 2005a: 141).

Additionally, there have been important critiques regarding Beck's rejection of the continued importance of the distribution of goods in shaping life chances. John Scott provided substantial evidence to show how 'class situations' continue to exercise a powerful causal effect on life chances (Scott 2002: 27–8). Scott argued that one's class situation continues to be a key 'determinant of the resources available for attaining other life chances' (Scott 2002: 28). There continue to be important differentials in health, education, and possession of basic commodities based on class, with those in higher classes exhibiting significantly better health and significantly greater education levels (Reid 1998 in Scott 2002: 28).

Despite the importance of much of this research, one of the outcomes of the critiques of Beck's claims regarding class and risk was that, because Beck got his specific claims about risk and inequality wrong, there is not much that the risk society theory can offer to better understand contemporary inequalities (Curran 2013a, 2018). Nevertheless, as discussed below, there have been some recent attempts to rethink the theory of risk society to enable it to illuminate rather than obscure the intensification of class inequalities via risk processes.

1.2   Problems of Incommensurability

A second primary challenge that the study of risk and inequality has faced may be described as the 'incommensurability problem'. On the one hand, the study of the distribution of goods, in particular, the distribution of income and wealth, has the advantage of an already provided set of *technologies of commensurability*. These technologies of commensurability include the ability to measure income and wealth in money and the corresponding existence of currency markets and financial markets that commensurate the value of different monies and assets into a single dimension. This makes it much more straightforward to compare many types of advantages and the ability to acquire these advantages on markets between individuals and groups within and between countries.

Risks on the other hand, do not exhibit similar types of commensurability. Comparing across the risks of crime, climate change, and financial precarity is much more difficult. Even finding an adequate index to compare risks *within* these dimensions is very difficult even in ordinal, let alone cardinal terms. Summing up across these dimensions to provide any kind of picture of overall risk burden, much less changes in risk burdens over time presents itself as a very difficult task. This problem is even further intensified by the massive elasticity of the term 'risk' itself. Almost anything and everything can embody risks in some way, so capturing the distribution of risks in a way that is not subject to the criticism of arbitrary selection criteria is particularly fraught. As such, research into the configurations of contemporary risk and inequality faces a series of significant theoretical and methodological challenges.

1.3   One Proposed Approach: Risk-Class Analysis

One attempt to address both the theoretical and the methodological challenges of studying key relations between risk and inequality is that of risk-class analysis. Emerging from a debate with Ulrich Beck regarding the claim that risk society processes are actually intensifying, rather than undermining or reproducing, class inequalities, Beck coined 'risk-class' as a new type of risk and inequality analysis (Curran 2013a, 2013b; Beck 2013).[2] While the concept of 'risk-class' was initially used only to describe the unequal burden of risks, the concept was quickly expanded to include both the inequalities associated with both the unequal benefits from the production of risk *and* the unequal distribution of damages from these risks (Curran 2015).[3]

Through focusing specifically on socially produced risks and the inequalities that emerge from both the production and distribution of risks, this approach has sought to build on Beck's analysis of how the systematic production of risks is changing contemporary political economy, while also seeking to bring a more empirically oriented approach to charting the relation between class position and risk position than Beck had done. While the incommensurability challenge continues to loom, research tracking some of the key relations between risk and inequality has already been carried out in the areas of climate change, environmental risk and justice (Curran 2016, 2018, 2021; Tyfield 2018), the 2008 financial crisis (Curran 2015), low-carbon innovation (Curran and Tyfield 2020), and data-driven governance (Curran and Smart 2021). Nevertheless, this research is still in its infancy and is waiting for a more integrated analysis across different risks, even if some initial steps have been taken in this regard (Curran 2016). As such, this is an exciting time for this still-emerging field. It is in this space, where there is a massive amount of research that speaks to the inequalities of many different risks, but which does not necessarily theorize the specificities of risk and the formations of risk and inequality that are emerging, that this handbook resides.

2. OVERVIEW OF THE HANDBOOK

Given the incipient nature of the study of risk and inequality, this handbook includes a series of exciting contributions to the study of risk and inequality. Overall, the picture is of a vibrant area of potential study, in which a lot of directly relevant research has been completed, while also promising more innovative work in the future. This section provides a brief introduction to the collection, while highlighting some of the key contributions of the chapters in this collection.

2.1 Part I: Different Dimensions of Risk

In Part I, there are five chapters tackling many of the different types of risks that are characteristic of twenty-first-century societies and some of the key inequalities associated with them.

One of the key trends in terms of changes in the risk profiles of societies across the world since the 1980s has been the emergence of what may be called 'financialization'. The shift towards financial markets and banking as a source of income and wealth for individuals, profits for corporations, and economic growth for states has led to a massive sea change in the distribution of economic outcomes. Thibault Darcillon, in his chapter 'Finance, risk, and inequality', examines some of the key shifts in risk and inequality emerging from this process. He shows how, amongst OECD countries, increases in the financial sector, changes in corporate governance rules, and the diffusion of new financial values for households – all features associated with financialization – have developed alongside increases in both risk for households and inequality between households. Darcillon then proceeds to identify some of the possible routes through which financialization may have increased both risk and inequality. Firstly, he shows how the expansion of the financial sector has displayed a sharp increase in relative wages in finance, which in turn has helped increase overall inequality. Secondly, he reveals how financial development and the rise of stock options, amongst other changes, has affected firm behaviour in many ways, in terms of both risk and inequalities. Darcillon then proceeds to show how the relation between finance, risk, and inequality is fundamentally conditioned by politics. Peeling behind pictures of financialization as an autonomous process, he demonstrates how the distributive issues raised by financialization are fundamentally political choices. And likewise, the political decisions made in regard to financialization and the mediation of its consequences fundamentally affect the balance of power across social groups in society. Darcillon then proceeds to show higher income and risk is similarly associated with increased support for redistribution. As his chapter sets out in very clear ways, risk cannot be considered simply a technical process managed and determined by experts, but rather is fundamentally a political and economic phenomenon.

In 'Dimensions of risk and environmental inequality', David N. Pellow examines some of the key analytical and normative dimensions of existing configurations of environmental risk and inequalities. He proposes reframing environmental injustice as a practice akin to warfare, which states, corporations, and other institutions perpetrate against disadvantaged communities. Furthermore, he proposes reframing institutional racism as a form of institutional violence. For Pellow, this reframing may further aid in gaining widespread support for activism and policy changes to address these challenges. Likewise, he proceeds to build on this reframing to tie environmental injustice to anti-imperialism and even to anarchist accounts of social transformation. Specifically highlighting the potential of anarchist political ecology, he suggests this may be a path to addressing existing social and ecological crises outside of institutional mechanisms of problem solving. For Pellow, a core appeal of anarchist political ecology is how it seeks to challenge all forms of oppression and domination, including class, race, species, and human domination of nature. As such, he argues that the problems of environmental risk and of inequality need to be addressed, not as separate issues, but together in a path that does not employ the coercive power of the state, seeking rather to pursue transformative change without the state. In this way, Pellow seeks to develop a new 'generative way of framing' vulnerable communities, as well as raising important issues about the extent to which problems of risk and inequality need to be addressed together, rather than as two separate issues.

Philipp Rehm, in his chapter 'Risk and (welfare state) politics', raises important issues regarding how modern democracies have come to insure so many of the risks that individuals face. Quipping (from Paul Krugman) that modern democracies are akin to insurance companies with an army, Rehm examines how it is the case that, despite the many challenges facing the provision of insurance against many of the main risks of modern life, such a large number of democracies have done so. In particular, he shows how modern democracies have established mandatory social policy programs for each of the four types of risks citizens face (accident, unemployment, health, old age). He proceeds to raise the paradox that, while each social policy in each country came to fruition in a different way, there is a massive amount of commonality in terms of types of risks that states insure. Rehm then proceeds to propose a 'majority politics of risk' as a key mechanism for securing this relative commonality of outcomes. Thinking about the 'politics of risk', he raises important questions regarding trends that could militate against the continued risk pooling necessary for broad insurance programs, as further detailed information on individuals and their behaviour may help to undermine previous cases of information asymmetry between insurer and insured. Highlighting the progressively fine-grained info from GPS-trackers in cars to track in real time actual driving behaviour, Rehm highlights the possibility of how other insurance domains, including home, health, and life, are increasingly experiencing similar developments. As we see in his analysis of the politics of risk, emerging risk technologies have potential distributive impacts that can be fundamental to analyses of configurations of risk and inequality.

Klaus Rasborg, in his chapter 'Changing risks, individualisation and inequality in a recast welfare state', examines some of the key theoretical approaches to the relationship between contemporary risks, individualization, and inequalities. He first investigates Beck and Giddens' claim that the welfare state is increasingly under strain in contemporary societies as new types of risks cannot be effectively managed by traditional welfare policies. He then proceeds to outline the Foucauldian approaches of Ewald and Dean, which understand the risk technology of insurance as a key form of contemporary governmentality and the types of responsibilization that are developing with the increasing privatization of contemporary risks. Lastly, he investigates the types of approaches manifested by Bonoli, Taylor-Gooby, Standing, and Wacquant, where new social risks are linked more closely not to the 'risk society' as a movement within modernity, but rather to more specific changes in the welfare state and the labour market. In particular, Rasborg raises interesting questions regarding whether increasing individualization should be understood in the classless way that Beck and Giddens do, or rather as itself a further source of stratification, as Bonoli, Taylor-Gooby, Standing, and Wacquant do. Rasborg outlines how these new risks and the forms of individualization associated with these risks are not only intensifying existing inequalities but also creating new class formations in the precariatization of certain social groups. Likewise, he shows how, despite Beck's rejection of class, concepts such as 'risk-class' and 'emancipatory catastrophism' provide the potential to theorize key connections between risk, individualization, and inequalities. He then ties these conceptual innovations back to existing comparative welfare research in a way that suggests future potential pathways for theoretical and empirical research.

In the next chapter, 'Digital risk and inequality', Elizabeth Cameron and Dean Curran examine the different approaches to the relationship between digital risk and inequality. Surveying Bourdieusian, Marxist, and intersectionality, amongst other approaches, they identify a massive amount of research that speaks to inequalities associated with a variety of different types of digital risks. From the acquisition of digital technologies to successfully leveraging the ability to participate in the digital realm, to cyber-risks, the already least advantaged again and again suffer the burdens of these risks. Cameron and Curran then proceed to take a closer look as well at some of the primary beneficiaries of these inequalities. Specifically, they highlight how digital corporations and their major shareholders continue to extract massive value from the digital economy. Core to the chapter is that the basic framework of the digital economy tends to happen *to* users, with very little distribution of agency as to how this basic framework of the digital economy proceeds. The authors then also highlight the way in which this asymmetry in terms of control and design leads not only to inequalities in risks but also to a fundamental undermining of most users' ability to even be able to adequately assess the risks that they face. Given how much dynamism there has been in the academic field of the digital, they conclude by calling for more integrative research across different digital risks to better identify novel configurations of risk and inequality and the cumulative impacts they are having on different groups in society.

Each of these chapters tackles a different basic dimension of risk – from financial to environmental to social, to economic and digital risks. Engaging in both an overview of the existing research and in conceptual innovation, they speak to a variety of different questions regarding the growth of risk in several domains of entrenched inequalities, which have in turn further intensified inequalities. Furthermore, they also raise important normative issues regarding the justice of these changes and how society should understand the different projects that increase risk and inequality, as well as those projects that seek to address these nexuses of risk and inequality.

2.2   Part II: Theorizing Risks and Inequality

The second part of this handbook contains a series of chapters that take a closer look at different theoretical approaches that attempt to develop new approaches to capture the intersection of risk and inequality.

In the first chapter, 'Actor, structure and inequality: an intersectional perspective of risk', Katarina Giritli Nygren, Anna Olofsson, and Susanna Öhman build on their already groundbreaking research in the field of risk to discuss some of the key challenges facing an intersectional approach to risk. Through an intersectional frame they examine three key aspects of risk theorizing: the definition of risk; risk and power; and risk and inequality through three different theoretical approaches: a system-centred one, a process-centred one, and finally a group-centred one. Emphasizing the ambivalence of dichotomies such as structure and agency, they highlight how these different approaches lead to different framings of inequalities. In pursuing a relational approach to risk and inequality, they highlight how risk can be understood as a governing principle producing risk regimes, or alternatively in a performative way, or, again alternatively, in an embodied manner. Each of these three approaches in turn highlights different methods for understanding the nexus of risk and inequality through an intersectional framework. The chapter then proceeds to highlight the ambivalence associated with applying the historical framing of risk to other contexts (such as the global South) when this frame of risk originates from the global North. In this way Nygren, Olofsson, and Öhman highlight the ongoing dynamism of intersectional research in its attempts to tackle the structural and the lived experience of risk inequalities in the contemporary world.

In the next chapter, 'Risk and new realities: social ontology, expertise and individualization in the risk society', Philip Walsh seeks to address some of the metatheoretical issues relating to the theorization of risk and risk society and how these in turn are related to theorizations of inequality. He proceeds to investigate the implications of understanding the theory of risk society through a critical realist perspective. Walsh highlights how both the macro, emergent characteristics of risk and risk as an aspect of how people manage uncertainty in the world involve social constructionist elements. Yet, as he argues, these constructionist elements are still broadly consistent with a critical realist approach. Walsh then proceeds to identify the ways in which the risk society thesis has reshaped our understanding of inequalities related to contemporary ecological crisis, the breakdown of nation-state boundaries in the face of forced cosmopolitanization, the inequalities of expertise and their impacts, and the broad-ranging effects of individualization on relationships. While questioning Beck's use of 'risk' as a concept to unlock almost any social problem, Walsh highlights the ongoing fundamental importance of Beck's risk society for social science.

In the following chapter, 'Corporations, class and the normalization of risk', Laureen Snider and Steven Bittle address some key themes relating to the political economy of risk. They argue that 'risk' in contemporary society cannot be understood outside of the capitalist class relations that shape both the production and distribution of risks. They proceed to highlight limitations not only in Beck's original rejection of the relevance of class but even in his reformulated accounts that allow for greater influence of class, due to his account of class as being constituted by two opposing groups. Instead, they argue that we need to focus class analysis on the process of producing surplus labour. In this way, this approach focuses on the structure of pre-existing economic categories embodying class interests, rather than the specific individuals who may occupy these different categories. They then go on to highlight how risk regulation is itself a key site of the production of risk, where corporate elites are able to protect themselves from the consequences of producing these risks, while dumping risks on others. Building on Whyte's conception of 'state regimes of permission', they highlight how, even when regulation is put into place, it does not tend to undermine the capitalist class interests secured by risk production. Highlighting the fundamental limitations of corporate social responsibility (CSR) as a means of self-regulation, they emphasize how the cultural hegemony of the corporate structure continues to shape the terrain of power associated with systemic risk production by corporations. They then proceed to argue for the primacy of class and that increased focus on *class* risk, rather than *risk* class will enable a better understanding of the power imbricated with contemporary risk.

In the final chapter in Part II, 'Risk and trust: ethnomethodological orientations to risk theorizing', Patrick Watson aims to address some of the key relations between risk and trust through an ethnomethodological approach. One of the key aspects of risk in contemporary society is how it connects to questions of trust. Building on theorizations of these threads developed by Luhmann, Giddens, and Garfinkel, Watson hopes to tease out some of the key connections between understandings of risk and trust and to highlight, in previously underexplored ways, how ethnomethodological research may contribute to better understanding the connection of risk and trust. He then proceeds to employ discussions by Turowetz and Rawls to investigate some of the key connections between trust and inequality. He also addresses some of the key tensions that emerge when expertise is mistrusted, especially when this mistrust is manifested by already-marginalized populations. In this way, Watson highlights how the connection between risk and inequalities is generated not only at the macro, systematic level but also at micro-interactional levels.

As all of the chapters show, there are a series of important, novel ways to theorize the relationship between risks and inequalities. Moreover, they show how there are many potential vibrant debates in these fields including how to understand the intersectionality of risk; the relation of risk, realism, and constructionism; class, corporations, and risk; and risk and trust. Again, in developing new frames of analysis of risk and inequality, not only up for grabs is which theories to adopt, but also which phenomena to focus upon, as well as which tools to better illuminate these processes.

2.3   Part III: Special Topics and New Areas of Research

The third part of this handbook addresses a series of special topics, as well as new areas of potential study. Some of the topics in this part include precariatization in the global South, epistemic inequality and the global South, the new urban crisis, GMO food, and the risks of a retrotopian world. As varied as the topics are, they speak to a common set of concerns regarding how existing political, economic, and cultural processes in the contemporary world are, in a variety of different ways, generating a set of risk processes that are intensifying already entrenched inequalities.

In the first chapter, 'Inequality rising: the gendered impacts of precarious labor and financialization', Ghazal Zulfiqar and Aleena Shafique examine the impacts on gender inequality of the rise of a new, highly interdependent global economy. The chapter examines how this global economy, driven by neoliberal governments, transnational corporations, and global institutions (such as the IMF and World Bank) has shaped the development of global production networks. In this environment of heightened competition, the results have been uneven development and precarious labour. Focusing on changes in the global South in the labour market – specifically increasing informalization and feminization – and the rising formalization of credit, Zulfiqar and Shafique highlight how these two new features feed each other, thus further intensifying the precarity that women in the global South experience. Zulfiqar and Shafique proceed to emphasize the productivity of risk as the pursuit of 'bottom billion capitalism' generates a new kind of poverty capital, while also intensifying risk for others. The authors then go on to question the World Bank's 'smart economic agenda', which lauds the redirecting of work and credit away from poor men towards poor women, as a means of securing gender equality and greater growth. However, as they show, dumping onto women to an even greater level, the burden of social reproduction threatens to yield greater poverty, inequality, and risk for women and their households. In this way, Zulfiqar and Shafique extend the theoretical analysis of risk and inequality towards the global South and towards global development in a way that suggests this as an important area of future potential research.

In the following chapter, 'Beyond the spirit of the new urban crisis: risk-class and resonance', David Tyfield tackles some important issues relating to how to understand the emerging urban crisis by utilizing the dual concepts of risk-class and resonance. Risk-class, derived from debates revolving around risk society, and resonance, deriving from Hartmut Rosa's recent work, together provide, according to Tyfield, the basis for tackling emerging forms of sociality and power associated with the emergence of a middle risk-class in the 'developing world'. Seeking to develop frames that can speak to issues of simplicity and complexity, and alienation and fear, Tyfield highlights how existing theoretical frames are found wanting in addressing the rapidity and unpredictability of existing change. Critiquing reproductivist studies of inequality, Tyfield emphasizes that the contemporary complexity of risk defies such reductionist approaches. Highlighting not only the power of risk-class, Tyfield also seeks to bring in the conception of 'emancipation' as necessarily a fundamental aspect of contemporary risk studies, thus highlighting both the threat and the hope in existing social–material transformations.

In the following chapter, 'Science, food, and risk: ecological disasters and social inequality under the GMO regime', Md Saidul Islam examines the critical nexus between the 'establishment of science', food regimes, and social and ecological risk through the exemplar of the emergence of genetically modified organisms (GMOs). Focusing specifically on how science is responsible for an increasingly large share of the risks and disasters faced in the contemporary world, Islam highlights how existing food regimes are increasing risk and inequality. These industrial food regimes, relying on scientific technocracy, are undergirded and oriented to the interests of the already powerful, specifically large corporations. Discussing the Janus-faced nature of science as both producer of risk and as a necessary means of addressing the risks, Islam highlights in the case of food regimes, how science has both brought about significant increases in agricultural productivity, while also generating the possibility of disastrous outcomes. Likewise, the patent system, which was intended to encourage corporations to increase innovation in agro-biotechnology, has, on the other hand, turned into a means for corporations to further consolidate their market position, thus keeping out potential competitors. Islam then proceeds to argue that retailers, farmers, NGOs, and consumers all have a legitimate basis for critique here and Islam suggests the food justice movement as one potential pathway to pursue in remedying the production of risk and of inequality from these food regimes.

In the following chapter, 'Risk society and epistemic inequality: rising voices from the "Global South" in global governance', Joy Y. Zhang highlights a key form of inequality of significant importance in the risk society – the *epistemic inequality* within science. As Zhang emphasizes, while this inequality has a huge impact on lives around the world, it is often indiscernible in the public sphere. Zhang argues that, taking the idea of a 'multi-centred world' seriously requires questioning the hegemonic status of Western science. Zhang stresses that, in a world that celebrates diversity, we should question why some approaches to science are 'naturally' given more socio-political legitimacy than others. In particular, Zhang argues that we need to rethink what is a valid scientific question and what counts as scientific evidence. In that vein, building on Beck's discussion of the metamorphosis of world orders, Zhang argues that consciousness of risk can open up, rather than close down, our engagement with alternative reasonings. Looking specifically at debates revolving around alternative approaches to neuroscience, Zhang maintains that existing cosmopolitanization augurs a more equal future, with alternative scientific reasoning also gaining further legitimacy and credibility.

In the final chapter in this part, 'The political economy of climate vulnerability: searching for common ground in a retrotopian world', David Champagne addresses the issue of the impact of climate hazards and injustice. In particular, he proceeds to argue that a reified notion of climate vulnerability threatens to obscure key aspects of contemporary climate injustice. Building on a cultural political economy approach to climate vulnerability, Champagne highlights the idea of the loss of a shared planet as a frame of reference and, following Bauman, how this has led to the rise of 'retrotopia'. The nostalgia for the past, such as the Thirty Glorious Years, as manifested in retrotopian thinking, is then critiqued. Alternatively, Champagne proposes to analyse the heterogeneous meaning-making process ongoing in local communities. In this way, by engaging with conflict, solidarity, and resistance regarding climate vulnerability, Champagne argues that it is possible to free ourselves from a retrotopian worldview to address the ongoing challenge of intensifying climate vulnerability.

As these chapters show, there is a multitude of different potential novel areas of study at the intersection of risk and inequality. From gendered precarity in the global South, to risk-class and resonance, to existing food regimes, the epistemic inequality of the global South, and the risks of a retrotopian world, the new potential areas of study of risk and inequality are extremely wide-ranging and at the intersection of the cutting edge of a variety of different fields. In this way the 'productivity' of risk as a paradigm for understanding shifts in contemporary inequalities is well demonstrated in this collection.

3.   CONCLUSION

The collection of chapters shows that there are a multitude of important issues related to contemporary risk and inequality. From the environment to finance and the global economy, to the city, and to epistemic power, there are a variety of different topics that involve risk and inequality. Yet one of the questions that may be asked is, where do we go from here? While the study of inequalities is undergoing another renaissance, the question that emerges is, what is the role of the study of risks in this renaissance? As Beck has previously argued, there is a definite bias towards 'goods' in the study of inequalities (Beck 2013). Even other scholars, who have addressed the question of risks and inequalities, have often emphasized the level of continuity between inequalities in goods and that of risks (Mythen 2005a; Atkinson 2007a, 2007b, 2010). If the logic of the distribution of risks tracks the distribution of goods, it raises the question, how necessary is the separate study of risks?

There are a couple of different potential responses to this question. First, even if the distribution of risks does not overturn the existing hierarchies associated with the distribution of goods, this does not mean that it may not modify or complicate this distribution in some way. As has been previously argued, the intensification of the social distribution of risks may not only reproduce class inequalities; it may *intensify* them (Curran 2013a). In this way, the rise of an increasingly precarious world may further undermine the living standards of the already most disadvantaged – as such, even if it does not significantly change the ordinal hierarchy of living standards, it is still of immense relevance. This is particularly the case when those who are in poor and precarious situations may be near 'tipping points', where further burdening of them can cause cascading disadvantage in their life circumstances, which may not have occurred without this additional disadvantage. Consequently, insofar as we are aiming to identify the core contributors to individuals' and groups' living standards, or rather their capabilities to secure basic functioning, the distribution of risks that threaten the means of these functionings is fundamental.[4]

There is another key reason to consider the contribution of the distribution of risks to inequalities as a necessary area of study, in addition to the study of the distribution of goods, which is the normative importance of risks. This is that, in general, there is greater normative urgency to redress a harm done to someone, rather than a denial of a benefit of a comparable level. In that sense, insofar as the distribution of risks produces harm, it is of special moral urgency to chart these relations of harm, as a basis for better redressing them. Consequently, engaging in the 'space of risks', in addition to the 'space of goods' is necessary to adequately address the normative and analytical challenges of inequality in the twenty-first century.

Now admittedly, a need is not the same as the solution of a need. Nevertheless, as this collection shows, there is a variety of important eligible research questions with which to engage in these areas of research. Likewise, there is a variety of different innovative theoretical and empirical approaches to chart the different configurations of risk and inequality. While still early in its development, this collection suggests a rich future for this area of study insofar as critical social science continues to address the foundational social and material problems of the twenty-first century.

NOTES

1. As Savage (2000: 44) points out, interestingly enough it was economists who first identified the growth in economic inequality since the 1980s.
2. 'Dean Curran introduces the concept of "risk-class" to radicalize the class distribution of risk and charts who will be able to occupy areas less exposed to risk and who will have little choice but to occupy areas that are exposed to the brunt of the fact of the risk society' (Beck 2013: 63).
3. For further discussions, see Christophers (2015) and Dorn (2016).
4. For discussions of the importance of functionings, and the means to these functions, see Sen 1981, 1985, 1993, 1999; Nussbaum 1992.

REFERENCES

Abedi, V., Olulana, O., Avula, V., Chaudhary, D., Khan, A., Shahjouei, S., Li, J. and Zand, R. (2021) 'Racial, Economic, and Health Inequality and COVID-19 Infection in the United States', *Journal of Racial and Ethnic Health Disparities* 8:732–742.

Ahmed, F., Ahmed, N., Pissarides, C. and Stiglitz, J. E. (2020) 'Why Inequality Could Spread COVID-19', *Lancet* 5(5, E240). https://doi.org/10.1016/S2468-2667(20)30085-2

Atkinson, A. B., Piketty, T. and Saez, E. (2011) 'Top Incomes in the Long Run of History', *Journal of Economic Literature* 49:3–71.

Atkinson, W. (2007a) 'Beck, Individualization and the Death of Class: a Critique', *British Journal of Sociology* 58(3):349–366.

Atkinson, W. (2007b) 'Beyond False Oppositions: a Reply to Beck', *British Journal of Sociology* 58(4):707–715.

Atkinson, W. (2010) *Class, Individualization and Late Modernity: In Search of the Reflexive Worker*. Basingstoke: Palgrave Macmillan.

Bauman, Z. (2000) *Liquid Modernity*. Cambridge: Polity.

Beck, U. (1987) 'The Anthropological Shock: Chernobyl and the Contours of the Risk Society', *Berkeley Journal of Sociology* 32:153–165.

Beck, U. (1992[1986]) *Risk Society: Towards a New Modernity*. London: Sage.

Beck, U. (1999) *World Risk Society*. Cambridge: Polity.

Beck, U. (2002) 'The Terrorist Threat: World Risk Society Revisited', *Theory, Culture & Society* 19(4):39–55.

Beck, U. (2013) 'Why "Class" is Too Soft a Category to Capture the Explosiveness of Social Inequality at the Beginning of the 21st Century', *British Journal of Sociology* 64(1):63–74.

Bullard, R. (1990) *Dumping in Dixie: Race, Class, and Environmental Quality*. Boulder, CO: Westview Press.

Carson, R. (2002[1962]) *Silent Spring: 40th Anniversary Edition*. Boston, M.A.: Houghton Mifflin.

Case, A. and Deaton, A. (2020) *Deaths of Despair and the Future of Capitalism*. Princeton, N.J.: Princeton University Press.

Christophers, B. (2015) Value Models: Finance, Risk, and Political Economy. *Finance and Society* 1(2):1–22.

Collins, P. H. and Bilge, S. (2016) *Intersectionality*. Cambridge: Polity.

Curran, D. (2013a) 'Risk Society and the Distribution of Bads: Theorizing Class in the Risk Society', *British Journal of Sociology* 64(1):44–62.

Curran, D. (2013b) 'What is a Critical Theory of the Risk Society? A Reply to Beck', *British Journal of Sociology* 64(1):75–80.

Curran, D. (2015) 'Risk Illusion and Organized Irresponsibility in Contemporary Finance: Rethinking Class and Risk Society', *Economy and Society* 44(3):392–417.

Curran, D. (2016) *Risk, Power, and Inequality in the 21st Century*. Basingstoke: Palgrave Macmillan.

Curran, D. (2018) 'Environmental Justice meets Risk-Class: the Relational Distribution of Environmental Bads', *Antipode* 50(2):298–318.

Curran, D. (2021) 'Risk Mismatches and Inequalities: Oil and Gas and Elite Risk-Classes in the U.S. and Canada', *Sociologica* 15(2):57–74.

Curran, D. and Smart, A. (2021) 'Data-Driven Governance, Smart Urbanism and Risk-Class Inequalities: Security and Social Credit in China', *Urban Studies* 58(3):487–506.

Curran, D. and Tyfield, D. (2020) 'Low-Carbon Transition as Vehicle of New Inequalities? Risk-Class, the Chinese Middle Class and the Moral Economy of Misrecognition', *Theory, Culture, and Society* 37(2):131–156.

Dorn, N. (2016) 'Where There's Muck, There's Brass—and Class: Financial Market Regulation and Public Policy', in G. A. Antonopoulos (ed.), *Illegal Entrepreneurship, Organized Crime and Social Control* (311–330). AG Switzerland: Springer.

Douglas, M. and Wildavsky, A. (1982) *Risk and Culture: An Essay on the Selection of Technological and Environmental Dangers*. Berkeley, CA: University of California Press.

Engelen, E., Ertürk, I., Froud, J., Johal, S., Leaver, S., Moran, M., Nilsson, A. and Williams, K. (2011) *After the Great Complacence: Financial Crisis and the Politics of Reform*. Oxford: Oxford University Press.

Furedi, F. (1997) *Culture of Fear*. London: Cassell.

Furlong, A. and Cartmel, F. (2007[1997]) *Young People and Social Change: New Perspectives*, 2nd edition. Buckingham: Open University Press.

Giddens, A. (1990) *Consequences of Modernity*. Stanford, CA: Stanford University Press.

Giddens, A. (1994) 'Living in a Post-Traditional Society', in U. Beck, A. Giddens, and S. Lash (eds), *Reflexive Modernization: Politics, Tradition and Aesthetics in the Modern Social Order* (56–109). Cambridge: Polity.

Goldthorpe, J. H. (2002) 'Globalization and Social Class', *West European Politics* 25(3):1–28.

Ibarrán, M. E. and Ruth, M. (2009) 'Climate Change and Natural Disasters: Economic and Distributional Impacts', in M. Ruth and M. E. Ibarrán (eds), *Distributional Impacts of Climate Change and Disasters: Concepts and Cases* (46–66). Cheltenham, UK and Northampton, MA, USA: Edward Elgar Publishing.

Jessop, B. (2002) *Future of the Capitalist State*. Cambridge: Polity.

Lash, S. (1994) 'Reflexivity and Its Doubles: Structure, Aesthetics, Community', in U. Beck, A. Giddens, and S. Lash (eds), *Reflexive Modernization: Politics, Tradition and Aesthetics in the Modern Social Order* (110–73). Cambridge: Polity.

Lash, S. (2000) 'Risk Culture', in B. Adam, U. Beck, and J. van Loon (eds), *The Risk Society and Beyond: Critical Issues for Social Theory* (33–46). London: Sage.

McMylor, P. (1996) 'Goods and Bads', *Radical Philosophy* 77:52–53.

Mythen, G. (2005a) 'Employment, Individualization and Insecurity: Rethinking the Risk Society Perspective', *The Sociological Review* 8(1):129–149.

Mythen, G. (2005b) 'From Goods to Bads? Revisiting the Political Economy of Risk', *Sociological Research Online* 10(3), www.socresonline.org.uk/10/3/mythen.html (accessed 08.08.2011).

Mythen, G. (2007) 'Reappraising the Risk Society Thesis: Telescopic Sight or Myopic Vision?', *Current Sociology* 55(6):793–813.

Nussbaum, M. (1992) 'Human Functionings and Social Justice: In Defense of Aristotelian Essentialism', *Political Theory*, 20:202–246.

Outhwaite, W. (2009) 'Canon Formation in Late 20th-Century British Sociology', *Sociology* 43(6):1029–1045.

Piketty, T. (2014) *Capital in the Twenty-First Century*. Cambridge, M.A.: Harvard University Press.

Piketty, T. and Saez, E. (2003) 'Income Inequality in the United States, 1913–1998', *Quarterly Journal of Economics* 118(1):1–39.

Redefining Progress (2004) 'African Americans and Climate Change: an Unequal Burden', Oakland, CA: Redefining Progress, http://www.sustainlex.org/BlackCaucusfullCBCF_REPORT_F.pdf (accessed 11.12.2011).

Roth, S. (2018) 'Introduction: Contemporary Counter-Movements in the Age of Brexit and Trump', *Sociological Research Online* 23(2):496–506.

Saez, E. (2012) 'Striking it Richer: The Evolution of Top Incomes in the United States (Updated with 2009 and 2010 Estimates)', March 2, http://elsa.berkeley.edu/users/saez/saez-UStopincomes-2010 .pdf (accessed 16.04.2013).

Savage, M. (2000) *Class Analysis and Social Transformation*. Buckingham: Open University Press.

Schneier, B. (2018) *Click Here to Kill Everybody: Security and Survival in a Hyperconnected World*. New York, NY: Norton.

Scott, A. (2000) 'Risk Society or Angst Society? Two Views of Risk, Consciousness and Community', in B. Adam, U. Beck, and J. van Loon (eds), *The Risk Society and Beyond: Critical Issues for Social Theory* (33–46). London: Sage.

Scott, J. (2002) 'Social Class and Stratification in Late Modernity', *Acta Sociologica* 45(1) 23–35.

Sen, A. K. (1981) *Poverty and Famines: an Essay on Entitlement and Deprivation*. Oxford: Clarendon Press.

Sen, A. K. (1985) *Commodities and Capabilities*. Amsterdam: North-Holland.

Sen, A. K. (1993) 'Capability and Well-Being', in M. Nussbaum and A. Sen (eds), *The Quality of Life* (30–53). Oxford: Clarendon Press.

Sen, A. K. (1999) *Development as Freedom*. New York: Oxford University Press.

Tett, G. (2009) *Fool's Gold: How Unrestrained Greed Corrupted a Dream, Shattered Global Markets, and Unleashed a Catastrophe*. London: Abacus.

Tett, G. (2015) *The Silo Effect: The Peril of Expertise and the Promise of Breaking Down Barriers*. New York, NY: Simon & Schuster.

Tyfield, D. (2018) *Liberalism 2.0 and the Rise of China: Global Crisis, Innovation and Urban Mobility*. Abingdon: Routledge.

Volscho, T. W. and Kell, N. J. (2012) 'The Rise of the Super-Rich: Power Resources, Taxes, Financial Markets, and the Dynamics of the Top 1 Percent, 1949 to 2008', *American Sociological Review* 77(5):679–699.

Walker, G. (2012) *Environmental Justice: Concepts, Evidence and Politics*. Abingdon: Routledge.

Wilkinson, R. and Pickett, K. (2010) *The Spirit Level: Why Equality is Better for Everyone*, London: Penguin Books.

Wynne, B. (1996) 'May the Sheep Safely Graze? A Reflexive View of the Expert–Lay Knowledge Divide', in S. Lash, B. Szerszynski, and B. Wynne (eds), *Risk, Environment and Modernity: Towards a New Ecology* (44–83). London: Sage.

PART I

DIFFERENT DIMENSIONS OF RISK

2. Finance, risk, and inequality

Thibault Darcillon

1. INTRODUCTION

Since the 1980s, financial and banking activities have continuously risen in most OECD countries. Along with financial development, income inequality—measured by the Gini coefficient or the top income shares—has increased (see Figure 2.1), thereby contributing to a modification of the allocation of risk as well. Structural changes (*i.e.* globalization, technological progress, and financialization) have increased instability on labor markets, particularly for some categories of workers (Rodrik, 1997). A growing literature has provided increasing evidence that financial liberalization and financial development (on the global and domestic levels) have contributed to higher income inequality (*e.g.* Jaumotte, Lall, and Papageorgiou, 2013; Godechot, 2016; Jauch and Watzka, 2016). First, financial liberalization and financial development directly determine the relative size of the financial sector (which includes the scope of the financial markets and the banking activities). An expansion of the financial sector can have strong implications on the distribution of income and risk. Additionally, financial development is also likely to affect how firms decide to finance their investment projects and how risk is allocated among shareholders, managers, and workers—which refers to the corporate governance structure. In this respect, Jacoby (2007) states that inequality and the allocation of risk between owners and corporate stockholders (creditors, suppliers, and employees) are two different labor–market outcomes tied to finance. Finally, financial development by increasing credit access to a larger number of households could stimulate households' accumulation in financial assets with large disparities across households, affecting the distribution of income and risk. As a result, the growth of the financial sector *per se*, a change in corporate governance rules and practices in nonfinancial companies and a diffusion of new financial values for households—all associated with the process of financialization (van der Zwan, 2014)—have strong direct implications on income and risks.

In addition, labor markets have also shown profound mutations particularly since the 1980s: trade density union rates have declined in all OECD countries, collective wage bargaining institutions have become increasingly decentralized, and the level of employment protection has also been reduced. All these transformations have then participated in the emergence of new inequalities or risks for workers. For instance, trade unions' weakening has an overall impact on the dispersion of wages and may have contributed to higher labor market segmentation. Moreover, it has become more difficult for governments to reduce inequality and risks by efficient redistributive policies because tax rates—and especially on top incomes—have continuously declined over time, particularly since the 1980s. It can then be argued that labor market mutations and changes in tax policy—which both play a significant role in the allocation of income and risk—can be related to the rise in finance, thereby indirectly contributing to the increase in inequality and risk.

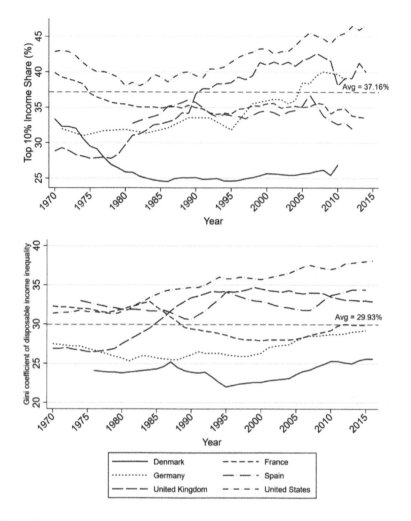

Note: The first variable measures the share of national income (which refers to gross total income, including pre-tax and pre-transfer labor, business and capital incomes but excluding realized capital gains) held by the 10% richest households. Data on top income share are taken from the World Inequality Database (WID). Then, inequality in disposable (post-tax, post-transfer) income is measured by Gini coefficient. Data on Gini coefficient are provided by the Standardized World Income Inequality Database (SWIID) built by Solt (2016) on the basis on the Luxembourg Income Study

Figure 2.1   Measures for income equality

Finally, we stress in this chapter the role of politics to understand how finance is related to the distribution of income and risk. In this line, Jacoby (2007, p.9) argues, 'the relationship between financial markets and labor markets (*i.e.* risk and inequality) is mediated by politics, which occurs at the national level in disputes over redistribution and regulation, and at the corporate level, where the key players—workers, managers, and owners—press singly or in coalition for alternative forms of governance.' More particularly, adopting a political economy perspective, we focus on the role of *political mediation*, which tries to relate particular expectations from different sociopolitical groups with heterogeneous interests and policymakers interested in building a viable sociopolitical strategy (Amable and Palombarini, 2009). First, a large series of contributions has shown that politics has shaped financial liberalization and development (Hoffman, Postel-Vinay, and Rosenthal, 2007; Quinn and Toyoda, 2007) and corporate governance structures (Roe, 2003; Gourevitch and Shinn, 2005) over time. Second, changes in labor markets (Potrafke, 2010) and in tax systems (Scheve and Stasavage, 2016) have also been driven by politics. In that sense, politics directly contributes to the distribution of income and risks. Figure 2.2 displays the mechanisms underlying the relationship between finance, the distribution of risk and income by distinguishing the channels through which finance is associated with risk and inequality (solid arrows) and politics-related channels (dashed arrows).

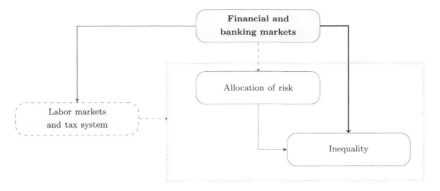

Note: Solid arrows indicate the channels through which the increasing influence of the financial and banking activities is likely to affect the distribution of risk and income. Dashed arrows indicate the different channels which are related to politics

Figure 2.2   Finance, risk, and equality: a complex tangle of mechanisms

The structure of this chapter is as follows. Section 2 presents how finance can differently affect risk and inequality. First, I explore the direct effect of the different dimensions of financialization on the distribution of risk and income. Second, I investigate two institutional changes that can be directly attributable to financialization and that can have strong implications on income and risk: labor market institutions and tax systems. Then, section 3 analyzes the role of politics in understanding the relationship between finance, risk, and income. First, changes in financial systems, labor market regulation, and tax systems can be considered direct outcomes of political choices. Second, how governments have decided to respond to a continuous increase in risk and inequality can also be treated as political choices. Finally, section 4 provides concluding remarks.

2.   HOW DOES FINANCE AFFECT RISK AND INEQUALITY?

First, one can argue that the process of financialization—which refers to the growth of the financial sector *per se*, a change in corporate governance rules and practices in nonfinancial companies, and a diffusion of new financial values for households—can have a direct impact on the distribution of income and risk (section 2.1). Then, this process of financialization is likely to affect central institutional arrangements that play a central role in the distribution of income and risk: labor market institutions and taxation (section 2.2).

2.1   Financialization, the Growth in Inequality, and the Allocation of Risk

The implications of financial development in terms of inequality and risk are driven by different dynamics. First, the rise of the financial sector can be described as a primary source of inequality and risk. The growth of the financial services industry resulting from a reduction in financial regulation at the global and domestic levels should stimulate financial actors' earnings—thereby contributing to the overall inequality—and should impact the allocation of risk (section 2.1.1). In addition, financial development has strong implications in terms of inequality and risk with regard to affecting simultaneously corporate governance rules and practices in nonfinancial corporations as well as households' savings choices (section 2.1.2).

2.1.1   The expansion of the financial sector

Financial deregulation reforms that occurred in the 1970s–1980s in most OECD countries strongly contributed to the rise in the size of the financial sector, measured by the finance's share of gross value added or by the (absolute or relative) share of wages going to financial-sector workers (see Figure 2.3). Then, the rise of income inequality within the financial sector eventually contributed to overall income inequality (Godechot, 2012; Philippon and Reshef, 2012; Denk, 2015; Boustanifar, Grant, and Reshef, 2018). A series of papers has shown that the extension of the financial activities can be responsible for increasing income inequality between high-skilled and low-skilled workers, by contributing to the increase in the employment level and wages of skilled labor (Jerzmanowski and Nabar, 2013; Larrain, 2015). In this regard, Philippon and Reshef (2012) find that financial deregulation in the United States has caused an increase in skill intensity and in wages in the financial sector. This has resulted in excess wages in finance and then an increase in wage differentials between the workers working in the finance industry and those working in the rest of the economy. More recently, Boustanifar, Grant, and Reshef (2018) find evidence of this argument for a large sample of OECD countries. As a result, the rise in the financial sector has strongly contributed to the increase in the top 1% income shares in the United States (Bakija, Cole, and Heim, 2012), in the United Kingdom (Bell and Van Reenen, 2014), and in France (Godechot, 2012).

Beyond the growth in overall size, the financial sector has also shown higher diversification, with the emergence of new actors—such as asset managers (*i.e.* professional fund managers). For instance, the US Employee Retirement Security Act of 1974 has indirectly stimulated the growth of a diversified number of funds, such as hedge funds, private equity (PE) and venture capital (VC). Financial mutations have also induced profound transformations in the banking activities in a context of higher competitive pressure in times of continuous financial and banking deregulation. These evolutions have strong implications in terms of inequality and risk. First, as documented by Mazzucato (2018), the number of 'high-net-worth individuals'

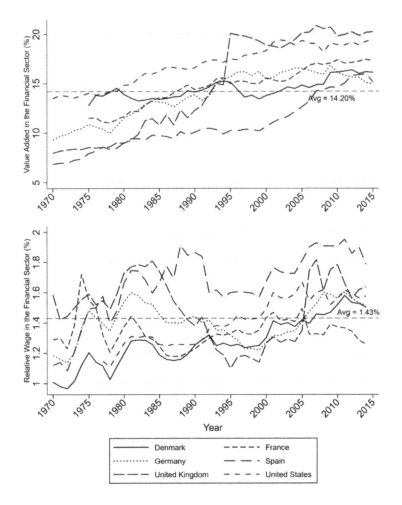

Note: Value added in the financial sector is calculated as the proportion of value added in total economy (all sectors). Relative wages in the financial sector are expressed in the percentage of total wages. See Boustanifar et al. (2018)}. Financial sector refers here to the financial intermediation, real estate and insurance (FIRE) activities. Data on value added are taken from EU-KLEMS Database (Version 2017) (See Jäger, 2017)

Figure 2.3   Value added and wages in the financial sector (in %)

has gradually increased over time worldwide. Moreover, the oligopolistic nature of banking (especially among the derivatives markets)—resulting from a strong concentration of the financial industry—is closely linked to banks' greater ability to extract rents, thereby reflected higher earnings (Mazzucato, 2018), and this as the financial sector expands as well as the cost of financial services (Bazot, 2018). Second, the gradual deregulation of finance and the subsequent rise in financial and banking activities raise concerns about financial stability, especially following the development of securitization operations. This has resulted in higher financial instability with increasing systemic risk (and this although management risks are assumed to be shared with these operations). Higher financial instability increases the probability of financial crisis, which can impose a huge cost in terms of social welfare.[1]

2.1.2   The financialization of nonfinancial corporations and the rise in households' financial wealth

The increasing size of the financial sector can be attributable to different demand factors, such as new financing needs from nonfinancial corporations and new savings choices from households.

Financial deregulation reforms have contributed to the continuous increase in stock market activities (Figure 2.4). One can argue that stock market development has affected the level of risk in nonfinancial corporations and its allocation among owners, creditors, suppliers, executives, and employees with strong impact on inequality and risk. This allocation can be mutually influenced by the firm's financial structure (debt *versus* equity) and by capital ownership structure (Perotti and von Thadden, 2006). Blockholders (*i.e.* large shareholders with at least 5% of shares) and minority shareholders may have opposed risk preferences: blockholders are more favorable of strong regulation in the economy (notably on product markets and on labor markets) compatible with long-term innovative strategies based on cooperative relationships as in the post-war era. In the post-war era, ownership of major enterprises was concentrated among blockholders in most European countries and in Japan. In the Anglo-Saxon countries, capital structure ownership was dispersed among abundant small and medium-size outside investors with a weak institutional voice due to their fragmentation. In fact, a strong degree of market regulation was consistent with the 'retain-and-reinvest' model of corporate resource allocation (Lazonick and O'Sullivan, 2000) in which profits are first used to reinvest in productive capacities; then, corporations retain their earnings and their talent in order to share the gains of innovative enterprise with a broad base of employees. As a result, this model contributes to producing weak income dispersion.

By contrast, minority shareholders are more supportive of strong financial market liquidity, compatible with higher product and labor market flexibility and short-term innovative strategies based on competitive relationships since the 1970s–1980s. At that time, a new model of corporate resource allocation was emerging: the 'downsize-and-distribute' model, in which corporate executives seek to downsize the labor force to then distribute the earnings to shareholders. This results from the growing role in company strategies of asset management companies (especially the large investment and pension funds) and large firms specializing in investment banking and from the emergence of 'shareholder value' as a central corporate governance principle. This new model of corporate resource allocation based on increasing financial development produces higher employment instability and income inequality (Lazonick, 2015), in particular through the adoption of performance-related pay. Financial development, by broadening the pool of external investors, improves risk-sharing and encourages firms to adopt more profitable and riskier strategies, and this including for non-listed firms (Thesmar and Thoenig, 2004). In this case, firms have higher incentives to introduce specific income schemes, such as performance-related pay, which are indexed on the firms' profits. This kind of incentive pay realigns executive and shareholder interests, with the ultimate aim of maximizing shareholder value (MSV) following the theoretical apparatus developed by Friedman (1970) and the two agency theorists Jensen and Meckling (1976). As a result, directors saw their share of the companies' income significantly rise over the last two decades, especially in forms of stock options or stock awards (Boyer, 2005) as reflected by a sharp increase in buybacks (Lazonick, 2015). According to the agency theory, the aim of buybacks is to increase the value of shares in undervalued shares and to minimize any threat of hostile takeovers, and this with the ultimate objective to maximize shareholder value.

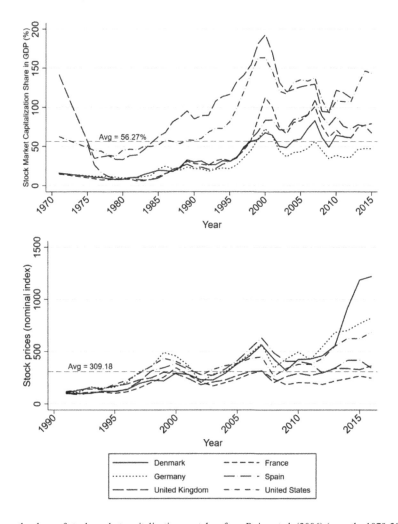

Note: Data on the share of stock market capitalization are taken from Roine et al. (2006) (over the 1970-2006 period) and the World Bank's Global Financial Development Database (GFDD) (over the 2007–2015 period). Data on stock prices are provided by the Jordà-Schularick-Taylor Macrohistory Database (Jordà, Schularick and Taylor, 2017).

Figure 2.4   Measures of stock market activity

In the United States, the falling trend in the rate of retained profits since the early 1980s has been coupled with a negative contribution of equity issues to the financing of investment due to equity repurchases (van Treeck, 2009). It resulted in a continuous rise in the CEO-to-worker compensation ratio, especially in the US, where stock-based pay is now the dominant component of top executive pay, and a reduced tenure of management. Beyond specific performance-related pay designed for managers, firms also can have incentives to adopt individual or collective bonuses for employees (*e.g.* employees stock ownership plan). Overall, the introduction of this kind of scheme is likely to make incomes more volatile (OECD, 2011) and to produce higher income inequality, especially across workers with different skill levels. More particularly, financial globalization has been identified as a central factor to the continuous increase in income (and employment) volatility (Buch and Pierdzioch, 2014; Furceri, Loungani, and Ostry, 2018).[2]

The increasing expansion of the financial sector has triggered a gradual transformation in households' saving behavior in most OECD countries, again with large implications in terms of inequality and risk. The purpose of financial deregulation in the 1970s–1980s was to boost households' saving by increasing interest rates. At the same time, financial development has allowed households to diversify their portfolios to riskier and more profitable assets (compared with more traditional saving products). As a result, the share of financial assets (Figure 2.5) held by households has continuously grown over time, in the form of stocks and bonds. This evolution can reflect the 'democratization of finance', whereby large parts of the population (including low-income households) have an easier access to financial products and services at the microeconomic level. As underlined by van der Zwan (2014), this dimension is directly related to the cultural diffusion of new values associated with investment, risk, and indebtedness (Toporowski, 2009). Accordingly, the variety of financial products and services (such as capital-funded pension plans, consumer credit, and other mass-marketed financial products) consumed by households has considerably increased in many countries. Due to these transformations, there are large inequalities in savings across households (Fesseau and van de Ven, 2014). For instance, higher credit availability to low-income households allows them to increase their borrowings (and then to get more indebted) with the ultimate aim of defending their consumption level (Kumhof and Rancière, 2010; Azizi and Darcillon, 2014). In this regard, financialization can also be reflected by easy credit and high levels of household debt (Jacoby, 2007).

As a result, as financial development increases savings ability for top earners, and this at the expense of low-income households, higher credit availability implies a risk transfer from top earners (with increasing financial assets) to low-income households (with higher debt-in-income ratios), particularly whereby derivative markets—and especially mortgage markets—are very large and active, such as in the US. Indeed, derivative markets can be used to raise the flow of capital by providing a protection against any kind of risks—referring to better risk management and higher efficiency at the microeconomic level. Consequently, high-income individuals (with high savings ability) can acquire new financial products that can be allocated in the form of loans (such as mortgage loans) for low-income households (with lower savings ability). In other words, finance plays here its traditional role of intermediary, thereby transferring resources from actors who have them to those who need them more. However, even though derivative products allow for risk spread for final users (*i.e.* borrowers and lenders), these products also create dangerous risk concentration within derivative markets, implying major potential consequences at the macroeconomic level. For instance, an excessive volume of financial transactions (such as mortgage transactions) is associated with higher probability of banking/financial crisis, contributing to new risks particularly for the most vulnerable individuals, *i.e.* low-income households (with lower savings ability), especially when the latter are particularly indebted. As shown by Fesseau and van de Ven (2014), low-income households have become increasingly indebted, reflected by negative saving rates. In that sense, low-income households are more likely to be affected by aggregate risks in times of crisis.

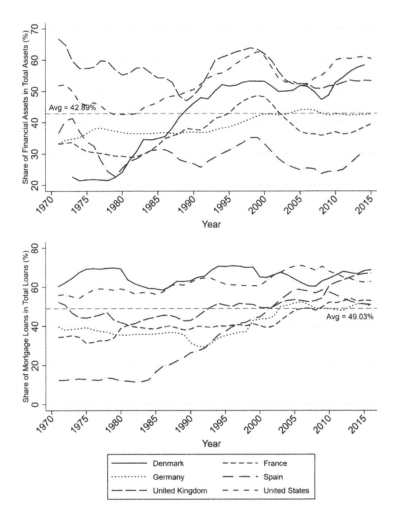

Note: Total assets refers to the private (financial and nonfinancial) assets held by households at the national level. Data on assets are provided by World Wealth and Income Database (WID). Then, we compute the mortgage loans to non-financial private sector as the share of total loans to non-financial private sector (all Depository Institutions). Data on loans are provided by the Jordà-Schularick-Taylor Macrohistory Database (Jordà, Schularick and Taylor, 2017).

Figure 2.5   *Household assets and mortgage loans*

2.2   Institutional Changes, Inequality, and Risk in the Age of Financialization

Due to strong institutional interactions, the increasing influence of the financial and banking activities has also affected other institutional areas, such as labor markets or taxation. These institutional side effects can then have strong implications on the distribution of risk and income. We first explore the impact of finance on labor market institutional arrangements. Then, we investigate the potential effect of finance on taxation.

2.2.1   Finance and labor market institutions

A large literature in labor market economics has paid strong attention to the role of labor market institutions—such as the employment protection legislation, the union density and coverage, the degree of centralization or coordination of wage bargaining as well as unemployment benefits and more broadly to redistribution policies—in the reduction in labor market fluctuations (Wasmer, 2006) as powerful 'automatic stabilizers' and in income inequality (*e.g.* Card, Lemieux, and Riddell, 2004; Koeniger, Leonardi, and Nunziata, 2007). Most OECD countries have experienced an overall reduction in the level of employment protection legislation (on regular and/or temporary contracts) and a gradual decentralization of wage bargaining (Figure 2.6).

First, it can be argued that the rise in the financial activities and financial markets may have played a significant role in the overall reduction in labor market regulation shown in Figure 2.6. From this perspective, Darcillon (2015b) shows that the increasing influence of the financial institutions and financial markets has exerted strong pressures on labor markets towards more eroded/decentralized bargaining institutions and more flexible employment relations. More specifically, the diffusion of shareholder value as a principle has changed industrial relations in a direction towards the decentralization of collective bargaining institutions (as in Germany) and to a weakening of the unions' power (as in the United Kingdom and in the United States), thereby leading to an 'erosion–decentralization' of collective bargaining institutions. In addition, employment relations have become more flexible by making wages and employment adjustment variables (Boyer, 2011). As higher employment protection levels reduce the firm's financial returns, it conflicts with shareholder's interests to increase short-term corporate profitability.

Second, financial and labor markets have strong mutual interactions. In that sense, any change in financial markets should affect labor market dynamics, and reciprocally (Amable and Ernst, 2005), thereby jointly impacting the distribution of income and risk. For instance, higher financial market liquidity reduces the incentives for shareholders to invest in specific (financial) assets (*i.e.* favoring investments on a larger time horizon), which in turn will reduce workers' incentives to invest in specific skills.[3] For instance, in the Anglo-Saxon countries, flexible labor markets combined with large financial activities produce higher levels of inequality and instability compared with the continental or northern European countries. In the same line, Darcillon (2016a and 2016b) finds that labor market institutions play a significant role in mitigating the increase in income inequality (measured by the Gini coefficient) and the increase in labor market fluctuations (in terms of wages or employment) both associated with higher stock market and credit development. In other words, the effects of an increase in the financial and banking activities on inequality and risk are amplified by low levels of labor market regulation (*i.e.* weak trade unions or low level of employment protection).

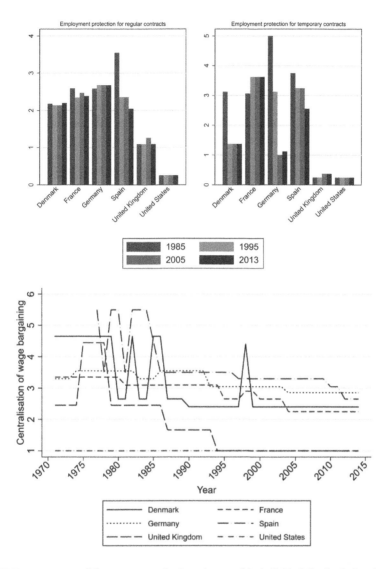

Note: The OECD proposes two different measures for the strictness of the individual dismissal of workers on regular contracts (EPR) and on temporary contracts (EPT). Scores on EPR are calculated on the basis of different aspects, such as procedural inconveniences, notice and severance pay, and difficulty of dismissal. EPT refers to the regulation of fixed-term contracts and to the regulation of temporary work agencies. The variable on the actual degree of centralization of wage bargaining is based on the frequency or scope of additional enterprise bargaining, the articulation of enterprise bargaining, the derogation, and the general opening clauses in collective agreement. This variable is provided by the Data Base on Institutional Characteristics of Trade Unions, Wage Setting, State Intervention and Social Pacts, 1960–2014 (Visser, 2016).

Figure 2.6   Measures for labor market institutions

Another labor market outcome tied to finance is labor market segmentation: some workers are protected through permanent contracts whereas workers with temporary contracts or unemployed workers have lower protection (Rueda, 2007). It has been shown that changes in financial or corporate governance regulation can amplify labor market segmentation with potential effects on inequality and risk (Jackson, Höpner, and Kurdelbusch, 2006; Rueda and Barker, 2007; Barker, 2010). For instance, in the case of Germany, Vitols (2004) and Höpner (2007) show that shareholder value practices have been made compatible with the traditional system of codetermination, which provides a large institutional power to trade unions to represent the interests of the 'insider' workers. This has resulted in higher institutional power and higher wages for 'insiders' (through the adoption of variable pay combined with reduced taxes on stock options), thereby creating higher inequality, and resulting in higher instability for 'outsiders' (in a logic of economic adjustment).[4]

2.2.2   Finance and Taxation

In addition to labor market institutions, tax policy has been long identified as a central driver of inequality, especially at the top distribution of income. For instance, Piketty (2014) shows that top income shares were particularly low in the United States during the post-war era, when marginal top tax rates were very high. By contrast, top income shares began to increase when marginal top tax rates were reduced. As displayed in Figure 2.7, most OECD countries have experienced a gradual decline in marginal top tax rates with large cross-country differences.

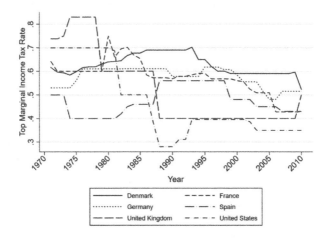

Note: Data are provided by Piketty, Saez and Stantcheva (2014) which propose a historical series mainly derived from the OECD Database. This dataset provides yearly data on the top marginal income tax rate.

Figure 2.7   *Marginal top tax rates, 1970–2013*

Then, it could be argued that the rise in the financial sphere has encouraged governments to reduce personal incomes for top earners. In fact, financial deregulation in the 1970s contributed to the growth in the share of finance industry in GDP, thereby leading to increased incomes, especially for top earners (who are overrepresented in the financial sector). In this way, due to higher incomes, bargaining power for top earners has gradually increased (whereas in parallel workers' bargaining power has declined along with mutations of labor markets). Finally, top earners can use their bargaining power to press for reduced tax rates on their incomes through their political connections. To sum up, financial deregulation appears as one of the most important factors driving down top tax rates (Darcillon, 2018). In this new environment of higher competitive pressures associated with a more deregulated financial sector, tax policy has been weakened to mitigate the increase in inequality.

As a consequence, labor market institutions and taxation, two central institutional arrangements in the reduction in inequality and risk, are strongly connected to the transformations in the financial systems. In that sense, changes in different institutional areas are cumulative and have mutual influence among them. Cumulatively, all these structural changes should produce higher inequality and instability.

3.   WHY DOES POLITICS MATTER?

Increasing influence of finance is expected to have different effects across sociopolitical groups due to the heterogeneity in their socioeconomic interests. In other words, financial liberalization/development and finance-related institutional changes have strong distributive effects in terms of income and risk. Using a political economy approach, one can argue that the relationship between finance and inequality and the allocation of risk is mediated by politics (or political mediation). A process of political mediation occurs when policymakers decide to select some social demands and finally results in the implementation of particular institutions (*i.e.* financial and banking regulation) or economic policies (Amable and Palombarini, 2009). Consequently, any institutional change implies a modification in the balance of power across social groups. For instance, any change in corporate governance regulation should alter the balance of power within the firm between managers, workers, and shareholders (Pagano and Volpin, 2005; Darcillon, 2015a).

   Following this political economy approach, any change in regulation in financial structures (banks and financial markets) or in corporate governance structures can be seen as political choices (section 3.1). In this sense, government ideological orientation has contributed to shaping the nature and the scope of financial reforms. Moreover, changes in labor market regulation and in tax systems can be seen as political outcomes as well. In addition, how governments decide to respond to higher income and risk can also be interpreted as political choices (section 3.2). As a response to higher inequality, governments can either implement redistributive policies (potentially by increasing public debt) or promote financial development with easy credit policies (potentially by increasing private debt).

3.1   Financial and Banking Deregulation as Political Choices

The rise in the financial sector since the 1980s can be considered as the direct outcome of radical regulatory changes during the 1970s. These regulatory changes imply high levels of distributive conflicts that are then solved in the political arena at two different yet intertwined levels: (1) international sociopolitical conflicts where countries battle over international capital flows (as reflected, for instance, by increased tax competition across countries), which will shape international financial regulation and influence the volume of international financial transactions; (2) domestic sociopolitical conflicts where states (through government regulation) and markets struggle over access to resources, thereby contributing to shaping domestic regulation on financial markets, product and labor markets, corporate governance, education, and training systems through institutional complementarities (Hall and Soskice, 2001; Amable, 2003, 2016). A large literature has explored the political economy determinants of capital account liberalization (at the international level) and financial and banking deregulation (at the domestic level). It has been shown that right-wing governments have been strong supporters of financial liberalization (Kastner and Rector, 2005; Quinn and Toyoda, 2007; Burgoon, Demetriades, and Underhill, 2012), and this is in line with the capital holders' interests because strongly integrated financial markets guarantee a more efficient resource allocation and allow for a better risk diversification for them. Increasing trade openness has also contributed to changes in preferences, especially for commercial banks. Changes in preferences in the financial actors combined with profound mutations in the macroeconomic context in the 1970s (*i.e.* the demise of the Bretton Woods System of adjustable peg exchange rates in 1974), which contributed to alter the needs from businesses (in terms of financing) and from households (in terms of savings). The subsequent capital account liberalization followed by a deregulation in the financial and banking systems implemented by governments in the 1970s–1980s resulted from these changes in political preferences following a traditional process of political mediation (*i.e.* policymakers will select the demands that will be satisfied and those that will not).

In addition, the firm's financial structure will determine the capital ownership structure (Hall and Soskice, 2001), which also triggers strong distributive transfers between different socioeconomic groups, such as shareholders, workers, and managers (Stockhammer, 2004; Gourevitch and Shinn, 2005; Pagano and Volpin, 2005). In the economies where financial markets are particularly developed and active, it will be easier for firms to raise capital funds through equity, thereby resulting in a more dispersed capital ownership structure (such as in the US). Conversely, firms have higher incentives to finance their projects through bank loans in countries with a dominant banking structure. As a result, firms' finance and then corporate governance affects voters because it affects corporate decisions, which drive the creation and distribution of national income. Then, in line with Gourevitch and Shinn (2005), Pagano and Volpin (2005), and Darcillon (2015a), regulatory changes in corporate governance and in financial systems are supported by a coalition of different sociopolitical groups, which will influence the allocation of risk at the firm level, thereby resulting in a new political mediation and in redefining the balance of power at the domestic level. In the post-war era, when financial and banking regulation was strong, a 'corporatist' alliance between workers and managers emerged, resulting in stable jobs and pay increase for workers and in strong discretionary power and protection for managers. Consequently, the emergence of global capital markets and the subsequent financial and banking deregulation encouraged the creation of an 'investor' alliance between minority shareholders and managers, resulting in higher inequality and instability (through the introduction of various incentive mechanisms or the creation of an active market for corporate governance). Finally, a new 'transparency' alliance has been emerging since the 1990s in most OECD countries between some workers and shareholders (with greater oversight of managers), thereby producing higher labor market segmentation (Darcillon, 2015b) and then increased inequality. Workers are in fact more likely to join this 'transparency' alliance if they perceive pro-minority shareholder corporate governance rules as good for jobs and wages for some workers (Jackson, Höpner, and Kurdelbusch, 2006). Moreover, workers have higher incentives to support this new alliance if they become more concerned with returns on assets if they acquire more private pension assets and, more generally, financial wealth (Perotti and von Thadden, 2006). As argued by Boyer (2000), the decision for workers to save or spend is increasingly influenced by the prospect of gains on the financial markets *via* equity holdings or pension funds, especially in a finance-led growth regime marked by stagnating real wages. Finally, workers and outside investors can ally with greater oversight of managers, as in the case of the US after the Enron crisis in the early-2000s with the adoption of the Sarbanes–Oxley Act in 2002.

Finally, as preciously underlined, households' preferences for the financial system (*i.e.* financial market depth and scope) can widely differ across households due to inequality in access to financial markets (Hoffman, Postel-Vinay, and Rosenthal, 2007). Top incomes (*i.e.* large investors and entrepreneurs) have large access to widely diversified markets (including international markets) while low-income households (*i.e.* low-skilled workers or unemployed) have, in contrast, little financial wealth, weak human capital, and no tangible assets avaliable for collateral. The middle class (*i.e.* small investors/medium- and high-skilled workers) has more financial wealth and more human capital than low-income households but less diversified assets than top incomes. This last group can generate strong demand for new financial institutions and financial products and can then influence governments' decisions to liberalize the financial structures with the aim of promoting the expansion of the financial and banking activities. This results in the development of new financial intermediaries (such as mutual funds, branch banks, or interregional mortgage funding) in order to reduce the cost of diversification for middle-class households. Furthermore, a change in the distribution in financial wealth is also likely to alter the balance of power within the firm, thereby affecting the firm's financing and corporate governance structure.

In a political economy approach, government ideological orientation can influence the decision to liberalize the financial structures. As the utility of political parties should reflect the interests of the groups they represent, right-wing and left-wing parties should then defend different positions regarding financial reforms. Right-wing governments are more likely to support financial deregulation reforms with the ultimate aim of reducing government intervention in the economy. By contrast, left-wing governments should oppose financial deregulation reforms because they are supposed to defend the interests of their traditional electorate. Figure 2.8 provides some evidence for the left–right cleavage hypothesis: right-wing governments are more likely to adopt financial or pro-minority shareholder reforms. Moreover, left-wing governments also support higher government intervention to reduce income differences: income inequalities are likely to be smaller under left-wing governments than under right-wing governments (Pontusson, Rueda, and Way, 2002). In fact, left-wing governments (respectively right-wing governments) are more (resp. less) prone to support trade unions and to increase the level of employment protection (Potrafke, 2010). Moreover, progressive governments can be more likely to increase the cost of taxation for rich citizens (Scheve and Stasavage, 2016). For instance, in the United States, Republican governments are more statistically associated with strong reductions in statutory tax rates on personal incomes (such as in 1986 or in 2001). Some patterns can be observed in the United Kingdom (during the Thatcher era) or in France. Combining these two findings, left-wing governments are more associated with reduced income inequality and risk.

3.2   More Finance or More Redistribution in Response to Higher Inequality and Instability?

The rise of the financial sector has affected different institutional arrangements, thereby contributing to modifying the effects of institutional combinations. Subsequently, all these changes might lead to a new socioeconomic model whereby finance plays a more central

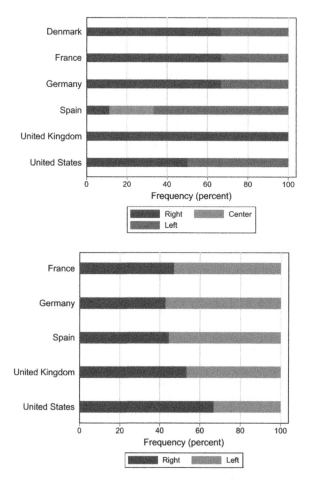

Note: Financial reforms refer to a reduction in financial regulation at least in one of the following dimensions credit controls; interest rate controls; entry barriers; state ownership in the banking sector; capital account restrictions; prudential regulations and supervision of the banking sector and securities market policy). This variable has been proposed by Abiad, Detragiache and Tressel (2010). Pro-minority shareholder reforms refer to an adoption of corporate governance reforms which increase the degree of legal protection for minority shareholders. This variable has been created by Darcillon (2015b). Finally, government ideological orientation is calculated by a categorical variable capturing the chief executive party orientation (Left/Center/Right). This variable is provided by the World Bank's Database of Political Institutions 2017 (DPI2017) (See Cruz, Keefer and Scartascini, 2018).

Figure 2.8   *Regulatory changes in finance/corporate governance and government ideological orientation*

position and is linked to higher inequality and socioeconomic instability. In turn, the continuous rise in income inequality has been caused by various tensions on the existing institutional arrangements, which will also modify the expectations of sociopolitical groups. In this new environment of growing instability, new risks have emerged—especially for 'unprotected' or low-skilled workers. More particularly, some categories of workers who are especially exposed to higher risks can increase their support for more generous redistribution and social protection policies.

According to Rodrik (1997), support for redistribution—to reduce risk exposure—should increase as long as instability or income inequality are becoming more significant. Using survey data on the role of government in the reduction in income inequality, it can be seen in Figure 2.9a that the share of people in favor of higher redistribution has increased from the 1980s to nowadays in the OECD countries. Whereas people increasingly support redistribution, redistributive policies have become less effective in correcting market income inequality over the same period in most OECD countries (see Figure 2.9b). This drop in effectiveness of tax policy can be seen as a result of multiple structural changes, such as rising globalization and technological change (Causa and Hermansen, 2017). Financialization can be described as an additional source. As shown in section 2.2, the rise in the financial sector is strongly associated with an increase in top 1% income shares. First, the rise in the financial sector by triggering an increase in capital incomes benefits more proportionately top earners because capital incomes are more concentrated in the top distribution of the income (Piketty and Saez, 2007), thus leading to high interpersonal inequality of incomes. Second, the financialization of the nonfinancial corporations and the rise in rich households' wealth have also contributed to making it more difficult in practice to distinguish between capital and labor incomes, with, for instance, the growth of stock options (Saez and Zucman, 2016). As a result, high labor and capital income earners tend to increasingly be the same people, intensifying overall income inequality (Milanovic, 2016, pp. 185–6): the traditional labor/capital conflict (*i.e.* implying a negative correlation between labor and capital incomes) has shifted in the United States to a strong complementarity between labor and capital (*i.e.* reflecting a positive correlation between the two types of incomes).

A context of higher inequality and instability can produce a higher preference and party fractionalization. As the result of increased inequality and instability, preferences for redistribution have become more heterogeneous (Alt and Iversen, 2017), reflecting higher diffuse socioeconomic interests across social groups. In parallel, an increase in inequality could also produce higher party fractionalization or even party polarization (Pontusson and Rueda, 2008). In addition, heterogeneity across preferences for redistribution is then likely to affect welfare state generosity particularly when the degree of fractionalization of the party system increases (Amable, Gatti, and Guillaud, 2008). Conversely, it can be argued that a polarization is likely to reduce any consensus on taxation and redistribution (Rajan, 2010). In this context, US policymakers in the 1990s have promoted financial development—and more specifically easier access to credit (through easy credit policies)—especially for middle-class and low-income households, in response to increasing inequality. In that context, the financial sector was further deregulated in the 1990s by the Clinton administration (labeled as left in Figure 2.8). Easing credit policies have been encouraged with the aim of sustaining the aggregate demand due to stagnating incomes since the early 1990s (Boyer, 2011; Piketty, 2014). Subsequent financial development provides higher opportunities for citizens and firms to become more heavily indebted (Streeck, 2014). In this respect, recent literature has stressed the central role of the increase in inequality in the emergence of the US *subprime* financial crisis (Rajan, 2010; van Treeck, 2014). Furthermore, trade and financial globalization—beyond their impact of labor income instability—reduce governments' capacity to raise taxation. In that context, it could be more difficult for government to fund and enforce public policies (and social protection policies). Accordingly, it could increasingly be appealing to governments to promote private financial transactions by deregulating financial markets that would be able to provide efficient insurance against growing labor income risks and to satisfy the increasing demand for higher social protection (Bertola and Lo Prete, 2013).

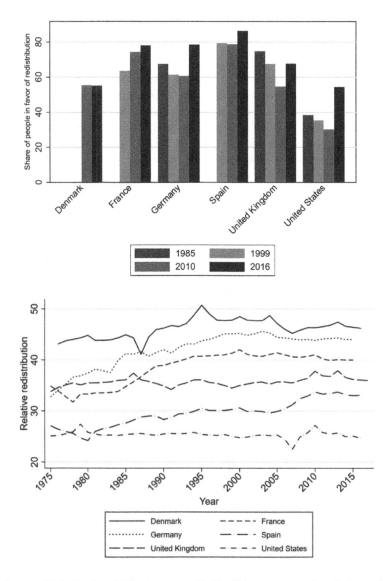

Note: Attitudes on redistribution on redistribution are provided by different programs from the International Social Survey Programme (ISSP) dataset (ISSP). Support for redistribution is calculated by the number of respondents per country who express in favor and strongly in favor of government intervention to reduce the differences in income between people with high incomes and those with low incomes as a share of the total number of respondents per country. Relative redistribution is measured by the difference between market-income inequality and net-income inequality, divided by market-income inequality. Data on relative redistribution are taken by the Standardized World Income Inequality Database (SWIID) built by Solt (2016) on the basis on the Luxembourg Income Study.

Figure 2.9   Measures for redistribution

4.   CONCLUDING COMMENTS

Since the 1980s, financial and banking activities have continuously risen in most OECD countries, while income inequality and risk have also increased over the same period. Using an interdisciplinary literature, the aim of this chapter was to examine how the process of financialization—the growth of the financial sector *per se*, a change in corporate governance rules and practices in nonfinancial companies, and a diffusion of new financial values for households—can be associated with higher inequality and risk in the OECD countries over the last three decades.

First, I identified direct channels through which finance may have contributed to higher inequality and risk: (1) the expansion of the financial sector has shown a sharp increase in relative wages in finance, thereby strongly contributing to overall wage inequality; (2) financial development has also affected how firms decide to finance their investment projects, impacting corporate governance structures, with strong implications for the distribution of income and risk (*i.e.* through stock options); and (3) financial development can also stimulate a larger number of households to consume financial products and to increase their financial assets. In addition, a growing literature has emphasized intertwined influences between finance and inequality: the process of financialization—through the expansion of the financial sector and its impact on the distribution of value added of the nonfinancial corporations—has strongly affected the distribution of income. Moreover, some authors (*e.g.* Rajan, 2010; Streeck, 2014; and van Treeck, 2014) argue that financialization has also been driven by increased income inequality. Then, additional institutional arrangements—such as labor market institutions (*i.e.* trade unions and employment protection legislation) and tax systems—have a traditional reducing effect on income inequality and risk. Among other factors, financialization has also played a role in weakening labor market regulation—reflecting a decreased workers' bargaining power (or rather, for some workers)—and in tax rates (especially for top incomes), indirectly contributing to higher income inequality and risk.

Second, the relationship between finance, income inequality, and risk is mainly determined by politics. Financial deregulation reforms and the subsequent financial development involve in fact high distributive conflicts that will then be resolved in the political arena. Distribution conflicts of one reform may result from the post-reform heterogeneity of gains (Alesina and Drazen, 1991). These conflicts are then structuring the balance of power between social groups in the economy. In this respect, any change in financial (or corporate governance) regulation—by altering the balance of power across social groups—can be seen as a political choice reflecting specific sociopolitical expectations. Following this political economy approach, right-wing governments are more likely to promote financial and labor market deregulation with strong implications for the allocation of income and risk. Furthermore, higher income and risk is associated with increased support for redistribution. How governments decide to respond to higher income and risk—by promoting more traditional redistributive policies or by facilitating credit access to a larger number of households—can be considered as a political choice. As intertwined relationships between finance and inequality (*i.e.* finance contributes to increasing inequality, which finally contributes to higher financial development) are mainly based on political mechanisms, the financial sector has continuously expanded, including after the major financial crisis in 2008.[5]

NOTES

1. Financial crises can have a negative impact on GDP growth, with consequences for unemployment. In addition, as in the case of the 2007/08 financial crisis, public debt can be positively affected with different government funded bailout programs, which are good examples of 'privatizing losses and socializing losses.' Sawyer (2018) provides a detailed review about the relationship between financialization, financial crisis, and inequality.
2. Furceri *et al.* (2018) show that labor share was reduced by capital account liberalization episodes, especially in industries with higher external financial dependence and with a higher elasticity of substitution between capital and labor.
3. In that context, workers would be likely to reduce their support for strong levels of employment protection legislation, thereby weakening the institutional power of trade unions, which will impact the dispersion of wages or incomes.
4. Figure 2.6 shows that employment protection level for workers with temporary contracts gradually declined from 1985 to 2013, whereas the employment protection level for workers with permanent contracts became stagnant over the same period.
5. Additional factors can be relevant to explain the rise in finance. First, globalization may have played a central role during the first phase of financial development in the 1960s/1970s. Second, technological change particularly during the 1990s then had a significant influence on the development of the financial sphere.

REFERENCES

Abiad, A., E. Detragiache, and T. Tressel (2010), 'A New Database of Financial Reforms', *IMF Staff Papers*, 57, 281–302.
Alesina, A. and A. Drazen (1991), 'Why Are Stabilizations Delayed?', *The American Economic Review*, 81(5), 1170–1188.
Amable, B. (2003), *The Diversity of Modern Capitalism*, Oxford: Oxford University Press.
Amable, B. (2016), 'Institutional Complementarities in the Dynamic Comparative Analysis of Capitalism', *Journal of Institutional Economics*, 16(1), 79–103.
Amable, B. and E. Ernst (2005), 'Financial and Labour Market Interactions: Specific Investment and Labour Market Activity', *Center for Empirical Macroeconomics*, Working Paper No. 93.
Amable, B. and S. Palombarini (2009), 'A Neorealist Approach to Institutional Change and the Diversity of Capitalism', *Socio-Economic Review*, 7(1), 123–143.
Amable, B., D. Gatti, and E. Guillaud (2008), 'How Does Party Fractionalization Convey Preferences for Redistribution in Parliamentary Democracies?', *PSE Working Paper*, No. 2008-42.
Alt, J. and T. Iversen (2017), 'Inequality, Labor Market Segmentation, and Preferences for Redistribution', *American Journal of Political Science*, 61, 21–36.
Azizi, K. and T. Darcillon (2014), 'The Political Economy of Easy Credit Policies', *Journal of Income Distribution*, 23(3–4), 84–105.
Bakija, J., A. Cole, and B.T. Heim (2012), 'Jobs and Income Growth of Top Earners and the Causes of Changing Income Inequality: Evidence from U.S. Tax Return Data', Department of Economics Working Papers, Williamstown, Williams College.
Barker, R.M. (2010), *Corporate Governance, Competition, and Political Parties: Explaining Corporate Governance Change in Europe*, Oxford: Oxford University Press.
Bazot, G. (2018), 'Financial Consumption and the Cost of Finance: Measuring Financial Efficiency in Europe (1950–2007)', *Journal of the European Economic Association*, 16(1), 123–160.
Bell, B. and J. Van Reenen (2014), 'Bankers and Their Bonuses', *The Economic Journal*, 124(574), F1–F21.
Bertola, G. and A. Lo Prete (2013), 'Finance, Governments, and Trade', *Review of World Economics*, 149, 273–294.
Boustanifar, H., E. Grant, and A. Reshef (2018), 'Wages and Human Capital in Finance: International Evidence, 1970–2011', *Review of Finance*, 22(2), 699–745.

Boyer, R. (2000), 'Is a Finance-Led Growth Regime a Viable Alternative to Fordism? A Preliminary Analysis', *Economy and Society*, 29(1), 111–145.

Boyer, R. (2005), 'From Shareholder Value to CEO Power: The Paradox of the 1990s', *Competition & Change*, 9(1), 7–47.

Boyer, R. (2011), *Les financiers détruiront-ils le capitalisme?*, Paris: Economica.

Buch, C.M. and C. Pierdzioch (2014), 'Labor Market Volatility, Skills, and Financial Globalization', *Macroeconomic Dynamics*, 18(5), 1018–1047.

Burgoon, B., P. Demetriades, and G.R.D. Underhill (2012), 'Sources and Legitimacy of Financial Liberalization', *European Journal of Political Economy*, 28(2), 147–161.

Card, D., T. Lemieux, and W.C. Riddell (2004), 'Unions and Wage Inequality', *Journal of Labour Research*, 25, 519–559.

Causa, O. and M. Hermansen (2017), 'Income Redistribution through Taxes and Transfers across OECD Countries', OECD Economics Department Working Papers 1453, OECD Publishing.

Cruz, C., P. Keefer, and C. Scartascini (2018), Database of Political Institutions 2017 (DPI2017), Inter-American Development Bank. Numbers for Development.

Darcillon, T. (2015a), 'Corporate Governance Reforms and Political Partisanship: An Empirical Analysis in 16 OECD Countries', *Business and Politics*, 17(4), 661–667.

Darcillon, T. (2015b), 'How does Finance Affect Labor Market Institutions? An Empirical Analysis in 16 OECD Countries', *Socio-Economic Review*, 13(3), 477–504.

Darcillon, T. (2016a), 'Do Interactions between Finance and Labour Market Institutions Affect the Income Distribution?', *LABOUR: Review of Labour Economics and Industrial Relations*, 30(3), 235–257.

Darcillon, T. (2016b), 'Labor-Market Volatility and Financial Development in the Advanced OECD Countries: Does Labor Market Regulation Matter?', *Comparative Economic Studies*, 58(2), 254–278.

Darcillon, T. (2018), 'Finance, Tax Policy, and Top Income Shares: Cross-Country Evidence, 1960–2010', mimeo.

Denk, O. (2015), 'Financial Sector Pay and Labour Income Inequality: Evidence from Europe', OECD Economics Department Working Papers, No. 1225, OECD Publishing, Paris.

Fesseau, M. and P. van de Ven (2014), 'Measuring Inequality in Income and Consumption in a National Accounts Framework', *OECD Statistics Brief*, November, No. 19.

Friedman, M. (1970), 'The Social Responsibility of Business is to Increase Its Profits', *The New York Times Magazine*, September 13.

Furceri, D., P. Loungani, and J. Ostry (2018), 'The Aggregate and Distributional Effects of Financial Globalization: Evidence from Macro and Sectoral Data', IMF Working Paper No. 18/83, International Monetary Fund.

Global Financial Development Database (GFDD) (2017), June 2017 Version, World Bank.

Godechot, O. (2012), 'Is Finance Responsible for the Rise in Wage Inequality in France?', *Socio-Economic Review*, 10(3), 447–470.

Godechot, O. (2016), 'Financialization Is Marketization! A Study of the Respective Impacts of Various Dimensions of Financialization on the Increase in Global Inequality', *Sociological Science*, 30(3), 710–729.

Gourevitch, P.A. and J. Shinn (2005), *Political Power and Corporate Control: The New Global Politics of Corporate Governance*, Princeton, NJ: Princeton University Press.

Hall, P.A. and D. Soskice (2001), 'An Introduction to Varieties of Capitalism', *in* Peter A. Hall and David Soskice (eds), *Varieties of Capitalism: The Institutional Foundations of Comparative Advantage*, Oxford, Oxford University Press, pp. 1–68.

Hoffman, P.T., G. Postel-Vinay, and J.-L. Rosenthal (2007), *Surviving Large Losses: Financial Crises, the Middle Class, and the Development of Capital Markets*, Cambridge, MA: The Belknap Press of Harvard University Press.

Höpner, M. (2007), 'Corporate Governance Reform and the German Party Paradox', *Comparative Politics*, 39(4), 401–420.

International Social Survey Programme (ISSP), GESIS Data Archive, Cologne.

Jackson, G., M. Höpner, and A. Kurdelbusch (2006), 'Corporate Governance and Employees in Germany: Changing Linkages, Complementarities, and Tensions', *in* Howard Gospel and Andrew

Pendleton (eds), *Corporate Governance and Labour Management: An International Comparison*, Oxford: Oxford University Press, pp. 84–121.

Jacoby, S.M. (2007), 'Finance and Labor: Perspectives on Risk, Inequality, and Democracy', mimeo.

Jäger, K. (2017), 'EU KLEMS Growth and Productivity Accounts 2017 Release: Description of Methodology and General Notes', The Conference Board, September 2017, revised July 2018.

Jauch, S. and S. Watzka (2016), 'Financial Development and Income Inequality: A Panel Data Approach', *Empirical Economics*, 51(1), 291–314.

Jaumotte, F., S. Lall, and C. Papageorgiou (2013), 'Rising Income Inequality: Technology, or Trade and Financial Globalization?', *IMF Economic Review*, 61, 271–309.

Jensen, M.C. and W.H. Meckling (1976), 'Theory of the Firm: Managerial Behavior, Agency Costs and Ownership Structure', *Journal of Financial Economics*, 3(4), 305–360.

Jerzmanowski, M. and N. Malhar (2013), 'Financial Development and Wage Inequality: Theory and Evidence', *Economic Inquiry*, 51, 211–234.

Jordà, Ò., M. Schularick, and A.M. Taylor (2017), 'Macrofinancial History and the New Business Cycle Facts', *in* Martin Eichenbaum and Jonathan A. Parker (eds), *NBER Macroeconomics Annual 2016, volume 31*, Chicago, IL: University of Chicago Press.

Kastner, S. and C. Rector (2005), 'Partisanship and the Path to Financial Openness', *Comparative Political Studies*, 38(5), 484–506.

Koeniger, W., M. Leonardi, and L. Nunziata (2007), 'Labour Market Institutions and Wage Differentials', *Industrial & Labour Relations Review*, 60(3), 340–356.

Kumhof, M. and R. Rancière (2010), 'Inequality, Leverage and Crises', IMF Journal Working Paper, WP/10/268.

Larrain, M. (2015), 'Capital Account Opening and Wage Inequality', *Review of Financial Studies*, 28(6), 1555–1587.

Lazonick, W. (2015), 'Labor in the Twenty-First Century: The Top 0.1% and the Disappearing Middle-Class', *Institute for New Economic Thinking*, Working Paper No. 4, February.

Lazonick, W. and M. O'Sullivan (2000), 'Maximizing Shareholder Value: A New Ideology for Corporate Governance', *Economy and Society*, 29(1), 13–35.

Mazzucato, M. (2018), *The Value of Everything: Making and Taking in the Global Economy*, London: Allen Lane.

Milanovic, B. (2016), *Global Inequality: A New Approach for the Age of Globalization*, Cambridge, MA: The Belknap Press of Harvard University Press.

OECD (2011), 'Earnings Volatility: Causes and Consequences', *OECD Employment Outlook 2011*, Paris: OECD Publishing.

Pagano, M., and P.F. Volpin (2005), 'The Political Economy of Corporate Governance', *The American Economic Review*, 95(4), 1005–1030.

Perotti, E. C. and E. L. von Thadden (2006), 'The Political Economy of Corporate Control', *Journal of Political Economy*, 114 (1), 145–175.

Philippon, T. and A. Reshef (2012), 'Wages and Human Capital in the U.S. Financial Industry: 1909–2006', *The Quarterly Journal of Economics*, 127(4), 1551–1609.

Piketty, T. (2014), *Capital in the 21st Century*, Cambridge, MA: Harvard University Press.

Piketty, T. and E. Saez (2007), 'How Progressive is the U.S. Federal Tax System? A Historical and International Perspective', *Journal of Economic Perspectives*, 21(1), 1–24.

Piketty, T., E. Saez, and S. Stantcheva (2014), 'Optimal Taxation of Top Labor Incomes: A Tale of Three Elasticities', *American Economic Journal: Economic Policy*, 6(1), 230–271.

Pontusson, J. and D. Rueda (2008), 'Inequality as a Source of Political Polarization: A Comparative Analysis of Twelve OECD Countries', *in* Pablo Beramendi and Christopher J. Anderson (eds), *Democracy, Inequality and Representation*, Russell Sage Foundation, pp. 312–353.

Pontusson, J., D. Rueda, and C. Way (2002), 'Comparative Political Economy of Wage Distribution: The Role of Partisanship and Labour Market Institutions', *British Journal of Political Science*, 32, 281–308.

Potrafke, N. (2010), 'Labor Market Deregulation and Globalization: Empirical Evidence from OECD Countries', *Review of World Economics (Weltwirtschaftliches Archiv)*, 146(3), 545–571.

Quinn, D.P. and A.M. Toyoda (2007), 'Ideology and Voter Preferences as Determinants of Financial Globalization', *American Journal of Political Science*, 51(2), 344–363.

Rajan, R.G. (2010), *Fault Lines: How Hidden Fractures Still Threaten the World Economy*, Princeton, NJ: Princeton University Press.

Rodrik, D. (1997), *Has Globalisation Gone Too Far?*, Washington DC: Institute for International Economics.

Roe, M. (2003), *Political Determinants of Corporate Governance: Political Context, Corporate Impact*, Oxford: Oxford University Press.

Roine, J., J. Vlachos, and D. Waldenström (2009), 'The Long-Run Determinants of Inequality: What Can We Learn from Top Income Data?', *Journal of Public Economics*, 93(7), 974–988.

Rueda, D. (2007), *Social Democracy Inside Out: Partisanship and Labor Market Policy in Industrialized Democracies*, Oxford: Oxford University Press.

Rueda, D. and R.M. Barker (2007), 'The Labor Market Determinants of Corporate Governance Reform', *CLPE Research Paper*, No. 5/2007, April.

Saez, E. and G. Zucman (2016), 'Wealth Inequality in the United States since 1913: Evidence from Capitalized Income Tax Data', *Quarterly Journal of Economics*, 131(2), 519–578.

Sawyer, M. (2018), 'Financialisation, Financial Crisis and Inequality', *in* Philip Arestis and Malcolm Sawyer (eds), *Inequality*, International Papers in Political Economy, Cham: Palgrave Macmillan, pp. 43–87.

Scheve, K. and D. Stasavage (2016), *Taxing the Rich: A History of Fiscal Fairness in the United States and Europe*, Princeton, NJ: Princeton University Press.

Solt, F. (2016), 'The Standardized World Income Inequality Database', *Social Science Quarterly*, 97(5), 1267–1281.

Stockhammer, E. (2004), 'Financialisation and the Slowdown of Accumulation', *Cambridge Journal of Economics*, 28, 719–741.

Streeck, W. (2014), *Buying Time: The Delayed Crisis of Democratic Capitalism*, London: Verso.

Thesmar, D. and M. Thoenig (2004), 'Financial Market Developments and the Rise in Firm Level Uncertainty', London: Centre for Economic Policy Research.

Toporowski, J. (2009), 'The Economics and Culture of Financial Inflation', *Competition & Change*, 13(2), 145–156.

van der Zwan, N. (2014), 'Making Sense of Financialization', *Socio-Economic Review*, 12(1), 99–129.

van Treeck, T. (2009), 'The Political Economy Debate on "Financialization": A Macroeconomic Perspective', *Review of International Political Economy*, 16(5), 907–944.

van Treeck, T. (2014), 'Did Inequality Cause the U.S. Financial Crisis?', *Journal of Economic Surveys*, 28(3), 421–448.

Visser, J. (2016), ICTWSS Database, version 5.1. Amsterdam: Amsterdam Institute for Advanced Labour Studies (AIAS), University of Amsterdam. September.

Vitols, S. (2004), 'Negotiated Shareholder Value: The German Variant of an Anglo-American Practice', *Competition and Change*, 8, 357–374.

Wasmer, E. (2006), 'Interpreting Europe–US Labour Market Differences: The Specificity of Human Capital Investments', *The American Economic Review*, 96(3), 811–831.

World Wealth and Income Database (WID), consulted on March 2018.

3. Dimensions of risk and environmental inequality

David N. Pellow

INTRODUCTION

Environmental justice studies scholarship is founded on evidence and claims of unequal exposure to environmental risk. That is, research demonstrates that particular populations (low income, Indigenous, female, people of color, immigrants, communities of the global South, houseless persons, etc.) are more likely to face a range of environmental risks than other groups as a result of public policies and industry practices that reflect and reinforce ideologies of differential valuation, including racism, nativism, patriarchy, classism, and other systems of power that require and produce hierarchy among humans and between humans and ecosystems. And while most of the literature has focused on various aspects of environmental disadvantage, more recent work has begun to explore the phenomenon of environmental privilege (Farrell 2020; Murphy 2016; Taylor 2009), which some argue is not only the flipside but also the driving force behind environmental inequality (Park and Pellow 2011). Another important area of inquiry documents the ways in which military activities produce enormous harms to ecosystems and human health (Clark and Jorgenson 2012; Gould 2007; Hooks and Smith 2004), including disproportionate impacts on some populations. Building on both of these bodies of work, this chapter argues that we might productively cast environmental injustice as a form of warfare for three reasons: (1) it involves direct assaults by states and state-supported organizations on entire communities; (2) it results in massive harm to those human communities and ecosystems; (3) it is a practice designed to maintain the health of those populations that are highly valued—people who matter—at the expense of those whose lives matter less because they are differentially valued as such. Virtually every aspect of environmental injustice reflects the logic of warfare in that it reveals how government and corporate sector activities place different populations under conditions of highly uneven risk of exposure to a spectrum of environmental threats, which directly contribute to and reinforce disparate and unjust public and environmental health outcomes and environmental privileges. This framing of environmental injustice contributes to the literature on environmental justice studies and the scholarship on health disparities by offering an innovative and urgency-inducing way of thinking about the seriousness and long-term impacts of public policy and state-sponsored and institutionalized violence.

In what follows, I present some of the key developments in the literatures around environmental justice as it relates to privilege and militarization. I then present three cases of environmental racism as "warfare." The first is an examination of nuclear violence perpetrated by the U.S. military on Indigenous peoples in the United States and in the Pacific Islands. The second is a consideration of medical experiments on Black incarcerated persons at a Pennsylvania prison that involve direct chemical attacks on this population. Finally, I consider the classic environmental racism problem of disproportionate pollution in residential communities of color in the U.S. and use that example as a way of thinking through even the most seemingly unspectacular and ordinary forms of institutional racism as de facto warfare that seeks to preserve and enhance the health of White America at the expense of people of color through state and corporate violence.

ENVIRONMENTAL PRIVILEGE, MILITARIZATION, AND ECOLOGY

Environmental justice scholarship has evolved and blossomed into a major field of study. EJ studies has a primary focus on the consequences of government policy and corporate practices that result in widespread, documented, and persistently uneven impacts on communities around the world that are already suffering from economic, racial, gender, cultural, spatial, or other forms of marginalization (Bullard 2000; Mohai, Pellow, and Roberts 2009; Ray 2013; Schlosberg and Carruthers 2010; Sze 2020; Taylor 2016). This research tends to assume or leave undertheorized the driving forces behind these trends, broadly attributing these inequities to racism, socioeconomic inequality, or some combination of the two. And while we generally find merit in those assessments, other scholars have developed a framing of the problem that is more specific to the context of environmental justice politics, and that brings us to the concept of *environmental privilege*.

Environmental privilege is a term used to explain how elite communities generally enjoy relatively cleaner and healthier air, water, food, and greater access to green space and sites of recreation and leisure with coveted environmental amenities. These communities enjoy environmental privilege because they also enjoy social, economic, and racial–cultural privileges (which reinforce each other) and can take those unearned benefits for granted while other populations must mobilize and fight vehemently to simply reduce the rate, depth, and breadth of environmental injustice expansions within their communities. Environmental privilege is something that elite communities expect and desire, and it is therefore the flipside of environmental disadvantage. In other words, environmental privilege is a key driving force that helps explain why environmental injustice is so routine and ubiquitous across the social and geographic landscape in virtually any nation on earth (Gould and Lewis 2016; Park and Pellow 2011; Taylor 2016). The concept of environmental privilege builds on Laura Pulido's (2000) groundbreaking work in which she argued that the EJ studies literature had (up until that time) failed to take seriously the problem of white privilege as a primary driver of environmental racism. For Pulido, this oversight was extremely significant because the power of white privilege explains why environmental racism is so deeply entrenched in society, as it yields material payoffs for whites and is reinforced by cultural expectations and institutional power. In this chapter, I seek to explore how environmental privilege is a motivator and outcome of state and corporate violence or, to put it more bluntly, warfare.

Environmental social scientists have documented the myriad ways in which military activities and the broader phenomenon of militarization have enormous consequences for ecosystem health and human health. Scholars have, for many years, described the innumerable ways in which militaries not only imperil human populations but also involve the widescale destruction of plants, nonhuman animals, and massive impacts on marine and river systems. As Kenneth Gould (2007, p. 331) writes, "militarization is the single most ecologically destructive human endeavor," and as Renner (1991, p. 132) noted decades ago, the world's armed forces are, collectively, the single largest polluter on the planet. As of 1950, the U.S. military became the world's largest purchaser of oil (Shearer 2011). For many years, U.S. military expenditures have made up the largest share of that nation's national budget, resulting in all fifty U.S. states' economies being linked to the military industrial complex and ushering in an enduring commitment to what has become a permanent war economy (Clark and Jorgenson 2012). What this means is that the U.S. military has enormous and negative impacts on global ecosystems even during peace time (*ibid.*).

Gregory Hooks and Chad Smith (2004) proposed the idea of the Treadmill of Destruction to describe the expansionary tendencies of military institutions that operate in ways that are destructive of ecosystems and that tend to perpetuate environmental injustices against Indigenous peoples in the U.S. Scholars have similarly documented the long histories of the intersections of U.S. militarization and conquest in Indigenous communities, which has resulted in the irradiation of land, peoples' bodies, and their homes (Kuletz 2002; Malin 2015; Powell 2018; Voyles 2015).

Building on these two strands of scholarship, I contend that environmental racism is akin to warfare, even in the absence of overt military activities, and that one of its primary purposes and outcomes is to reinforce environmental privilege. In what follows, I present three cases that support this thesis.

BOMBING THE INDIGENOUS PEOPLES OF NORTH AMERICA AND THE PACIFIC

Radiating Diné Lands

At the dawn of the U.S. entry into World War II, President Franklin D. Roosevelt authorized the development of a secret undertaking to develop an atomic bomb—the Manhattan Project. The awful and awesome power of such a weapon would only be realized with massive inputs of uranium, and the one place within the borders of the U.S. with well-documented and voluminous deposits of that dense, gray radioactive metal was Navajo/Diné land in the Four Corners region. In the end, the majority of uranium used in this effort actually came from Canada and the Congo, but the mining practices in the U.S. Southwest left their mark on both the Indigenous Diné people and their lands. Today, there are upwards of some 2,000 abandoned uranium mines, mills and tailings piles, which are generally unsecured and poorly marked. Over the decades, some 3,000 Indigenous miners performed the hard work of extracting uranium from the earth and processing it into "yellowcake." That substance was the raw material for the nearly 1,000 bombs tested on Western Shoshone Indigenous lands in the U.S. and on the peoples and ecosystems of several Pacific islands.

The afterlife of uranium remains and continues to commit violence for generations. Diné families have had to contend with sick and dying family members who either worked in the mines or were contaminated by uranium residues because of close contact with those who did. Rates of lung cancer and respiratory disease in these communities rose suddenly and dramatically as a result of the mining industry activities in the region. Moreover, researchers have found exceedingly high rates of other diseases believed to be caused by uranium exposure as well, including tuberculosis, fibrosis, silicosis, birth defects, testicular and ovarian cancer, and neuropathy. These communities have been exposed to water laced with uranium and arsenic, and nearly 1,000 homes and other structures have been found to contain radioactive substances because they were built with debris or rocks extracted from the mines. This is the definition of a sacrifice zone. These Indigenous communities were knowingly placed on the front lines of environmental harm to advance U.S. national security and global military dominance. At that time, the lethal dangers of uranium had been well known for hundreds of years, and were documented by scientists in the late 19th and early 20th centuries (Voyles 2015). Notably, as early as the 1950s (before the effects of uranium presented themselves), scientists found that the rate of cancer among Diné people was so low that some medical researchers posited the idea that this population might have "cancer immunity" (Powell 2018, p. 52). Sadly, that theory would soon be debunked.

A number of advocacy groups emerged in the wake of public disclosures of uranium's horrifying effects on human and environmental health. These groups mobilized for federal regulation to control and reduce the impacts of the industry, to insist on the thorough and safe clean-up of toxic sites, and to exercise some power over the future of this sector, with varying degrees of success (Malin 2015). Many energy justice and environmental justice activists in Diné country have worked to strengthen federal regulations on uranium-related illness compensation policies that discriminated against or excluded Diné people, and have also pushed their tribal government to embrace and develop alternatives to toxic, extractive energy such as wind and solar power (Powell 2018).

Nuclearizing the Pacific

The vast expanse of Pacific Island nations that make up the regions of Micronesia, Melanesia, and Polynesia consist of thousands of islands and atolls, and multiple cultures and languages. Since the mid-1940s, this region has been used as a nuclear arms laboratory by colonial powers that have detonated nuclear bombs and performed intercontinental missile tests in the area (Weisgall 1994). The U.S., Britain, and France have all participated in these practices, which have resulted in countless forms of violence done to human and nonhuman life, including the problem of "jelly fish babies" in the Marshall Islands—humans born without eyes, heads, arms, or legs (Kuletz 2002, p. 128). To this day, in the so-called "post-colonial" era, wealthy nations are using the region as a dumping ground for the hazardous wastes associated with chemically intense industries and militarization. Valerie Kuletz argues that this nuclearization was deliberate and had a purpose: the development of military knowledge for the benefit, security, and protection of powerful global North nations:

> The post-World War II nuclear testing regimes in the Marshalls were in many ways typical of a colonial occupation. The difference was in the kind of raw material that was taken from the colonized site and brought back to the colonial mother country. Instead of gold, timber, or sugar, the Americans obtained scientific knowledge about radiation and nuclear weapons (Kuletz 2002, p. 128).

The fact that human beings—Indigenous peoples—were living in these areas meant that the U.S., France, Britain, and other nations created the conditions under which their scientists could study the effects of radiation on human beings and ecosystems, invaluable knowledge for nuclear powers seeking geopolitical advantage. In 1946, the U.S. military relocated Bikinians from the Bikini Atoll to the island of Rongerik, more than 100 miles away, in order to remove them from the testing site (Miller 1986). The U.S. promised to return these nuclear refugees afterwards. In the meantime, Operation Crossroads—the name given to the nuclear test on the atoll—proceeded, while many Bikinians starved on Rongerik island because there was insufficient food from the local flora and fauna (Weisgall 1980). The military did not return the people to the atoll, and instead relocated them again and again. They were never returned to the Bikini atoll and, by 1963, when the Limited Test Ban Treaty was signed, the U.S. had exploded 67 nuclear bombs in the Marshall Islands, rendering their homes uninhabitable (Gerrard 2015).

These activities gave rise to the Nuclear-Free and Independent Pacific Movement (NFIP), a regional network of activists seeking environmental justice and sovereignty from colonial powers whose goal has been to use the Pacific region as a laboratory to develop, expand, and better understand the nature of nuclear weapons to maintain their geopolitical and military dominance. The NFIP succeeded in pushing for the development and ratification of the South Pacific Nuclear Free Zone Treaty (commonly known as the Treaty of Rarotonga), which bans the testing, use, and possession of nuclear weapons within the borders of that zone. The nations that have ratified the treaty include: Australia, the Cook Islands, Fiji, Kiribati, Nauru, New Zealand, Niue, Papua New Guinea, Samoa, Solomon Islands, Tonga, Tuvalu, and Vanuatu.

The case of the radiated Four Corners region and the nuclearized Pacific region underscores how military activities have been—and continue to be—used in ways that involve targeting entire communities for institutional and ecological violence, and for the purpose of strengthening environmental privilege and martial dominance. In the next section I present a case of environmental injustice that extends the reach of this thesis into the U.S. prison system.

ENVIRONMENTAL RACISM IN PRISON AS CHEMICAL WARFARE

Scholars have recently documented a number of connections between prisons and environmental injustice concerns, including the fact that many prisons are beset with contaminated water and/or are located on or near toxic sites (Pellow 2017). These linkages are even more disturbing and direct when we consider the deliberate use of toxins on prisoners' bodies. Dictionary.com defines "chemical warfare" as follows: "the use of chemical agents as a weapon of war or terror." The Merriam-Webster Dictionary defines it as "tactical warfare using incendiary mixtures, smokes, or irritant, burning, poisonous, or asphyxiating gases" and, according to that same source, a chemical weapon is defined simply as "a weapon used in chemical warfare." I believe these definitions accurately and appropriately describe the practice of using chemicals on the bodies and communities of incarcerated persons *as well as* the broader realities of environmental racism/injustice that affect communities beyond the prison walls around the world.

While a number of scholars and journalists have reported on medical experimentation against vulnerable people—including prisoners (see Hornblum 1998 and Washington 2006)—few if any of those approaches have taken an environmental or environmental justice perspective on this matter, and that gap is of great significance because an EJ framing opens up the possibilities for analysis and action that are much broader than a medical, public health, or state-based rights-focused perspective.

During the 1950s and 1960s, University of Pennsylvania professor and dermatologist Dr. Albert Kligman exposed scores of inmates at Holmesburg Prison in Pennsylvania to high doses of dioxin, the most toxic substance known to science and the main poisonous ingredient in Agent Orange. The Dow Chemical Company paid Kligman $10,000 to conduct these experiments with the purported goal of measuring the toxicity effects of this chemical compound best known for the U.S. military's widespread usage of it during the U.S. war in Viet Nam. The company sought to determine the "threshold" or minimum level of exposure that could produce chloracne.[1] Other similar experiments occurred at that same prison from 1950 to 1974 (Blivaiss 1998). The inmates as "research subjects" were paid $2 to $3 per day for lending their bodies to these projects. Since they were paid, some observers claimed the prisoners gave their consent—a view disputed by many critics, including Allen Hornblum (1998), author of an exposé on the prison. Hornblum and others point out that, because the prisoners were never fully informed of the risks associated with the procedures, this was a clear violation of the rules of consent under the Nuremberg Code of 1947. Albert Kligman even noted, at the time he conducted his research, "informed consent was unheard of. No one asked me what I was doing. It was a wonderful time" (Goodman 1998). As Kligman destroyed his research records when the program was shut down in 1974, the best estimate is that "thousands" of inmates took part in the experiments over the years (*ibid.*).

What might an environmental justice perspective on prisons and chemical warfare look like? Let us first consider the institutions involved in these practices. Many of the institutions whose products were being tested on the incarcerated are some of the world's most infamous polluters, including the U.S. military and Dow Chemical, and their products are known to contaminate ecosystems and human bodies and communities. Dioxin is the deadly chemical compound that is a core component of Agent Orange, the most commonly used herbicide by U.S. military forces to eliminate forest cover and crops used by North Vietnamese and Viet Cong troops from 1961 to 1971. In what was called Operation Ranch Hand, the U.S. military dumped some 20 million gallons of Agent Orange and other pesticides on Laos, Viet Nam, and Cambodia during the war, with Agent Orange being the most potent and highest percentage of that total volume at 65% or 13 million gallons. Operation Ranch Hand caused physical deformities in tens of thousands of children, destroyed 14 percent of Viet Nam's forests, and produced great suffering among military service personnel from all sides of the conflict. The Vietnamese government recently reported that more than seventy thousand of its citizens suffer from medical diseases related to Agent Orange exposure. Other estimates are closer to one million because many people who suffer are those who were not even born at the time (New York Times 2003).

Dioxin's reach is a powerful example of "slow violence" (Nixon 2011) in that it is a highly persistent chemical compound that lasts for many years in waterways, soil, and the food chain. Slow violence need not be intentional—it can be the unintended result of decisions made by government or corporate officials who may not have foreseen the far-reaching effects of certain institutional policies and practices. The main point is that it is the kind of harm that occurs over extended periods of time and that, therefore, tends to escape routine observation and documentation. Dioxin's slow violence is observable—if we pay close attention—as it accumulates in fatty tissue in the bodies of birds, fish, and other animals, and humans tend to be exposed to it through consuming fish, shellfish, eggs, meat, dairy, poultry, and from incinerator emissions. It is universally known to be a carcinogen and studies of laboratory animals have demonstrated that it is extremely toxic even in minute doses.

Despite the fact that the US Environmental Protection Agency (USEPA) "believed that there was no safe levels of dioxin exposure" because "herbicides spread on pastures, farmlands, and forests could promote stillbirths, birth defects, and cancer" (Hornblum 1998, p. 173) and the fact that the agency is the federal institution responsible for regulating pesticides and herbicides, the Environmental Protection Agency (EPA) responded to prisoners' demands to do a full-scale investigation by quietly narrowing that effort to interview only a fraction of the persons involved in the Holmesburg experiments. The agency eventually reached the conclusion that evidence of dioxin exposure causing any significant health problems among Holmesburg prisoners was unfounded (Hornblum 1998, pp. 163–183). This is just one of many examples of the USEPA refusing to render a finding of abuse or criminal behavior when marginalized communities have been concerned about the inundation of toxic chemicals (Lombardi, Buford, and Greene 2015).

It is also noteworthy that, while a prison is at the center of this story, so is a university—the University of Pennsylvania. Scholar–activist Julia Oparah (Sudbury 2009) reminds us that universities and prisons have a long history of entanglement, including the development of entire fields of research that have generally supported the prison industrial complex and the billions of dollars that academic institutions have invested in the private prison system (Williams 2015). Also at the center of this story is the institution of medicine and how so many of medical scientific "advances" have been achieved at the expense of vulnerable human and nonhuman populations.

The U.S. Army was implicated in the Holmesburg Prison experiments insofar as it had been working with Dow Chemical on the effects of various chemicals on humans, so Kligman's contracts with Dow indirectly linked the Holmesburg Prison experiments with the U.S. military. For example, the U.S. military had, along with the CIA, already been deeply involved in chemical warfare against Black communities through the MK-ULTRA project—an effort to unleash genetically modified mosquitos on the all-African American communities of Carver Village in Florida and Georgia, with the intent of testing the viability of spreading infectious diseases through using the insects as biological/chemical weapons vectors (see Washington 2006, pp. 359–383). In 1999, Dow Chemical purchased Union Carbide, the company responsible for a toxic chemical gas leak that killed thousands of people in Bhopal, India beginning in 1984.

It is important to also point out that the inadequacies and racist violence within the prison "medical" system reflect and shape what we find in the "health care" system *outside* of the prisons and their associated consequences. For example, the scholarship on health disparities has, for decades, revealed that people of color and low-income populations consistently have greater morbidity and mortality than whites and affluent communities, which cannot be fully explained by economics, "health behaviors," or biology (Gee and Payne-Sturges 2004; Institute of Medicine 1999). Moreover, the health care system in the U.S. and globally is frequently implicated in contributing to ecological harm and environmental injustices as it is the leading source of materials burned in medical waste incinerators—which are often located in vulnerable communities and are a major producer of dioxin emissions (Health Care Without Harm 2001). Furthermore, the health care sector routinely uses toxic materials in furniture, cleaning supplies, and medical delivery devices in hospitals and clinics (Health Care Without Harm 2014). No less important and perhaps even more challenging is the fact that millions of consumers use similar toxic materials in their homes each day (Breast Cancer Prevention Partners 2018).

If prisons are, as I believe the evidence makes abundantly clear, sites of torture by virtue of being systems of total control and incapacitation, chemical warfare via medical experimentation is a *compounding* practice—a torture chamber within a torture chamber; a form of abuse and violence occurring within a system that is already innately abusive and violent. The interrelationships among the organizations and institutions involved in the Holmesburg prison experiments reveal an ecology of power and a productive opening into EJ approaches to change making because if EJ requires confronting not just the prison but all of the institutions, organizations, and practices that fuel it and make it possible, this case reveals quite clearly that not only was the prison perpetrating environmental racism and torture but so was Dow Chemical, the U.S. military, the University of Pennsylvania, and the US Environmental Protection Agency. This is an ecology of torture and hierarchy that cannot be ignored in our campaigns and investigations of prisons, as Julia Oparah (Sudbury 2009) has argued persuasively. These horrific experiments were therefore not actually taking place in isolation from other major institutions in this society, which offers an opportunity to see those linkages as points of intervention and alliance building for change. For example, we continue to witness examples of torture, medical neglect, and cruel and unusual punishment in prisons today, which are supported directly by taxpayer dollars, government agencies, and private institutions (Pellow 2017; Pellow et al. 2019). These observations are critical because they underscore that environmental justice approaches must involve multi-sited efforts to confront violence across multiple institutions.

Resistance: This is What Environmental Justice Looks Like

Former Holmesburg prisoner and research subject Leodus Jones launched and led Community Assistance for Prisoners, an organization that advocates for current and formerly incarcerated persons in the state of Pennsylvania. He declared, "These tests were unfair; they were barbaric …. We were lied to; we were used and were exploited. We were human guinea pigs" (Lowe 1998). Jones and his group led street demonstrations and protests to demand free medical treatment, compensation for suffering and pain, and funds for rehabilitation programs. He and 300 former inmates brought lawsuits against the city of Philadelphia, the University of Pennsylvania, Albert Kligman, Dow Chemical, and Johnson & Johnson for the lingering physical and psychological effects associated with the experiments, and for not informing them of the associated risks. These experiments became the focus of Allen Hornblum's 1998 book *Acres of Skin*, in which he detailed examples of exposure to various cosmetics, powerful skin creams, dioxin, and high doses of LSD that occurred at the prison. The majority of the plaintiffs in the legal case were low-income African–American men, some women, all in poor health and experiencing trouble breathing, and many suffering from gynecological complications, infections, and skin rashes. And while their lawsuit was ultimately unsuccessful, they have put this issue on the radar of human rights, healthcare rights, and prisoner rights movements. This is of critical importance given that, despite a number of state and federal laws that were believed to have ground the use of prisoners in medical experiments to a halt, in recent years evidence emerged that medical experimentation on prisoners had continued in several states, including Arkansas, Connecticut, Florida, Maryland, Rhode Island, South Carolina, and Texas. The University of Texas Medical Branch, the University of Miami, the University of Florida, Yale University, and Brown University have all been the subjects of investigations that have led to findings that reporting and oversight for protecting imprisoned research subjects were lacking. The University of Texas Medical Branch (UTMB) case has been reported in the media as one that was particularly concerning. In July 2000, the federal Office of Human Research Protections (a division of the Department of Health and Human Services) suspended federally sponsored research projects at UTMB because of a failure to follow basic regulations and protocols designed to protect human research subjects. Of the 300 studies brought to a halt that month, 195 of them involved Texas prisoners (Talvi 2001), many of which were clinical drug trials, including those for HIV positive persons (Ward and Bishop 2001). These and many other cases have led legal scholars to conclude that medical experimentation on prisoners remains an ongoing trend in the U.S. (Reiter 2009).

A liberal–reformist approach to this problem would likely argue that we need only to propose stronger regulations to protect prisoners. In other words, the problem is deregulation, and the solution is more regulation. My view is that this is misguided. The problem is the prison itself, which is a form of torture and warfare that an EJ approach would demand an end to. As one observer put it with respect to experimentation, "Instead of asking how prison research should be done ... they should be asking if it should be done at all" (Talvi 2001). In the third case below, I consider a more everyday instance of environmental racism to explore how a more familiar story can also be reframed as warfare on people of color.

A "CLASSIC" CASE OF ENVIRONMENTAL RACISM

In June of 2020, Donald Trump proposed one of numerous rollbacks in federal pollution control legislation that his administration perpetrated for years. Of the more than a hundred such proposals, that particular one included efforts to curtail limitations on carbon dioxide emissions from power plants and motor vehicles (Popovich, Albeck-Ripka, and Pierre-Louis 2020). These proposals were of particular concern to environmentalists and EJ activists because communities of color are disproportionately impacted by coal-fired power plants and vehicle pollution because those plants and highways are, on average, in closer proximity to those communities than to white communities. Greenpeace USA decried this effort in a mass emailing:

> For decades Black and Brown communities have borne the disproportionate impacts of pollution. More coal plants, refineries, and chemical processing facilities are built in communities of color than in white communities—this environmental racism has to stop.
> So imagine my outrage when I saw Donald Trump's announcement this morning that he was rolling back pollution controls at the Environmental Protection Agency (EPA). Donald Trump's anti-environment agenda is also a racist one. We are in the middle of a pandemic caused by a virus that targets the lungs and makes it harder to breathe. The impacts of COVID-19 can be worse for those who experience air pollution. This is one reason the health crisis means more Black, Brown, and Indigenous lives are lost. We are fighting against extractive industries that have wrecked our climate while treating communities of color and working-class communities as sacrifice zones. This executive order is another manifestation of the white supremacy that has driven Trump's policymaking from day one, and it will have deadly consequences .... Trump is trying to sneak in roll backs to pollution protections. And air pollution can make COVID-19 deadlier, particularly for Black and Brown communities that live closer to dirty factories and freeways. (Allen 2020)

In many ways, this series of environmental regulatory rollbacks constitutes what I would call a "classic" example of environmental racism. It is "classic" because it is so familiar and such a longstanding practice under the weak environmental regulatory system in the U.S. It involves institutional actors making policy changes that have disparate impacts on communities of color, which will exacerbate morbidity and mortality in those populations, not only through the increase in the volume of particulate matter and air pollution, but also through the intensification of anthropogenic climate change, which also has uneven and unjust impacts on communities of color and Indigenous communities (Bhavnani et al. 2019; Porter et al. 2020). In other words, this is a case of environmental policy making that puts marginalized communities at greater risk. Most scholarly treatments of this case would essentially end there, but in this chapter I seek to go further in reframing the scourge of environmental racism.

Building on the two earlier cases presented above, I contend that this kind of "classic" act of environmental injustice can be thought of not only as an instance of environmental racism but also as an act of warfare because: (1) it involves direct assaults by states and state-supported organizations on entire communities; (2) it results in massive harm to those human communities and ecosystems; (3) it is a practice designed to maintain the health of those populations that are highly valued—people who matter to elites in positions of political and economic power—at the expense of those whose lives matter less because they are differentially valued as such. That last point reflects the importance of pinpointing the enduring quest for environmental privilege as a motivating force behind environmental racism and injustice. What this framing facilitates is a grasp not just of the phenomenon of environmental privilege, but more importantly, how it is routinely weaponized. When we reframe environmental racism as warfare (not merely as an act of war but as a broader process of militarization), we can more clearly see how dominant institutions view those who suffer from and experience these ills, not as "environmental justice communities" or innocent people experiencing unfair environmental harms, but as military targets and enemies whose communities, bodies, territories, and identities must be contained, neutralized, and frequently destroyed.

Environmental social science scholarship on militarization demonstrates that the socioecological impacts of military activities have far-reaching consequences for both people and ecosystems. And some of that research reveals how militarization has uneven, environmentally unjust consequences for some populations. This chapter has taken these ideas a step further to argue that environmental injustice itself is a form of warfare because it weaponizes environmental privilege through state and institutional violence.

The argument that environmental racism is a form of warfare raises a key question: since warfare is an intentional act (or series of acts) of violence, does the same logic truly apply to environmental policy? In the case of environmental racism, the answer is both yes and no. Specifically, in those cases where environmental racism is the result of interlocking institutional (i.e., market and governmental) forces that produce uneven and harmful consequences within communities of color, one could definitely argue that animus or ill-intent is often not in evidence. But there are far too many cases where the intention *is* in fact present. The cases of military experimentation in the Pacific and the Holmesburg Prison experiments are clear examples of this, as are scores of other cases of environmental racism where documents and statements of ill-intent are on the record (see Bullard and Wright 2012; Cerrell Associates 1984). But many "traditional" or "classic" cases of environmental racism do not always fit this scenario, so it should be stated that my argument framing these policies and practices as warfare does have its limits.

Ironically, as with institutional racism more generally, environmental racism and injustice take a considerable toll on the very populations deemed worthy of protection and privilege because the massive production of chemical pollutants and other forms of ecologically harmful agents ultimately knows no boundaries. As Ulrich Beck famously argued in his "risk society" thesis, there is a "boomerang" effect wherein those populations responsible for producing environmentally damaging chemicals that are frequently transported or dumped far away from wealthy communities, are still exposed to those threats in the end (Beck 1995). So if institutional forms of environmental racism could be said to be a type of warfare, then, sadly, one could also argue that it constitutes a war on ourselves and our planet.

CONCLUSION: FROM ENVIRONMENTAL JUSTICE TO ANARCHIST POLITICAL ECOLOGIES

If, as I have argued here, environmental injustice can be reframed as a practice involving warfare, one could similarly reframe environmental justice activism as a practice that may be most effective if it focuses on pursuing peaceful means of social change that target the ways in which states, corporations, and other institutions perpetrate violent activities against communities. That is to say, rather than simply viewing environmental racism as another form of institutional racism, if we see it as a form of institutional violence, scholars and activists may succeed in mobilizing new and previously untapped sources of public sentiment and support for the movement and for progressive policy making (including, for example, anti-war/peace and human rights movements).

Going even further, perhaps this reframing must also extend to ways of thinking of environmental justice as an anti-imperialist and anarchist vision of change. Given that the state is an apparatus that is inextricably bound to capitalism, scholars have increasingly considered perspectives that are not just critical of markets via anti-capitalist theory, but that also suggest an embrace of anarchism. One emergent theoretical and activist–scholar development in that direction is anarchist political ecology, a refusal of formal institutional mechanisms to solve our socioecological crises because such pathways invariably serve to reinforce the power of the very institutions that have given rise to our crises in the first place (Springer forthcoming). Anarchist political ecology argues that all forms of oppression and domination—not only classism or racism, but also speciesism and anthroparchy (human domination)—must be challenged. While environmental justice scholarship and activism have traditionally eschewed openly anarchistic leanings, there are indications that changes are afoot. EJ scholars like Pulido (2016 and 2017), Pellow (2016 and 2017), and others have begun to openly call for theoretical and political engagements that no longer envision an environmental justice that is reliant on state power and state intervention. And the *Principles of Environmental Justice*, which is a sort of founding document or manifesto for the EJ movement, contains very strong leanings in this direction, as it articulates a program of change that targets virtually all known forms of oppression (see www.ejnet.org/ej/principles.html). Whatever direction EJ scholarship and politics may take in the future, my view is that it will behoove researchers and activists to think deeply about the role of militarization and institutional violence as driving forces behind environmental injustice and as a generative way of framing how we think and act to confront these challenges and risks facing vulnerable communities.

NOTE

1. This is a particularly horrifying example of how threshold levels for toxic exposure to certain substances can be determined.

REFERENCES

Allen, L. (2020), 'Stop Trump's environmental racism', Greenpeace USA. June 5.

Beck, U. (1995), *Ecological Enlightenment: Essays on the Politics of the Risk Society*, Amherst, New York: Humanity Books.

Bhavnani, K, Foran J, Kurian P. A, and Munshi, D. (Eds.) (2019), *Climate Futures: Re-Imagining Global Climate Justice*, London: Zed Books.

Blivaiss, N. (1998), 'Decades old prison tests stir controversy', *The Daily Pennsylvanian*. November 19.

Breast Cancer Prevention Partners (2018), *Right to Know: Exposing Toxic Fragrance Chemicals in Beauty, Personal Care, and Cleaning Products*, Campaign for Safe Cosmetics.

Bullard, R. (2000), *Dumping in Dixie: Race, Class, and Environmental Quality*, Boulder, Colorado: Westview Press. 3rd edition.

Bullard, R and Wright, B. (2012), *The Wrong Complexion for Protection: How the Government Response to Disaster Endangers African American Communities*, New York: New York University Press.

Cerrell Associates (1984), *Political Difficulties Facing Waste-to-Energy Conversion Plant Siting*, California Waste Management Board.

Clark, B. and Jorgenson, A. (2012), 'The treadmill of destruction and the environmental impacts of militaries', *Sociology Compass*, **6**(7), 557–569.

Farrell, J. (2020), *Billionaire Wilderness: The Ultra-Wealthy and the Remaking of the American West*, Princeton, New Jersey: Princeton University Press.

Gee, G. and D. Payne-Sturges (2004), 'Environmental health disparities: A framework integrating psychosocial and environmental concepts', *Environmental Health Perspectives*, **112**(17), 1645–1653.

Gerrard, M.B. (2015), 'America's forgotten nuclear waste dump in the Pacific', *SAIS Review of International Affairs*, **35**(1), 87–97.

Goodman, H. (1998), 'Studying prison experiments research', *Baltimore Sun*. July 21.

Gould, K. (2007), 'The ecological costs of militarization', *Peace Review: A Journal of Social Justice*, **19**(4), 331–334.

Gould, K., and Lewis, T. (2016), *Green Gentrification: Urban Sustainability and the Struggle for Environmental Justice*, New York: Routledge.

Health Care Without Harm (2001), *Non-Incineration Medical Waste Treatment Technologies*, Washington, D.C.

Health Care Without Harm (2014), *Global Reach, Enduring Change*, Impact Report. Washington, D.C.

Hooks, G. and Smith, C.L. (2004), 'The treadmill of destruction: National sacrifice areas and Native Americans', *American Sociological Review*, **69**(4), 558–576.

Hornblum, A. M. (1998), *Acres of Skin: Human Experiments at Holmesburg Prison*, New York: Routledge.

Institute of Medicine (1999), *Toward Environmental Justice: Research, Education, and Health Policy Needs*, Committee on Environmental Justice. Washington, D.C.: National Academies Press.

Kuletz, V. (2002), 'The movement for environmental justice in the Pacific Islands', in Adamson, J., Evans, M., and Stein, R. (Eds.), *The Environmental Justice Reader*, Tucson, Arizona: University of Arizona Press, pp. 125–144.

Lombardi, K., Buford, T., and Greene, R. (2015), 'Environmental Justice, Denied', Center for Public Integrity. August 3.

Lowe, H. (1998), 'Former Inmates Protest They Say They Still Suffer from Experiments Performed on Them in Philadelphia Prisons', *Philadelphia Inquirer*. November 6.

Malin, S. (2015), *The Price of Nuclear Power: Uranium Communities and Environmental Justice*, New Brunswick, New Jersey: Rutgers University Press.

Miller, R. (1986), *Under the Cloud: The Decades of Nuclear Testing*, New York: The Free Press.

Mohai, P., Pellow, D.N., and Roberts, J.T. (2009), 'Environmental Justice', *Annual Review of Environment and Resources*, **34**, 405–430.

Murphy, M. (2016), 'Mapping Environmental Privilege in Rhode Island', *Environmental Justice*, **9**(5), 159–165.

New York Times (2003), 'More Were Exposed to Agent Orange', *New York Times*, April 17.

Nixon, R. (2011), *Slow Violence and the Environmentalism of the Poor*, Cambridge, Massachusetts: Harvard University Press.

Park, L. S., and David N. P. (2011), *The Slums of Aspen: Immigrants vs. the Environment in America's Eden*, New York: New York University Press.

Pellow, D. N. (2016), 'Toward a critical environmental justice studies: Black Lives Matter as an environmental justice challenge', *DuBois Review*, **13**(2), 221–236.

Pellow, D N. (2017), *What Is Critical Environmental Justice?* Cambridge, UK: Polity Press.

Pellow, D. N., Vazin, J., Austin, M.A., and Johnson, K. (2019), *Capitalism in Practice: Free Market Influences on Environmental Injustice in America's Prisons*, Annual Report by UCSB's Prison Environmental Justice Project, an initiative of the Global Environmental Justice Project. September.

Popovich, N., Albeck-Ripka, L., and Pierre-Louis, K. (2020), 'The Trump Administration is reversing 100 environmental rules: Here's the full list', *New York Times*. May 20.

Porter, L., L. Rickards, B. Verlie, K. Bosomworth, S. Moloney, B. Lay, B. Latham, I. Anguelovski, and D. Pellow (2020), 'Climate justice in a climate changed world', *Planning Theory & Practice*, DOI: 10.1080/14649357.2020.1748959.

Powell, D. (2018), *Landscapes of Power: Politics of Energy in the Navajo Nation*, Durham, North Carolina: Duke University Press.

Pulido, L. (2000), 'Rethinking environmental racism: White privilege and urban development in Southern California', *Annals of the Association of American Geographers*, **90**(1), 12–40.

Pulido, L. (2017), 'Geographies of race and ethnicity II: Environmental racism, racial capitalism, and state-sanctioned violence', *Progress in Human Geography*, **41**(4), 524–533.

Pulido, L, Kohl, E., and Marie-Cotton, N. (2016), 'State regulation and environmental justice: The need for strategy reassessment', *Capitalism Nature Socialism*, **27**(2), 12–31.

Ray, S.J. (2013), *The Ecological Other: Environmental Exclusion in American Culture*, Tucson, Arizona: University of Arizona Press.

Reiter, K. (2009), 'Experimentation on prisoners: Persistent dilemmas in rights and regulations', *California Law Review*, **97**(2), 501–566.

Renner, M. (1991), 'Assessing the military's war on the environment', in Linda Starke (ed.), *State of the World*, New York: W.W. Norton & Company, pp. 132–152.

Schlosberg, D. and Carruthers, D. (2010), 'Indigenous struggles, environmental justice, and community capabilities', *Global Environmental Politics*, **10**(4), 12–35.

Shearer, C. (2011), *Kivalina: A Climate Change Story*, Chicago, IL: Haymarket Books.

Springer, S., *Undoing Human Supremacy: Anarchist Political Ecology in the Face of Anthroparchy*.

Sudbury, J. (2009), 'Challenging penal dependency: Activist scholars and the Antiprison Movement', in Julia Sudbury and Margo Okazawa-Rey (Eds.), *Activist Scholarship: Anti-Racism, Feminism, and Social Change*, Boulder, Colorado: Paradigm Publishers, pp. 17–35.

Sze, J. (2020), *Environmental Justice in a Moment of Danger*, Berkeley, California: University of California Press.

Talvi, S.J.A. (2001), 'The prison as laboratory', *In These Times*, December 7.

Taylor, D. (2009), *The Environment and the People in American Cities, 1600s–1900s: Disorder, Inequality, and Social Change*, Durham, North Carolina: Duke University Press.

Taylor, D. (2016), *Toxic Communities: Environmental Racism, Industrial Pollution, and Residential Mobility*, New York: New York University Press.

Voyles, T. (2015), *Wastelanding: Legacies of Uranium Mining in Navajo Country*, Minneapolis, Minnesota: University of Minnesota Press.

Ward, M. and Bishop, B. (2001), 'Becoming guinea pigs to avoid poor prison care, ill inmates urge each other to join experiments', *Austin American-Statesman*. December 17.

Washington, H. (2006), *Medical Apartheid: The Dark History of Medical Experimentation on Black Americans from Colonial Times to the Present*, New York: Anchor Books.

Weisgall, J. (1980), 'The nuclear nomads of Bikini', *Foreign Policy*, **39**, 74–98.

Weisgall, J. (1994), *Operation Crossroads: The Atomic Tests at Bikini Atoll*. Annapolis, Maryland: Naval Institute Press.

Williams, A. (2015). 'Afrikan Black Coalition Accomplishes UC Prison Divestment!' http://afrikanblackcoalition.org/2015/12/18/afrikan-black-coalition-accomplishes-uc-prison-divestment/

4. Risk and (welfare state) politics

Philipp Rehm[1]

INTRODUCTION

Modern democracies are insurance companies with an army.[2] How did they end up that way? Why did modern democracies develop far-reaching social insurance systems that cover most citizens from the main adversities of modern life? This is a puzzling pattern in need of an explanation.[3] After all, the creation of social insurance institutions faces a double-challenge: the *social choice problems* typical for political decision-making and the *information problems* typical for insurance arrangements. Worse, some of the same factors that facilitate social choice (or collective action) undermine the actuarial necessities of risk pooling. In particular, social choice problems are more readily resolved under conditions of *homogeneity*: smallness, coherence, and similarity facilitate cooperation and democratic decision-making. In contrast, insurance requires *heterogeneity*: large numbers, diversity, and uncorrelated risks make risk-pooling schemes work (de Swaan 1988: 146; Platteau 1991: 159).

How was this 'social insurance dilemma' overcome? Why, against the odds, did all of today's modern democracies set up mandatory social policy programs against the main risks their citizens face? Existing scholarship answers these questions by pointing to what modern democracies have in common: they are democratic and they are industrialized.

Explanations that focus on *democratization* suggest that the welfare state is a child of the democratic (class) struggle. Through enfranchisement (Lindert 2004; Meltzer and Richard 1978) and electoral success (Esping-Andersen 1985; Stephens 1979), actors championing the welfare state—such as unions and social democratic parties—gained political power and advanced the cause. The main weakness of these *political* explanations is that they cannot account for the commonality of the experience. Left party power is not a necessary—and perhaps not even a sufficient condition—for welfare state emergence and expansion. These approaches do not analyze welfare state politics from an insurance perspective and therefore overlook the importance of information problems.

Explanations that focus on *industrialization* suggest that the suffering and destitution brought by industrialization posed 'social questions' to which the welfare state was the answer. Perhaps the most elegant formulation in this spirit posits that risk-averse citizens prefer insurance but private insurance markets cannot exist in the presence of well-known information challenges (Barr 2012). Thus, the welfare state—mandatory public insurance—is an efficient solution to this problem. Elegant as they are, the main weakness with these *economic*, functionalist explanations[4] is their reliance on efficiency as a key mechanism. However, efficiency does not bring about political outcomes (Iversen and Rehm 2022). Instead, coalition-building and majority decision-making does. These approaches do not analyze politics and therefore overlook social choice problems.

In this chapter, I want to combine insights from both economic and political approaches to shed light on the 'social insurance dilemma' and sketch a framework to analyze the politics of risk. I first summarize the standard argument for the existence of mandatory social insurance schemes, as developed in economics (section 2). The information problems identified in this economic literature are crucial, but mostly glossed over in political science. I then lay out an alternative framework, which pays attention to both social choice and information problems (section 3). The framework yields several mechanisms that should be relevant for overcoming the 'social insurance dilemma' and I examine their plausibility (section 4). In particular, I explore whether the framework can make sense of the transition from voluntary mutual aid societies to mandatory social insurance arrangements (section 5). As informational problems are key for understanding (social) insurance, the ongoing information revolution might give us insights about the future of 'risk and politics' (conclusion).

Information Problems and Social Insurance: The Standard Argument

An elegant view of the welfare state, developed in economics, interprets it as an efficient solution to informational problems that prevent the existence of private insurance markets for personal risks. The argument goes something like this (Barr 2001, 2012; Sinn 1995): risk-averse individuals are willing to buy private insurance at actuarially fair rates to cover their potential loss.[5] As most people are risk averse, there is broad demand for insurance.

Obviously, the demand for insurance can be met by commercial insurance only when the latter exists. For most of history, that was simply not the case. Before the invention of commercial insurance—and, even later, the welfare state—people coped with the adversities of life with mostly informal arrangements that can be described as 'hunger insurance' (Platteau 1991). Those arrangements were limited and existed only at the local level, such as the household or village (Thane 1996). On the one hand, the small scale helped in setting up insurance arrangements (or coping strategies), and to monitor their participants' behavior (to avoid free-riding and moral hazard). On the other hand, the small scale undermined the insurance logic, which requires pooling of diverse and uncorrelated risks. Those whose survival was at the whim of nature understood the importance of spatial diversification, and attempts of spatial risk pool diversification are documented, going all the way back to pre-capitalist village societies. But those coping arrangements were difficult to achieve and maintain—diversifying the risk pool is a challenging task (Platteau 1991).

Even when actuarial knowledge and bureaucratic capacities had advanced to a degree that commercial insurance became feasible in theory and common in some domains, it was not always viable. Many threats to workers' livelihood that emerged or became salient during the Industrial Revolution—workplace accidents, unemployment, sickness, old age—are (or were) difficult for commercial insurance to insure. For private insurance markets to be viable, certain conditions regarding risks, and information about risks, need to hold.

A first precondition for the existence of robust private insurance markets is that the probability of bad events needs to be uncorrelated for risk pooling to work. Good risks—those that were spared from experiencing a bad event—support bad risks, and not everybody can be unlucky at the same time. For example, if most insured houses in an insurance company's portfolio burn down in the same wildfire, the company will go bankrupt. In that sense, risk pools need to be diverse. This does not mean that everybody's probability of experiencing a bad risk has to be dissimilar ex ante, although it typically is. But it does mean that unlucky policy holders need to be balanced by lucky policy holders in an insurance company's portfolio. With respect to personal risks, one reason why private insurance often does not exist is the correlation of risks. A good example is unemployment insurance, which private insurance companies do not offer.

A second precondition for the existence of robust private insurance markets is symmetric information. In this situation, the insurance company and the customer have the same actuarially relevant information. However, this is often not the case: drivers know how they drive, but car insurance companies do not; people know their health and dietary behavior, but life insurance companies do not; and so on. Asymmetric information of this sort can lead to adverse selection and/or moral hazard.

Adverse selection occurs when those with a higher probability of needing insurance are more likely to take out insurance. For example, life insurance companies prefer to insure people with high life expectancy, because these customers pay premiums for a longer time. But life insurance policies are more attractive for people who have reasons to believe that they will die early. As those 'bad risks' are selecting to take out life insurance, the company has to increase its premiums, which makes life insurance even less attractive to people with high longevity. Asymmetry in information and the resulting problem of adverse selection are well understood in the economics literature, and frequently cited as the main reason why robust private insurance markets often do not exist (Akerlof 1970; Boadway and Keen 2000; Przeworski 2003; Rothschild and Stiglitz 1976; Stiglitz 1982).

Moral hazard occurs when people with insurance behave less well than they would if they did not have insurance. For example, drivers might drive more aggressively because they do not bear the (full) costs of an accident, once they have insurance. As another example, people may not internalize the costs of bad dietary behavior, if they have health insurance.

In the economics literature, the challenge of asymmetric information is well understood, as are some potential solutions. There are three types of solutions to deal with asymmetric information. First, in some cases, private insurance markets can emerge despite asymmetric information if a *pooling equilibrium* can be achieved. In those cases, an insurance company classifies customers in risk groups (i.e. the company does not rely on individual-level risk levels, which are unobservable). For example, life insurance companies usually use age and gender (among other things) to classify people into risk groups. If, however, it is illegal to charge different rates for women and men—as is the case in some countries and U.S. states— the insurance company would have to charge either the 'male premium' (which is higher, because male life expectancy is lower) or a 'pooled rate', which is somewhere between the actuarially fair premiums for men and women. In either situation, life insurance is too expensive for women, relative to a situation in which the insurance company is allowed to discriminate by gender. Even in this very simple scenario, a life insurance market may not exist, at least not for women. In reality, risk classification is complex, and if information asymmetries exist, pooling equilibria are usually not sustainable.

In some cases, a second potential solution to the problem of asymmetric information emerges if insurance companies can offer contracts that incentivize customers to select the appropriate policy, generating a *separating equilibrium*. For example, assume that insurance companies want to sell policies with low premiums to good drivers and policies with higher premiums to bad drivers—but they cannot distinguish good from bad drivers. In this case, bad drivers simply take out the cheaper policy, which bankrupts the insurer—the adverse selection problem. However, insurance companies could use auxiliary means to nudge bad drivers to take out the more expensive policies. For instance, the cheaper policy could have high deductibles, which are attractive for good drivers but less so for bad drivers. But separating equilibria often do not exist.

A third solution to the adverse selection problem is *mandatory insurance*. This is as blunt a solution as it is common: to avoid adverse selection, people are prevented from making a choice. They are simply forced to get insurance coverage. Prominent examples of this approach include car insurance, home/fire insurance, liability insurance in many professions—and the system of social insurance programs known as the welfare state. In the latter case, the actuarial principle of tying premiums to risk is entirely abandoned: premiums are typically proportional to income (which is observable), not risk (which is not observable). After all, most social policy programs are financed either through contributions or through general taxes, both of which are proportional to income.

In the elegant view developed in economics, therefore, mandatory risk pooling is an efficient solution to the adverse selection problem caused by information asymmetries. In other words, the welfare state—which is a system of mandatory social insurance programs—exists because risk-averse citizens prefer to have insurance yet private insurance markets cannot satisfy this demand (chiefly because they are not economically viable). Mandatory risk pooling overcomes the adverse selection problem, and therefore constitutes an efficient outcome. This is the solution to the information problem.

This admirably clear and elegant explanation of why welfare states exist—in all rich democracies, no less—relies on efficiency as the central mechanism that brings about social choice. Yet, efficiency typically does not bring about political outcomes. Can the economic explanation be reconciled with a world in which political outcomes require majority support? What is the solution to the social choice problem? Differently put, under which conditions does an up–down vote on the adoption of mandatory social insurance garner majority support?

Risk and (Welfare State) Politics: A Framework

Once established, most social policy programs enjoy widespread popular support (Brooks and Manza 2006; Rehm 2016). But does a majority of citizens support the adoption of social insurance programs before they exist? The answer is far from obvious. On the one hand, it is clear that some citizens support socialization of risks, namely those with high risks (and low income, if premiums are tied to income) (Baldwin 1990; Dryzek and Goodin 1986; Ewald 1986, 1991; Iversen and Soskice 2001; Mares 2003; Swenson 2002). On the other hand, there is a potentially sizeable group that would prefer private insurance arrangements, even if they are imperfect, or no insurance coverage at all. Mandatory risk pooling may be an efficient solution to the information problems that plague private insurance markets, but it is not everybody's preferred choice. The welfare state is not a pareto improvement for every citizen.

No historical survey data exist to investigate the empirical patterns of popular support for social policy adoption.[6] In this section, I therefore explore the theoretical conditions under which the socialization of risk *should* enjoy majority support. To simplify this task, I will make several assumptions:

- Regarding *income and risk*, I will assume that people vary only in terms of risk exposure, not in terms of income. Therefore, people are assumed to have the same degree of risk aversion, to have the same amount of income, and to face the same (insured) loss.

- Regarding *politics* (the *social choice problem*), I will assume that policies are decided by majority rule in a one-dimensional space. This generates a tractable decision-making process: the median (risk) voter is decisive and her preferred policies are being implemented. This is a radical simplification of complex political processes, but it resonates well with a widely shared intuition about democracy: political decisions need the support of electoral majorities (Iversen and Soskice 2006).
- Regarding *information*, I will generally focus on the realistic case of asymmetric information—people have private information about their risk, and they cannot credibly share it with a third party, though average risk is observable—but I briefly discuss other scenarios as well.[7]

These simplifications regarding risk, politics, and information allow for a characterization of the demand side for insurance. In particular, the following three insights follow. First, the realistic assumption of risk aversion yields that people desire insurance—or alternative risk coping mechanisms—if they are exposed to risk. Since almost all people are, and historically were, exposed to risk, we should observe many historical examples of risk coping strategies. This turns out to be a well-studied topic in anthropology and economics, and there is wide agreement that risk exposure was and is a central motivation for developing risk coping mechanisms (Platteau 1991).

Jean-Philippe Platteau summarizes and synthesizes the work that describes and interprets risk coping strategies in pre-industrial societies. What are the main characteristics of 'traditional systems of social security' and how did they come about? There are competing views on the motivations of peasants to support risk coping institutions. The 'moral economy' approach (Scott 1976) assumes that people within a community subscribe to a 'subsistence ethic' (Platteau 1991: 114) because it is the right thing to do, i.e. for moral reason. In contrast, the 'political economy' approach suggests that 'the calculations of peasants [are] driven by motives in a risky environment' (Popkin 1979: 32–3), i.e. by egoistic insurance considerations. These views are difficult to distinguish empirically, because 'selfish peasants can well adopt apparently altruistic behaviour' (Platteau 1991: 177). In fact, formal models assuming altruistic motivations are near-identical to those that assume insurance motivations (Alt and Iversen 2017). However, whether for altruistic or egoistic reasons, there is agreement that risk exposure was and is a central motivation for peasants in pre-industrial societies to develop risk coping institutions.[8] The resulting 'traditional systems of social security and hunger insurance' were 'imperfect [but] worked reasonably well in situations of moderate hardship' (Platteau 1991: 118).

A second insight that follows from the assumptions is that demand for insurance increases with risk exposure. Risk coping mechanisms have always existed. However, even if they were adequate in pre-industrial societies (a big if), they were ill equipped to deal with the intensification and proliferation of risk during the Industrial Revolution. The transition from agricultural to industrial societies not only disrupted traditional risk coping mechanisms—such as care provided by the family, local community, or by charity (Thane 1996: 20)—it also generated new kinds of risks (such as unemployment) and increased the incidence of existing risks (such as workplace accidents). Thus, we should expect that people intensified their efforts to develop risk coping strategies during the Industrial Revolution. This is consistent with the historical record (de Swaan 1988: 144).

Lacking adequate social protection through the state or market, workers during the period of industrialization set up voluntary mutual aid arrangements to cope with risk. Mutual aid (or friendly) societies became quite common. By the end of the 19th century, they had millions of members and covered up to half of all male adults in England/Wales and Prussia (de Swaan 1988: 144). However, as discussed below, these mutual aid societies suffered from serious shortcomings that led to their demise.

A third insight that follows from the assumptions is that the distribution of risk[9] within a society determines whether there is majority support for social insurance (though it is not necessarily the only determinant). Theoretically, the distribution of risk could have four different shapes: (1) it could be unknown, i.e. the case of uncertainty; (2) it could be a point, i.e. everybody has the same risk exposure; (3) it could be top-heavy, i.e. a majority has high risk exposure; and (4) it could be bottom-heavy, i.e. a majority has low risk exposure. In the next section, I will argue that, theoretically, in each of these cases of different risk distributions there are plausible scenarios in which a majority supports the adoption of socialized insurance. Moreover, I will argue that each case is historically plausible.

Risk Distributions and Majority Support for Social Insurance Adoption

Uncertainty

The case of uncertainty occurs when the risk distribution is not known (Knight 1921). It resembles the famous 'original position' behind the 'veil of ignorance' (Rawls 1971). Although information is symmetric in the case of uncertainty—nobody knows anything—private insurance cannot exist because there is no useful information to calculate actuarially accurate premiums. Hence, the only way to gain insurance coverage is through socializing it. Since everybody is risk averse, we can expect widespread support for mandatory risk pooling in the case of uncertainty.

Historically, 'total wars' that affected a country's entire population might empirically approximate this theoretical scenario. The framework's prediction in this situation is that mandatory risk pooling garners broad majority support. Indeed, wars played an important role in the development of the welfare state (Castles 2010; Cutler and Johnson 2004; Dryzek and Goodin 1986; Obinger and Schmitt 2020). Different authors provide different answers to the question why warfare and social policymaking often coincide (Rehm 2016: 8). But one important mechanism that existing scholarship has identified is the similarity of risk, or the experience of uncertainty (Dryzek and Goodin 1986).

Equal risk exposure

If everybody has the same risk exposure, the risk distribution becomes a point. In this scenario, it makes sense to distinguish two cases. First, it could be that risks are correlated, as in a pandemic, or due to a potential earthquake, or due to some other national catastrophe. If so, private markets typically cannot prevail. A majority of citizens should support socializing risk, as this is the only option to secure insurance coverage. In fact, given that everybody benefits from social insurance ex ante, everybody should support mandatory risk pooling (given an actuarially fair pricing).

Historically, perhaps the closest example to this case are pandemics and public policies to contain them. Public good provision—in the form of sanitation—in the face of an epidemic like cholera might be an example (de Swaan 1988: 62). However, this scenario is not a good description of the birth of the modern welfare state.

Second, it could be that risks are equal but uncorrelated. If so, and because there is no asymmetric information (everybody has the same risk exposure), private markets can exist. Whether or not there is majority support for the socialization of risk depends on whether private insurance or social insurance is more efficient. Due to economies of scale and the lack of a profit motive in public insurance, the latter might indeed be more efficient and would enjoy majority support. While risk distributions can be more or less equal, it is difficult to think of a real-world example in which risk exposure is identical but risk is uncorrelated. Perhaps the risk of needing subsistence in old age (i.e. a pension) in societies with very equal life expectancy among the population would describe this scenario.

Overall, then, equal risk exposure can theoretically explain widespread support for mandatory risk pooling, but it does not seem to be a good empirical explanation for the emergence of the modern welfare state.[10]

Top-heavy (left-skewed) risk distribution
In the case of top-heavy (left-skewed) risk distributions, the median (voter's) risk exposure is higher than average (=mean) risk. While the details depend on assumptions and modeling choices, average (mean) risk is roughly the point of the risk distribution that separates net-benefit winners from net-benefits losers in systems that are not financed by premiums proportional to risk (i.e. social insurance systems). Citizens with below-average risk subsidize citizens with above-average risk, compared with a system in which premiums are proportional to risk (i.e. private insurance).

Even if private markets exist—either because information is symmetric or because some sort of pooling equilibrium exists despite asymmetric information—the median voter (and hence a majority of citizens) prefers mandatory risk pooling because her premiums are subsidized by the lower-risk minority. In fact, in a partial private market, the median risk person may not be able to buy insurance at all, either because the market refuses to insure bad risks or because it charges rates that are unaffordable. Once again, this leads to majority support for socializing risk.

Possible empirical examples of top-heavy risk distributions include deep recessions, depressions, and pervasive technological change. In these situations, a majority of people face (or at least perceive) a high probability of a bad event—such as unemployment—and therefore benefit from forcing good risks to be part of the risk pool. Social insurance is either the only or the more affordable option for the median voter, and hence enjoys majority support.

Historically, deep recessions and depressions are often associated with significant social policy innovation (Castles 2010) and the vagaries of technological change have been linked to widespread support for welfare state expansion (Iversen and Cusack 2000; Rehm 2020). As such, the situation of top-heavy risk distributions—or 'risk flips' (Rehm 2016)—is a rare but potentially important case for the emergence and expansion of the welfare state. The emergence of the modern American welfare state with the Social Security Act from 1935 is the posterchild for this recurring theme.[11]

Bottom-heavy (right-skewed) risk distribution
When the median voter (and hence a majority) has below-average risk, the risk distribution is bottom-heavy. This is very likely the commonest of the four cases of risk distributions. In

terms of majority support for social policy adoption, it is definitely the most complicated case. In particular, whether or not there is majority support for private or social insurance depends on information (a)symmetries, among other things (Iversen and Rehm 2022).

In social insurance—where premiums are not based on actuarial criteria—the median voter may end up subsidizing higher-risk citizens (because, as mentioned, below-average risks subsidize above-average risks), but the median voter may end up being subsidized herself (by lower-risk citizens). It is therefore not obvious whether or not the median voter is interested in mandatory risk pooling.

There are situations in which the median voter prefers social insurance, even when the risk distribution is right-skewed: If no private market exists, a majority may prefer social insurance to no insurance. Whether or not this is the case depends on specifics (such as the degree of risk aversion). But history is full of attempts to set up risk coping institutions, which suggests that many people prefer social insurance to no insurance.

A majority may prefer social insurance to commercial insurance in a partial private market. In particular, social insurance may be cheaper for the median voter because mandatory risk pooling compels low risks to subsidize higher risks (including the median voter).

If private markets are viable—for example because of symmetric information and uncorrelated risks—the social insurance premium may still be lower than the actuarially fair premium, once again because lower-risk citizens are compelled to subsidize higher-risk citizens in social insurance.

What these cases have in common is that the median voter may support social insurance as a more attractive option compared with no insurance or commercial insurance. In the latter case, the mandatory nature of social insurance compels good risks to subsidize worse risks, including the median voter.

This case of bottom-heavy (right-skewed) risk distributions—a situation in which mandatory risk pooling may or may not enjoy majority support—describes 'normal' times. Social policy development is unlikely to experience 'big bangs' or bursts of activity. Mandatory risk pooling can garner electoral majorities under some conditions, but progress is likely slow, non-linear, and laborious, and it is best described as a trial-and-error process.

Does this fourth case—majority support for risk socialization in the presence of bottom-heavy risk distributions—have historical plausibility? To explore this question, I next focus on the transition from mutual aid societies (MASs) to welfare states because MASs were the last step in the transition 'from individual providence by private savings [to] collective forms of insurance against income loss to nationwide compulsory social security arrangements' (de Swaan 1988: 165). As the direct precursors to social insurance, MASs allow us to study the transition from private voluntary mutual aid societies to public mandatory social insurance. Like all risk coping institutions, they had to deal with adverse selection, moral hazard, and correlated risks (Leeuwen 2016).[12]

Before the Welfare State

Mutual aid societies

Mutual aid societies (MASs)—also termed fraternal, friendly, benevolent, or mutual benefit societies—still exist, but their heyday was the 19th century. These societies emerged in many countries and provided rudimentary forms of social protection, often for a large share of the (male) workforce (Leeuwen 2016: 5–6). By the end of the 19th century, they had millions of members and covered up to half of all male adults in England/Wales and Prussia (de Swaan 1988: 144). Scholars of mutual aid societies[13] explain their popularity with the social and economic disruptions brought by the Industrial Revolution. Rapid technological and social change led to widespread status/social insecurity and economic insecurity, and MASs ameliorated both (Rimlinger 1982: 151).

With respect to status security, MASs created 'a sense of belonging' (Hoogenboom et al. 2018: 258), provided a space for socialization (Brodie 2014; Joyce 1980), and offered a 'discourse of respectability' (Cordery 1995) in the fight for recognition for the new class of laborers. One sign of respectability was a decent burial, and this presumably explains why most MASs offered burial insurance. The expenses—for festivities and burials—were covered by regular contributions by the members, or by ad hoc collections.

With respect to economic security, MASs attempted to mitigate some of the many risks that workers experienced during the Industrial Revolution. In fact, while MASs were 'combinations of social clubs and financial institutions' (Glenn 2001: 638), the provision of insurance became increasingly their raison d'être. They provided members with sickness, accident, burial, and life insurance policies (Glenn 2001: 638), with burial insurance the commonest and sickness insurance the most important (Andersson and Eriksson 2017: 6). MASs were typically the only way to gain some sort of insurance coverage since there were neither public nor—initially—commercial options.[14] Private savings—the bourgeoisie's preferred way to address the social question—were not a viable option simply because workers lacked money (de Swaan 1988: 161). (As they say, the root cause of poverty is that poor people do not have enough money.)

How did MASs deal with the problems resulting from asymmetric information, namely adverse selection and moral hazard? MASs were (typically) small, and organized around some (more or less homogenous) trait, such as occupation, workplace, ethnicity, or religion. There are several advantages to small size and homogeneity. First, these make collective action—such as founding and running a mutual aid society—easier since collective action problems are more easily overcome in small groups of like-minded people with similar traits. Members of homogenous groups have similar needs (and risk), and they trust each other. Second, small size and homogeneity are advantageous for monitoring (which reduces moral hazard) and screening (which lowers adverse selection). Therefore, MASs were quite well equipped to deal with moral hazard and adverse selection problems (Gottlieb 2007: 278; Thane 2012: 413).

However, MASs also had several deficiencies. First, basic bookkeeping skills and actuarial knowledge were not well developed at the time. As a result, MASs often went bankrupt due to miscalculation or fraud. For example, one recurring problem was that the treasurer—often the owner of the bar where the society would meet—would run away with the accumulated savings. Second, a small and homogenous risk pool with voluntary membership is susceptible to the problem of correlated risks: if one member needs a benefit, chances are that another member needs a benefit as well. Thus, 'the social homogeneity which made for mutual solidarity among members also caused a concentration of risks and sooner or later an accumulation of claims' (de Swaan 1988: 146). This led to either bankruptcy, an increase in contributions, or a decrease in benefits. These scenarios made it unattractive for good risks—healthy, young workers—to join MASs,[15] especially once commercial insurance had become available to these workers.

Overall, the financial practices of many MASs were simply not sound. Typically, member contributions/fees were too low, relative to obligations. Due to increasing life expectancy, this was not a big problem for burial insurance, but it was a grave challenge for sickness insurance. Essentially, MASs continuously needed to recruit new, young, good risks in order to stay solvent, but this turned out to be increasingly difficult. In fact, the financial arrangements of many MASs were so dire that they have been described as 'Ponzi schemes' (Gottlieb 2007: 275–6).

In sum, MASs could deal with the problems of adverse selection and moral hazard quite well. However, because of the problems of correlated risks and unsound financial practices, they often went bankrupt and were generally not attractive for good risks (young and healthy workers). They also were inaccessible to large segments of the population—mainly women and poor workers. They 'were the preserve mainly of regularly employed, better paid men' (Thane 2012: 413), 'although the enormous growth in coverage during the nineteenth century must have lessened this problem' (Leeuwen 2016: 255). In my theoretical framework's language, MASs covered mainly the middle part of the risk distribution. Bad risks did not have access (they were screened out), while good risks had few incentives to join MASs, especially as time went on—they simply opted out. Once commercial insurance companies gained expertise and the public's trust (de Swaan 1988: 150), they became an appealing option for 'good risks', which targeted good risks with attractive conditions. This further worsened the situation for MASs.

From MASs to social insurance
Voluntary MASs were an important risk coping institution for many workers, but eventually they were replaced by mandatory social insurance programs, presumably with majority support. What led to the demise of MASs? Why did collective social insurance emerge? The literature continues to debate this open question.[16] There are two explanations. Both point out a correlation between the demise of MASs and the emergence of the modern welfare state; they differ in their interpretation of this correlation (Gottlieb 2007: 275).

Some scholars argue that increased state involvement in the form of regulation and social policy legislation put MASs out of business (Beito 1990, 2000; Siddeley 1992). They argue that the 'legal or coercive impediments […] constrained fraternal societies from effectively countering new private and governmental competitors' (Beito 1990: 726) and that the leadership of MASs opposed social insurance. However, such explanations overlook the serious deficiencies of MASs (see above). They also fail to consider that many MASs were pushing for regulation and ignore the different interests of MASs' members and their leadership (Glenn 2001: 647).

Other authors argue that the deficiencies of MASs led to their demise and that social insurance emerged because of failures of mutualism, not the other way round (Glenn 2001; Harris 2018). Given the stark problems of MASs, this second explanation strikes me as more plausible. As discussed above, MASs were fraught with financial problems that often led to bankruptcy (Glenn 2001: 646). For that and other reasons, MASs failed to keep or attract good risks (Beito 1990: 725; Gottlieb 2007: 271, 275–6; Thane 2012: 414). From a risk-distribution perspective, MASs neither covered good risks (who opted out) nor bad risks (who were screened out), leaving middle-risk (male) workers as their main constituency. The middle-risk workers could not access commercial insurance, either because it did not (yet) exist, or because commercial insurance was targeted to good risks.

Over time, the situation for existing MASs worsened. Increasing life expectancy and the ageing of its members intensified the financial problems of MASs. For the same reasons,

MASs became less and less attractive for good risks. Moreover, once commercial insurance companies gained expertise and the public's trust (de Swaan 1988: 150), they became an appealing option for 'good risks', which were targeted with attractive conditions. This further deprived the mutual aid societies of the best risks and left them with the actuarially least attractive members, leading to their demise. This left many workers without risk coping institutions and made mandatory risk pooling their preferred choice. Faced with failing mutual aid arrangements and exclusion from commercial insurance markets, many workers supported social insurance. It is worth quoting de Swaan's seminal work at length on this important development:

> As modern means of communication and publicity created a nationwide market, commercial insurers began to reach out to a public which had traditionally supplied the members of the workers' funds. The mutual societies found themselves outpriced, their potential clients usurped by the commercial societies and their actual members increasingly isolated on relatively unfavorable terms. The commercial-insurance market threatened to do to them what the autonomous mutual-aid funds had done before to a lower [income and higher risk] social stratum: exclude them and join on better terms with more attractive company. This perspective forced the workers to abandon mutualism and opt against commercialism in favor of the one most encompassing and least voluntary solution: compulsory national insurance under state control. (de Swaan 1988: 150)

This provides a plausible explanation for the emergence of mandatory social insurance even in the presence of bottom-heavy risk distributions: MASs' deficiencies and demise made mandatory risk pooling an attractive proposition for a majority of the population—consisting of those covered by MASs and those excluded from them—even at the cost of also covering bad risks. Mandatory membership forces good risks into the pool, and they subsidize those that are worse off.

CONCLUSION

All of today's modern democracies established mandatory social policy programs (of various kinds) for each of the main four risks citizens face (accident, unemployment, health, old age). They did so despite the centrifugal tensions described as the social insurance dilemma in the introduction. This is a remarkable pattern. While there surely are many important idiosyncrasies specific to every single case—every social policy program in every country came about in its own specific way—the commonality of the experience raises the possibility that some mechanisms are common to many cases. The framework sketched above—a majority politics of risk—offers such mechanisms.

The prominent role of risk distributions in this framework seems justified since all four theoretical cases of risk distributions can explain why countries set up social insurance. Theoretically, majority support for mandatory risk pooling follows relatively easily in the cases of uncertainty (risk is unknown); equal risk; and top-heavy risk distributions. Majority support in the case of bottom-heavy risk distributions—probably the most common case—is more difficulty to explain. Yet, a plausible theoretical explanation exists: given the (lack of) alternatives, a majority supports social insurance as mandatory membership forces 'good risk' into the pool, thereby subsidizing those worse off.

Taking seriously both social choice and information problems helps us to understand the past of welfare state politics. It also helps us to make predictions about its future. Risk exposure will continue to exist, and it will continue to powerfully motivate people. As has historically been the case, old risks may alleviate or exacerbate, and new risks may emerge. However, what will (likely) qualitatively change in the future is information about information. From an actuarial perspective, two aspects of information are of interest: its level and its shareability (Iversen and Rehm 2022). Both of these aspects are increasing in many domains. As a result, the asymmetric information problem—which is critically important from an insurance perspective—may be mitigated, or it may even disappear.

The car insurance market provides a glimpse into the future. Since its inception about a hundred years ago, the car insurance market has had to deal with a central problem: insurance companies want to charge higher rates for worse drivers, yet they cannot observe driving behavior. If the insurance company offers two insurance contracts—one with low premiums, for good drivers; the other with high premiums, for bad drivers—all drivers have incentives to take out the low-premium contract. This adverse selection will bankrupt the insurance company. Until recently, therefore, car insurance companies have charged premiums based on verifiable traits that correlate with proneness to accidents, such as car type, horsepower, age, gender, credit score, and zip-code.

However, about a decade ago, car insurance started using GPS trackers to objectively observe and transmit—often in real time—actual driving behavior, such as miles driven, speed, speed relative to speed limits, hard braking events, cornering forces, and so on. Based on algorithms that predict accident proneness with these data, premiums can be tailored to individual driving behavior. Therefore, people's insurance premiums reflect their actual driving behavior, leading to actuarially fair premiums (in expectation). In many countries, car insurance companies have started to offer these appropriately labeled 'pay-as-you-drive' (PAYD) or 'pay-how-you-drive' (or telemetric) contracts. Since they are attractive to good drivers, we can expect more and more safe drivers to switch to these PAYD products. This will make traditional car insurance more expensive, which will further attract better risks to PAYD products, and so on. This dynamic ends when PAYD is the only available insurance option. Within a few years, the ability to track and therefore objectively observe and share individual driving behavior already has fundamentally altered the car insurance market, and it is likely to completely transform it within the next few years.

Other insurance domains experience similar developments, including in home, health, and life insurance. In the health and life insurance market, more and more companies rely on devices (such as smart watches) that track individual behavior (such as number of steps taken) and conditions (such as pulse and heartbeat) to calculate premiums. More importantly, advances in predictive medicine yield objective insights about health risks. As a recent newspaper article quipped: 'The Doctor Will See Your Future Now' (Forbes, April 16, 2018).

If the asymmetric information problem can be solved, private insurance markets will be viable in more areas, and they may be an attractive alternative for good—and even some middling—risks that are currently compelled to subsidize bad risks via mandatory national risk pooling. Whether or not these developments will erode majority support for social insurance theoretically depends on a host of factors and therefore remains to be seen. But because winners and losers of social policy will be more easily identifiable, we can expect that the role of risk in politics will intensify in the future.

NOTES

1. This essay benefitted much from, and draws on, joint work with Torben Iversen (Iversen and Rehm 2022). I thank Dean Curran for helpful comments.
2. Paul Krugman uses this quip; he attributes it to Peter Fisher in 2002 (then Undersecretary of the Treasury).
3. In contrast, it is not difficult to understand that modern democracies—or, indeed, most countries—have armies: in light of existential external threats, pooling resources to provide the public good of a common defense is in everybody's interest, and free-riding is relatively easy to avoid (through taxation, a draft system, and so on). Moreover, only states that resolved their external security challenges successfully survived.
4. Another prominent explanation in this tradition is per 'Wagner's law': as countries get richer, the activities and expenditures of their governments increases (Peacock and Wiseman 1961).
5. The actuarially fair premium is $(1+\alpha) \times p \times L$, where α is a 'loading factor' (money raised to cover the expenses of the insurance company), p is the risk, and L is the expected loss. For example, if the probability of one's house burning down is 0.01 in a given year, and the value of the house is 300,000, risk-averse individuals are willing to pay more than $0.01 \times 300,000 = 3,000$ in premiums to insure the house.
6. An interesting account of support for public unemployment insurance in the early 20th century can be found in Hanna (1931). According to this mostly anecdotal 'data,' support for unemployment insurance adoption was widespread.
7. More generally, symmetric information refers to the scenario in which all relevant parties have the same actuarially relevant information. This includes the cases in which nobody knows anything (uncertainty), everybody knows everything (perfect information), or other situations in which actuarially relevant knowledge is the same for the relevant parties.
8. Along similar lines: '[I]t is scarcity and not sufficiency that makes people generous, since everybody is thereby insured against hunger … in a community where everyone is likely to find himself in difficulties from time to time' (Evans-Pritchard 1940: 85).
9. In previous and related work, I have called the distribution of risk exposure 'risk pool' or 'risk inequality' and argued that higher risk inequality (more unequal distribution of risk exposure) leads to more dissimilar—or polarized—preferences regarding (social) insurance (Rehm 2011); lower overall support for social policy; and ultimately less generous welfare states (Rehm 2016). The distribution of risk is of theoretical interest also in other contributions that have informed this manuscript (Iversen and Rehm 2022; Stone 2009).
10. However, more equal distribution of risk is associated with lower polarization about social policy; less opposition and higher support for social policy; and more generous welfare states (Rehm 2016).
11. 'Risk flips' are temporary, which means that the median voter is only temporarily a high-risk type. This raises the question why the median voter does not reverse mandatory risk pooling once the risk distribution returns to its normal, right-skewed shape (see next case). I believe the answer has to do with the stickiness of institutions and policies. Moreover, once a social insurance program exists, the costs of switching to a private system may be so high that abandoning the program is too expensive.
12. Before the emergence—and eventual near-universal adoption—of mandatory social insurance programs of one kind or another in today's modern democracies, other risk coping institutions existed (and continue to exist). They included the following: (1) The family, which 'was almost certainly the first resort,' and help for one's kin was motivated by affection, duty, or reciprocity expectations (Thane 1996: 19). (2) When the family was unable to help—either because it was too poor to help, or not available due to death or emigration—'the local community could be an important source of support' (Thane 1996: 19). Neighbors and friends could help with food, shelter, clothing, and other basic needs. Moreover, pawnshops and shopkeepers sometimes provided credit (Thane 1996: 20). (3) After family and community resources were exhausted, charity was the next step (Thane 1996: 20). This included begging, church-provided assistance, and official poor relief. The sources of funding varied, and included taxes, the church, and the rich. Even when official poor relief was available, these efforts were local, complex, and stingy. (4) Some people in some countries had access to social protection provided by guilds (roughly 18th century) or friendly/mutual aid soci-

eties (roughly 19th century). These four means of social protection emerged roughly in the above order.

13. MASs are seldom analyzed from an insurance perspective, though there are important exceptions (Emery and Emery 1999; Glenn 2001; Gottlieb 2007; Guinnane and Streb 2011; Hechter 1988; Leeuwen 1997, 2016; Linden 2008, 2017; Pearson 2002; Siddeley 1992). There are country-specific studies, including for Britain (Brodie 2014; Cordery 2003; Harris 2018; Hennock 2007), the Netherlands (Leeuwen 2016), and Germany (Hennock 2007)—and many more on these and other countries. There are also volumes on regions (Cunningham and Grell 2002; Grell et al. 2005; Grell and Cunningham 2002).

14. Even when commercial insurance existed, it was not accessible to everyone. For example, commercial insurance discriminated against bad risks but also often excluded African–Americans (regardless of risk type). The American 'fraternal societies' were a reaction to that.

15. However, some socio-demographic trends countered these problems: "But lower benefits—or higher contributions—might drive out good risks. This did indeed occur in some cases during epidemics or when the society's membership aged. It could, and did, lead to bankruptcy in a few instances, though on the whole, the nineteenth century saw an enormous growth in mutualism. Like their predecessors and successors, friendly societies were ill-equipped to deal with correlated risks in the case of unemployment or ill health, but fortunately the epidemiological transition saw a reduction in the number of epidemics' (Leeuwen 2016: 264).

16. Here are some examples. (1) 'Although the decline in cooperative societies coincides with the implementation of social insurance, we still do not know whether there exists a causal relation between them. Several explanations have been proposed but most of them either have not been tested or have important drawbacks' (Gottlieb 2007: 271). (2) 'At this point, the state of the research does not offer easy answers to the important question of why fraternal and other mutual aid institutions have lost so much ground in the last half century or more. The literature has been cursory and suggestive at best' (Beito 1990: 725). (3) 'At the height of fraternal insurance in America, consumers could choose from a wide array of insurance arrangements. In addition to fraternal insurance, a consumer could choose commercial insurance similar to what is common today. Industrial insurance, with premiums collected door-to-door on a weekly basis, was another low cost option for the workingman. Many trade unions also offered insurance. Today's insurance industry, however, is characterized by a much more restricted range of options. Indeed, consumers have very little choice in what has become a two-tiered system consisting of, first, costly commercial insurance usually linked to employment, and second, the government's "social safety net." Disentangling the factors and processes that led from a situation with a considerable number of options to this restrictive two-tier system is a daunting task. [This is an area] in which much more research is needed' (Siddeley 1992: 15).

REFERENCES

Akerlof, G. A. (1970), 'The Market for "Lemons": Quality Uncertainty and the Market Mechanism', *The Quarterly Journal of Economics*, **84** (3), 488–500.

Alt, J. and T. Iversen (2017), 'Inequality, Labor Market Segmentation, and Preferences for Redistribution', *American Journal of Political Science*, **61** (1), 21–36.

Andersson, L. F. and L. Eriksson (2017), 'Sickness Absence in Compulsory and Voluntary Health Insurance: The Case of Sweden at the Turn of the Twentieth Century', *Scandinavian Economic History Review*, **65** (1), 6–27.

Baldwin, P. (1990), *The Politics of Social Solidarity: Class Bases of the European Welfare State, 1875-1975*, New York, NY: Cambridge University Press.

Barr, N. (2001), *The Welfare State as Piggy Bank: Information, Risk, Uncertainty, and the Role of the State*, Oxford, UK: Oxford University Press.

Barr, N. (2012), *Economics of the Welfare State*, 5th edn, Oxford, UK: Oxford University Press.

Beito, D. T. (1990), 'Mutual Aid for Social Welfare: The Case of American Fraternal Societies', *Critical Review*, **4** (4), 709–36.

Beito, D. T. (2000), *From Mutual Aid to the Welfare State: Fraternal Societies and Social Services, 1890-1967*, Durham, NC: University of North Carolina Press.

Boadway, R. and M. Keen (2000), 'Redistribution', in A. Atkinson and F. Bourguignon (eds), *Handbook of Income Distribution*, Amsterdam: Elsevier, pp. 679–789.

Brodie, M. (2014), '"You Could Not Get Any Person to be Trusted Except the State": Poorer Workers' Loss of Faith in Voluntarism in Late 19th Century Britain', *Journal of Social History*, **47** (4), 1071–95.

Brooks, C. and J. Manza (2006), 'Why Do Welfare States Persist?', *The Journal of Politics*, **68** (4), 816–27.

Castles, F. G. (2010), 'Black Swans and Elephants on the Move: The Impact of Emergencies on the Welfare State', *Journal of European Social Policy*, **20** (2), 91–101.

Cordery, S. (1995), 'Friendly Societies and the Discourse of Respectability in Britain, 1825–1875', *Journal of British Studies*, **34** (1), 35–58.

Cordery, S. (2003), 'Into the State', in S. Cordery (ed), *British Friendly Societies, 1750–1914*, Springer, pp. 152–74.

Cunningham, A. and O. P. Grell (2002), *Health Care and Poor Relief in Protestant Europe 1500–1700*, Abingdon, UK: Routledge.

Cutler, D. and R. Johnson (2004), 'The Birth and Growth of the Social Insurance State: Explaining Old Age and Medical Insurance across Countries', *Public Choice*, **120** (1–2), 87–121.

de Swaan, A. (1988), *In Care of the State: Health Care, Education and Welfare in Europe and the USA in the Modern Era*, Oxford, UK: Oxford University Press.

Dryzek, J. and R. E. Goodin (1986), 'Risk-Sharing and Social Justice: The Motivational Foundations of the Post-War Welfare State', *British Journal of Political Science*, **16** (1), 1–34.

Emery, G. and H. Emery (1999), *Young Man's Benefit: The Independent Order of Odd Fellows and Sickness Insurance in the United States and Canada, 1860–1929*, vol. 7, Montreal: McGill-Queen's Press–MQUP.

Esping-Andersen, G. (1985), *Politics Against Markets: The Social Democratic Road to Power*, Princeton, NJ: Princeton University Press.

Evans-Pritchard, E. E. (1940), *The Nuer: A Description of the Modes of Livelihood and Political Institutions of a Nilotic People*, New York; Oxford: Oxford University Press.

Ewald, F. (1986), *L'état providence*, Paris: Grasset.

Ewald, F. (1991), 'Insurance and Risk', in G. Burchell, C. Gordon, and P. Miller (eds), *The Foucault Effect: Studies in Governmentality*, Chicago, IL: University of Chicago Press, pp. 197–210.

Glenn, B. J. (2001), 'Understanding Mutual Benefit Societies, 1860-1960', *Journal of Health Politics, Policy and Law*, **26** (3), 638–51.

Gottlieb, D. (2007), 'Asymmetric Information in Late 19th Century Cooperative Insurance Societies', *Explorations in Economic History*, **44** (2), 270–92.

Grell, O. P. and A. Cunningham (2002), *Health Care and Poor Relief in 18th and 19th Century Northern Europe*, Abingdon, UK: Routledge.

Grell, O. P., A. Cunningham, and B. Roeck (2005), *Health Care and Poor Relief in 18th and 19th Century Southern Europe*, Abingdon, UK: Routledge.

Guinnane, T. W. and J. Streb (2011), 'Moral Hazard in a Mutual Health Insurance System: German Knappschaften, 1867–1914', *The Journal of Economic History*, **71** (1), 70–104.

Hanna, H. S. (1931), *Unemployment-Benefit Plans in the United States and Unemployment Insurance in Foreign Countries*, Washington, D.C.: U.S. Government Printing Office.

Harris, B. (2018), 'Social Policy by Other Means? Mutual Aid and the Origins of the Modern Welfare State in Britain during the Nineteenth and Twentieth Centuries', *Journal of Policy History*, **30** (2), 202–35.

Hechter, M. (1988), *Principles of Group Solidarity*, Berkeley, CA: University of California Press.

Hennock, E. P. (2007), *The Origin of the Welfare State in England and Germany, 1850–1914: Social Policies Compared*, Cambridge, UK: Cambridge University Press.

Hoogenboom, M., C. Kissane, M. Prak, P. Wallis, and C. Minns (2018), 'Guilds in the Transition to Modernity: The Cases of Germany, United Kingdom, and the Netherlands', *Theory and Society*, **47** (3), 255–91.

Iversen, T. and T. Cusack (2000), 'The Causes of Welfare State Expansion: Deindustrialization or Globalization?', *World Politics*, **52** (3), 313–49.

Iversen, T. and P. Rehm (2022), *Big Data and the Welfare State. How the Information Revolution Threatens Solidarity*, New York, NY: Cambridge University Press.

Iversen, T. and D. Soskice (2001), 'An Asset Theory of Social Policy Preferences', *American Political Science Review*, **95** (4), 875–95.

Iversen, T. and D. Soskice (2006), 'Electoral Institutions, Parties and the Politics of Class: Why Some Democracies Distribute More than Others', *American Political Science Review*, **100** (2), 165–81.

Joyce, P. (1980), *Work, Society and Politics: The Culture of the Factory in Later Victorian England*, Brighton, UK: Edward Everett Root.

Knight, F. H. (1921), *Risk, Uncertainty and Profit*, New York: Hart, Schaffner and Marx.

Leeuwen, M. H. D. V. (2016), *Mutual Insurance 1550–2015: From Guild Welfare and Friendly Societies to Contemporary Micro-Insurers*, London, UK: Palgrave Macmillan.

Linden, M. van der (2008), *Workers of the World: Essays Toward a Global Labor History*, Leiden: BRILL.

Linden, M. van der (2017), 'Mutualism', in M. van der Linden and K. Hofmeester (eds), *Handbook Global History of Work*, Berlin; Boston: De Gruyter Oldenbourg, pp. 491–504.

Lindert, P. H. (2004), *Growing Public. Social Spending and Economic Growth since the Eighteenth Century*, New York, NY: Cambridge University Press.

Mares, I. (2003), *The Politics of Social Risk. Business and Welfare State Development*, New York, NY: Cambridge University Press.

Meltzer, A. H. and S. F. Richard (1978), 'Why Government Grows (and Grows) in a Democracy', *Public Interest*, **52** (Summer), 111–18.

Obinger, H. and C. Schmitt (2020), 'World War and Welfare Legislation in Western Countries', *Journal of European Social Policy*, **30** (3), 261–74.

Peacock, A. T. and J. Wiseman (1961), *The Growth of Public Expenditure in the United Kingdom*, Princeton, NJ: Princeton University Press.

Pearson, R. (2002), 'Moral Hazard and the Assessment of Insurance Risk in Eighteenth and Early-Nineteenth-Century Britain', *Business History Review*, **76** (1), 1–35.

Platteau, J.-P. (1991), *Traditional Systems of Social Security and Hunger Insurance: Past Achievements and Modern Challenges*, Oxford, UK: Oxford University Press.

Popkin, S. L. (1979), *The Rational Peasant: The Political Economy of Rural Society in Vietnam*, Berkeley, CA: University of California Press.

Przeworski, A. (2003), *States and Markets: A Primer in Political Economy*, New York, NY: Cambridge University Press.

Rawls, J. (1971), *A Theory of Justice*, New York, NY: Cambridge University Press.

Rehm, P. (2011), 'Social Policy by Popular Demand', *World Politics*, **63** (2), 271–99.

Rehm, P. (2016), *Risk Inequality and Welfare States. Social Policy Preferences, Development, and Dynamics*, New York, NY: Cambridge University Press.

Rehm, P. (2020), 'The Future of Welfare State Politics', *Political Science Research and Methods*, **8** (2), 386–90.

Rimlinger, G. V. (1982), 'The Historical Analysis of National Welfare Systems', in R. L. Ransom, R. Sutch, and G. M. Walton (eds), *Explorations in the New Economic History*, New York: Academic Press, pp. 149–67.

Rothschild, M. and J. Stiglitz (1976), 'Equilibrium in Competitive Insurance Markets: An Essay on the Economics of Imperfect Information', *The Quarterly Journal of Economics*, **90** (4), 629–49.

Scott, J. C. (1976), *The Moral Economy of the Peasant: Rebellion and Subsistence in Southeast Asia*, New Haven, CT: Yale University Press.

Siddeley, L. (1992), 'The Rise and Fall of Fraternal Insurance Organizations', *Humane Studies Review*, **7** (2), 13–16.

Sinn, H.-W. (1995), 'A Theory of the Welfare State', *Scandinavian Journal of Economics*, **97** (4), 495–526.

Stephens, J. D. (1979), *The Transition from Capitalism to Socialism*, London, UK: Macmillan.

Stiglitz, J. E. (1982), 'Self-selection and Pareto Efficient Taxation', *Journal of Public Economics*, **17** (2), 213–40.

Stone, R. W. (2009), 'Risk in International Politics', *Global Environmental Politics*, **9** (3), 40–60.

Swenson, P. A. (2002), *Capitalists against Markets: The Making of Labor Markets and Welfare States in the United States and Sweden*, Oxford, UK: Oxford University Press.

Thane, P. (1996), *The Foundations of the Welfare State*, Abingdon, UK: Routledge.

Thane, P. (2012), 'The Ben Pimlott Memorial Lecture 2011: The "Big Society" and the "Big State": Creative Tension or Crowding Out?', *Twentieth Century British History*, **23** (3), 408–29.

Van Leeuwen, M. H. (1997), 'Trade Unions and the Provision of Welfare in the Netherlands, 1910–1960', *Economic History Review*, 764–91.

5. Changing risks, individualisation and inequality in a recast welfare state

Klaus Rasborg

1. INTRODUCTION

In the classic industrial society – or 'first modernity', in the terminology of German sociologist Ulrich Beck – the most important task of the welfare state was to secure individuals against the social risks arising from the increasing industrialisation, de-ruralisation and urbanisation at the end of the 19th and beginning of the 20th century (Bengtsson et al. 2016a: 3–4; Bengtsson et al. 2016b: 235–36; Harsløf and Ulmestig 2013: 6).[1] Through social transfers, the classic welfare state secured in particular against four predominant types of risk, which were largely determined by the industrial society, namely unemployment, sickness, work-related accidents and old age (Harsløf and Ulmestig 2013: 1). However, as a consequence of the social and economic changes that have taken place in the transition to post-industrial society – or 'second (reflexive) modernity', in Beck's terminology – new social risks are confronting most people across their life course. Examples of such risks include increased job insecurity in the flexible labour market; new family patterns (the dual-income family, broken families, single parents, etc.); demographic shifts (more elderly people); privatisation/outsourcing of social services; new health risks related to diet, smoking, alcohol and exercise; new forms of crime; international terrorism and risks related to the environment and climate change (Bonoli 2005, 2007; Taylor-Gooby 2004: 2–5, 7–11; Taylor-Gooby 2008). In the social sciences we can distinguish among three different approaches to analysing new, or changing, social risks and explaining who is affected by them. Firstly, a 'risk society perspective' that points to the changing role of the welfare state in a 'risk society' characterised by increasing individualisation and the emergence of new types of classless (egalitarian) risks (Beck 1992, 1999; Giddens 1994, 1998a, 1998b); secondly, a 'governmentality perspective' that focuses on risk and insurance as management technologies that are linked to a dismantling of the welfare state (Dean 1999; Ewald 1991b; Foucault 1991; cf. Rasborg 2020); and, thirdly, a 'social stratification perspective', where variables such as gender, class and ethnicity are key in order to explain which groups are affected by social risks and how the welfare state acts upon this (Bonoli 2005, 2007; Standing 2014; Taylor-Gooby 2004: 13–14, 23–24; Taylor-Gooby 2008; Wacquant 2008).

The chapter shows how each of the three perspectives, despite differences, contributes to the understanding of key aspects of changing risks and how these are related to increased individualisation and the emergence of new forms of inequality in contemporary society. Firstly, it outlines key elements of the risk-oriented approach to the analysis of the transformation of the welfare state (the risk society perspective) (sections 2 and 3). Next, in section 4, it looks at how the transformation of the welfare state is going hand in hand with the emergence of new and more individualised forms of risk management aimed at shaping and managing human behaviour (the governmentality perspective). Section 5 shows how the advent of new social risks is also linked to structural changes in the labour market and the family in post-industrial society with a resulting risk of precarisation, poverty and marginalisation (the social stratification perspective). Section 6 moves on to examine the extent to which there can be said to be empirical evidence for Beck's thesis of classless and egalitarian risks, taking inequality in health and climate change as examples. Finally, the concept of 'risk class' (Beck, Curran), and the related concept of 'geo-social classes' (Latour), are discussed as a possible point of departure for drawing up an analysis of the intersections among risk, inequality and class in contemporary society (section 7).

2.　THE CLASSIC WELFARE STATE

A core element in the classic welfare state as it arises in industrial society, is that of social citizenship, which, according to Marshall, is constituted by civil, political and social rights (Marshall 1950: 10–11, 14). Following Marshall, these rights can be seen as part of a historical evolution: in the 18th century civil rights evolved – that is, the classical freedom rights (freedom of speech, freedom of assembly, property rights, etc.). In the 19th century political rights were fostered – that is, the right to political participation at all levels of society; and in the 20th century social rights came to the fore, in sum, 'the whole range from the right to a modicum of economic welfare and security to the right to share to the full in the social heritage and to live the life of a civilised being according to the standards prevailing in the society' (Marshall 1950: 11, 28–29; cf. Esping-Andersen 1990: 21). Taken together, these rights form the basis of modern social citizenship that modifies market demands and diminishes the class differentiations of industrial society. A prerequisite for this, however, is that citizenship rights are associated with certain obligations, not least the obligation to work, to pay taxes and insurance contributions, to educate oneself, and to perform military service (Marshall 1950: 77–78).[2]

Based on the insights of Marshall, and of Titmuss (1974), Esping-Andersen points out that modern social citizenship is shaped differently in different 'welfare regimes'. Thus, following Esping-Andersen, we can distinguish between Scandinavian (universal) (e.g. Denmark, Norway, Sweden and Finland), Middle European (corporate) (e.g. Germany, France and Italy) and Anglo-Saxon (residual) (e.g. Great Britain, the USA, Canada and Australia) welfare regimes (Esping-Andersen 1990: 26–29; Titmuss 1974: 30–32). According to Esping-Andersen, the different (ideal-typical) regimes each determine a specific pattern of social stratification – that is, the class differentiations in society – and a certain degree of 'de-commodification', being the degree to which the welfare state enables that 'individuals, or families, can uphold a socially acceptable standard of living independently of market participation' (Esping-Andersen 1990: 37). Since de-commodification refers to the extent to which the welfare state, through transfer payments, creates 'market immunity', it can be seen as an indicator of the degree of redistribution – and thus solidarity – in the welfare state.

In Scandinavian, universalist, rights-based or institutional–redistributive welfare states, de-commodification is relatively high and social stratification is consequently low, as de-commodification is institutionalised in a relatively expanded social citizenship, which gives citizens the right to economic and social security regardless of their market status (e.g. unemployment benefits, cash benefits, sickness benefits and pensions) (Esping-Andersen 1990: 21–23). The Anglo-Saxon (liberal) model, conversely, is characterised by a lesser degree of redistribution and, consequently, greater inequality and more pronounced class divisions in society. Somewhere in between lies the corporate model, which is founded on labour market-based insurance schemes (e.g. occupational pensions) and where a large part of the redistribution is undertaken by the family, the church, private associations and relief organisations etc., with consequent rather distinct status differentiation in society (Esping-Andersen 1990: 51–54, 69–77).

As indicated above, an essential characteristic of the classic (universal rights-oriented) welfare state is that, unlike the market principle of equivalence, it is based on a principle of solidarity, which means that – in contrast to the corporate model – there is no specified 'rights account' that establishes a specific relationship between 'input' (taxes and insurance contributions) and 'output' (social benefits) (Andersen 1991: 76, 116). Redistribution, however, does not solely take place between income groups (vertical redistribution) but also over life cycles – that is, between generations (horizontal redistribution) (Andersen 1991: 129–37).

3.   THE TRANSFORMATION OF THE WELFARE STATE IN THE 'RISK SOCIETY'

In relation to the classic welfare state, whose contours are outlined above, today the role of the welfare state is changing as a result of the transition from industrial to post-industrial society (or a highly developed 'risk society') in which new social risks arise that it must address. This has been pointed out by social theorists such as Beck, Giddens and Dean (Beck 1999; Dean 1999; Giddens 1994, 1998a, 1998b, 2000, 2007; cf. Ejrnæs and Rasborg 2019). In addition, it has been shown that the welfare state not only acts upon new social risks, but in some cases itself plays a part in creating them (e.g. the creation of poverty as a result of cuts in social benefits in order to increase the incentive to work) (Harsløf and Ulmestig 2013: 18; Ulmestig and Harsløf 2013: 267, 270–72, 276). Thus, it is claimed, in today's 'risk society' we are moving away from the classic welfare state based on the satisfaction of needs in order to create 'safety from cradle to grave', and towards a recast welfare state that, to a much greater extent, is based on 'risk promotion' (Harsløf and Ulmestig 2013: 12–16; Kemshall 2002: 40). That is, 'the welfare state has become a risk society as a result of processes of globalisation and individualisation, which has led to the birth of a new "risk culture"' (Veen 2011: 17–18), a risk culture that can also be described as amounting to an increasing conversion of risks from the societal macro-level to the individual micro-level (Bengtsson et al. 2016a: 5; Bengtsson et al. 2016b: 240–42).

In a risk perspective, the welfare state can be viewed as a collective insurance system that offsets the individual risks of unemployment, disease and aging. Correspondingly, the social foundations of the welfare state can be said to consist of: (1) a perception of risks as *social* – that is, a product of socio-economic factors in advanced capitalism rather than individual misfortune or personal failure; (2) the willingness to share risks – that is, solidarity; and (3) a translation of both the former into a strategy of risk management and into welfare state policies (Veen 2011: 14–18; Veen, Achterberg and Raven 2011; Veen and Yerkes 2011: 191).

Among the above-mentioned social theorists, Giddens, not least, has focused on the transformation of the welfare state from a risk perspective, since the theme of risk 'unites many otherwise disparate areas of politics: welfare state reform, engagement with world financial markets, responses to technological change, ecological problems and geopolitical transformations' (Giddens 1998b: 64).

The point of departure for Giddens' analysis of the transformation of the welfare state is that its (alleged) crisis is not only fiscal but also has to do with, 'the lack of possibilities for controlling a risk society' (Giddens 2000: 155; cf. Beck 1998: 16). Following Giddens, the modern welfare state is built around three pillars: (1) work; (2) (nation-state) solidarity; and (3) risk management (Giddens 1994: 136–37). According to Giddens, it is being put under pressure in all three areas, for the following reasons. Firstly, it is no longer possible to build a society that, in the traditional sense, is based on full employment (cf. Beck 2000). Secondly, in a globalised, open economy the welfare state is increasingly dependent on international market fluctuations, which means that a traditional, Keynesian, demand-oriented crisis management is no longer able to solve the economic problems. Thirdly, the highly developed risk society confronts the institutional structures of society with a number of new problems that the classic welfare state has difficulty in solving. In Giddens' view, many analyses of the welfare state have focused excessively on the first two points, seeing the welfare state as a 'solidarity project' that is largely a result of the collective struggle of the working class for better living conditions (Giddens 1994: 139; cf. Esping-Andersen, above).

We must, therefore, says Giddens, focus more on the third point above and conceive the welfare state as, 'a pooling of risks rather than resources. What has shaped the solidarity of social policy is that "otherwise privileged groups discovered that they shared a common interest in reallocating risks with the disadvantaged"' (Giddens 1998b: 116). Thus, in Giddens' view, the welfare state was originally an 'insurance state' that protected people against the risks of industrial society: 'The welfare state, or at least its social security systems, could be seen as a giant insurance company, and it is also affected by shifting patterns of risk' (Giddens and Pierson 1998: 106; cf. Beck 1998: 15–16).

However, as a consequence of the transition to post-industrial society or highly developed risk society, from the 1960s and onwards the welfare state has been increasingly confronted with new types of risks, which Beck and Giddens refer to as 'manufactured uncertainty' and 'high-consequence risks' (Giddens 1994: 78, 152, 219). Following Beck and Giddens, these risks are characterised by the fact that they are not 'external' but rather a product of post-war welfare state modernisation. That is, they represent a man-made generalised uncertainty that may have far-reaching – in some cases irreversible – consequences, which cannot be calculated and thus cannot be insured (e.g. environmental risks, health risks, financial risks and terror risks) (Beck 1999: 76–77).

Hence, in the risk society new forms of risk arise that put the welfare state under pressure. The traditional welfare state is, according to Giddens, characterised by the fact that it compensates via transfer payments for damages *after* they have arisen (e.g. cash benefits as compensation for loss of income due to unemployment) (Giddens 1994: 18). Thus, the welfare state has served as, 'a kind of repair mechanism, which intervened when problems arose' (Giddens 2000: 155). However, such *reactive* welfare policies are not well suited to addressing the problems faced by the welfare state in a society characterised by new types of risks:

> In a world of more active engagement with health, with the body, with marriage, with gender, with work – in an era of manufactured risk – the welfare state cannot continue on in the form in which it developed in the post-1945 settlement. The crisis of the welfare state is not purely fiscal, it is a crisis of risk management in a society dominated by a new type of risk. (Giddens 1998a: 32–33)

Examples of these new types of risks include health risks, new forms of family and of cohabitation (broken families, single parents, etc.), and job insecurity in the flexible labour market.

Lifestyle-related diseases that many people suffer from in late-modern welfare society are, for example, not external 'strokes of fate' (external risks), but rather a result of life-political choices of individuals regarding diet, smoking, alcohol and exercise. Rather than acting upon these diseases once they have emerged (reactive welfare policies), the welfare state must, in Giddens' view, focus much more on prevention – that is, seeking to prevent them from occurring at all.

In other words, the reactive welfare policies of the classic welfare state must, according to Giddens, be replaced by 'generative politics' – that is, more proactive welfare policies that focus on prevention and strengthening of personal resources (empowerment) rather than intervention once the damage is done: 'The cultivation of human potential should as far as possible replace "after the event" redistribution' (Giddens 1998b: 101). In this way citizens must, to a greater extent, be able to take responsibility for their own health – that is, make responsible life-political decisions regarding the new types of risks they are faced with in late modern risk society (Giddens 1994: 15, 93–94). As examples of generative politics, Giddens mentions, among other things, preventive health programs, measures to reduce traffic accidents, family policies, therapeutic measures in order to combat domestic violence and measures to prevent crime (Giddens 1994: 153–57).[3] This development is also reflected in the concept of the 'competitive state', where the short-term demand-oriented policies of the welfare state are replaced by more proactive, long-term supply-oriented policies aimed at securing the future of the welfare state (Pedersen 2011: 27–28).

Thus, in Giddens' view, generative politics – in connection with life politics and positive welfare – must strengthen the citizens' personal resources and capacity for independent risk management in a society characterised by constant change and uncertainty (Giddens 1994: 18; Giddens 2007: 96–100). For example, better competences in relation to health could enable many people to live healthier, longer and better lives. As Giddens points out, this would make a bigger difference to life chances than the transfer of economic resources (Giddens 1995: 27). A prerequisite for this, however, is an institutional adjustment that includes not least the welfare state, which must be adapted to a more reflexively organised society. According to Giddens, the welfare state should not primarily be based on intervening and assembling the pieces after the damage has occurred; instead, it should be much more oriented towards facilitating that people themselves organise their lives by means of their own efforts and commitment – that is, a more individualised risk management (Giddens 2000: 155).

Giddens' analysis of the transformation of the welfare state also forms the basis for his ideas about the 'third way', which in Great Britain formed the ideological basis for Tony Blair's New Labour. Key elements are breaking with 'rights thinking' and a renewal of civil society. The principle of public support has, according to Giddens, led citizens to neglect their personal responsibilities (Giddens 1998b: 37, 114–15). The relationship between rights and obligations in the welfare state must therefore be reconsidered so that rights are more closely linked to obligations. Social benefits should not function as a passive safety net, but rather as an active stepping stone to reintegration in the labour market (Giddens 1998b: 36–37, 65–66). The welfare state should first and foremost provide 'self-help' assistance (*Enabling Government*), and here social partnerships and a bigger involvement of the voluntary (third) sector in solving social tasks can play an important role (Giddens 1998b: 78–86). The ideal is an 'inclusive society', where equality is conceived in terms of social inclusion (Giddens 1998b: 101–11).[4]

Even if Giddens and Beck agree on the diagnosis of individualisation in late modernity (Rasborg 2021: ch. 4), Beck, in contrast to Giddens, emphasises that increasing individualisation and incalculability of risk increases social insecurity since it leads to an 'uninsured society': 'Risk society is *uncovered* society, in which insurance protection *decreases* with the scale of the danger – and this in the historic milieu of the "welfare state", which encompasses all spheres of life, and of the fully comprehensive society. Only the two together – uncovered *and* comprehensively insured society – constitute the politically explosive force of risk society' (Beck 1999: 85). Beck thus, in line with Dean, Standing and Wacquant (cf. below), seems to place more emphasis on the negative aspects of the individualisation of risk.

4.   RISK AND INSURANCE AS MANAGEMENT TECHNOLOGIES OF THE WELFARE STATE

Significant formulations of the role of risk in connection with the transformation of the welfare state can also be found in recent French (and French-inspired) social theory (cf. Rasborg 2012, 2021: chs. 2 and 3). A central figure here is Mitchell Dean, who, with inspiration from, among others, Michel Foucault and Francois Ewald, points out that risk is inextricably linked to insurance, which is about 'making the incalculable calculable' (Dean 1999: 183–84; Ewald 1991b: 204–5). Thus, here risk is linked with insurance technology and the advent in modern society of new forms of governance that are about making social reality calculable and thus controllable (Dean 1999: chs. 8 and 9).

As shown above, Beck and Giddens believe that 'external' risks in industrial society are, basically, calculable, whereas the high-consequence risks and manufactured uncertainty of late-modern risk society are increasingly incalculable. However, this opposition between calculable and incalculable risks is criticised by Dean for conceiving risk as a social fact ('a thing') whose inherent characteristics change during the development of modern society. In this, Dean draws on Ewald, who precisely breaks with such a realist, or essentialist, understanding of risk when he points out: 'Nothing is a risk in itself; there is no risk in reality. But on the other hand, anything *can* be a risk; it all depends on how one analyses the danger, considers the event' (Ewald 1991b: 199). In other words, following Ewald, that something is a risk is not an intrinsic property of the given phenomenon, but rather expresses a certain way of observing it – that is, from an insurance point of view. Thus, for Ewald, there is an inseparable connection between risk and insurance (Ewald 1991b: 198). Insurance is, as he says, the technology of risk, and this is what makes it meaningful at all to say that something is a risk. According to this actuarial concept of risk, risks are characterised by being: (1) calculable; (2) collective; and (3) constituting a capital (Ewald 1991b: 201–5).

Consequently, if something has to be a risk, it must be made subject to insurance calculation models (statistics and calculations of probability) (Ewald 1991b: 201–2). Moreover, it must be possible to chart how the damage is distributed among given populations (Ewald 1991b: 202–3). Finally, it must be possible in terms of insurance to provide economic compensation for damages, which can only with difficulty be priced (e.g. the loss of a body part as a result of a work accident). This is calculated by means of calculation models that determine how much compensation a given damage (e.g. a given degree of disability) triggers (Ewald 1991b: 204–5). Hence, according to Ewald and Dean, risk cannot be understood independently of insurance, which, as mentioned, is about 'making the incalculable calculable' (Dean 1999: 183–84).

For the same reason, as Dean points out, it does not make sense to speak of incalculable risks, because if risks are defined in terms of insurance, it follows by definition that they must be calculable (because otherwise they would not be risks): 'It is thus not possible to speak of incalculable risks, or of risks that escape our modes of calculation, and even less possible to speak of a social order in which risk is largely calculable and contrast it with one in which risk has become largely incalculable' (Dean 1999: 177). Since insurance is exactly about pricing damages, which can only with difficulty be priced in terms of economic compensation, in principle everything can be made a risk from an insurance point of view: 'For insurance rationality, everything can be treated as a risk and the task of insurers has been both to "produce" risks and to find ways of insuring what has previously been thought to be uninsurable' (Dean 1999: 184).

Consequently, in Dean's view, risk is closely connected with governance since the attempt to make reality calculable by means of probability is precisely an attempt to order it so that it becomes controllable (Dean 1999: 177–79). Where Beck and Giddens primarily locate the origin of risk in socio-economic development, in Dean's (radical constructivist) approach it is, rather, associated with the emergence in the modern welfare state of new forms of government aimed at shaping and guiding human behaviour (cf. Foucault 1991).

On this basis, the emergence of the welfare state in the late 19th century is seen by Ewald and Dean as a collective insurance against the unintended consequences of the industrial society (unemployment, work accidents, disease, etc.). In other words, since the welfare state socialises risks, it becomes a key insurance technology in relation to risks in modern society (Dean 1999: 191). Hence, according to Ewald and Dean, the insurance principle is constitutive for the social contract – and thus solidarity – in modern society (Dean 1999: 185–88; Ewald 1991a: 288, 291–92; Ewald 1991b: 207, 209–10).

Conversely, today, neo-liberal (or advanced liberal) forms of governmentality are, in Dean's view, associated with an increasing individualisation, decentralisation and privatisation of the collective risk management of the welfare state that aimed at equalising the individual risks of unemployment, illness and old age (Dean 1999: 191; cf. Achterberg and Raven 2011). These new forms of governmentality, however, do not work through an overt (repressive) power, but rather through a more tacit, creative and facilitating power whose purpose, according to (Foucault and) Dean, is to get individuals to govern themselves by increasingly taking responsibility for their own individual risk management (e.g. private health insurance and pension savings, workfare policies, smoking cessation courses, alcohol rehabilitation, guidance on healthy diet and exercise, etc.) (Dean 1999: 192–97).

That is, we are witnessing new forms of 'self-governance', which, in Foucault's sense, express a 'normalising power' (Foucault 1979, 1991) that aims to normalise and reintegrate vulnerable and potentially 'dangerous' groups in society (the long-term unemployed, cash benefit recipients, drug and alcohol abusers, etc.) and make them responsible (Dean 1999: 168, 170–71, 173–74; cf. Castel 1991; Standing 2014). The role of the welfare state and the professional treatment system thus becomes to provide the basis for,

> multiple 'responsibilization' of individuals, families, households, and communities for their own risks – of physical and mental ill-health, of unemployment, of poverty in old age, of poor educational performance, of becoming victims of crime. Competition between public (state) schools, private health insurance and superannuation schemes, community policing and 'neighbourhood watch' schemes, and so on, are all instances of contriving practices of liberty in which the responsibilities

for risk minimization become a feature of the choices that are made by individuals, households and communities as consumers, clients and users of services. (Dean 1999: 166)

According to Dean this takes place through, on the one hand, 'technologies of agency' aimed at improving the ability of individuals to participate, consent and act (contracting, outsourcing, action plans, etc.) and, on the other, 'technologies of performance' that seek to optimise these skills by making them calculable and comparable (performance indicators, benchmarking, quasi-markets, etc.) (Dean 1999: 167–70, 172–73). Key to contemporary risk management is also 'case-management risk', which is linked to clinical assessments of the 'riskiness' of vulnerable groups, for example the likelihood of a mentally ill person committing a violent act. Here, risk assessment forms the basis for a number of therapeutic, observational and discipli-nary measures aimed at rehabilitating vulnerable and 'deviant' groups, or at least, 'lower[ing] the dangers posed by their risk of alcoholism, drug dependency, sexual diseases, criminal behavior, long-term unemployment and welfare dependency' (Dean 1999: 189; 168–70).

Vulnerable groups 'at risk' are thus made subject to technologies of agency, in order to turn them into active citizens who are able to manage their own risks (Dean 1999: 167–68). However, this, according to Dean, increasingly leads to a division between active citizens capable of handling their own risk, and vulnerable and underprivileged groups who fail to do so and therefore must be subjected to therapeutic and resocialising interventions (Dean 1999: 167–68; cf. Abrahamson 2016: 26). This does not necessarily reflect a traditional class division – e.g. 'the dangerous classes' versus the wage labour class – but rather, 'the warp and weft of risk within a population' (Dean 1999: 167). But as 'high-risk' categories often overlap with social class divisions, the governmentality approach to risk can, as Dean says, 'be thought of as re-inscribing and recoding earlier languages of stratification, disadvantage and marginalization' (Dean 1999: 167).

At a descriptive level, Dean and Giddens seem to agree that today the emergence of a new risk structure is associated with a transformation of the welfare state, which to a greater extent creates a framework for self-management of risk by citizens. The decisive difference between them is that Giddens (normatively) perceives this development as a necessary renewal of the welfare state facilitated by generative politics and positive welfare, whereas in Dean's view it reflects,

> a set of political programmes and formulas of rule that represent a major retraction of social rights and the ideal of a welfare state that drove social provision for much of the now receding century. At the end of the nineteenth century in France the socialization of risk was linked to the invention of social forms of government. In the twilight of the twentieth century, we might say that the individualization of risk is linked to new forms of liberal government. (Dean 1999: 191)

Hence, compared with Giddens' 'positive' analysis of the transformation of the welfare state, Dean, as can clearly be seen from the quotation above, is much more critical of the conse-quences of (late) modern forms of risk management.

Nevertheless, despite these differences, Beck, Giddens, Ewald and Dean share a basic assumption, namely that the modern welfare state can be perceived as a collective insur-ance system that offsets the individual risk of unemployment, illness, etc. Scandinavian, institutional–redistributive welfare states, such as Denmark, Sweden, Norway and Finland, cannot, however, be said to be based on pure insurance principles. Although some social benefits – e.g. the unemployment benefit system – are, in principle, built up as an insurance system, to which the employee him/herself pays a contribution (a premium), it is in fact the state that finances the major part (Andersen 1999: 46, note 10). Public welfare benefits financed through income taxes differ from private insurance in that private insurance typically divides policyholders into risk classes so that those who have the greatest risk of being affected by illness, accident, unemployment, etc., either pay a higher premium or have a larger excess. Conversely, those who have the least risk pay less. Thus, in private insurance there is only solidarity *within* risk classes, whereas there is no solidarity *between* those who have a low risk and those who have a high risk of being exposed to the insurance event (Andersen 1991: 134; Esping-Andersen 1999: 38–39; Kvist 2016: 52; Veen 2011: 15–16).

For that reason, the solidarity of the (institutional–redistributive) welfare state is more extensive than the insurance model, since it is based not solely on solidarity *within* risk classes, but also on solidarity *between* risk classes – that is, the healthy pay to the sick, the employed to the unemployed, the young to the elderly, etc. (Esping-Andersen 1999: 41; Greve 2016: 132). Consequently, both the risk/insurance and the citizenship approach can be said to reveal significant aspects of the welfare state: where the former captures the principle of risk equalisation within risk classes, the latter better captures the fact that the de-commodifying welfare state is based on a more comprehensive solidarity that is rooted in the ideal of making everyone a full citizen of society (*Social Citizenship*) (Andersen 1999: 42–43, note 6).

5.   NEW SOCIAL RISKS IN THE POST-INDUSTRIAL SOCIETY

The new risk structure analysed by Beck, Giddens and Dean has been described by other social theorists as 'new social risks' (Bonoli 2005, 2007; Taylor-Gooby 2004, 2008; cf. Harsløf et al. 2013). These theorists have pointed out that changes in the labour market, globalisation and the transformation of the welfare state have created a growing risk of being marginalised in the labour market and becoming poor (Bonoli 2005, 2007; Standing 2014: 11; Taylor-Gooby 2004, 2008; Wacquant 2008). The concept of new social risks relates to socio-economic changes that have taken place in the post-industrial society, such as women's growing labour market participation, increased flexibility and job insecurity in the labour market, growing income inequality, increased immigration, and demographic change (Bonoli 2005, 2007; Taylor-Gooby 2004, 2008). The new social risks include a lack of balance between family and work, loss of care, unstable family relationships, social isolation and lack of educational competencies. According to Taylor-Gooby, the groups that are particularly vulnerable to the new social risks are young people, immigrants, families with children, single parents and the low skilled (Taylor-Gooby 2004, 2008).

The notion of new social risks has been criticised for the fact that the risks just mentioned do not differ significantly from the 'old' risks of industrial society such as unemployment, poverty and social exclusion (Harsløf and Ulmestig 2013: 1–2, 15–16). However, decisive differences between 'new' and 'old' risks are to be found in the mechanisms that cause social marginalisation and exclusion, as well as in the policies aimed at mitigating risks. As we have seen in the foregoing, the role of the welfare state in industrial society was to ensure full employment and secure individuals against disease, unemployment and old age through income transfers, whereas the role of the welfare state today is increasingly to enable citizens to participate in the labour market. According to Peter Taylor-Gooby, the transformation of the welfare state points in the direction of a 'social investment state' aimed at investing in people's productive potential so that risk groups can become active in the labour market (Taylor-Gooby 2004, 2008). Investments in childcare, health, further education/upskilling and active labour market policy combined with labour market reforms must ensure that the individuals can be integrated into the labour market and thereby counteract social exclusion. Thus, the transition from 'old' to 'new' risks is not, as with Dean, perceived as identical to a dismantling of the welfare state based on social justice and a security principle, but rather with its restructuring in terms of a 'competitive state' or a 'social investment state' based on 'work first' policies and investment in human capital in order to promote labour market inclusion (Abrahamson 2016: 25–26, 34–36; Pedersen 2011; Veen and Yerkes 2011: 193–94, 203).

A more pessimistic analysis of the new risks and uncertainties in post-industrial society is, apart from Dean, also found in Guy Standing (2014) and Loïc Wacquant (2008). According to Standing, increased flexibility, growing income inequality and a dismantling of the welfare state's universal benefits have created a new class – 'the precariat' – located at the bottom of the class structure and characterised by permanent employment insecurity and income insecurity, low mobility, and little opportunity to organise collectively. In today's flexible labour market, the employment and job security that wage workers had in the post-war industrial society, where the state sought to create full employment by stimulating demand and where companies secured permanent employment to a larger degree, is diminishing. Today, employment policies seek to make the workforce more productive by creating incentives to move from public support to employment. Due to increasing demands for flexibility, permanent full-time employment is increasingly being replaced by more flexible types of employment such as temporary contracts, project appointments and part-time employment. As a result, seven forms of security that, following Standing, characterised 'industrial citizenship' are increasingly undermined, namely: (1) labour market security; (2) employment security; (3) job security; (4) work security; (5) skill reproduction security; (6) income security; and (7) representation security (Standing 2014: 17; cf. Beck 2000, 2005; Rasborg 2021: chs. 6 and 8; Sennett 1998; Wacquant 2008: 234–36, 244–47).

Standing thus to a large degree shares Beck's view that increasing job insecurity is caused by the emergence of a 'system of flexible and pluralized underemployment' (Beck 1992: 140–49; cf. Standing 2014: 26) – that is, a deregulation of the labour market, which Beck also refers to as 'Brazilianization of the West' or 'precarious work' (*prekäre Arbeit*) (Beck 2000: 1–9, 13, 54, 88).[5]

Standing and Wacquant also emphasise that the new types of risks and job insecurity in the flexible labour market are associated with a transformation of the welfare state. Where the classic welfare state – as we have seen above – provided social security by insuring the citizens against risks such as unemployment, illness and old age through income transfers, the state is now increasingly subjected to a competition logic where it, through incentives, attempts to provide citizens with qualifications and skills in order to enable them to adapt to the demands of a knowledge-based economy. In other words, the welfare state changes from de-commodifying the workforce – that is, modifying market demands – to increasingly re-commodifying it by encouraging the unemployed to become active in the labour market (Standing 2014: 71; Veen, Achterberg and Raven 2011: 37–38; Wacquant 2008: 252, 267–70). Thus, in order to increase the incentive to work, the redistributive welfare state has, according to Standing and Wacquant, increasingly been replaced by a neo-liberal 'paternalistic workfare state' characterised by lower social benefits and a disciplining of vulnerable groups such as the unemployed, homeless, immigrants, etc. (Standing 2014: 246–51; Wacquant 2008:

267–70, 276–79; cf. Abrahamson 2016: 25–26, 34–36; Bauman 1998; Veen and Yerkes 2011: 193–94, 203).

6.   CHANGING RISKS, INEQUALITY AND CLASS

A basic element in Beck's theory of the risk society is, as already mentioned, the claim that risks, unlike wealth, are individualised, classless and egalitarian, since we are all affected by the global environmental, finance and terrorist risks of the 'world risk society' (climate change, financial crises, international terrorism, etc.). As Beck puts it: 'poverty is hierarchic, smog is democratic' (Beck 1992: 36). However, it is well documented that a number of risks still reflect familiar patterns of inequality. For example, if we look at health risks, which, as we have seen above, play a decisive role in Giddens' argument about the necessity for a more individualised risk management, there is solid evidence that they are unequally distributed depending on social conditions (family conditions, social position and harder impact of illness on the more vulnerable) (Christensen et al. 2013; Diderichsen et al. 2011: 7, 26–28; Eikemo et al. 2016). According to several empirical studies, the lowest social groups (low education, income and occupational status) are far more vulnerable and likely than the highest social groups (high education, income and occupational status) to incur diseases such as chronic obstructive lung disease, heart disease, dementia, lung cancer and depression. Altogether, these diseases account for two-thirds of the inequality in health in the Danish welfare society – which is sometimes referred to as an 'ideal society' in other countries – which is reflected in the average life-expectancy in terms of lost years of life (Diderichsen et al. 2011: 7). That is, even though the average life expectancy as such has risen in all highly developed industrial societies, it does not increase equally for all social groups. A comparison of the average life expectancy of the richest and the poorest quarters of the Danish population (income quartiles) shows that there is a difference in life expectancy between the highest and the lowest strata in society of 9.9 years for men and 6.2 years for women (Diderichsen et al. 2011: 33). Over time this has increased, especially for men, since the difference in 1987 was 5.5 years for men and 5.3 years for women (Diderichsen et al. 2011: 33, 66).

Inequality in health applies not only in Denmark, but, with national variations, also in the other European countries and the USA and Canada (Diderichsen et al. 2011: 15–16; Eikemo et al. 2016; Pintelon et al. 2013; Wilkinson and Pickett 2010: 82). Moreover, in large comparative empirical studies of several European countries it is emphasised that individual lifestyle factors – which Giddens, as we have seen, puts a strong focus on – are not in themselves sufficient to explain inequality in health: 'This is because health and health inequalities are deeply rooted in the social stratification systems of modern societies. Income redistribution policies or action towards an improvement of physical working conditions in manual occupations may be equally effective policies to obtain healthier lives' (Eikemo et al. 2016: 14). In other words, there is a marked – and increasing – inequality in health that does not support Beck's thesis on 'democratic' – individualised, classless and egalitarian – risks.

Regarding this, Beck's counter-argument might be that it is not social risks, but above all environmental risks that are 'democratic' (Beck 2016: 86–95).[6] But here too, problems arise, as several empirical studies show that the effects of environmental risks such as, for example, particle pollution in the air are socially unequal as well, since they interact with – and reinforce – a number of diseases (e.g. 'smoker's lung', asthma and cardiovascular diseases), which less privileged people already have an increased risk of contracting (Diderichsen et al. 2011: 85). Similarly, Dean Curran has argued that environmental risks are correlated with social inequality and class, since the possibilities of resisting, or escaping, climate disasters such as drought, cloudbursts, floods, violent storms and hurricanes – which most climate scientists put in context with man-made global warming – depend on economic capacity and thus social position (class) (Curran 2013a; Curran 2013b; Curran 2016: 100–105). That being so, risks are not classless, but on the contrary interact with class, and risk and class can mutually reinforce each other, which Curran seeks to capture with the concepts of 'risk position' (Curran 2013a: 49, 52; Curran 2013b: 75–76, 79; Curran 2016: 87) and 'risk class' respectively (Curran 2018: 36). Thus, not only social risks, but also environmental risks seem largely to be socially stratified. In other words, the smog is not democratic, as claimed by Beck, but rather hierarchic (cf. Rasborg 2021).

Nevertheless, despite the criticism, Beck basically maintains his argument that although risks are in many cases embedded in a global inequality structure – described as an asymmetry between those who produce the risk and those who are affected by it (Beck 2015: 76; Beck 2016: 38–39) – the general trend is that they become so extensive and boundless that they transcend class positions (e.g. climate change, global warming) (Beck 2016: 79–96). Moreover, he emphasises that, contrary to what he claimed in his early writings, the world risk society is not a 'catastrophe society', but rather is characterised by a constant anticipation of possible disasters, which is a general condition of reflexive modern society (Beck 2009b: 9–11, 14; Beck 2013: 69–70).[7] Finally, Beck points out that in order to understand the new global inequalities it is necessary to cut the theoretical ties to the nation state which, in his view, characterises traditional class theory. In other words, not only the class concept, but also the related 'methodological nationalism' must be transcended and replaced by 'methodological cosmopolitanism' in order to understand the new and more complex inequalities associated with global risks (Beck 2007; Beck 2013: 71–72; cf. Beck 2009a, 2009c, 2010, 2011, 2016: 79–80; Beck and Grande 2010).

In order to better understand this new global complexity, Beck, in his most recent writings, introduced the concept of 'risk class', which is closely connected to the concepts of 'metamorphosis' and 'emancipatory catastrophism' (Beck 2013: 63, 68; Beck 2015; Beck 2016: 79–96). With the notion of 'emancipatory catastrophism', Beck seems to insist that, even in the case of the worst possible incident – in the disaster and/or anticipation of the disaster – there is potential for change, as it raises awareness of the relationship between, for example, climate change and social and racial inequality. As an example, Beck mentions the hurricane named Katrina that in 2005 moved from northern Cuba across Florida to New Orleans and in total cost over 1,800 lives. According to Beck this led to a 'social catharsis' as Katrina connected – the previously separate – climate disasters with social and racial inequality – whereby it created the basis for the emergence of a new normative horizon of global justice (Beck 2015: 79–81; Beck 2016: 118–22). With the concept of 'risk class' Beck – like Bruno Latour with his related concept of 'geo-social classes' (Latour and Riquier 2018) – precisely seeks to understand this connection between climate change, social inequality and class. He points out that social inequality and class are today made subject to a social change that has become so radical, discontinuous and unpredictable that it assumes the character of a 'metamorphosis' (Beck 2015, 2016). As a consequence: 'classes are metamorphosed into risk-classes, nations into risk-nations and regions into risk-regions' (Beck 2016: 80). With the notion of risk-class Beck thus attempts to shed light on the intersection of risk positions and class positions in contemporary society (Beck 2016: 81). However, unlike the traditional class concept that, following Beck, is descriptive, the concept of risk class also contains a normative dimension, by thematising how the climate crisis leads to an increasing awareness of the link between climate change and social/racial inequality, which provides the basis for normative ideas about social justice, cf. the example above (Beck 2016: 81).

At first glance, it might appear as if Beck now, in the light of the criticism, is moderating his general rejection of the concept of class. However, if we take a closer look, we discover that he maintains that 'risk positions' – or 'RISKclass' in Beck's terms – are increasingly prevalent in relation to 'class positions' – or 'riskCLASS' in Beck's terms – in contemporary society (Beck 2013: 63, 68; Beck 2016: 84–96). Beck thus – still – seems to perceive global risks as an 'overarching' structure that increasingly obfuscates class differences (but not social inequality) (cf. Curran 2018: 37–38). Or put differently: he still seems to insist on perceiving risk and class – as well as individualisation and class (Atkinson 2007, 2010) – as mutually exclusive ('either–or') rather than as interdependent ('both–and'). A general point in Beck's theory of modernity is that where a dichotomous 'either–or' logic was dominating in industrial society/first modernity, a much more ambivalent 'both–and' logic is prevalent in the risk society/second modernity (Beck 1994: 177; Beck 1997: 13, 21, 24, 32, 38). But when it comes to risk and class – as well as individualisation and class – Beck, paradoxically, maintains the 'either–or' logic of first modernity rather than the 'both–and' logic of second modernity (cf. Rasborg 2017, 2018, 2021).

7.   CONCLUSION

In this chapter three different approaches to the analysis of changing risks, individualisation and inequality in contemporary welfare society have been identified. Firstly, we looked at Beck and Giddens' claim that the welfare state is put under pressure in the risk society, as it is confronted with new types of risks that cannot be adequately addressed by traditional (reactive) welfare policies. Welfare policies are therefore, according to Beck and Giddens, increasingly concerned with a more individualised 'risk management'. Next, the focus was on Foucault, Ewald and Dean's alternative approach, which perceives risk and insurance as related to contemporary forms of governmentality and, on this basis, argues that today's individualisation, decentralisation and privatisation of risks is associated with a dismantling of the classic (solidaristic) welfare state. Finally, we investigated how, according to Bonoli, Taylor-Gooby, Standing and Wacquant, new social risks are also linked to more specific changes in the welfare society and the labour market in terms of flexible work, job insecurity, growing inequality, new family patterns, an aging population, etc.

Unlike Beck and Giddens, who claim that new social risks have become classless (individualised), Bonoli, Taylor-Gooby, Standing and Wacquant maintain a stratification perspective pointing to specific groups – such as immigrants, young people, single parents and the unskilled – who are at particular risk of being marginalised. Somewhere in between lies Dean, with his observation that more individualised forms of risk management give rise to an increasing polarisation, which to some extent overlaps with a social class division, between high- and low-risk groups. As a consequence of new social risks, according to Standing and Wacquant, a precariat is emerging that is described as a growing class living in permanent employment and income insecurity. Thus, Taylor-Gooby, Standing and Wacquant point out that the de-commodifying welfare state is increasingly transformed into a social investment state, or a competitive state, that manages social risks through re-commodification. However, the assessment of the transformation of the welfare state is different. Where Giddens and Taylor-Gooby see the transformation of the welfare state as an opportunity to prevent social risks through generative politics and social investments, Dean, Wacquant and Standing perceive the increased uncertainty as a result of the transition to a neo-liberal workfare state.

Empirically, as shown, there is not particularly good evidence for Beck's thesis on classless and egalitarian risks. On the contrary, a large number of studies show that changing risks such as inequality in health and climate change are embedded in a pattern of inequality, which to a much greater extent supports the stratification perspective (cf. Pintelon et al. 2013). On the other hand, the risk-oriented approach to the welfare state points out a significant weakness in the 'traditional' welfare state research, namely that it has not adequately addressed the challenges that environmental and climate change represent in relation to the welfare state. From the risk society perspective, at least two key areas can thus be identified where social and environmental risks and risk politics intertwine: 'First environmental risks do and probably will, to a much higher degree than today, turn into social and health risks. Second, the social investment state and the environmental investment state may be at conflict with each other in terms of attracting financial support or they may, in combination, create a high-profile competition state on the global market' (Bengtsson et al. 2016b: 246).

With the notion of 'risk class' (and the related concepts of 'metamorphosis' and 'emancipatory catastrophism'), Beck, in spite of his general rejection of the class concept, seems to open up for a thematisation of the interconnections between social, environmental and class-related differentiations in contemporary society. However, since the notion of 'risk class' – as well as the related notion of 'geo-social classes' (Latour) – is rather rudimentary and insufficiently defined, further development and clarification is required if it is to be useful in further studies of the forms of differentiation that are linked to changing social risks. A prerequisite for this, however, is that the concept of 'risk class' is detached from its 'risk bias', which (a priori) assigns the 'risk logic' a priority in relation to the 'class logic'. In this way, in accordance with Beck's own 'both–and' logic, it will be possible to maintain an analytical openness to the fact that risk and class are not necessarily mutually exclusive ('either–or'), but rather, as shown in this chapter, interact in complex ways in contemporary society ('both–and'). As such, the concepts of 'risk class', 'class risk' and 'risk category' are not new, but are already used in comparative welfare research (Baldwin 1990: 10–54; Esping-Andersen 1999: 40–41). As a first step in the conceptual strategy proposed here, it could therefore be fruitful to clarify the various meanings in which the terms are used in welfare research and risk research respectively.

NOTES

1. I would like to thank Professor Anders Ejrnæs for his kind permission to draw on parts of our joint work on new social risks and the transformation of the welfare state (Ejrnæs and Rasborg 2019).
2. An underlying premise of Marshall's understanding of citizenship is that it is tied to the nation state, which is clear when he states: 'the citizenship whose history I wish to trace is, by definition, national' (1950: 12). However, this premise – which is a good example of what Beck understands by 'methodological nationalism' (Beck 2005; Beck and Grande 2010) – is increasingly becoming untenable in today's globalised societies, not least where increasing EU integration makes it possi-

ble for EU citizens to work and achieve social benefits (such as child allowance, educational support and unemployment benefits) in EU countries other than their countries of origin. In other words, social rights are no longer exclusively tied to the nation state, wherefore, among others, Beck, Giddens and Held advocate that today we must conceive a global or 'cosmopolitan' citizenship (Beck 2005; cf. Delanty 2009: 111–31; Rasborg 2021: ch. 7).

3. In practice, it seems difficult to maintain a sharp distinction between 'reactive' and 'generative' policies, since the welfare state's 'reactive' core services such as unemployment benefits and cash benefits can also be said to contain preventive (generative) elements, as they minimize the risk that unemployment leads to a more serious social déroute (cf. Andersen 1996). In addition, the idea of prevention had already been built into Nordic welfare states from an early stage.

4. Many of the reform measures in the Danish welfare state in the 1990s, where the Danish Social Democracy held the government power for a long period, are reminiscent of Giddens' third way. Examples include active labour market policy (workfare), increased involvement of volunteer work in solving social tasks, and an emphasis on corporate social responsibility.

5. With the concept of 'precarious work', Beck may in a sense be said to 'anticipate' Standing's 'precariat'. However, a key difference between the two concepts is that where the precariat, according to Standing, designates a 'new' class at the bottom of the class hierarchy (Standing 2014: 13), Beck does not believe that the new forms of inequality and job insecurity should be understood in class terms (cf. above).

6. This counter-argument has not been plucked out of thin air, but was made by Beck himself in personal communication with the author of this chapter.

7. In his early writings, Beck stated: 'The risk-society is, therefore, a catastrophe-society, in which exceptional circumstances threatens to become normality' (Beck 1989: 90).

REFERENCES

Abrahamson, P. (2016), 'Denmark from an international perspective', in T. Torbenfeldt Bengtsson, M. Frederiksen and J. Elm Larsen (eds), *The Danish Welfare State: A Sociological Investigation*, London/New York: Palgrave Macmillan, pp. 25–39.

Achterberg, P. and Raven, J. (2011), 'Individualisation: a double-edged sword. Does individualisation undermine welfare state support?', in R. van der Veen, M. Yerkes and P. Achterberg (eds), *The Transformation of Solidarity: Changing Risks and the Future of the Welfare State*, Amsterdam: Amsterdam University Press, pp. 49–68.

Andersen, B. Rold (1991), *Velfærdsstaten i Danmark og Europa. Kendsgerninger og myter om den offentlige sektor*, Copenhagen: Fremad.

Andersen, J. Goul (1996), 'Velfærdssystem, marginalisering og medborgerskab', *Dansk Sociologi* 7(1), 7–41.

Andersen, J. Goul (1999), 'Den universelle velfærdsstat under pres – men hvad er universalisme?', *GRUS* 20(56/57), 40–62.

Atkinson, W. (2007), 'Beck, individualization and the death of class: a critique', *The British Journal of Sociology* 58(3), 349–66.

Atkinson, W. (2010), *Class, Individualization and Late Modernity: In Search of the Reflexive Worker*, London/New York: Palgrave Macmillan.

Baldwin, P. (1990), *The Politics of Social Solidarity: Class Bases of the European Welfare State 1875–1975*, Cambridge: Cambridge University Press.

Bauman, Z. (1998), *Work, Consumerism and the New Poor*, Buckingham: Open University Press.

Beck, U. (1989), 'On the way to the industrial risk-society? Outline of an argument', *Thesis Eleven* 23, 86–103.

Beck, U. (1992), *The Risk Society: Towards a New Modernity*, London: Sage.

Beck, U. (1994), 'Self-dissolution and self-endangerment of industrial society: what does this mean?', in U. Beck, A. Giddens and S. Lash (eds), *Reflexive Modernization: Politics, Tradition and Aesthetics in the Modern Social Order*, Cambridge: Polity Press, pp. 174–83.

Beck, U. (1997), *The Reinvention of Politics: Rethinking Modernity in the Global Social Order*, Cambridge: Polity Press.

Beck, U. (1998), 'Politics of Risk Society', in J. Franklin (ed.), *The Politics of Risk Society*, Cambridge: Polity Press, pp. 9–22.

Beck, U. (1999), 'Risk society and the welfare state', in U. Beck, *World Risk Society*, Cambridge: Polity Press, pp. 72–90.

Beck, U. (2000), *The Brave New World of Work*, Cambridge: Polity Press.

Beck, U. (2005), *Power in the Global Age: A New Global Political Economy*, Cambridge: Polity Press.

Beck, U. (2007), 'Beyond class and nation: reframing social inequalities in a globalizing world', *The British Journal of Sociology* 58(4), 679–705.

Beck, U. (2009a), 'Critical theory of world risk society: a cosmopolitan vision', *Constellations* 16(1), 1–22.

Beck, U. (2009b), *World at Risk*, Cambridge: Polity Press.

Beck, U. (2009c), 'World risk society and manufactured uncertainties', *Iris: European Journal of Philosophy and Public Debate* 1(2), 291–99.

Beck, U. (2010), 'Climate for change, or how to create a green modernity?', *Theory, Culture & Society* 27(2–3), 254–66.

Beck, U. (2011), 'We do not live in an age of cosmopolitanism but in an age of cosmopolitisation: the "global other" is in our midst', *Irish Journal of Sociology* 19(1), 16–34.

Beck, U. (2013), 'Why "class" is too soft a category to capture the explosiveness of social inequality at the beginning of the twenty-first century', *The British Journal of Sociology* 64(1), 63–74.

Beck, U. (2015), 'Emancipatory catastrophism: what does it mean to climate change and risk society?', *Current Sociology* 63(1), 75–88.

Beck, U. (2016), *The Metamorphosis of the World*, Cambridge: Polity Press.

Beck, U. and Grande, E. (2010), 'Varieties of second modernity: the cosmopolitan turn in social and political theory and research', *The British Journal of Sociology* 61(3), 409–43.

Bengtsson, T. Torbenfeldt, M. Frederiksen and Larsen J. Elm (2016a), 'Is risk transforming the Danish welfare state?', in T. Torbenfeldt Bengtsson, M. Frederiksen and J. Elm Larsen (eds), *The Danish Welfare State: A Sociological Investigation*, London/New York: Palgrave Macmillan, pp. 3–21.

Bengtsson, T. Torbenfeldt, M. Frederiksen and Larsen J. Elm (2016b), 'Risk dynamics and risk management in the Danish welfare state', in T. Torbenfeldt Bengtsson, M. Frederiksen and J. Elm Larsen (eds), *The Danish Welfare State: A Sociological Investigation*, London/New York: Palgrave Macmillan, pp. 235–49.

Bonoli, G. (2005), 'The politics of the new social policies: providing coverage against new social risks in mature welfare states', *Policy & Politics* 33(3), 431–49.

Bonoli, G. (2007), 'Time matters: postindustrialization, new social risks, and welfare state adaptation in advanced industrial democracies', *Comparative Political Studies* 40(5), 495–520.

Castel, R. (1991), 'From dangerousness to risk', in G. Burchell, C. Gordon and P. Miller (eds), *The Foucault Effect: Studies in Governmentality*, Hemel Hempstead: Harvester Wheatsheaf, pp. 281–98.

Christensen, A.I. et al. (2013), *Danskernes Sundhed. Den nationale Sundhedsprofil 2013*, Copenhagen: Sundhedsstyrelsen.

Curran, D. (2013a), 'Risk society and the distribution of bads: theorizing class in the risk society', *The British Journal of Sociology* 64(1), 44–62.

Curran, D. (2013b), 'What is a critical theory of the risk society? A reply to Beck', *The British Journal of Sociology* 64(1), 75–80.

Curran, D. (2016), *Risk, Power and Inequality in the 21st Century*, London/New York: Palgrave Macmillan.

Curran, D. (2018), 'Beck's creative challenge to class analysis: from the rejection of class to the discovery of risk-class', *Journal of Risk Research* 21(1), 29–40.

Dean, M. (1999), *Governmentality: Power and Rule in Modern Society*, London: Sage.

Delanty, G. (2009), *The Cosmopolitan Imagination: The Renewal of Critical Social Theory*, Cambridge: Cambridge University Press.

Diderichsen, F., I. Andersen and C. Manuel (2011), *Ulighed i sundhed – årsager og indsatser*, Copenhagen: Sundhedsstyrelsen.

Eikemo, T.A. et al. (2016), 'Social Inequalities in Health and their Determinants: Topline Results from Round 7 of the European Social Survey', ESS Topline Results Series, Issue 6.

Ejrnæs, A. and Rasborg, K. (2019), 'Velfærdsstaten og arbejdsmarkedets transformation og nye sociale risici', in B. Greve (ed.), *Socialvidenskab*, Copenhagen: Nyt fra samfundsvidenskaberne, pp. 177–204.

Esping-Andersen, G. (1990), *The Three Worlds of Welfare Capitalism*, Cambridge. Polity Press.

Esping-Andersen, G. (1999), *The Social Foundations of Postindustrial Economies*, Cambridge: Polity Press.

Ewald, F. (1991a), 'Die Versicherungs-Gesellschaft', in U. Beck (ed.), *Politik in der Risikogesellschaft. Essays und Analysen*, Frankfurt/M: Suhrkamp, pp. 288–301.

Ewald, F. (1991b), 'Insurance and risk', in G. Burchell, C. Gordon and P. Miller (eds), *The Foucault Effect: Studies in Governmentality*, Hemel Hempstead: Harvester Wheatsheaf, pp. 197–210.

Foucault, M. (1979), *Discipline and Punish: The Birth of the Prison*, New York: Vintage Books.

Foucault, M. (1991), 'Governmentality', in G. Burchell, C. Gordon and P. Miller (eds), *The Foucault Effect: Studies in Governmentality*, Hemel Hempstead: Harvester Wheatsheaf, pp. 87–104.

Giddens, A. (1994), *Beyond Left and Right: The Future of Radical Politics*, Cambridge: Polity Press.

Giddens, A. (1995), 'Anthony Giddens' livspolitik. Et kommenteret interview ved Carsten Jensen', *Social Kritik* 6(37), 18–27.

Giddens, A. (1998a), 'Risk society: the context of British politics', in J. Franklin (ed.), *The Politics of Risk Society*, Cambridge: Polity Press, pp. 23–34.

Giddens, A. (1998b), *The Third Way: The Renewal of Social Democracy*, Cambridge: Polity Press.

Giddens, A. (2000), 'The post-traditional society and radical politics: an interview with Anthony Giddens', in L.B. Kaspersen (ed.), *Anthony Giddens: An Introduction to a Social Theorist*, Oxford: Blackwell Publishers, pp. 143–56.

Giddens, A. (2007), *Europe in the Global Age*, Cambridge: Polity Press.

Giddens, A. and Pierson, C. (1998), *Conversations with Anthony Giddens: Making Sense of Modernity*, Cambridge: Polity Press.

Greve, B. (2016), *Velfærdssamfundet – en grundbog*, 4. Udgave, Copenhagen: Hans Reitzels Forlag.

Harsløf, I. and R. Ulmestig (2013), 'Introduction: changing social risks and social policy responses in the Nordic welfare states', in I. Harsløf and R. Ulmestig (eds), *Changing Social Risks and Social Policy Responses in the Nordic Welfare States*, London/New York: Palgrave Macmillan, pp. 1–24.

Harsløf, I., S. Scarpa and S. Nygaard Andersen (2013), 'Changing population profiles and social risk structures in the Nordic countries', in I. Harsløf and R. Ulmestig (eds), *Changing Social Risks and Social Policy Responses in the Nordic Welfare States*, London/New York: Palgrave Macmillan, pp. 25–49.

Kemshall, H. (2002), *Risk, Social Policy and Welfare*, Buckingham: Open University Press.

Kvist, J. (2016), 'Social investment as risk management', in T. Torbenfeldt Bengtsson, M. Frederiksen and J. Elm Larsen (eds), *The Danish Welfare State: A Sociological Investigation*, London/New York: Palgrave Macmillan, pp. 41–55.

Latour, B. and C. Riquier (2018), 'For a terrestrial politics: an interview with Bruno Latour', *Eurozine*, 6 February (https://www.eurozine.com/terrestrial-politics-interview-bruno-latour, accessed October 20th, 2021).

Marshall, T.H. (1950), *Citizenship and Social Class and Other Essays*, Cambridge: Cambridge University Press.

Pedersen, O.K. (2011), *Konkurrencestaten*, Copenhagen: Hans Reitzels Forlag.

Pintelon, O., B. Cantillon, K. van den Bosch and C.T. Whelan (2013), 'The social stratification of social risks: the relevance of class for social investment strategies', *Journal of European Social Policy* 23(1), 52–67.

Rasborg, K. (2012), '"(World) risk society" or "new rationalities of risk"? A critical discussion of Ulrich Beck's theory of reflexive modernity', *Thesis Eleven* 108(1), 3–25.

Rasborg, K. (2017), 'From class society to the individualized society? A critical reassessment of individualization and class', *Irish Journal of Sociology* 25(3), 229–49.

Rasborg, K. (2018), 'From "the bads of goods" to "the goods of bads": the most recent developments in Ulrich Beck's cosmopolitan sociology', *Theory, Culture & Society* 35(7–8), 157–73.

Rasborg, K. (2020), 'Risk', in Peter Kivisto (ed.), *The Cambridge Handbook of Social Theory*, Cambridge/New York: Cambridge University Press, Vol. 2, pp. 313–32.

Rasborg, K. (2021), *Ulrich Beck: Theorising World Risk Society and Cosmopolitanism*, London/New York: Palgrave Macmillan.

Sennett, R. (1998), *The Corrosion of Character: The Personal Consequences of Work in the New Capitalism*, New York: W.W. Norton.

Standing, G. (2014), *The Precariat: The New Dangerous Class*, London: Bloomsbury.

Taylor-Gooby, P. (2004), 'New risks and social change', in P. Taylor-Gooby (ed.), *New Risks, New Welfare: The Transformation of the European Welfare State*, Oxford/New York: Oxford University Press, pp. 1–28.

Taylor-Gooby, P. (2008), 'The new welfare settlement in Europe', *European Societies* 10(1), 3–24.

Titmuss, R.M. (1974), *Social Policy*, London: Allen and Unwin.

Ulmestig, R. and I. Harsløf (2013), 'Discussion: the take on new social risks in the Nordic welfare states', in I. Harsløf and R. Ulmestig (eds), *Changing Social Risks and Social Policy Responses in the Nordic Welfare States*, London/New York: Palgrave Macmillan, pp. 266–81.

Veen, R. van der (2011), 'Risk and the welfare state: risk, risk perception and solidarity', in R. van der Veen, M. Yerkes and P. Achterberg (eds), *The Transformation of Solidarity: Changing Risks and the Future of the Welfare State*, Amsterdam: Amsterdam University Press, pp. 13–30.

Veen, R. van der, P. Achterberg and J. Raven (2011), 'Contested solidarity: risk perception and the changing nature of welfare state solidarity', in R. van der Veen, M. Yerkes and P. Achterberg (eds), *The Transformation of Solidarity: Changing Risks and the Future of the Welfare State*, Amsterdam: Amsterdam University Press, pp. 31–47.

Veen, R. van der and M. Yerkes (2011), 'Towards a new welfare state settlement? The transformation of the welfare state solidarity', in R. van der Veen, M. Yerkes and P. Achterberg (eds), *The Transformation of Solidarity: Changing Risks and the Future of the Welfare State*, Amsterdam: Amsterdam University Press, pp. 191–206.

Veen, R. van der, M. Yerkes and P. Achterberg (2011), 'Introduction', in R. van der Veen, M. Yerkes and P. Achterberg (eds), *The Transformation of Solidarity: Changing Risks and the Future of the Welfare State*, Amsterdam: Amsterdam University Press, pp. 7–11.

Wacquant, L. (2008), *Urban Outcasts: A Comparative Sociology of Advanced Marginality*, Cambridge: Polity Press.

Wacquant, L. (2010), 'Crafting the neoliberal state: Workfare, prisonfare and social insecurity', *Sociological Forum* 25(2), 197–220.

Wilkinson, R. and K. Pickett (2010), *The Spirit Level: Why Equality is Better for Everyone*, London: Penguin Books.

6. Digital risk and inequality
Elizabeth Cameron and Dean Curran

Sociologists are increasingly undertaking the work of articulating the ways in which people understand, assume, and manage digital risks amidst backdrops of social stratification and inequalities, both online and offline. A central consideration of our discussion is that, like offline realms, digital spaces and the ways digital technologies are used reflect existing social patterns and practices rather than having an inherently unequal quality to themselves. And as with offline life, the ways digital realms can be unequal are diversely patterned, not always obvious, and reflective of power relations.

We begin by examining some of the key dimensions and present discussions in the existing literature with respect to digital risk and inequality. A wide umbrella of topics generally concerning data, algorithms, and artificial intelligence (often with regard to their rapid enmeshment with offline life and dual potential as socially emergent risk amplifiers and mediators) is reviewed. Numerous theoretical frameworks have been applied to the sociological study of digital risk and inequalities. Most prominently and presented in the next section are Bourdieusian, Intersectional, and briefly, Marxian approaches. The extension of key Bourdieusian concepts such as capital and habitus to digital spheres of life has considerably advanced the literature looking at how the process of social reproduction translates to the digital. Intersectional perspectives draw attention to the multidimensional ways digital risks and inequalities manifest, both tangibly in the lives of individuals as well as through overarching oppressive relational structures that wield digital technologies as tools of domination, or control (and limit) access to its benefits. These analyses have been particularly useful for examining the ways algorithms and smart technologies are used and the often-stratified impacts for users. The theoretical section is rounded out with a discussion about digital risk and inequality as taken up by Marxian perspectives, which incorporate digital contexts into their considerations of the present, globally hegemonic capitalist mode of production.

We then present a section of Special Topics, in which we summarize important conversations happening about inequalities of access, knowledge, and resources within digital life, and ground the presented theoretical discussions with several examples from the literature that examine digital risks and inequalities in health care, education, and within youth populations. The chapter concludes with a summary of the present gaps in the literature and areas for future research, as well as some considerations of the particular challenges and opportunities digital risk and inequality scholars may encounter.

KEY DIMENSIONS AND DISCUSSIONS IN EXISTING LITERATURE

Issues Concerning Data, Algorithms, and Artificial Intelligence

Questions about inequalities resulting from the global advent of "Big Data", algorithms, and artificial intelligence have generated a considerable amount of research. There are concerns related to virtually all aspects of mass data procurement and use, with some going as far as to argue current practices threaten democracy (O'Neil, 2016) and to ask whether a "Big Data Divide" exists (Andrejevic, 2014). There are wide-ranging discussions related to data profiling (particularly, profiles built by algorithms), data collection through surveillance (concerning both the practices of various actors, and the technologies they use), online user privacy, and security (digital risks associated with being online, in the context of protecting data once collected, and digital infrastructure); see below: Blank and Lutz (2016), Crawford and Schutz (2014), Eubanks (2018), Gangadharan (2012 and 2017), Lerman (2013), Madden et al. (2017), and Moon (2018).

There is a gap between the ability to collect data and the oversight of how those data are used. The consequences of incomplete or flawed data collection and analysis (by digital algorithms, people, or a combination) typically fall on those from whom it has been collected rather than those who collect, store, and utilize data. As has been shown in other areas of study of risk mismatches, such as finance and oil and gas production, when mistakes are made the powerful can generally transfer the risks to others (Curran, 2015, 2021). Conversely, those who tend to benefit (in the form of profits, information, political/social capital, etc.) are those who do the data collection, store it, or control its use once mined, and regulations or non-private control of these processes is extremely limited compared with the rapidly expanding abilities of digital technologies that increasingly permeate daily activities in post-industrial societies. The ways data are used once they are collected presents multiple dimensions of possible inequalities, including their ownership and the outcomes of their use in policy and/or legal decisions that may discriminately harm some populations and not others. As Lerman (2013) points out, there are risks to both being left out of the conversation and being included.

Several discussions about who owns and gets to use personal health data collected from apps on wearable or mobile devices illustrate these points. The "far-reaching controls over data ownership" (Sherwani and Bates, 2021, p. 31) that mobile health app companies have put people at risk in ways that are varied and difficult to anticipate, as Sherwani and Bates (2021) point out using the example of Strava, a personal training and social networking app that allows users to share their running or cycling route location via heat map, which inadvertently revealed secret U.S. military operations in Syria and Iraq. O'Loughlin et al. (2019) discuss inequalities of power and control between application owners and users by examining data collection and privacy practices of mobile apps intended to help users with depression, while Singh et al. (2016) provide a discussion about inequalities in the actual health conditions that are addressed by "mHealth apps" (we revisit this later in the chapter, under Special Topics). Borthwick et al. (2015) raise important questions about the "quantified self" that "wearable personalized learning technologies" – which are highlighted as particularly useful for students with physical limitations – generate, as well as the implications of present reliance on "outside vendors" for storage and analysis of this data (p. 85). There are additional considerations for educators, who may or may not incorporate potentially equalizing (or simply useful) technological options into their classrooms due to inequalities in access or privacy concerns (Borthwick et al., 2015). Kostkova et al. (2016) also discuss the "quantified self", interrogating it as an outcome of data sharing on mobile applications and the wide-ranging implications for users. In all these cases, risks are generated by both inclusion in surveillance capitalist systems (Zuboff, 2019) and from potential exclusion from the services these systems provide.

In pursuing an overarching analysis of the existing literature on digital risk and inequality, we find much of the literature argues that increasing reliance on information organized and synthesized by algorithms has had a disproportionately negative impact on already-marginalized groups, largely due to this technology's ability to amplify existing inequalities and human biases on a mass scale. These issues are often raised in response to arguments positing the potential for these technologies to improve the lives of these same groups and daily life in post-industrial societies generally, and are an effort to bring these populations into a conversation where they have been excluded; see below: Birhane and Cummins (2019), Gran et al. (2019), Hampton (2021), Noble (2018), and Obermeyer et al. (2019). Several studies demonstrate algorithms are being utilized in a diverse number of ways by private industries, governments, law enforcement, and in the legal system (see Crawford and Schultz 2014, Curran and Smart 2020, Eubanks 2018, Madden et al. 2017, and Noble 2018), while others mention or directly articulate how artificial intelligence technologies are disrupting and will disrupt life as we know it, particularly global labour landscapes (Curran, 2018). Gran et al. (2019) raise the question of whether or not awareness of algorithms could constitute a new digital divide, and argue it is important to investigate not only how aware people are of algorithms, but how they are understood, given their increasing weight in shaping our experiences online. The highly cited book *Algorithms of Oppression* (Noble, 2018) has evidently provided key developments in this discourse. We expect it will be necessary and valuable for sociologists to pursue diverse avenues of future research concerning the social employment of algorithms and artificial intelligence, and that seeks to identify risks before these technologies are integrated into social life where possible as well as ways to reduce the negative impacts of those already in play.

THEORETICAL APPROACHES: BOURDIEUSIAN, INTERSECTIONAL, AND MARXIAN

In aiming to grasp the novel dimensions of inequalities from emerging configurations of digital risk, this chapter outlines the research from several of the key theoretical frameworks, including Bourdieusian, Intersectional, and Marxian. As suggested below, all of these can provide important insights into how digital innovation is affecting inequalities.

Bourdieu

As Ignatow and Robinson (2017) put it, Pierre Bourdieu's work has become "central" to theorizing inequality and stratification in sociology. Their aptly titled article "Pierre Bourdieu: theorizing the digital" provides an excellent summary of how a Bourdieusian framework has been and can be applied to the study of digital inequalities, both theoretically and methodologically. They argue Bourdieu's work provides a useful ontological stance that accounts for realism and social constructionism, allowing the interrelationships and entanglements of seemingly discrete social phenomena to be empirically studied. Bourdieu's work stands out as a theoretical framework for consideration partly because of the significant amount of literature that has already employed his ideas to research digital phenomena through a social lens. In particular, Bourdieu's interrelated notions of field theory, capitals (particularly digital or "information capital": van Dijk, 2005), and habitus have been intensely developed in digital sociology, and widely applied in the study of information and communication technologies (ICTs) (Ignatow and Robinson, 2017). Indeed, many of these articles were published in leading journals such as *New Media & Society* and *Information, Communication & Society*; see: Gangadharan (2017), Haight et al. (2014), Ignatow and Robinson (2017), Ragnedda et al. (2019), Robinson (2009), and van Deursen and van Dijk (2019).

Much of the literature that applies Bourdieu's concepts to digital life and beyond interrogates how ICTs are understood and used practically by individuals, as well as how they exist as part of ongoing, but slightly-below-the-surface class reproduction processes. There is plenty of research that uses Bourdieu's theory of capitals to understand how inequalities, digital or otherwise, are reproduced by digital activities, technologies, and infrastructure. One theme that emerges in this discussion is how ICTs and other digital aspects of life may be beneficial in some ways at the same time as they perpetuate class or other social divides, or how they are often beneficial to some while harming others. As such, this research on digital risk complements research on other studies focusing on "risk-class", which highlight how the intensification of risks, such as climate change, is imbricated with the production of social wealth and goods (Curran, 2021). Several studies report on this observation that the advantages of digital technologies are often accompanied by the unanticipated or unaddressed consequence of actually reproducing existing inequalities and privileges both online and offline.

Digital capital

One of Bourdieu's most influential theoretical contributions is his conception of cultural and social capitals, or the internalized or externalized resources and connections that can be accumulated and invested to negotiate one's position in a field and acquire additional resources (Bourdieu, 1986). This is accomplished through their conversion to other forms of capital, primarily economic. This conversion process is integral to social reproduction in Bourdieu's theory, particularly the reproduction of social inequalities between a dominating and dominated classes as capital becomes concentrated in the upper classes and a hard-won resource among others. Observing the diffusion of digital technologies into everyday life over the past 30 years or so, scholars have come to theorize digital capital as a secondary, distinct form of capital, one that bridges the gap between online and offline "worlds" (Ragnedda and Ruiu, 2020). Massimo Ragnedda defines digital capital as "the accumulation of digital competencies and digital technologies" (Ragnedda et al., 2019, p. 794), and the same authors have developed an index that accounts for differences in digital skills and competencies to empirically measure digital capital (2019). Calderón Gómez (2020) provides a detailed explanation of the Bourdieusian capital conversion process in a digital context through the experiences of young people in Madrid, and operationalizes many of Bourdieu's concepts described here in the discussion. It should be briefly noted that digital capital is sometimes used interchangeably, or to refer to a similar idea, as van Dijk's (2005) "information capital", defined as "the financial resources to pay for computers and networks, technical skills, evaluation abilities, information-seeking motivation, and the capacity for implementation" (pp. 72–3, as quoted in Ignatow and Robinson, 2017, p. 952).

Discussions about digital capital are often tied to conversations about digital divides, and challenge previous arguments that these stratification patterns would be amended by patching gaps in access, infrastructure, or skills. Sims (2014) argues that well-meaning interventions to level access to ICTs oversimplify and distort the relationships between digital media and social inequalities. And even in wealthy countries with high digital connectivity, scholars have found digital divides persist and actually "continue to expand even after physical access [to the internet] is universal" (van Deursen and van Dijk, 2019, p. 369). Differential access to devices, additional materials, and financial resources continue to impact the skills, uses, and outcomes for internet users even after an internet connection is made (see van Deursen and van Dijk, 2019, pp. 369 and 371). Ragnedda (2017) has questioned whether a third digital divide exists, one that concerns the relationships between online behaviour and digital skills and social status offline, although that particular discussion was framed in Weberian terms. However, other scholars have taken up the same question from an explicitly Bourdieusian approach and examined digital capital's interface with economic, cultural, and social capitals and subsequent impacts for individuals' life chances rather than solely discussing digital inequalities in terms of access to or literacy of technologies. As Calderón Gómez (2020) notes, several authors have found not only do individuals' digital outcomes differ by technology use, but digital capital can be leveraged to affect life chances offline. Calderón Gómez (2019) previously took up Bourdieu's work to develop the idea of "technological capital", which describes how people's socioeconomic status relates to different methods of accessing and using ICTs, specifically. Bourdieu's theory of capitals has been particularly useful for Calderón Gómez's research "because of its suitability for theorizing the interconnection between social practices, based on subjects' dispositions (schemes for action), and social structure, which emerges from continuous position-taking in a hierarchized space of social positions" (Calderón Gómez, 2020). Calderón Gómez also underlines Bourdieu's assessment that economic capital is "the most basic form of digital inequality, imposing material barriers to access" (Calderón Gómez, 2020), emphasizing the interconnection between digital and non-digital capitals. If digital inequalities translate to social life, or at least have a possibility to influence it, a lack of digital capital means being left out of the advantages these technologies provide for others online as well as in other areas of life. This is a familiar logic from digital inequality literature that may not adopt an explicitly Bourdieusian approach, but often documents the implications of being left out of the advantages or burdened with the disadvantages of an increasingly complex digital society.

The interconnections between digital and non-digital capitals are further illuminated by cultural capital inequalities, which are not only reflected in digital spaces but interact with digital capital as individuals negotiate their field positions both on- and offline. Despite claiming to be democratizing, social media platforms tend to amplify (through algorithms, settings, and other mechanisms) the views of groups rich in cultural capital, such as academics, political and media figures on Twitter or entertainment and media personas on YouTube and Instagram, while censoring, or hiding content from others with less – people of colour or LGBTQ2IA+ communities, for example. However, it is the widespread availability of these digital platforms to those beyond cultural elites that makes it possible for those with less or little cultural capital to change their social location by amassing and leveraging digital and cultural capital, often by creating or distributing cultural products (this may be themselves, or "content" they create) and gaining large and/or passionate followings – and along with them, social or cultural influence that has impacts on- and offline. Although the lessening of cultural capital inequalities can be accomplished online by counter-elites who gain digital and cultural capital through rejecting mainstream cultural values, practices, or norms, it would be amiss to ignore the way proponents of misinformation take advantage of this same process, and the broader impacts this can have in a society. This is evident in the spread of misinformation about vaccinations, which certainly existed before the COVID-19 pandemic; however, it is also the case that polarization over COVID-19 vaccinations has rapidly festered to global proportions during the most digitally connected time in history, and this is arguably due in part to both digitally intensified political and cultural polarization and how some counter-elites have been able to exploit these divides to emerge online as enrichened cultural capitalists.

Although field theory was somewhat neglected in explicit analysis, its core concepts and assumptions are foundational to much of the literature using Bourdieusian frameworks (see Ignatow and Robinson, 2017; Calderón Gómez, 2020). Discussions drawing on field theory have often looked at the ways digital and other forms of capital constrain and enable individual actors to position themselves in both digital and non-digital fields, as we have outlined above. Bourdieu also theorized the use of exclusion by upper classes to constitute and demarcate their dominance in a given field, and prevent others from gaining access to group membership or additional capital (Bourdieu, 1987). This has also been extended to a digital context: Helsper (2012) argues digital exclusion and social exclusion are mutually influential in certain aspects using a corresponding fields model. On one hand, access, skills, and attitudes in offline exclusion fields influence digital exclusion, while the "relevance, quality, ownership, and sustainability of engagement with different digital resources" mediate patterns of exclusion in offline realms on the other (Helsper, 2012). In other words, digital fields have become a reproductive site of social inequalities, but offline life is also mediated by online behaviour and comes to mirror online stratification patterns.

Habitus

Bourdieu's theory of social reproduction has been invaluable to digital inequality researchers, and explanations of class-shared tastes and habitus (the embodied form of social structure which also structures this structure: Calderón Gómez, 2020) are especially illuminating for questions about online behaviour, attitudes towards and adoption of technology (or lack of), as well as capturing portraits of the digital landscape through a sociological lens. Kvasny (2002) provides a conceptual framework for empirically studying digital inequality that is rooted in Bourdieu's theory of social and cultural reproduction, and argues cultural capital is a crucial concept in this research because "the Internet reflects the culture, tastes, preoccupations, styles and interests of the middle class" (Kvasny, 2002, p. 1801). Kvasny (2005) later used habitus to demonstrate how, in the US, "predominant views of information technology and its use may unwittingly reproduce social inequities" (para. 75), as relatively disadvantaged persons are betrayed by "the prevailing digital divide rhetoric of empowerment and opportunity [as achievable] through production-oriented uses of IT" (para. 75).

Robinson (2009) applied a Bourdieusian approach to digital inequality in a study of economically disadvantaged American youth, and found the internalized "informational orientation or habitus" of the participants varied by the quality of their internet access (p. 491). Those with high-quality access had playful and exploratory attitudes, and those with low-quality access took task-oriented stances towards internet use. Applying Bourdieu's famous phrasing, Robinson (2009) describes this as a "taste for the necessary", and develops a theory of what they term "information habitus" (p. 492). When applied to digital contexts, the notion of habitus has been conceptualized in several ways: in their review of Bourdieu's theory in digital sociology, Ignatow and Robinson (2017) summarize several studies that examine differences in digital activities using the term digital habitus, whereas Papacharissi and Easton (2013) discuss the "social media habitus". A recent study in Germany examined how the digital habitus of teachers hindered transitions to online learning during the COVID-19 pandemic, reporting that "traditional skepticism for innovation" was reinforced by the teachers' digital, cultural, and educational habitus (Blume, 2020). Overall, when it comes to questions of how people actually navigate and understand their social environments through the use of digital technology or resources (and online fields), digital habitus is a widely applicable concept.

Bourdieu's theoretical frameworks are useful for conceptualizing digital inequalities as embedded in, mutually shaping, and reproducing social life. These inequalities become embodied through the habitus of individuals, which both structure and are structured by their context. However, rather than a solely economic or material focus, a Bourdieusian framework makes it possible to consider the different actors, institutions, technologies, and reified but non-material social structures and resources that organize the digital society and allow individuals to take action within it. If taking up an action-oriented framework, a Bourdieusian approach might address questions of individuals' levels of risk perception or risk-aversion online, and how these dispositions shape their position in a given field and thus the digital inequalities or privileges they experience during the life-course. There is little to no research that applied Bourdieu's theories to discussions of algorithms, Big Data, or artificial intelligence (AI). Future research in this area that applies Bourdieu's theory will hopefully turn its attention to how digital inequalities are reproduced beyond the individual level in a globalized world. The intersectional approaches discussed next consider these topics in greater depth.

Intersectional Approaches

While Bourdieu's work pays particular attention to the reproductive mechanisms of inequalities (and chiefly through a class lens), intersectional approaches allow the author to address the often-complicated nexus of social positionalities and multiple forms of oppression that digital actors exist within (Collins and Bilge, 2020; Crenshaw, 1991). Intersectionality locates patterns of discrimination and privilege that are stratified across social identities as rooted in larger oppressive systems of power (such as racism, patriarchy, and colonialism), which is particularly important given the increasingly transnational character of the increasingly globalized world (Purkayastha, 2012). Intersectional approaches have been highly influential in critical and feminist theory (particularly, Black feminist theory), but attention has also been turned in recent years to the role digital worlds play in creating a "matrix of domination" that upholds hegemonic status quos (Collins and Bilge, 2020). There is already substantial discussion of technologies, algorithms, and other non-social phenomena that form parts of the digital society, and their implications for shaping and stratifying the larger social ordering within which individuals are positioned (as well as how individuals understand and conduct themselves in relation to this context) are explicitly considered. In two notable examples, Costanza-Chock (2018) documents the embodied experiences of non-heteronormative individuals who exist in digital "matrixes of domination" (referencing Collins' highly influential concept: Collins and Bilge, 2020) from an auto-ethnographic perspective, while Madden et al. (2017) examine the intersection of privacy, poverty, and Big Data as a "matrix of vulnerabilities". While this research investigates the impacts of algorithms and artificial intelligence on specific populations, recent work in this area has also directed efforts towards developing policy frameworks and recommendations to dismantle digital inequalities in the context of post-colonial and Black feminist theory (Hampton, 2021; Mohamed et al., 2020). McMillan Cottom (2016) discusses algorithmic stratification as a gatekeeper and mediator to digital interactions, and argues Black cyberfeminist theory is an exceptional tool for refining "digital sociology's understanding of identities, institutions and political economies in the data age."

There is a breadth of intersectional literature concerning digital inequality in a variety of contexts, such as entrepreneurship, risk, law, health, race and ethnicity, gender, and media. The latter three were by far the most fleshed-out areas of study, but the diversity of literature speaks to the many ways intersectional theory can be applied in digital inequality research. Often, authors used intersectional frameworks in tandem with other theoretical concepts or ontologies. As mentioned above, Calderón Gómez (2019) has taken up Bourdieu's work to develop the idea of technological capital to describe how people's socioeconomic status relates to different methods of accessing and using ICTs, but does so through an explicitly intersectional approach, examining differential access and use of ICTs by young people in Spain along several socio-structural variables (gender, age, education, and employment situation) (p. 945). Similarly, Ragnedda and Ruiu (2020) have written a book that looks at the digital divide from a Bourdieusian theoretical perspective and employ the concept of digital capital to "shed light on the multidimensionality and intersectionality of digital inequalities" (p. 6), which are "firmly intertwined" with social inequalities (p. 5). The same text also explores whether traditional forms of social inequalities are merely replicated in the digital sphere or if digital inequalities have their own dynamics of inequalities. Liu (2021) looks at the interplay between the use of digital technologies (namely, the internet), social identities, and health outcomes (loneliness and quality of life) among older adults in the UK, arguing an "intersectional perspective of cumulative disadvantages can help social workers better understand how the multiplicative effect of multiple identities socially excludes the vulnerable adults" (p. 3077).

As Zheng and Walsham (2021) write in the abstract for their study of digital inequalities under the COVID-19 pandemic, intersectional perspectives adopted from feminist studies are useful for highlighting "the intersection and entanglement between digital technology, structural stratifications and the ingrained tendency of 'othering' in societies" (p. 100341). Intersectional perspectives generally cast digital technologies and risks as multifaceted, and their character contingent on the particular way they are entangled with, or present, in individuals' lives alongside the rest of the milieu of social life. Technologies and digital "innovations" can be wielded as oppressive tools at the same time they provide benefit, or at least, functional or practical returns, and often produce and reproduce social orders that harm some while privileging others. Of primary concern in the intersectional literature is the identification and understanding of digital inequalities – how they take shape, diffuse, perpetuate, and affect – so that they can be made visible, avoided, or improved. For example, Henne and Troshynski (2019) argue intersectional methodologies in criminology research are important if "technosocial entanglements emblematic of ongoing shifts in social control" (p. 55) (such as the prevalence and ongoing sophistication process of surveillance and policing technologies) are to be addressed.

Intersectional inequalities have also been studied in the context of risk and digital behaviour studies. Milioni et al. (2014) ask how young people's online experiences in Cyprus are shaped by socioeconomic factors (gender, education, and income) and investigate how ethnicity could be an important factor when it comes to the kinds of activities people participate in online.

Dodel and Mesch (2018) make an important contribution to discussions of cyber-safety behaviours and digital inequality research that is neither explicitly Bourdieusian nor intersectional; their work cites many of the authors and studies in this summary and provides an example of the applicability of multidimensional approaches to inequality in digital risk research. The authors found multiple factors (age, gender, education, and quality of access) were associated with digital security skill levels among internet users in Israel, ultimately arguing that social and digital disparities are reproduced in the use of measures to prevent online threats, and the digitally disadvantaged are thus positioned to be at greater risk (Dodel and Mesch, 2018). However, Giritli Nygren and Olofsson (2014) critically reviewed how health-risk research has used intersectional approaches since the early 2000s and concluded that, despite increasing arguments for the "necessity" of intersectional perspectives in this field of research, they are generally underutilized. To overcome this, the authors argue "for a new approach that echoes the 'doing gender' of gender studies: doing risk" (p. 1112).

Intersectional approaches offer some of the most explicit critiques of digital inequalities and the social processes that perpetuate them. Despite acknowledging the advantageous possibility of many digital technologies, intersectional theorists are concerned with the way digital inequalities are structured by social relations, which are embedded in less-than-neutral domains of power and result in tangible effects to health, safety, and mobility (Collins and Bilge, 2020). Sloane (2019) argues, "the hype around 'ethics' as panacea for remedying algorithmic discrimination is a smokescreen for carrying on with business as usual." Similarly, Dy et al (2016) challenge "the notion that the internet is a neutral platform for entrepreneurship". Using an interpretivist approach, the authors raise "how the privileges and disadvantages arising from intersecting social positions of gender, race and class status are experienced by UK women digital entrepreneurs" (p. 286). Digital entrepreneurship was a common area of focus amongst intersectional discussions of digital inequality. Leung (2018) presents qualitative research about the experiences of digital entrepreneurs in Taiwan in the context of its political, social, and economic history in *Digital Entrepreneurship, Gender and Intersectionality: An East Asian Perspective* (Palgrave Macmillan, 2018), and Wahome and Graham (2020) further contribute to this conceptualization of digital entrepreneurship as a less-than-neutral mechanism of social inequality through case studies of digital entrepreneurs in several African cities, finding that "popular and academic spatial imaginaries and discourses, for example those that cast the digital economy as borderless and accessible, do not correspond with the experience of many African entrepreneurs" (p. 1123). Additionally, they argue, "enacting the metaphoric identities that coincide with these imaginaries and their discourses is a skillset that determines which (and how) actors can participate" and these identities reflect "the inherent coloniality of the digital, capitalist discourse" surrounding digital entrepreneurship (p. 1123).

Without taking on an explicitly intersectional perspective, Haight et al. (2014) examine differences in internet access and online activity through a multidimensional approach, particularly in terms of how demographic factors affect social networking site adoption and usage. They found,

> access to the internet reflects existing inequalities in society with income, education, rural/urban, immigration status, and age all affecting adoption patterns. Furthermore … inequality in access to the internet is now being mimicked in the level of online activity of internet users. More recent immigrants to Canada have lower rates of internet access; however, recent immigrants who are online have significantly higher levels of online activity than Canadian born residents and earlier immigrants.

Additionally, women perform fewer activities online than men. People's use of [social networking sites] differs in terms of education, gender, and age.

While intersectional and multidimensional approaches to digital risk and inequality have already made a significant contribution, this area of research promises to continue to develop cutting-edge analyses.

Marxian Theory

Amiss so far has been thorough consideration of the global capitalist economy and its trans-national character. The book *Marx in the Age of Digital Capitalism* (Fuchs and Mosco, 2015) provides a useful overview of the many applications Karl Marx's work has for studying various aspects of the 21st-century political economy. Viewing digital risk and inequality from a Marxian perspective casts digital inequalities as by-products of the capitalist mode of production, which ultimately affords advantages to whoever controls the means of production and successfully dominates the masses, or Proletariat. Some authors argue this working class has become the "Cybertariat" in the age of digital labour (Huws, 2003). There has been plenty of discussion of how digital workers are "unduly" affected by the risks and costs associated with the gig economy and digital labour (Graham et al., 2017). Marxian concepts are also useful for understanding labour relations that have been disrupted by digital technologies even if the labour is not digital, or alternatively, is "digital immaterial labour" (Kologlugil, 2015).

As the ruling class who control digital technologies and infrastructure (the means of production in capitalist digital society) are also the benefactors, the assumption of Marxian theoretical positions would be that this class will design and implement these products to be more effective for their interests of accumulating wealth and maintaining control and power over the Proletariat class. The depiction of algorithmic or surveillance technologies that collect data as a necessary and helpful addition to individuals' lives while they may be used to reproduce this class domination could be considered a kind of false consciousness, and the lack of control or ownership individuals have over these data a form of alienation. Fuchs (2019) argues the development of algorithms and "digital machines" that gather volumes and varieties of data at speeds never before possible has resulted in a "specific quality of digital capitalism", which Fuchs terms "Big Data Capitalism" (p. 53). Recently, attention has also shifted towards "Industry 4.0", referring to a transformation in manufacturing processes and technologies that incorporate automation and data exchange and may include cyber-physical systems, cloud computing, and smart factories (Lasi et al., 2014). As Rainnie and Dean (2020) argue, "i4.0" has resulted in "platform capitalism, which already has implications for workers in the Global South and which, via i4.0's digital integration with production, will potentially have significant implications for the quality of work in the Global North" (p. 16).

SPECIAL TOPICS

Issues of Access, Knowledge, and Resources

When it comes to accessing web-connected technologies and resources or opportunities to develop the necessary competencies to use them, there is considerable stratification across personal demographics, socioeconomic classes, geographic locations, and of course many other factors. One study framed the digital divide as a class–power divide (Schradie, 2020), while others argue some groups, such as people with intellectual disabilities, have digital gatekeepers that restrict or monitor their behaviour online with the intention to mitigate potential risks, but in fact hinder the development of knowledgeable users (Chadwick, 2019). Stratification across digital literacy levels (Gangadharan, 2017) and discussions about "digital citizenship" (Moon, 2018) in a digital society also provide areas of investigation. One study examined geographical remoteness as a factor in digital inclusion or exclusion in rural Australia (Park, 2017). Park (2017) found physical and material factors, as well as personal attitudes, contributed to varying levels of digital literacy and use, even in a population that is generally isolated. A qualitative study by researchers in Spain revealed the importance of libraries as digital-levelling spaces for populations without sufficient access to digital technologies or infrastructure such as the internet (Gómez-Hernández et al., 2017). Interestingly, one study found well-educated users could be at increased risk online compared with less-educated peers, a finding the authors attribute in part to the concerns and attitudes towards online privacy a person holds (Blank and Lutz, 2016). There is also recent critical discourse about whether or not things like digital finance actually expose poorer populations to risks that outweigh the potential or advertised benefits (Ozili, 2020).

Overall, these digital divides exist globally and within counties and particular populations (Norris, 2001). They manifest across multiple dimensions: geographical, socioeconomic status, race and ethnicity, generationally, cultural backgrounds, cognitive ability, political borders, age, gender, sexuality, and more. Most concern and present research seems to concentrate on formulating better understandings of the impacts of AI, algorithms, and "Big Data", and how the harms and benefits afforded from these technologies are stratified across human lives. We have not yet come across significant discussions of what policy changes, if any, have reduced inequalities related to digital risk in any part of the world, but there is a general sentiment that this is an important area of study and intersectional discourse is needed to inform policy-making and social understandings.

Healthcare, Education, and Youth

Healthcare planning and delivery, now challenged by a global pandemic, is an area where both digital risks and inequalities abound, according to a considerable number of sources investigating these relationships. In particular, increased reliance on telemedicine (Khilnani et al., 2020) and the use of algorithms in healthcare have led to inequalities and disproportionate risks for certain groups: for example, researchers found racial bias in the number of Black patients identified for extra care by a "widely used algorithm" in U.S. healthcare (Obermeyer et al., 2019). The COVID-19 pandemic has been demonstrated to exacerbate digital health inequalities by numerous studies, and these inequalities also come to increase COVID-19-related risks (Beaunoyer et al., 2020; Khilnani et al., 2020; Robinson et al., 2020). The earlier discussion in this chapter about inequalities of personal health data ownership and its use offers another example of this intersection between health care, health, and digital technologies. Singh et al.'s (2016) analysis of mobile health apps found a plethora of "mHealth" apps are available, but these only serve a handful of populations, such as people with an already high level of online engagement, and those seeking weight-related interventions, or help for depression (Singh et al., 2016). "The patients who could benefit the most", such as the elderly or those with chronic pain, are underrepresented (Singh et al., 2016).

There is also plenty of focus in the literature on the presence and implications of digital stratification and risk in childhood and adolescence, particularly concerning classrooms and education systems as both potentially mediating resources as well as risk amplifiers. As boyd (2014) writes in the aptly titled book *It's Complicated: The Social Lives of Networked Teens* (Yale University Press, 2014), "Society has often heralded technology as a tool to end social divisions, [but its] construction typically reinforces existing social divisions" (p. 156). Some of the recent relevant literature examines cognitive, social, and emotional harms and benefits to closing the "digital gap" in early childhood, as well as the role educational settings play in facilitating digital literacy and digital divides (Johnson, 2015; Katz et al., 2017; Moon, 2018). One study of interest investigated how children's immunization records are tracked with wearable technologies in India, with the author ultimately cautioning the use of such technologies in aid while balancing their potential benefits (Bergtora Sandvik, 2020). Again, as with every topic concerning digital inequalities, we can see a plethora of risks and dimensions of inequality at play that raise seemingly limitless avenues of research interests: data ownership and use among youth and in educational settings; the use of technologies including algorithms and AI software in classrooms; how intersections of race, class, gender, and other planes of stratification affect youth online; as well as how cultural and social capital and habitus set some children up to be well-versed digital citizens while others are relegated to the margins online, consistently or perhaps inconsistently with their social location offline (for further discussions relating to digital risk, inequality, youth, and education, see: Bergtora Sandvik, 2020; Blume, 2020; Borthwick et al., 2015; boyd, 2014; Calderón Gómez, 2019, 2020; Johnson, 2015; Katz et al., 2017; Milioni et al., 2014; Moon, 2018).

The COVID-19 pandemic has greatly accelerated the intertwining of digital technologies and education as classrooms around the world are intermittently shifted online, and remote work or learning has suddenly become a norm rather than a delivery method for distance education, remote communities, or the like. Youth who do not have digital devices to receive and submit their homework or listen to video lectures are quickly at risk of falling behind, and patchwork solutions such as sharing one device between several siblings or devices at the library are likely insufficient. While it quickly became normal for many students to attend classes online, resources and measures to assist them – particularly those who face digital literacy or access inequalities – have not been discussed as widely, nor has enough time passed to thoroughly evaluate the effects of this rapid acceleration of digital presences in everyday life on youth.

Outside the COVID-19 pandemic context, but perhaps providing an applicable insight, Katz et al. (2017) argue for a nuanced approach that balances calls from medical entities to broadly reduce technology overexposure among children with evidence that digital inequalities including lack of access inhibit a spectrum of social opportunities for children from low-income families, a demographic that Katz et al. (2017) note is increasingly overlapping with immigrants and people of colour in the American context. While there are always going to be examples of individuals who use digital technologies in extreme or harmful ways, it seems logical to extend Lerman's (2013) argument that in some cases being included digitally puts not only adults at less risk of being socially left out or stigmatized, but also youth, who must grapple with the increasingly necessitated use of digital technology in everyday life despite the particular socioeconomic or other stratifying factors contained within their social identity, and a lack of control over their daily routine (boyd, 2014).

CONCLUSION: GAPS, CONSIDERATIONS, AND AREAS FOR FUTURE RESEARCH

A considerable amount of the existing literature is concerned with risks that individuals or particular groups encounter through the use (or, in absence of use) of digital technologies that are increasingly married with everyday life, and a relatively large body of research has investigated how particular digital inequalities are (and come to be) patterned across demographic or otherwise-demarcated groups. Present discussions about digital risk and inequality are often framed at the individual level, addressing questions such as how people acquire the materials and skills to use digital technologies, or how this participation may be successfully leveraged by, or negatively impact, individuals or a particular population. A myriad of risk-types and ways digital risk may be stratified between individuals, groups, and around the globe have been identified, and scholars have begun to nominally chart the structural and systemic formations, social dynamics, and material arrangements that constitute what could be conceptualized as a field of digital risk. No matter how it is framed, it seems obvious but necessary to say that digital risk exists within, and cannot be looked at in isolation from, the rest of social and material life, as the digital is increasingly entangled with non-digital aspects of modern global capitalist societies in ways that make it hard to distinguish where the digital begins or ends.

Access to and use of digital technology is often spoken of in a humanitarian sense, as in people *ought* to be able to participate in the digital world (economically, politically, socially, etc.) where and how they want to. However, scholars have also recognized that much of the production and control over the digital, and thus digital risk, is in the hands of private corporations and a behemoth tech industry – all of which is ultimately driven by global capitalism, which bears no moral visions of equitable access and use, and in fact necessitates inequalities as a cost of growth. Rather than being some great equalizer, it is evident that the digital landscape acts as an amplifier of risk and inequality *as well as* a potential mediator. Intersectional theoretical approaches most explicitly demonstrate how digital inequalities come to mirror social hierarchies and imbalanced power relations online while simultaneously reproducing them offline, but this is also consistent in related Bourdieusian or expressly Marxian-informed literature.

Unfortunately, interventions and proposed actions, even if only for future areas of study, have generally not escalated beyond the scope of the symptoms of digital risks and inequalities, often neglecting to consider how the conditions that bring them to fruition might be addressed in any significant depth. This is understandable, firstly due to the real and urgent problems inequalities of a digital character may present at the individual or community level, and the speed at which digital innovations move in a globally connected world. Additionally, while conducting this review we observed that the primary actors involved in digital risk production (and upstream mitigation) may be named, but are largely absent within sociological research (though not entirely). The private corporations, governments, and other institutions that actually design, construct, and implement the digital infrastructure that individuals engage with and are engaged by are unlikely (perhaps unwilling) to provide access or unvetted information to social scientists about their processes, products, or plans for the future, so it is certainly to be anticipated that sociological research into these aspects of the digitized society has been limited – however, this highlights a significant gap in the existing body of knowledge concerning digital risk and inequality. It will be important going forward to continue to expand research beyond downstream manifestations.

This brings the discussion to a related observation we think deserves more consideration when framing discussions of digital risk and inequality. Currently, the digital world essentially happens *to* its users: people engage with it (personal devices, social media platforms, digitized labour positions, etc.), often without conscious choice, and adopt their online experiences as their own actions – and while the latter sentiment is true to an extent, most individuals have little to no say (or sophisticated understanding) over the actual digital technologies they encounter every day. And, while experiencing varying dimensions and degrees of risk and inequality as people living within digital societies, individuals are alienated from the data they produce, as well as knowledge, power, and the production capabilities of digital technologies – meaning they are unable to substantially assess their own risk, manage it, or fully reap the rewards from their participation in digital life. On the other hand, the actors and institutions that produce, facilitate, own, and control digital technologies only carry risk in a limited sense: systems, technologies, investments, and the like carry risks, but their incorporation, institutionalization, and layered bureaucracies provide a buffer so that risk is absorbed by an external, abstract entity. Individuals do not have this advantage, and with little power, take the risks of digital citizenship on personally – financially, in terms of their physical health, personal safety, etc. And it's not just the negative risk that is unequally beholden: these abstract entities, or their figureheads who are so financially insulated that they are practically untouchable, also stand to gain the most benefits compared with everyday people, municipalities, or nations – take your pick. Without a disruption to this imbalanced field of power relations, the inequalities researchers have identified will remain lamentations. Future discussions of digital risk must centre this imbalance and more clearly address this gap between the private, corporate, institutionalized, and hegemonic producers of digital risk and those who are actually at risk, if its inequalities are ever to be addressed.

In this chapter, we have summarized some of the most robustly researched topics concerning digital risk and inequality to date: health care planning and delivery, youth/elderly/racialized populations, AI and algorithmic technologies and disruptions to social life (in particular, labour), as well as the gathering, management, use, and ownership of data. However, this review is by no means exhaustive. When it comes to digital risk and inequality, there are seemingly limitless aspects to consider and research avenues to take. For example, examining the impacts of hyper-digital societies for the environment (and vice versa) in terms of unequal environmental risks such pursuits create could focus queries on upstream factors, such as how the development of digital technologies and their increasing integration into previously offline aspects of social life changes (and is shaped by) the physical environment in ways that differentially affect people or populations. Examining upstream factors of digital risks and inequalities, and extending analysis beyond particular individual circumstances, invites study of the broader conditions that shape the digital world and bring about the particular conditions that individuals come to experience – the actors and processes involved in production and distribution of digital technologies, as well as their uptake and use – and will provide a more complete view of the intensely complicated landscapes that make up modern global digitalized societies.

REFERENCES

Andrejevic, M. (2014), "The big data divide", *International Journal of Communication*, **8**(1), 17.

Beaunoyer, E., S. Dupéré and M. J. Guitton (2020), "COVID-19 and digital inequalities: reciprocal impacts and mitigation strategies", *Computers in Human Behaviour*, **111**(1), 106424.

Bergtora Sandvik, K. (2020), "Wearables for something good: aid, dataveillance and the production of children's digital bodies", *Information, Communication & Society*, **23**(14), 2014–2029.

Birhane, A. and F. Cummins (2019), "Algorithmic injustices: towards a relational ethics", *arXIV*, 1912.07376.

Blank, G. and C. Lutz (2016), "Benefits and harms from Internet use: a differentiated analysis of Great Britain", *New Media & Society*, **20**(2), 618–640.

Blume, C. (2020), "German teachers' digital habitus and their pandemic pedagogy", *Postdigital Science and Education*, **2**(1), 879–905.

Borthwick, A., and C. L. Anderson, E. S. Finsness and T. S. Foulger (2015), "Special article. Personal wearable technologies in education: value or villain?", *Journal of Digital Learning in Teacher Education*, **31**(3), 85–92.

Bourdieu, P. (1986), "The forms of capital", in John G. Richardson (ed.), *Handbook of Theory and Research for the Sociology of Education*, New York, NY: Greenwood, pp. 241–258.

Bourdieu, P. (1987), *Distinction: A Social Critique of the Judgement of Taste*, trans. R. Nice. Cambridge, MA: Harvard University Press.

boyd, d. (2014), *It's Complicated: The Social Lives of Networked Teens*, New Haven, CT: Yale University Press.

Calderón Gómez, D. (2019), "Technological capital and digital divide among young people: an intersectional approach", *Journal of Youth Studies*, **22**(70), 941–958.

Calderón Gómez, D. (2020), "The third digital divide and Bourdieu: bidirectional conversion of economic, cultural, and social capital to (and from) digital capital among young people in Madrid", *New Media & Society*, **23**(9), 2534–2553. https://doi.org/10.1177/1461444820933252

Chadwick, D. D. (2019), "Online risk for people with intellectual disabilities", *Tizard Learning Disability Review*, **24**(4), 180–187.

Collins, P.H., and S. Bilge (2020), *Intersectionality*, 2nd edn, Cambridge, UK: Polity Press.

Costanza-Chock, S. (2018), "Design justice, A.I., and escape from the matrix of domination", *Journal of Design and Science*. https://doi.org/10.21428/96c8d426

Crawford, K. and J. Schultz (2014), "Big data and due process: toward a framework to redress predictive privacy harms", *Boston College Law Review*, **55**(1), 93–128.

Crenshaw, K. (1991), "Mapping the margins: intersectionality, identity politics, and violence against women of color", *Stanford Law Review*, **43**(6), 1241–1300.

Curran, D. (2015), 'Risk illusion and organized irresponsibility in contemporary finance: rethinking class and risk society', *Economy and Society*, **44**(3), 392–417.

Curran, D. (2018), 'Risk, innovation, and democracy in the digital economy', *European Journal of Social Theory*, **21**(2), 207–226.

Curran, D. (2021), "Risk mismatches and inequalities: oil and gas and elite risk-classes in the U.S. and Canada", *Sociologica*, **15**(2), 57–74.

Curran, D. and A. Smart (2020), "Data-driven governance, smart urbanism and risk-class inequalities: security and social credit in China", *Urban Studies*, **58**(3), 487–506.

Dodel, M. and G. Mesch (2018), "Inequality in digital skills and the adopting of online safety behaviours", *Information, Communication & Society*, **21**(5), 712–728.

Dy, A., S. Marlow and L. Martin (2016), "A web of opportunity or the same old story? Women digital entrepreneurs and intersectionality theory", *Human Relations*, **70**(3), 286–311.

Eubanks, Virginia (2018), *Automating Inequality: How High-Tech Tools Profile, Police, and Punish the Poor*, London, UK: St. Martin's Press.

Fuchs, C. (2019), "Karl Marx in the age of big data capitalism", in Christian Fuchs and David Chandler (eds), *Digital Objects, Digital Subjects: Interdisciplinary Perspectives on Capitalism, Labour and Politics in the Age of Big Data*, London, UK: University of Westminster Press, pp. 53–72.

Fuchs, C. and V. Mosco (2015), *Marx in the Age of Digital Capitalism*, Leiden, The Netherlands: Brill.

Gangadharan, S. P. (2012), "Digital inclusion and data profiling", *First Monday*, 17(5). doi: 10.5210/fm.v17i5.3821.

Gangadharan, S. P. (2017), "The downside of digital inclusion: expectations and experiences of privacy and surveillance among marginal Internet users", *New Media & Society*, 19(4), 597–615.

Giritli Nygren, K. and A. Olofsson (2014), "Intersectional approaches in health-risk research: a critical review", *Sociology Compass*, 8(1), 1112–1126.

Gómez-Hernández, J. A., and M. Hernández-Pedreño and E. Romero-Sánchez (2017), "Social and digital empowerment of vulnerable library users of the Murcia Regional Library, Spain", *El Profesional de la Información*, 26(1), 20–32.

Graham, M., I. Hjorth and V. Lehdonvirta (2017), "Digital labour and development: impacts of global digital labour platforms and the gig economy on worker livelihoods", *Transfer: European Review of Labour and Research*, 23(2), 135–162.

Gran, A. B., P. Booth and T. Bucher (2019), "To be or not to be algorithm aware: a question of a new digital divide?", *Information, Communication, & Society*, 24(12), 1779–1796.

Haight, M., A. Quan-Haase and B. A. Corbett (2014), "Revisiting the digital divide in Canada: the impact of demographic factors on access to the internet, level of online activity, and social networking site usage", *Information, Communication & Society*, 17(4), 503–519.

Hampton, L. M. (2021), "Black Feminist Musings on Algorithmic Oppression", paper presented at Conference on Fairness, Accountability, and Transparency (ACM FAccT '21), Virtual Event, Canada, 3–10 March.

Helsper, E. (2012), "A corresponding fields model for the links between social and digital exclusion", *Communication Theory*, 22(4), 403–426. https://doi.org/10.1111/j.1468-2885.2012.01416.x

Henne, K. and E. I. Troshynski (2019), "Intersectional criminologies for the contemporary moment: crucial questions of power, praxis and technologies of control", *Critical Criminology*, 27(1), 55–71.

Huws, Ursula (2003), The Making of a Cybertariat: Virtual Work in a Real World, New York, NY: Monthly Review Press; and London, UK: The Merlin Press.

Ignatow, G. and L. Robinson (2017), "Pierre Bourdieu: theorizing the digital", *Information, Communication & Society*, 20(7), 950–966.

Johnson, G. M. (2015), "Young children at risk of digital disadvantage", in Kelly L. Heider and Mark Renck Jalongo (eds), *Young Children and Families in the Information Age*, Dordrecht: Springer, pp. 255–275.

Latz, V. S., C. Gonzalez and K. Clark (2017), "Digital inequality and developmental trajectories of low-income, immigrant, and minority children", *Pediatrics*, 140(2), 132–136.

Khilnani, A., J. Schulz and L. Robinson (2020), "The COVID-19 pandemic: new concerns and connections between eHealth and digital inequalities", *Journal of Information, Communication and Ethics in Society*, 18(3), 393–403.

Koloğlugil, S. (2015), "Digitizing Karl Marx: the new political economy of general intellect and immaterial labour", *Rethinking Marxism*, 27(1), 123–137.

Kostkova, P., and H. Brewer, S. de Lusignan, E. Fottrell, B. Goldacre, G. Hart, P. Koczan, P. Knight, C. Marsolier, R. A. McKendry, E. Ross, A. Sasse, R. Sullivan, S. Chaytor, O. Stevenson, R. Velho, J. Tooke (2016), "Who owns the data? Open data for healthcare", *Frontiers in Public Health*, 4(7). https://www.frontiersin.org/articles/10.3389/fpubh.2016.00007/full

Kvasny, L. (2002), "A Conceptual Framework for Examining Digital Inequality", paper presented at AMCIS 2002 Proceedings, Americas Conference on Information Systems.

Kvasny, L. (2005), "The role of the habitus in shaping discourses about the digital divide", *Journal of Computer-Mediated Communication*, 10(2), JCMC1025. https://doi.org/10.1111/j.1083-6101.2005.tb00242.x

Lasi, H., P. Fettke, H.-G. Kemper, T. Feld and M. Hoffmann (2014), "Industry 4.0", *Business & Information Systems Engineering*, 6(1), 239–242.

Lerman, J. (2013), "Big data and its exclusions", *Stanford Law Review*, 66(1), 55–63.

Leung, Wing-Fai (2018), *Digital Entrepreneurship, Gender and Intersectionality: An East Asian Perspective*, Cham, Switzerland: Palgrave Macmillan.

Liu, B.C.P.. (2021), "The impact of intersectionality of multiple identities on the digital health divide, quality of life and loneliness amongst older adults in the UK", *The British Journal of Social Work*, 51(8), 3077–3097.

Madden, M., M. Gilman, K. Levy and A. Marwick (2017), "Privacy, poverty, and big data: a matrix of vulnerabilities for poor Americans", *Washington University Law Review*, **95**(1), 53–125.

McMillan Cottom, T. (2016), "Black cyberfeminism: intersectionality, institutions and digital sociology", in Jessie Daniels, Karen Gregory and Tressie McMillan Cottom (eds), *Digital Sociologies*, Bristol, UK: Policy Press. https://ssrn.com/abstract=2747621

Milioni, D., V. Doudaki and N. Demertzis (2014), "Youth, ethnicity, and a 'reverse digital divide': a study of Internet use in a divided country", *Convergence: The International Journal of Research into New Media Technologies*, **20**(3), 316–366.

Mohamed, S., M. T. Png and W. Issac (2020), "Decolonial AI: decolonial theory as sociotechnical foresight in artificial intelligence", *Philosophy & Technology*, **33**(1), 659–684.

Moon, E. C. (2018), "Teaching students out of harm's way: mitigating digital knowledge gaps and digital risk created by 1:1 device programs in K-12 education in the USA", *Journal of Information, Communication and Ethics in Society*, **16**(3), 290–302.

Noble, S.U., (2018), Algorithms of Oppression: How Search Engines Reinforce Racism, New York, NY: New York University Press.

Norris, P. (2001), *Digital Divide: Civic Engagement, Information Poverty, and the Internet Worldwide*, Cambridge, UK: Cambridge University Press.

O'Loughlin, K., M. Leary, E. C. Adkins and S. M. Schueller (2019), "Reviewing the data security and privacy policies of mobile apps for depression", *Internet Interventions*, **15**(1), 110–115.

O'Neil, C. (2016), *Weapons of Math Destruction: How Big Data Increases Inequality and Threatens Democracy*, New York, NY: Crown.

Obermeyer, Z., B. Powers, C. Vogueli and S. Mullainathan (2019), "Dissecting racial bias in an algorithm used to manage the health of populations", *Science*, **366**(6464), 447–453.

Ozili, P. K. (2020), "Contesting digital finance for the poor: digital policy, regulation and governance", **22**(2), 135–151.

Papacharissi, Z. and E. Easton (2013), "In the habitus of the new", in J. Hartley, J. Burgess and A. Bruns (eds), *A Companion to New Media Dynamics*, Hoboken, NJ: Wiley-Blackwell, pp. 171–184.

Park, S. (2017), "Digital inequalities in rural Australia: a double jeopardy of remoteness and social exclusion", *Journal of Rural Studies*, **54**(1), 399–407.

Purkayastha, B. (2012), "Intersectionality in a transnational world", *Gender & Society*, **26**(1), 55–66.

Ragnedda, M. (2017), *The Third Digital Divide: A Weberian Approach to Digital Inequalities*, Abingdon, UK: Routledge.

Ragnedda, M., M. L. Ruiu and F. Addeo (2020), *Digital Capital: A Bourdieusian Perspective on the Digital Divide*, Bingley, UK: Emerald Publishing Limited.

Ragnedda, M. and M. L. Ruiu, F. Addeo (2019), "Measuring digital capital: an empirical investigation", *New Media & Society*, **22**(5), 793–816.

Rainnie, A. and M. Dean (2019), "Industry 4.0 and the future of quality work in the global digital economy", *Labour & Industry*, **30**(1), 16–33.

Robinson, L. (2009), "A taste for the necessary: a Bourdieuian approach to digital inequality", *Information, Communication & Society*, **12**(4), 488–507.

Robinson, L., and J. Schulz, A. Khilnani, H. Ono, S. R. Cotten, N. McClain, L. Levine, W. Chen, G. Huang, A. A. Casilli, P. Tubaro, M. Dodel, A. Quan-Haase, M. L. Ruiu, M. Ragnedda, D. Aikat and N. Tolentino (2020), "Digital inequalities in time of pandemic: COVID-19 exposure risk profiles and new forms of vulnerability", *First Monday*, **25**(7). https://journals.uic.edu/ojs/index.php/fm/article/view/10845

Robinson, L. and J. Schulz, H. S. Dunn, A. A. Casilli, P. Tubaro, R. Carvath, W. Chen, J. B. Wiest, M. Dodel, M. J. Stern, C. Ball, K.-T. Huang, G. Blank, M. Ragnedda, H. Ono, B. Hogan, G. S. Mesch, S. R. Cotten, S. B. Kretchmer, T. M. Hale, T. Drabowicz, P. Yan, B. Wellman, M.-G. Harper, A. Quan-Haase and A. Khilnani (2020), "Digital inequalities 3.0: emergent inequalities in the information age", *First Monday*, **25**(7). https://doi.org/10.5210/fm.v25i7.10844

Schradie, J. (2020), "The great equalizer reproduces inequality: how the digital divide is a class power divide", in B. Eidlin and M. A. McCarthy (eds), *Rethinking Class and Social Difference* (*Political Power and Social Theory, Vol. 37*), Bingley, UK: Emerald Publishing Limited, pp. 81–101.

Sherwani, S. and B. R. Bates (2021), "Role of wearable technology and fitness apps in obesity and diabetes: privacy, ownership, and portability of data", in Devjani Sen and Rukhsana Ahmed (eds), *Privacy*

Concerns Surrounding Personal Information Sharing on Health and Fitness Mobile Apps, Hershey, USA: IGI Publishing, pp. 31–59.

Sims, C. (2014), "From differentiated use to differentiating practices: negotiating legitimate participation and the production of privileged identities", *Information, Communication & Society*, **17**(6), 670–682.

Singh, K., and K. Drouin, L. P. Newmark, J. L. A. Faxvaag, R. Rozenblum, E. A. Pabo, A. Landman, E. Klinger and D. W. Bates (2016), "Many mobile health apps target high-need, high-cost populations, but gaps remain", *Health Affairs*, **35**(12), 2310–2318.

Sloane, M. (2019), "Inequality is the Name of the Game: Thoughts on the Emerging Field of Technology, Ethics and Social Justice", paper presented at the Weizenbaum Conference 2019, "Challenges of Digital Inequality – Digital Education, Digital Work, Digital Life", Berlin.

van Deursen, A. J. and J. A. G. M. van Dijk (2019), "The first-level digital divide shifts from inequalities in physical access to inequalities in material access, *New Media & Society*, **21**(2), 354–375.

van Dijk, J. A. G. M. (2005), The Deepening Divide: *Inequality in the Information Society*, Thousand Oaks, USA: SAGE Publications, Inc.

Wahome, M. and M. Graham (2020), "Spatially shaped imaginaries of the digital economy", *Information, Communication & Society*, **23**(8), 1123–1138.

Zheng, Y. and G. Walsham (2021), "Inequality of what? An intersectional approach to digital inequality under Covid-19", *Information and Organization*, **31**(1), 100341.

Zuboff, S. (2019), *The Age of Surveillance Capitalism*, New York, NY: Public Affairs.

PART II

THEORIZING RISKS AND INEQUALITY

7. Actor, structure and inequality: an intersectional perspective of risk

Katarina Giritli Nygren, Anna Olofsson and Susanna Öhman

INTRODUCTION

In this chapter, we use intersectionality to explore how the interplay between risk and inequality can be understood from three different approaches: (1) from a system-centred approach with the governance of risk at the forefront, including how the subject becomes possible through structure, for example, through interpellation and normalisation; (2) from a process-centred approach focusing on the performative aspects and performance of risk, thus how the subject as an actor negotiates and navigates among and between different discourses of risk; and, finally, (3) from a group-centred perspective, showing how it is possible to find the meeting point among risk, power and inequality beyond norms and hegemonic structures, or at least how this is played out in contemporary theorising. These three perspectives highlight the importance of both the external constraints on human beings – which are often conceived of as 'social structures', for example, collective habits formalised as legal rules, policy, norms, moral obligations and so forth, and the often-contrasting concept of 'action' or 'agency' – for better understanding risk and inequality. We will put together a jigsaw puzzle that at first glance might seem to fit together in its familiar division of concepts. Social theorists have batted structure and agency to and fro for generations; thus, are we, as agents, mere puppets in the web of these already-defined structures predisposing our scope of action, or are we free agents who define social structures (Connell 2004)? Mixing together pieces from different puzzles and using risk as a catalyst for an intersectional analysis of inequalities, we find the result is sometimes ambiguous.

In our approach towards intersectionality as well as towards risk, ambivalence is a key enabler because we use it as a critical standpoint for resignification; in this way, ambivalence could also be understood as a form of resistance. Regarding – for the epistemological questions of how to understand the relationship between discourse and reality – personal experiences of everyday life and aspects of wider social organisation and between interpreting and counting when analysing these different aspects of the social world, our answer is that it is important not to fall into the trap of reductionist thinking. We want to hold on to ambivalence and promote the necessity of shifting analytical positions; it is necessary to explore the discourses of risk, but it is as necessary to explore how risk is experienced. Just as with ambivalence, intersectionality is fundamental to this framework. Intersectionality and more broadly feminist theory, have been the theoretical field where we have found the knowledge and inspiration for the suggested conceptual toolbox. Thus, we apply the knowledges and concepts produced within gender studies by developing intersectional risk theory as a bricolage with its own patterns and expressions. It embraces ambivalent perspectives and contradictory realities and oblique knowledge relations; it is a relational approach that interrogates claimed positions and conditions. Central to this framework is the notion that individual actors and societies or structures fit together, an idea that must be problematised.

If the relation between individual actors and society must be an object of investigation, the question must be as follows: Where does risk fit in? Risk is a field of investigation, not necessarily as in an empirical examination, but more as in a theoretical exploration. Risk itself is a perfect example of ambivalence because it always exists within different viewpoints from which to evaluate whether there is or could be a threat. Views differ on how to assess and consider a possible threat, even more so when it comes to particular judgements on the relevance, meaning and implications of available risk information and which actions to consider. This is because our understanding of risk is time and context dependent and is based on norms, ideologies and individual experiences. Therefore, risk is neither 'real' nor merely a construction, but it has materialised consequences in people's everyday lives. What makes risk worth unpacking is the fluidity of the term, its inherent power and how, at least from a modernist view, it is entangled with inequality. This is also the reason for us to create a space in which to reconsider the theoretical understanding of risks and the ways in which such understandings intersect with other power relations, making it possible to construct and deconstruct the social (Foucault, 2007; Rose, 1996).

The last fundamental concept is inequality. Therefore, we will develop the interplay between risk and inequality from different angles and summarise our way of mixing pieces from different puzzles and carving the intersectional approach of inequality and risk into the picture. The result is skewed and ambiguous. However, we will not use violence to make the pieces fit together or try to hide the misfits; instead, we will do our best to tell a story that convinces the audience that the pieces do not necessarily need to fit. To be a subject (and body) today is to be dependent on the discourses, ideas, techniques and devices often established by norms and normality. In this context, it may be necessary to emphasise that this is not only about the ability of ideas and concepts to influence our notions or about social constructivism, but rather, it is about far more complicated interactions among materialities, practices, techniques, languages, ideas and much more. So where does this line of reasoning lead?

Saba Mahmood (2011) discusses the shortcomings of European and North American feminism, and we believe that risk research has similar shortcomings – that is, a lack of intellectual focus on problematising its own political starting point. The starting point of risk analysis and later on risk research more generally rests on its inheritance from the Enlightenment (Taylor-Gooby and Zinn, 2006); from the Enlightenment, we gained the concept of the autonomous will as a requirement for agency and self-realisation, which in itself relies on the liberal idea of the human being as a transcendental subject, one independent of historical and external conditions and that is able, through rational thought, to express rational requests. With intersectional risk theory, we try to open up the black box of risk and the individual subject and society, departing from an ambivalent knowledge position.

In this chapter, we will use an empirical example to illustrate intersectional risk theory. During the summer and autumn of 2015, the war in Syria led to an unusually large number of people seeking refuge in Sweden. This humanitarian crisis was translated into the language of risk in Swedish politics, migration and emergency systems as a large number of NGOs and citizens engaged to help migrants in need. This situation came at a time when right wing and racist ideology surfaced in the public debate in Sweden, and we will try to show how the analytical perspectives presented in this chapter can assist in analysing the intersections of risk, race and other categories of power.

This chapter is divided into two parts. Before we turn to the theoretical framework, intersectional risk theory and its theoretical genealogy, we will survey how power and inequality have been theorised in the sociology of risk and uncertainty. In the first part, we will present the four 'cornerstone' theories in sociological risk research, cultural theory, governmentality, risk society and systems theory, discussing how they picture risk, power and inequality. In the second part, we present intersectional risk theory and the gender theories on which intersectional risk theory is based. Intersectional risk theory puts gender, power and inequality at the centre of the analysis, and by disentangling the actor from structure and then reconnecting the two again, we use intersectionality as a way to explore how the interplay between risk and inequality can be understood from three different angles: systemic-, process- and group-centred perspectives. The chapter ends with a summary of the main arguments and our concluding remarks.

Risk, Uncertainty and Power

Our interest in risk, as well as many others', departs from risk's intrinsic relation to power and uncertainty (e.g., Beck, 1992; Douglas, 2002; Foucault, 2007, 2008). The relation is complex, but much originates from the concept's direction towards an uncertain future and the prospect of possible outcomes being either (when negative) manageable or avoidable or (when positive) reachable and obtainable. For example, Mary Douglas (2002) shows how risk is politicised in terms of liability (or blame) and consent. However, it is not only on a societal level that risk and power intersect; in every situation, from everyday life to transnational policy, the use of risk terminology aims at influencing something – perception, behaviour, policy and so forth. Needless to say, based on the assumption that there are no 'objective' truths, though not saying that there are no 'facts', risk terminology is part of belief systems and is influenced by particular interests, norms and ideologies. This is in line with Latour's (2003) master narrative, in which the security of the welfare state has made societies more sensitive to risks compared with earlier periods when safety was not taken for granted. This has resulted in the development of a risk paradigm through which these societies can understand themselves, other societies and global institutions. From this point of view, we have attempted to develop a theoretical framework that both embraces and questions the concept of risk and that problematises both its theoretical consequences and applications.

Gender, Class, Ethnicity and Risk Theory

As previously mentioned, many risk theorists have been occupied with the relationship between risk and power, but not as many have engaged in the relation between risk and inequality in terms of gender, class, ethnicity and so forth. Furthermore, although there are exceptions (e.g., Curran, 2016; Fitz-Gibbon and Walklate, 2017; Walby, 2015; Walklate, 1994), gender, class and ethnicity – as well as other concepts representing unequal relations of power – are rarely problematised. For example, the concept of gender is used in a variety of ways, both reproducing the role of difference and often ignoring feminist theory and empirical work. Thus, gender becomes 'black boxed' rather than opened up, problematised and understood in relation to risk, meaning that the concept can almost mean anything. If the concept means anything, it truly means nothing.

Table 7.1   *Typology 1: Theoretical frameworks of the definitions of risk, power and inequality*

	Risk (the grey boxes are from Zinn, 2008 pp.178–79)	Risk & Power	Risk & Inequality
Cultural theory	Risk is a danger for or transgression of symbolic orders	Risk reveals the relations of power in particular social organisations	Risk positions are conditional of social hierarchies, and that responsibility towards risk is defined within a limited cultural system
Governmentality	Risk is a specific way to manage uncertainty by calculative techniques and a specific way to govern society by allocating responsibility to a prudent subject	Risk is a particular way of comprehending problems and generating responses to them	Risks are techniques to maintain the normal and identify and manage deviance within systems of unequal power
Risk society	Risk is a hybrid, a real danger, constructed as objective issues, as well as a social construction of future possibilities and is thereby hypothetical	Risk has the power to influence social relations	Risk derives and intensifies social inequalities
Systems theory	Risk is the attribution of an undesired event to a decision		Inequality is at the centre of risk definitions and actions

One good exception is Kelly Hannah-Moffat and Pat O'Malley, who were among the first to recognise and systemise research in the relationship between gender and risk. In their edited collection from 2007, Hannah-Moffat and O'Malley (2007 p.8) acknowledge the importance of understanding the risk/gender nexuses because risk is shaped by, interacts with and (re)produces various configurations of inequality, such as gender, race, class and other inequalities:

> [G]ender and risk are mutually constitutive. Gendered knowledges, norms and hierarchies are linked with understandings of what constitutes a risk; the tolerance level of risk; the extent to which risk consciousness will be accepted or denied in public discourse or self-image; and whether risks are to be avoided and feared, regarded as just one of the costs of a certain lifestyle, or even valued as an experience and valorised as an opportunity for displays of courage and strength [...]. Despite the apparent obviousness of risk/gender nexus, research on risk has often proceeded as if it can be understood without clear reference to gender. (Hannah-Moffat and O'Malley, 2007 pp.5–6)

Hannah-Moffat and O'Malley (2007 p.25) also encourage feminist and risk scholars to overcome the dividing lines between cultural theory, governmentality, risk society and systems theory to instead focus on how they can complement each other. To take one step towards this goal, we will look at how these frameworks define risk, power and inequality, in addition to the risk theories we will add definitions of the same concepts from our own framework, including intersectional risk theory. Rather than identifying each framework's definition of risk, we use Zinn's definitions from 2008 (pp.178–79), where he systematically and convincingly harvests concise definitions from the frameworks (see Typology 1, Table 7.1). In the following, we will hence focus on each framework's view of power and inequality, from which we can identify definitions of these concepts and add them to Typology 1.

Cultural Theory of Risk

Cultural theory is based on the work of Mary Douglas, who uses her anthropological studies to explore the cultural meanings of danger and how danger is related to blame, sin and taboo. Cultural theory departs from an understanding of the world as socially constructed and offers ways to analyse people's understanding of risk and danger, where the individual is anchored in sociocultural relationships and the value systems of particular social groups (Tansey and O'Riordan, 1999). In no way denying the reality of hazards such as natural disasters or risks such as violence and crime, cultural theory contributes by providing knowledge of how phenomena like these, for example violence, are socially understood and acted upon in society, as well as in everyday life (Boholm, 2015). Douglas, along with others, develops a typology of social organisation, the so-called cultural biases. These cultural biases are derived from two dimensions of social organisation: the first dimension is called 'grid' and varies according to which individual behaviour is circumscribed by people's social positions. The second dimension is called 'group' and measures the level of solidarity among people. Together, the two dimensions create four ideal types; that is, cultures, which, according to the theory, can be used to understand the role of risk in society. The four cultures are usually described as individualist, fatalist, hierarchist and egalitarian cultures (Boholm, 2015).

Turning to looking at how risk, power and inequality are dealt with in this theory, Zinn (2008 p.178) interprets the definition of risk in cultural theory as 'a danger for or transgression of symbolic orders', thus, risk exists within the realm of social organisation and function as one way of social control. Furthermore, public perceptions and debates about risk are closely related to issues concerning power, justice and legitimacy (Douglas, 1992). Risks are defined in the process of holding those having power accountable and can be used as an analytic tool to reveal the structure for the accountability and responsibility of social organisations and relations (Tansey, 2004). Risk, or misfortune for that matter, demands an explanation, which starts the process of finding responsibility. Responsibility starts the forensic process because individuals must be separated into categories such as victims and offenders based on their relation to the particular risk, and in this process, social order, including gender divisions, social hierarchies and other power relations, can be upheld (Boholm, 2015 p.75). Thus, risk is a mechanism for social categorisation, division and cohesion. From this, we conclude that, in cultural theory, the association between risk and power can be defined according to the following: risk reveals the relations of power in particular social organisations (see Typology 1, Table 7.1).

Moving on to the relationship between risk and inequality, Douglas (1992) argues that culture will determine how inequality is dealt with in society or in particular institutions:

> Cultural analysis is a countervailing vision which warns what categories in each kind of culture are most likely to be at risk, who will be sinned against, and who will be counted as the sinner exposing the others to risk. [...] What is not true is that the same speculations are found in all cultures. In an individualist culture, the weak are going to carry the blame for what happens to them; in hierarchy, the deviants; in a sect, aliens and also faction leaders. (p.36)

In this way, cultural theory contributes by providing a situated understanding of risk, how risk is lived with in everyday life in a particular sociocultural setting (Hannah-Moffat and O'Malley, 2007 p.21) and how the attribution of risk, vulnerability and riskiness goes hand in hand with the existing social hierarchies. Therefore, the individual perceptions of risk, as well as how risks are defined and managed within different social organisations, will reflect a society's value system, including the unequal distribution of power among genders, classes, sexes and ethnicities. However, depending on the culture, the search for someone who is responsible, or can be blamed, can of course also be those in power.

Douglas' (1970) grid/group typology is the best-known categorisation of cultural systems, where, for example, the distribution of blame and responsibility depends on the system: responsibility is a matter for each person in an individualist cultural system, while it is collective responsibility in an egalitarian system. To capture this at the individual level, cultural theory has been used extensively in studies of risk perception (Dake, 1991; Olofsson and Öhman, 2015). However, this way of moving the theory away from one of the personality types, has been criticised already, by Douglas and Wildavsky (1982), who argue that the basic values that permeate certain contexts serve to shape the individual's perception of risk and that, hence, individual perception cannot be separated from the cultural system. This has been empirically supported in terms of its weak explanatory power between cultural biases and perceptions of risk (Sjöberg, 2000). Thus, at an individual level, it has been hard to show that a person's values or cultural biases have an impact on his or her perception of risk. However, relatively few cultural theorists or sociologists inspired by the work of Douglas incorporate gender studies into their analyses of risk. Returning to the relationship between risk and inequality within cultural theory, our interpretation is that risk positions are conditional on social hierarchies and that responsibility towards risk is defined within a limited cultural system (see Typology 1, Table 7.1). Thus, touching upon our empirical example about the association between risk and migration can be seen from a cultural theory perspective: when something, no matter what, is defined in terms of risk and danger, it becomes political. During the autumn of 2015, many people searched for shelter in Europe, and some 150,000 refugees came to Sweden. Initially, the Swedish attitude was positive and was in line with the national egalitarian bias; indeed, the Swedish prime minister went out in public, saying that Sweden would be open to anyone who needed help. However, as more and more countries in Europe closed their borders and the Swedish system for receiving refugees faltered, the political tone quickly changed. The public debate changed as well and was increasingly characterised by descriptions that hinted at crisis, risk and catastrophe. Soon, the situation was described as 'the refugee crisis', and in November 2015, Sweden closed its borders to those in need. Furthermore, behind this decision was not only a failing migration system, but also discourses that associated the refugees with 'the Other', a threat to the nation and, from a nationalist perspective, the antithesis of the definition of 'Swedish'. The traditional egalitarian stand was redefined as naive and, at the same time, reconnected to an understanding of equality as something that has to be protected against the arrival of 'foreigners' (Ericson, 2018). Analysing the situation using cultural theory, the border itself becomes a symbol for protecting the nation-state and the purity of the population against 'the Other' (Mackey, 1999).

Governmentality

Governmentality is the theoretical field most often used in risk research that overlaps with gender studies. There are several reasons for this, but an important one is the focus on governance and power in social relations that permeate governmentality studies and gender studies. Governmentality examines the ways risk is used in policy – directly or discursively – to control the population and change the world, analysing the implications of such control and what changes might occur because of these implications (Hannah-Moffat and O'Malley, 2007). Risk is seen as a particular way of comprehending problems and generating responses to them; thus, risk is how fear is coded, regulated and developed in particular biopolitics. The question of responsibility is often investigated, and studies in governmentality show how there has been a shift of responsibility in many societies from the state to the individual. Originating from the work of Foucault, not least his lectures about governance and security at the end of his career, his writings on governmentality and biopolitics have been further developed over the years (Dean, 1999). These developments include new concepts such as bioethics (Rose, 1996), risk colonialisation (Rothstein et al., 2006), critical security studies (Amoore, 2013) and algorithmic governmentality (Rouvroy and Stiegler, 2016), all of which try to better understand the relationship between the conceptualisations of risk and regulation of both societies and its inhabitants. Also here, we find a relativist view of risk: there is no risk in reality because nothing is a risk in and of itself, but anything can be considered to be a risk; it all depends on how one analyses a particular danger or event (Ewald, 1991 p.199).

The governmentality perspective questions dominant, top-down power concepts (O'Malley, 2004), and Zinn (2008 p.179) defines risk according to governmentality studies as 'a specific way to manage uncertainty by calculative techniques and a specific way to govern society by allocating responsibility to a prudent subject' (see Typology 1, Table 7.1). Thus, power is already part of the definition of risk. Power is instead conceptualised as increasingly exercised indirectly through discourses and calculative technologies, such as, for example, risk analyses, insurance risk calculations, epidemiology, risk management and so forth. To govern populations through the logic of risk puts the future into the present in terms possible (negative) events inflicting the process of governing, which can be described as a pre-emption of the future (e.g., de Goede, 2008), making things that have not yet happened seemingly calculable and thus manageable. To be able to know what should – and should not – be managed, one has to decide what is desirable, normal and optimal, and the acceptable limits that cannot be exceeded (Foucault, 2007). Governmentality can reveal how normalisation processes develop over time and thus also create unequal relationships between social positions, which hence become at risk or a risk. The power lies in defining social and other phenomena as risky and in making them governable (Belina and Miggelbrink, 2013 p.127). Therefore, the key question is how phenomena and (groups of) subjects are treated as a risk because to define something or someone as risky is a strategy of power that depoliticises this something or someone. Thus, it is expected that a security logic will not only control the areas associated with security and safety, such as borders, crime and health, but also extend to other areas, such as the labour market and organisational management (Giritli Nygren et al., 2015). In such governmentality work, attention is hence paid to the ways in which the increasingly prevalent adoption of risk as a framework of government – or a technology of power – creates new subjectivities and redefines relationships. There is a focus on how it invents new techniques for self-government (or 'techniques of the self') and for the government of others, creating and assigning responsibilities accordingly. Following Hannah-Moffat and O'Malley (2007 p.15), we define the relationship between risk and power in governmentality as a particular way of comprehending problems and generating responses to them (see Typology 1, Table 7.1).

Governmental research has mainly focused on law, regulation and policy; thus, it has primarily concentrated on the blueprint of societal organisation and less on the practical outcomes of such policy and regulation. Few have incorporated or engaged in gender theory or issues, but gender scholars and social scientists working on the questions of unequal social positions have extensively made use of governmentality (e.g., Ericson, 2018). However, feminist research undertaking a governmentality analysis has investigated the effects of policy not only on the kind of subjects they intend to make of their targets, but also on the discrepancy between these blueprints and the effects they have (e.g., Hannah-Moffat and O'Malley, 2007). Governmentality-inspired scholars have stressed the link between the development of statistical methods and risk governance, creating a sense of objectivity and new experts, where gender and other inequalities tend to be obscured and perpetuated. From this, we can define the relationship between risk and inequality in governmentality as techniques to maintain the normal and identify and manage deviance within systems of unequal power (see Typology 1, Table 7.1). Turning back to our empirical example about migration, governmentality helps us understand and analyse the implementation of risk governance and risk regulation regimes in migration policy (Hood et al., 2001). Without going into detail, one such example is the consequences of the reorganisation of the U.S. governmental structure to deal with migration after the attacks on the World Trade Centre in New York, September 11, 2001. In 2003, the Integration and Nationalization Service (INS), which was part of the Department of Justice, was reorganised into three bodies: the U.S. Citizenship and Immigration Services (USCIS), Immigration and Customs Enforcement (ICE), and Customs and Border Protection (CBP), all of which were organised under the then new Department of Homeland Security (DHS). This securitisation of migration has had major consequences in terms of how migrants, including travellers who in any way are associated with certain stigmatised places, ethnic groups or particular organisations, all over the world are monitored, managed and even detained (Amoore, 2013; de Goede, 2008). In Sweden, in 2015, the securitisation of migration was expressed in numerous ways. One way was that the NGOs and civilians who worked to support and help migrants (viewed as a threat to the nation) were themselves framed as security threats (Ericson, 2018).

Risk Society

The risk society theory is probably the most influential sociological theory of risk and uncertainty. It puts risk at the centre of social change as a driving force of both physical and social issues. Beck (1992) argues that modernity creates new kinds of global risks that are unknown to earlier societies based on technological and economic development, which runs in parallel with the failure of modern institutions to control the risks that they partly generated. What is new about these kinds of risks is that they are complex in terms of their causation, unpredictability and latent features, not being limited to time, space or social strata, 'insensible' (by human senses) and a result of human action. New risks are knowledge dependent and hence open to social definition and construction. This means that risks are a function of the ability of the social system (e.g., an organisation). That is, risk depends on institutions and actors rather than beforehand being constructed and controlled by technical systems. Furthermore, risks become political; that is, the consequences in terms of death and destroyed property combined with a lack of scapegoats creates conflicts and gives those with the ability to avert and manage these risks power. According to Beck (1992), risk awareness among the public creates new subpolitical movements that force politicians into action, reshaping politics. Today, in 2019, climate change is the risk that causes social movements like this; the 19-year-old Swedish girl Greta Thunberg might be seen as an example of such subpolitical movements. In 2018, she went on strike from school to encourage the Swedish government to adopt the UN Paris

Agreement. This action spread among the people, and many started following her example, and in 2019, she was, among other things, invited to speak at the UN Climate Action Summit.

In this framework, Zinn (2008 p.178) defines risk as a hybrid, a real danger that is constructed as objective issues and as a social construction of future possibilities, thereby making risk hypothetical. Beck understands risk as danger, and he assumes that new risks have a direct impact on the social at the same time; risk is the consequence of social entities, such as science, law, politics and mass media. In his early writing, especially, Beck (1992) tends to have an encompassing view of risk as the driving force of history, replacing welfare distribution during the modern era with risk production during the late-modern risk society. Since then, Beck has changed, or at least modified, this totalising view of risk and also acknowledges the role of, for example, social class (Beck, 2013). Still, risk and power are very close in the theory, and we choose to define this relationship as risk having the power to influence social relations (see Typology 1, Table 7.1).

From a gender perspective, Beck's focus on knowledge, particularly expert and scientific knowledge, then downscales the other types of knowledge – that is, lay, experience-based and emotional knowledge (Lupton, 1999). However, the theory has mostly been criticised for the assumptions of individualisation and risk replacing class inequalities (Mythen, 2004). Beck argues that, in modernity or class society, 'needs' is the organising principle, and welfare distribution is the main task of the political system, while in a risk society, this is replaced by 'anxiety and insecurity and the management of bads' rather than welfare (Beck, 1992). What is often misinterpreted, however, is that Beck argues that individualisation hides rather than changes social inequality and that inequality is driven out of new risks; in this way, risks are redefined in terms of an individualisation of social risks (Beck, 1992 p.100): 'Social crises appear as individual crisis which no longer (or are only very indirectly) perceived in terms of their rootedness in the social realm.' Hence, the individual is perceived as being responsible not only for his or her own failures or successes, but also for social crisis more generally, even though some individuals are subject to illnesses and hazards to a higher degree than others because of gender, class, race and so forth. The relationship between risk and inequality in the framework of risk society is further developed by Dean Curran (2016). Building on Beck's conceptualisation of risk positions, Curran argues that there is a systemic process structuring contemporary power relations resulting from the distribution of 'bads' (2016 p.8), for example, growing socially generated environmental and financial risks, and that risk intensifies class differences and, therewith, inequality. Based on this, we define the relationship between risk and inequality in a risk society simply as risk driving and intensifying social inequalities (see Typology 1, Table 7.1).

Using our example about migration, the ideas by Beck (1992) and Curran (2016) can contribute to the understandings of the entanglement of risk, migration and inequality. In particular, we look at the reasoning about how the uneven impact of the social production and distribution of risk – or the distribution of bads – and organised irresponsibility reinforce already unequal relations of power. Here, rather than individual class, or risk, differences, we find the roots in the colonial era, where countries in the Global North founded inequalities between continents, countries, regions and peoples still existing and exploited these peoples. Political leaders in affluent postcolonial nations today contribute to, or at least turn a blind eye towards, exploited resources, war and even genocide. Thus, the bads are unevenly distributed in the world, being the side-effects of some increasing their own resources and welfare. This is also an example of organised irresponsibility; hence, whole nations act to secure access to oil, land or other resources, but at the same time, these nations create unbearably or lethal living conditions for the local population, in the worst cases forcing people to leave their homes and countries. Inequality enhances exponentially between the refugee, who is entirely dependent on others for survival, and local citizens, who indirectly may have benefited from the cause of the flight to begin with. This vulnerability then to 'stick' to certain bodies, particularly bodies that are 'out of place' and/or coloured, creates a sense of conditional belonging (Wernesjö, 2019).

Systems Theory

A systemic perspective of risk is found both in the sociology of risk and uncertainty, being first developed by Luhmann in the late 1980s, and in the conceptualisations of ecologic and resilient systems, lately more known as complexity theory (Walby, 2015). Luhmann (1990) has a constructionist perspective; and in this perspective, risks are produced differently and depend on the self-referential logic of functional systems, such as science, law, religion and economy. Systems are self-regulating entities made up of communication but not just any communication: meaningful communication for the system. To achieve such communication, a different intermediate medium is needed, and in the case of risk, trust works as this medium. Without trust between the entities, communicating risk cannot be accomplished or fully understood within a system. Another key element in Luhmann's work on systems and risk is contingency and how this is related to uncertainty of the future. Here, Luhmann also discusses the 'double contingency', which indicates both the sender and receiver in a communication experience of uncertainty and how this uncertainty interacts with the capacity and need to trust other entities. As researchers, we can use second-order observations to observe how systems other than science observe, construct and manage risks. Departing from this, Zinn (2008 p.179) defines risk as the attribution of an undesired event to a decision (see Typology 1, Table 7.1).

Although Luhmann (1995) engages with the issue of power in the political system, social inequality is not something that he dwells upon. Instead, we turn to Sylvia Walby (2015), who combines the complexity theory with the early work by Yuval-Davis (2006) in her own systemic view of risk and crisis. Walby develops the system concept by allowing the systems to be overlapping and interacting with several sets of social relationships in and between different systems. She argues that the ontological basis of each of the social systems is autonomous and cannot be reduced to, for example, the economic system, but rather coexists in different systems. According to Walby (2007), there are two kinds of social system: institutionalised domains similar to those in Luhmann and previous system theorists, for example, economy, politics and science, and sets of social relations including gender, class, sexuality, ethnicity and so forth. Walby (2007 p.460) argues that these sets of social relations are constituted in institutional domains but 'not flattened to a culturally reductionist concept of identity, or economically reductionist concept of class', which, for example, means that individuals participate in institutional domains 'with a number of different sets of social relations', thus 'simultaneously existing multiple forms of inequality.' The four systems Walby (2015) defines are economy, polity, violence and civil society, in which all unequal social relations (gender, class, race) are present:

> These systems of social relations are constituted at different levels of abstraction; one level is emergent from another. An individual will participate with a number of different sets of social relations.

These are overlapping, non-saturating and non-nested systems of social relations. Gender is not contained within class relations; they are not nested. Gender relations are a separate system; it overlaps with class, but neither gender nor class fully saturates the institutional domains. (Walby 2007 p.460)

Gender is in the forefront in her analyses of the financial crisis in the late 2000s and its aftermath, and Walby (2015) argues that neoliberal ideology gender was – and still is – the axis of the crisis. Based on Walby's (2015) development of complexity theory and incorporation of intersecting inequalities, we define the relationship between risk and inequality as opposed to the previous theories and instead as risk being a driving force of inequality; hence, here, gender, class or other social positions are at the centre of risk definitions and actions (see Typology 1, Table 7.1). For the analysis of our empirical example of migration to Sweden, this would mean that we would look at how social relations such as gender and race intersect with different systems, for example, how the civic system intersects other systems, in defining potential risks. In Sweden, young boys' gender and culturally defined masculinity came into focus in the public debate, particularly within social media. They were assumed to have particular views of gender opposed to Swedish equality norms, 'becoming' a possible threat to girls and native boys (Herz 2019 p.446): 'Despite their different backgrounds, class, religion and age, these young men are collectively seen as a threat.'

The next section of this chapter presents intersectional risk theory. Like Walby, we also position gender and other lines of difference in the foreground for a better understanding and theorising of risk.

Intersectional risk theory: moving feminist theory to the foreground in studies of risk
As a concept, intersectionality grew from a critique of feminist research by black feminists during the 1970s and 1980s, which was originally based on the field's inability to address the multiple positions of the oppression of black women (see Crenshaw, 1989; Hill Collins, 1991). Since then, it has developed into a research field of its own, incorporating analyses of the conjunctions of marked and unmarked categories of privilege and oppression. Leslie McCall stresses the importance of intersectionality, calling it 'the most important theoretical contribution that women's studies, in conjunction with related fields, have made so far' (McCall, 2005 p.1771). There are numerous feminist overviews of the concept that provide thick descriptions of its origins and the varied ways in which it has been understood and applied (Choo et al., 2013; Hancock, 2007; Hill Collins and Bilge, 2016; Lutz et al., 2011; Prins, 2006).

The framework of intersectional risk theory that we suggest here has been developed out of a frustration of the current blindness towards feminist and critical race theory within the sociology of risk, here attempting to take on a critical feminist approach towards certain scientific and governmental practices of risk. It is a theoretical approach that moves feminist and intersectional theory to the centre of risk analysis (Giritli Nygren et al., 2020; Giritli Nygren and Olofsson, 2014; Montelius and Giritli Nygren, 2014; Olofsson et al., 2014). For this reason, we have worked to propose a perspective for the study of risks that adopts an intersectional approach that initiates an analysis of the intersecting processes of power and inequality, in which categories are viewed not as distinct but as fluid and permeable, thereby entangling them with the performative aspects of risk. Even though we term the intersectional risk theory, we think of intersectionality as both a theory and a political tool, a theory about how oppression works and a tool to generate transformative knowledge for social justice. Bilge (2013) expresses this in the following:

> Given the origins of intersectionality, it is important to ask what the introduction of this particular tool does for similarly subordinated groups in the local context of its introduction. Are these groups and individuals empowered in some way by the availability of this tool? Or, are they disempowered because the new tool is introduced in ways that erase their own thoughts and activism, and their own political standpoint shaped by multiple power differentials? (Bilge, 2013 p.410)

Therefore, it is important to always keep in mind the constitutive tension between white feminism as 'universal' feminism and women of colour in the development of intersectionality and to acknowledge the non-negotiable status of race and racialising processes in an intersectional analysis and praxis (Bilge, 2013).

Intersectional risk theory highlights the need for an intersectional analysis of the 'doings' of risk not only from the perspective of discourses that interpolate individuals into certain subject positions, but also from a perspective that acknowledges the power dimensions in the 'doings'. This is also related to the ongoing debate on how to understand the basis of inequality and its relation to embodied experiences, as well as materialistic and discursive explanations. Hence, we argue that risks are fundamentally related to the processes by which the norms of gender, ethnicity and class are socially, performatively and intersectionally represented in language, minds and bodies (Butler, 1990). From this, we extend the typology (see Typology 2, Table 7.2) by adding definitions of risk, risk and power, and risk and inequality from our perspective.

By applying an intersectional risk perspective, categorisations can be problematised, and inequality can be made visible. To explore phenomena within social discourses and practices, as well as within the context of power, we have argued that one needs to focus on practices that simultaneously (re)produce and obfuscate sociopolitical norms and positions as they occur in contemporary, hierarchical relations of power and knowledge. The theoretical framework we suggest includes a multifaceted conceptual apparatus for critical and feminist analyses of risk, power and inequality, here embracing ambivalence and departing from an intersectional perspective. We suggest an exploration of the social world of risk through a discussion of external constraints on human beings that are commonly described as 'social structures' – collective habits formalised as legal rules, policy, norms, moral obligations and so on to ensure the cohesion and continued reproduction of a given sociocultural system. Furthermore, we suggest that risk needs to be approached from the somewhat opposing concept of 'action' or 'agency', referring to the individual subject's intrinsic will and ability to act independently and to the possibility of change and resistance. In sociology, this agency–structure divide has been expressed in many ways, including individual/collective, person/society, micro/macro, desire/repression and creativity/constraint.

Choo and Ferree (2010) has distinguished between three ways of investigating intersectionality: system centred, process centred and group centred. Intersectionality studies as *system-centred* studies refers to research that holds intersectionality as a complex system where gender and race are embedded in a framework of global capitalism – the organisation of ownership, profit and the commodification of labour – trying to find the local and historically particular regimes of inequality. This approach is also associated with comparative and historical perspectives. The second style, intersectionality studies as *process-centred* studies, refers to research that views intersectionality as a process and power as relational, looking particularly at the way interactions between variables can multiply oppressions. This approach is sometimes used in comparative, multilevel analyses and has also been associated with attempts to draw attention to so-called unmarked groups. The third style, *group-centred* studies, looks at multiply marginalised groups and their perspectives, here theorising the ways

Table 7.2   *Typology 2: Theoretical frameworks of the definitions of risk, power and inequality, including intersectional risk theory*

	Risk (the grey boxes are from Zinn, 2008 pp.178–79)	Risk & Power	Risk & Inequality
Cultural theory	Risk is a danger for or transgression of symbolic orders	Risk reveals the relations of power in particular social organisations	Risk positions are conditional of social hierarchies, and that responsibility towards risk is defined within a limited cultural system
Governmentality	Risk is a specific way to manage uncertainty by calculative techniques and a specific way to govern society by allocating responsibility to a prudent subject	Risk is a particular way of comprehending problems and generating responses to them	Risks are techniques to maintain the normal and identify and manage deviance within systems of unequal power
Risk society	Risk is a hybrid, a real danger, constructed as objective issues and a social construction of future possibilities and is thereby hypothetical	Risk has the power to influence social relations	Risk derives and intensifies social inequalities
Systems theory	Risk is the attribution of an undesired event to a decision	The power of risk is dependent on the constitution of the social system	Inequality is at the centre of definitions and actions of risk
Intersectional risk theory	Risk is inseparable from gendered societal norms and value systems	Risk intersects with the exercise of power in all gendered aspects of social life and organisation	Risk enhances gendered inequalities

in which lived experiences of oppression cannot be separated into single issues of class, race and gender. This way of understanding intersectionality is closely related to standpoint theory, which is sometimes associated with projects concerned with giving voice to marginalised and silenced groups, focusing especially on the differences in experiences within a given category. These three dimensions, which are signified by intersectionality and the three different ways of understanding intersectionality, will be used as reference points for our exploration of what it would mean for risk researchers to practise intersectionality as a theoretical and methodological approach towards inequality.

A system-centred intersectional approach towards risk
It is important to explore how an intersectional risk analysis relates and departs from, but also how it contributes to, the understandings of risk as a governing principle of societies. This can be looked at not only as a tenet of the risk society thesis, but even more so in terms of risk regimes and as a technology for risk governmentality.

    We will explore theoretical accounts of how 'risk' – and more specifically the governance of risk and risk regulation – has become an, or even *the*, element of power that rules the current world, or at least the Global North, and its inhabitants, as such (re)producing inequalities in terms of health and wealth. Needless to say, Beck's emphasis on risk as a driving force in society is one such example, where risk becomes synonymous with power and even replaces other structural forces, such as class and gender. Without going into the risk society theory, in this chapter, we will look at a more recent interpretation of the work on risk society that has inspired analyses of risk and inequality, which show the entanglement of risk, power and inequality (e.g., Curran, 2016). However, the major part of this chapter will explore theoretical understandings of risk and inequality as being inspired by the governmentality perspective, including the colonialisation of risk and risk regimes, as well as how the conceptualisations of normalisation open up for an intersectional analysis of social structures and risk, bridging the gap between gender and risk theorising.

Risk regimes, and how risk analyses have become institutionalised, are more or less common sense in organisational and policy risk research (Hood et al., 2001). As mentioned previously, risk regimes are depicted as state regulatory institutions associated with the regulation of risks (Rothstein et al., 2006). The different domains of risks are regulated differently depending on the extent to which the risks are attributed to organisations or individuals, being either voluntary, compulsory, natural, social or man-made, or high- or low-tech. Furthermore, context – that is, the type and level of risk to be regulated – influences the content, being the regulatory stance, organisational structure, operating conventions and regulator attitudes, of risk regimes (cf. Power, 2007). Interestingly, these studies do not include feminist research on gender regimes, which were initially developed by Raewyn Connell in the mid-1980s in her work on gender and power, to investigate the relation between risk regimes, power and inequality, hereafter called 'gender risk regimes' (cf. gender risk regimes as an edgework by Laurendeau, 2008[1]). Gender regimes, as discussed by Connell (1987), identify a three-part structure to gender relations: labour, power and cathexis,[2] showing how social structures shape and constrain individual practices within institutional contexts. In this way, gender is seen as a dynamic construct of social power relationships that fall under specific historical circumstances, shaping people's lives in fundamental ways (Connell, 2002) and that itself is interwoven with the creation of power relationships, such as ethnicity, generation and class.

Risk regimes are similar to the concept of gender regimes in so far as they are defined as social institutions, regulation and discourses, but to better explore the understanding of risk regimes, we need to include practices that simultaneously regulate, (re)produce and hide sociopolitical norms and positions. Furthermore, if we return to the description of risk regimes, that the organisation of risk regimes is largely determined by (i) the institutional geography; (ii) the laws and regulations that apply in specific cases; (iii) the spread of ideas; and (iv) their practical implementation (Hood et al., 2001), it is evident that an understanding of how these practices are gendered, racialised and sexualised is needed. When thinking about migration after 2015 through the framework of the intersectional risk theory, the system-centred analysis can point to how unaccompanied minors came to be very much the focus within the heated Swedish debate about forced migration and integration related to masculinity, sexuality, age and ethnic cultures (Herz, 2019). This also shows directly how the logic of the current risk regimes and the rhetoric of 'crisis' and the minor refugee as a figure to care for or fear has a long and gendered history related to Swedish exceptionalism (Wernesjö, 2019).

A process-centred analysis of risk: the performative aspects and performance of risk

If we, as done in the previous section, propose that inequalities are manufactured by modes of governance, including the use of 'risk' as a regulatory regime, we do not only have to uncover its ideological underpinnings: we also need to look closer at the performative aspects of risk to acknowledge its inherent contradictions, resistance and the possibility of resignifying ideological interpellation (Montelius and Giritli Nygren, 2014). This is in line with Judith Butler's (1990, 1993) theorising on performativity: when developing her theory on the subject, she explicitly describes the interpellation scenario as an instance of performativity. What Butler's theoretical work has so powerfully elaborated on are the paradoxical conditions through which the accomplishment of subjecthood is made possible. Performativity itself does not refer to subjects 'doing gender' (or risk) because performativity is primarily a constitutive process. Although the term performance implies enactment or doing, performativity refers to the constitution of regulatory notions and their effects. For Butler (1993), the concept of performativity is an attempt to find a more embodied way of rethinking about the relationships between determining social structures and personal agency. Gender does not exist outside its 'doing', but its performance is also a reiteration of previous 'doings' that have become naturalised as gender norms.

In other words, subjectivity is not a state of being but rather is a state of doing. Referring to the absence of a 'gender identity' prior to gender 'expressions' in *Gender Trouble*, Butler writes, 'Identity is performatively constituted by the very 'expressions' that are said to be its results' (1990 p.25). When we engage with the 'doing gender' framework, we can draw attention to contestations and challenges within risk theory and create a space for engaging theoretically in a rethinking of the calculations of risk in everyday life and how it intersects with, for example, gender, class, sexuality and race.

People develop a situated consciousness of their position within relationships of power and act strategically to reproduce or resist the specific discursive and practical relationships that locate them either to rearticulate or disrupt, thereby making risk irrelevant (cf. Hernández Carretero and Carling, 2012; Wallman, 2001). This implies that the 'doings' of risk in everyday life largely involve a struggle over definition and the power to construct something as risk (or not) (Giritli Nygren et al., 2016).

If we return to our illustrative analysis of migration and unaccompanied minors, it is important to focus on both the performative and the performance aspects of risk. The developing discourse concerning the unaccompanied young men in Sweden and the major problems facing municipalities because of this influx have become redefined as a risk management issue – a kind of paradigm of suspicion by which the perceived threats of crime and immigration are raised (Olofsson and Rashid, 2011). In this case, risk is then the performative interpolating of these young unaccompanied men as potential threats; they are aware of the public's media image of them as a possible threat, which affects their performances in everyday life and how they look upon themselves and others. As shown in studies from their own perspective, this puts them in a gendered situation of questioning, of constantly having to defend themselves, their opinions and actions (Herz, 2019).

A group-centred intersectional analysis of risk: embodied experiences

Until now, we have tried to show how intersectional risk theory can be used to analyse the intersection of risk and inequality as a structural process. We have also looked at what these structures are doing with us and what we are doing with them by outlining the fruitful distinction (and combination) of performativity versus performance. In this chapter, we introduce a different phenomenological strand into the analysis of risk, which we describe as an existential standpoint phenomenology of risk. Taking our cue from scholars such as Dorothy Smith (1988) and Sandra Harding (2004), among others, we believe that being subordinated in everyday life gives rise to a specific kind of knowledge about how subordination works, which is not available for those who are privileged. Therefore, the beginning of research should not always be in the realm of abstract theoretical systems but can equally be based on the standpoint of everyday life. Standpoint then means a subjective position that 'creates a point of entry into discovering the social that does not subordinate the knowing subject to objectified forms of knowledge of society or political economy' (Smith, 2005 p.10). Looking at risk from the vantage point of everyday affective life offers an alternative approach to the master narratives about global conditions that sometimes circulate in risk studies. Talk of permanent war, states of exception and new security regimes, however important and useful these discussions might be, frequently operate at such a high level of abstraction that they fail to address the lived experiences of these systemic transformations.

With our aim of bringing feminist thinking into the sociology of risk and uncertainty, the emphasis is placed on the last line of research, namely the phenomenological, not on studies of risk perception or behaviour, hence departing from psychological or other perspectives of (rational) actors. Feminism engaging with the experiences of certain subject positions like that of women and/or of being a woman, such as standpoint theory and the existentialist feminism of Simone de Beauvoir, are ways of thinking that we find important to acknowledge regarding an intersectional analysis of risk. De Beauvoir [1948](1976) claims it is crucial to recognise the fundamental ambiguity of human existence to address the concrete reality of human existence, meaning that the individual must be aware of the paradox of his or her lived life and that this ambiguity is a constituent of human existence and, thus, cannot be denied.

Hence, standpoint theory can be summarised as a set of theoretical and epistemological propositions designed to produce alternative knowledge. This alternative knowledge is necessary because it destabilises the dominant androcentric knowledge production that excludes women and other unprivileged groups. Standpoint theorising is necessarily rooted in specific material conditions, such as, for example, women's experiences (cf. Smith, 1988).

Feminist theory, as a way of understanding the subordination of women, continues to remind us that what is important is not only how or what we know, but also what we do with that knowledge. This calls attention to the fact that women are not the only subordinate groups whose standpoint is valuable: standpoints of groups based in other orders – such as class, race and colonialism – are equally important if we are to understand the functioning of privilege and subordination and the ways in which these orders are used to construct one another.

There are, of course, studies within both feminist studies of phenomena that are approached as risks (such as prostitution, trafficking, sexual harassment, etc.) and within the field of risk and gender studies, where risk is researched from a kind of intersectional standpoint phenomenology. These studies often reveal how the subjective experiences of risk are related to gender in diverse ways and how the everyday contains multifaceted experiences of risk that go beyond the researchers' scope of attention. In this way, these studies illustrate, in line with our own arguments, how standpoint theory contributes to the understanding of risk phenomena. For example, a study of the everyday risks from the standpoint of unaccompanied asylum-seeking young men shows that their subjective experiences are affected not only by the legal context of asylum seeking, but also by their age and gender. Studying risk from this perspective means trying to find out how the risk phenomenon arises as a possible gender-specific phenomenon in people's lives.

Table 7.3   *Typology 3: Intersectional risk theory and definitions of risk, power and inequality, divided between the three different perspectives – system centred, process centred and group centred*

	Risk	Risk & Power	Risk & Inequality
Systems centred	Risk is a governing principle of societies producing gendered risk regimes	Risk is a dynamic construct of social power relationships under specific historical circumstances and is itself interwoven with the creation of power relationships such as gender, ethnicity and class	Risk regimes are conditional of gendered, racialised and classed hierarchies
Process centred	Risk is performative and a performance of norms	Risk is a particular way of comprehending problems and generating responses to them	Risks are techniques to maintain the normal and identify and manage deviance within gendered systems of unequal power
Group centred	Risk is an embodied phenomenological practice	Risk is an intersectional gender-specific phenomenon in people's lives	Gendered inequalities are at the centre of risk experiences and actions

CONCLUDING REMARKS

In this last section, we summarise our main arguments and make some concluding remarks. In Typology 3 (Table 7.3), our main arguments are transformed into definitions of risk, risk and power, and risk and inequality within the systems-, process- and group-centred perspectives. Risk theories are sometimes drawn from and, in turn, contribute to a particularly Western conceptualisation of risk analysis – one that is progressive, evidence-based and rational, and that is situated historically and socially within a post-Enlightenment tradition of modernity, postmodernity and development discourse. In addition, even though the understanding of risk has not been developed in other contexts with the same historical trajectory, through the historical phases of empires and the imperialism of certain scientific practices (including colonialism, postcolonialism and neocolonialism via discourse on development and aid), it has been put to use all over the world, informed by a progressive, scientific paradigm that is underpinned by an unchallenged assumption of objectivity (Desmond, 2015).

This has led us to question some of the underlying premises in the historical framing of risk as a construct of the post-Enlightenment Global North because there is a necessary ambivalence in how the concepts and understandings of the world originating from the Global North, for example, 'risk and uncertainty', are applied, understood and questioned in various contexts. Intersectional risk analysis can be said, on the one hand, to exemplify a 'northern' perspective, but on the other hand, it can be used as an opener for resignification, trying to embrace ambivalence from a critical standpoint. This is not about ambivalence as a sort of resigned pluralism or 'anything goes', but rather ambivalence as a conscious approach or a strategic positioning against fundamental power structures that define the world and 'knows' it. It is ambivalence in terms of opening up for contradictions, other interests, perspectives and stories that also describe those parts of the world that otherwise disappear and/or become colonised. It is an ambivalence, in other words, that allows seeing and consequently carrying a dialogue between different types of knowledge or can be seen as discussions or conversations that allow for multiple meanings.

Yeon Choo and Marx Ferree (2010), who have asked what it means for sociologists to practise intersectionality as a theoretical and methodological approach towards inequality, emphasise three dimensions of theorising that have become part of what intersectionality signifies: the importance of including the perspectives of multiply marginalised people; an analytical shift stating the importance of moving beyond the enumeration and addition of race, class, gender and other types of social subordination as separate factors into the analysis of their interactions; and a willingness to see multiple institutions as overlapping (cf. McCall, 2005). Furthermore, it is important to include an analysis of unmarked categories and the ways in which power and privilege are constituted. In relation to risk, this means to also investigate the ways in which risk as a concept might contribute to knowledge production that can sustain rather than challenge capitalist, racist and/or patriarchal structures. By using intersectional theory as a starting point, we believe that the everyday understanding and practices of risk, as well as discourses of risk, can be explored and better understood.

The ambivalent perspectives of contradictory realities, differential aspects and oblique relations of knowledge are opened up, and a relational perspective is applied both to what the position is claimed to describe and to how these parts relate to other positions in particular time/place settings. To make this critical analysis, intersectionality works as a way to demonstrate the ambivalence of dichotomies, such as structure and agency, as well as of the use of risk, to make new understandings of the world possible, liberating it from institutionalised conceptual frameworks of modernisation theory.

NOTES

1. Critical to what has become almost synonymous with risk taking in the sociology of risk – that is, edgework (often used for the analysis of voluntary risk taking in extreme sports and adventure, where risk is thought of as a thrill) – Laurendeau (2008) introduces Connell's (1987) gender regimes as an institutionally, or risk cultural, grounded understanding of why people engage in high risk sports and how this engagement might vary according to gender because risk and gender are always interwoven.
2. Cathexis refers to 'sexual social relationships' or men and women's emotional relationships with each other.

REFERENCES

Amoore, L. (2013), *The politics of possibility: Risk and security beyond probability*, Durham, NC: Duke University Press.
Beauvoir de, S. (1948), *The ethics of ambiguity*, New York: Citadel Press, reprinted (1976).
Beck, U. (1992), *Risk society: Towards a new modernity*, London: Sage.
Beck, U. (2013), 'Why "class" is too soft a category to capture the explosiveness of social inequality at the beginning of the twenty-first century', *British Journal of Sociology*, **64**(1), 63–74.
Belina, B. and J. Miggelbrink (2013), 'Risk as a technology of power', in Detlef Müller-Mahn (ed.), *The spatial dimension of risk*, London: Earthscan, pp.124–36.
Bilge, S. (2013), 'Intersectionality undone: Saving intersectionality from feminist intersectionality studies', *Du Bois Review*, **10**(2), 405–24.
Boholm, Å. (2015), *Anthropology and risk*, Abingdon: Routledge.
Butler, J. (1990), *Gender trouble: Feminism and the subversion of identity*, New York: Routledge.
Butler, J. (1993), *Bodies that matter: On the discursive limits of "sex"*, Routledge: London.

Choo, H. Y. and M. M. Ferree (2010), 'Practicing intersectionality in sociological research: A critical analysis of inclusions, interactions and institutions in the study of inequalities', *Sociological Theory*, **28**(2), 129–49.

Choo, S., K. W. Crenshaw and L. McCall (2013), 'Toward a field of intersectionality studies: Theory, applications, and praxis', *Signs*, **38**(4), 785–810.

Connell, R. (1987), *Gender and power: Society, the person and sexual politics*, Cambridge: Polity Press.

Connell, R. (2002), 'Studying men and masculinity', *RFR-DRF*, **29**(1/2), 43–55.

Connell, R. (2004), 'Encounters with structure QSE', *International Journal of Qualitative Studies in Education*, **17**(1), 10–27.

Crenshaw, W. K. (1989), *Demarginalizing the intersection of race and sex: A black feminist critique of antidiscrimination doctrine, feminist theory and antiracist politics*, University of Chicago Legal Forum 139.

Curran, D. (2016), *Risk, power and inequality in the 21st century*, New York: Palgrave Macmillan.

Dake, K. (1991), 'Orienting dispositions in the perception of risk: An analysis of contemporary world-views and cultural biases', *Journal of Cross-Cultural Psychology*, **22**, 61–82.

de Goede, D. M. (2008), 'The politics of preemption and the War on Terror in Europe', *European Journal of International Relations*, **14**(1), 161–85.

Dean, M. (1999), *Governmentality: Power and rule in modern society*, London: Sage Publications.

Desmond, N. (2015), 'Engaging with risk in non-Western settings: An editorial', *Health, Risk and Society*, **17**(3–4), 196–204. http://doi.org/10.1080/13698575.2015.1086482.

Douglas, M. (1970), *Purity and danger: An analysis of concepts of pollution and taboo*, New York: Praeger.

Douglas, M. (1992), *Risk and blame. Mary Douglas: Collected works 12*, London: Routledge.

Douglas, M. (2002), *Risk and blame. Essays in cultural theory*, London: Routledge.

Douglas, M. and A. Wildavsky (1982), *Risk and culture*, Berkeley, CA: University of California Press.

Ericson, M. (2018), '"Sweden has been naïve": Nationalism, protectionism and securitisation in response to the Refugee Crisis of 2015', Social Inclusion, **6**(4), 95–102.

Ewald, F. (1991), 'Insurance and risk', in G. Burchell, C. Gordon and P. Miller (Eds.), *The Foucault effect*, Chicago, IL: University of Chicago Press, pp.197–210.

Fitz-Gibbon, K. and S. Walklate (2017), 'The efficacy of Clare's Law in domestic violence law reform in England and Wales', *Criminology & Criminal Justice*, **17**(3), 284–300.

Foucault, M. (2007), *Security, territory, population*, London: Palgrave.

Foucault, M. (2008), *The birth of biopolitics: Lectures at the Collège de France, 1978–1979*, Basingstoke: Palgrave Macmillan.

Giritli Nygren, K. and A. Olofsson (2014), 'Intersectional approaches in health risk analyses: A critical review', *Sociology Compass*, 8/9, 1112–26.

Giritli Nygren, K., S. Fahlgren and A. Johansson (2015), 'Reassembling the "normal" in neoliberal policy discourses: Tracing gender regimes in the age of risk', *Nordic Journal of Social Research*, **6**, 24–43.

Giritli Nygren, K., S. Öhman and A. Olofsson (2016), 'Everyday places, heterosexist spaces, and risk in contemporary Sweden', *Culture, Health and Sexuality*, **18**(1), 45–57.

Giritli Nygren, K., A. Olofsson and S. Öhman (2020), *The framework of intersectional risk theory*. New York: Palgrave Macmillan.

Hancock, A. M. (2007), 'When multiplication doesn't equal quick addition: Examining intersectionality as a research paradigm', *Perspectives on Politics*, **5**(1), 63–79.

Hannah-Moffat, K. and P. O'Malley (eds.) (2007), *Gendered risks*, London: Routledge Cavendish.

Harding, S. (2004), *The feminist standpoint theory reader: Intellectual and political controversies*, New York: Routledge.

Hernández Carretero, M. and J. Carling (2012), 'Beyond "Kamikaze migrants": Risk taking in West African boat migration to Europe', *Human Organization*, **71**(4), 407–16.

Herz, M. (2019), '"Becoming" a possible threat: Masculinity, culture and questioning among unaccompanied young men in Sweden', *Identities*, **26**(4), 431–49.

Hill Collins, P. (1991), *Black feminist thought: Knowledge, consciousness, and the politics of empowerment*, New York: Routledge.

Hill Collins, P. and S. Bilge (2016), *Intersectionality*, London: Polity Press.

Hood, C., H. Rothstein and R. Baldwin (2001), *The government of risk: Understanding risk regulation regimes*, Oxford: Oxford University Press.

Latour, B. (2003), 'Is re-modernisation occurring—And if so, how to prove it? A commentary on Ulrich Beck', *Theory, Culture and Society*, **20**(2), 35–48.

Laurendeau, J. (2008) '"Gendered Risk Regime": A theoretical consideration of edgework and gender', *Sociology of Sport Journal*, **25**(3), 293–309.

Luhmann, N. (1990), 'Technology, environment and social risk: A systems perspective', *Industrial Crisis Quarterly*, **4**, 223–31.

Luhmann, N. (1995), *Social systems*, Stanford, CA: Stanford University Press.

Lupton, D. (1999), 'Archetypes of infection: People with HIV/AIDS in the Australian press in the mid-1990s', *Sociology of Health & Illness*, **21**(1), 37–53.

Lutz, H., M. T. Herrera Vivar and L. Supik (2011), *Framing intersectionality: Debates on a multi-faceted concept in gender studies*, Farnham: Ashgate Publishing.

Mackey, E. (1999), 'Constructing an endangered nation: Risk, race and rationality in Australia's native title debate', in D. Lupton (ed.), *Risk and sociocultural theory: New directions and perspectives*, Cambridge: Cambridge University Press, pp.108–30.

Mahmood, S. (2011), *Politics of piety: The Islamic revival and the feminist subject*, Princeton, NJ: Princeton University Press.

McCall, L. (2005), 'The complexity of intersectionality', *Signs*, **30**(3), 1771–1800.

Montelius, E. and K. Giritli Nygren (2014), '"Doing" risk, "doing" difference: Towards an understanding of the intersections of risk, morality and taste', *Health, Risk and Society*, **16**(5), 431–43.

Mythen, G. (2004), *Ulrich Beck: A critical introduction to the risk society*, London. Pluto Press.

O'Malley, P. (2004), *Risk, uncertainty and government*, London: The Glass House Press.

Olofsson, A. and S. Öhman (2015), 'Vulnerability, values and heterogeneity: One step further to understand risk perception and behaviour', *Journal of Risk Research*, **18**(1), 2–20.

Olofsson, A. and S. Rashid (2011), 'The white (male) effect and risk perceptions: Can equality make a difference?' *Risk Analysis: An International Journal*, **31**(6), 1016–32.

Olofsson, A., J. O. Zinn, G. Griffin, K. Giritli Nygren, A. Cebulla and K. Hannah-Moffat (2014), 'The mutual constitution of risk and inequalities: Intersectional risk theory', *Health, Risk & Society*, **16**(5), 417–30.

Power, M. (2007), *Organized uncertainty: Designing a world of risk management*, Oxford University Press On Demand.

Prins, B. (2006), 'Narrative accounts of origins: A blind spot in the intersectional approach?', *European Journal of Women's Studies*, **13**(3), 277–90.

Rose, N. (1996), 'The death of the Social? Refiguring the territory of government', *Economy and Society*, **25**(3), 327–56.

Rothstein, H., M. Huber and G. Gaskell (2006), 'A theory of risk colonization: The spiralling regulatory logics of societal and institutional risk', *Economy and Society*, **35**(1), 91–112. http://doi.org/10.1080/03085140500465865.

Rouvroy, A. and B. Stiegler (2016), 'The digital regime of truth: From the algorithmic governmentality to a new rule of law', *La Deleuziana: Online Journal of Philosophy*, **3**, 6–29.

Sjöberg, L. (2000), 'Factors in risk perception', *Risk Analysis*, **20**(1), 1–12.

Smith, D. (1988), *The everyday world as problematic: A feminist sociology*, Milton Keynes: Open University Press.

Smith, D. (2005), *Institutional ethnography: A sociology for people*, New York: AltaMira Press.

Tansey, J. (2004), 'Risk as politics, culture as power', *Journal of Risk Research*, **7**(1), 17–32.

Tansey, J. and T. O'Riordan (1999), 'Cultural theory and risk: A review', *Health, Risk and Society*, **1**(1), 71–90.

Taylor-Gooby, P. and J. Zinn (2006), 'The current significance of risk', in P. Taylor-Gooby and J. Zinn (eds.), *Risk in social science*, Oxford: Oxford University Press, pp.1–19.

Walby, S. (2007), 'Complexity theory, systems theory, and multiple intersecting social inequalities', *Philosophy of the Social Sciences*, **37**(4), 449–70.

Walby, S. (2015), *Crisis*, Cambridge: Polity Press.

Wallman, S. (2001), 'Global threats, local options, personal risk: Dimensions of migrant sex work in Europe', *Health, Risk & Society*, **3**(1), 75–87.

Walklate, S. (1994), 'Criminalising women?', *Criminal Justice Matters*, **18**(1), 20.

Wernesjö, U. (2019), 'Across the threshold: Negotiations of deservingness among unaccompanied young refugees in Sweden', *Journal of Ethnic and Migration Studies*, **46**(2), 389-404.

Yuval-Davis, N. (2006), 'Intersectionality and feminist politics', *European Journal of Women's Studies*, **13**(3), 193–209.

Zinn, J. (2008), 'Risk society and reflexive modernization', in J. O. Zinn (ed.), *Social theories of risk and uncertainty: An introduction*, Oxford: Blackwell Publishing Ltd, pp.168–210.

8. Risk and new realities: social ontology, expertise and individualization in the risk society
Philip Walsh

Ulrich Beck broke new ground with his 1992 book, *Risk Society: Towards a New Modernity*.[1] The various later iterations of the risk society thesis, captured in the titles of his subsequent books *World Risk Society* (1999) and *World at Risk* (2009), only added to the sense that the concept of risk identified links between crucial social and ecological changes that had hitherto appeared quite disparate from each other in an unprecedented way. Beck presented the proliferation of monetized markets, global climate change, post-national politics, cultural hybridization and homogenization, cosmopolitanism, religious fundamentalism, global terrorism and other features of our new hazardous world order, in terms of a single prism through which they could all be understood – or at least more effectively re-described. That prism was risk.

Social inequality was a central theme of the risk society thesis from the beginning, but the foci of concern altered during the course of Beck's subsequent career. His early focus on the ecological crisis led him to considerations of how addressing it would impact political institutions that, at least in Europe, had developed out of confrontations between capital and labour. His subsequent revisions of his project, in terms of the first and second modernities, of reflexive modernization and other frameworks led him into extensive engagement with the question of how new forms of knowledge impact inequality. Finally, Beck's later focus on intimate relations was also conducted with an eye towards the changing power relations between the genders and generations.

In this chapter, I take a broad lens to the link between risk and inequality. I first attempt a critical refinement of risk society theory by linking it to the critical realist paradigm. I argue that running Beck's concepts through the filter of realism clarifies some of the ambiguities that have beset the theory. I then consider how this refined version of the theory bears on inequalities that, broadly speaking, fall under the two types – or faces – of risk first analysed in *Risk Society*: risks associated with the changed relationship between scientific expertise on the one hand and with the intimate sphere on the other. For much of the chapter, I focus on Beck's risk trilogy of *Risk Society*, *World Risk Society* and *World at Risk*, which together constitute the theoretical keystone of his oeuvre. Towards the end, I turn to his later writings, with particular reference to *Distant Love* (2014), co-authored (as were the preceding works *Individualization: Institutionalized Individualism and its Consequences* (2001) and *The Normal Chaos of Love* (1995)) with his partner, the sociologist Elisabeth Beck-Gernsheim.

THE AMBIVALENCE OF RISK SOCIETY THEORY

Beck always cultivated a certain opaqueness in his various definitions of risk, together with the theory that he developed in order to understand it. This was certainly deliberate. As Hans Joas pointed out, there was something of the gadfly in his approach (2003, p. 171). 'Risk' and the 'Risk Society' are put to work as metaphors, descriptions, paradigms, rhetorical devices, a theory of social forces and psychological explanations, without ever spelling out which of these is paramount. As Joas notes,

> The concept of the 'risk society', which had been introduced in an ad hoc manner in order to describe specific phenomena, is tacitly treated as if it were a theoretical concept from which well-founded conclusions could be drawn. The theoretical definition of what constitutes the 'risk society', and how far we can go in speaking of an epochal change is confusingly accompanied by a mere listing of current phenomena. (p. 172)

Notwithstanding Joas' scepticism, I think the 'risk society' is a well-founded theoretical concept, but it has 'faces', which need to be distinguished from each other.[2] I think these distinct faces can be defended in realist terms, as existing at two different ontological levels of society. At the first level, risk exists as a property of certain macro-level phenomena, which I shall term social facts. Although the shortcomings of Durkheim's use of this term are well documented (Giddens, 1971; Lukes, 1972), it also has advantages that have been noted by critical realists (Sawyer, 2002; Smith, 2015). By insisting on social facts as a distinct order of phenomena, Durkheim affirmed the reality of entities and causal mechanisms that exceed the individual and have a degree of relative autonomy that make them genuine objects of knowledge. We do not need to also take on board Durkheim's rather narrow vision of social facts as *only* constraining, nor his confused distinction between social facts and their indices. Importantly, for realists, the reality of social facts allows us to identify their properties, including those that are emergent, and which give rise to social change. Insofar as they are *critical* realists, social facts are also potentially objects of evaluative critique. As I shall argue below, the first face of risk is best understood as an emergent property of certain social facts. But at the individual level, risk has another face; it exists as a *Weltanschauung*, or worldview,[3] which people draw on to make sense of their experiences. At both levels, I argue below, risk includes an element of *social construction*, but this has to be understood in two distinct senses relative to the two 'faces' of risk. Understanding the social constructionist element within risk in this double sense, it seems to me, is consistent with realist tenets, and with the broad thrust of Beck's own work. It is also consistent with understanding risk *critically*; that is, it clarifies Beck's evaluative stance towards many features of the risk society, but particularly inequality.

It is well to first dispense with what the risk society theory does not mean. It cannot refer straightforwardly to a determinant of social effects, such as globalization, individualization, detraditionalization[4] and so forth. It may be connected to such developments, but to identify it as such a determinant is misleading. Beck tempts us to do this when he compares it, as he sometimes does, to industrial society. This is wrong, since industrialization *can* be understood as a distinct determinant of major social changes. While we might contest what 'industrialism' means (see e.g., Bell, 1999; Giddens, 1971), there is broad agreement that the introduction of the factory system into national economies beginning in the late 18th century was a distinct phenomenon that gave rise to world-altering societal developments.[5] The concept of risk is not to be understood in the same way as industrialization, but this does not mean that Joas is correct to accuse Beck of defining risk society only in terms of a simple 'listing of current phenomena'.

To see why, we must understand the first 'face' of the risk society thesis as referring to a common feature of a range of social phenomena. Risk here refers to novel and/or unprecedented hazards and perils, the severity and effects of which are more or less unknown and/or unknowable, and that *this is itself an actionable, known fact about them*. In this sense, the perils associated with the Chernobyl disaster and the Y2K bug respectively can be seen as risk phenomena. Although both the actual negative effects of each turned out to be very different, the fact that both represented events with large but incalculable negative effects, and the fact that *this was known in advance* are emergent properties that constitute these phenomena as risky.[6] Industrialization no doubt produced unforeseeable effects, but these were not actively anticipated to a significant degree, nor did institutions, including a fully developed scientific-industrial and private insurance system, exist to take account of the effects. This is what distinguishes a phenomenon that is pervaded by risk; the relationship to the future is actively taken into account by actors associated with bringing it about. This, roughly, is what Beck means when he speaks of reflexivity. It is also what makes risk an intrinsically *social* fact. For the risk associated with these phenomena, and the actions taken on the basis of the knowledge of the possible effects, is a major factor in their *actual* effects. Insofar as it structures decision-making in such areas as public and environmental policy, financial planning, career advancement, intimate relationships, life-course planning and personal identity, the knowledge relation to the hazard is part of what constitutes it as an emergent social fact.

It might seem that this is where a social constructivist understanding of risk adheres, and where realism fails. Social constructivist understandings of risk are often derived from Mary Douglas' (1996; Douglas and Wildavsky, 1982) anthropological perspective, which emphasizes the latent values and presuppositions that underlie what is or what is not considered to be a risk. Douglas does not contest that certain natural facts (e.g., pollution) should be understood as hazardous phenomena (concordant with the definition offered above), but she argues that, in addressing a particular hazard as a risk, culturally specific considerations such as notions of purity and defilement enter into how we understand them. This means that some risks loom larger than others, not on the basis of the rational calculation of their likelihood and effects, but on the extent to which they tap into deeply held meanings that actors attribute to them.

Douglas' argument has been seen to offer insuperable challenges to a realist understanding of risk (see e.g., Strydom, 2002, p. 121) insofar as the conclusion that we are invited to draw is that what constitutes a risk is largely a consequence of the prevailing 'public interpretation of reality' (Mannheim, 1993, p. 404; cf. Strydom, 2002, p. 84). Since this public interpretation is produced via contested communication in the public sphere between diverse agents, motivated by pecuniary and political as much as genuinely normative concerns, risk must be understood as a 'discourse'. Actions taken in the face of risk on the basis of this discourse are therefore largely caused by the parties to the discourse, rather than by the risk phenomenon itself.

However, as Curran (2016) has pointed out, Douglas' approach is partial, choosing to focus *only* on how 'social structures shape which risks are selected as salient' (p. 24). The fact that a risk phenomenon includes our knowledge of it, and actionability relative to it, which may be structured by particular cultural meanings, does not in itself alter the reality of the underlying danger itself, although our actions may indeed alter it (this can be seen, for example, in the case of a bank run being triggered by a government attempting to head off a bank solvency crisis). Cultural meanings *are* relevant variables in any explanation of a risk phenomenon, since they enter into the chain of causation that allows knowledge and action. In this sense, it is possible, for instance, to examine the widespread fear that structured interest in the Y2K bug as a distinct social fact, independently of the question of whether the fear was justified. Similarly, in the case of Chernobyl, it is possible to examine the determinants of knowledge (or lack of knowledge) about nuclear meltdowns, as well as the presence or absence of action plans relative to them,[7] and to include these as emergent properties of the Chernobyl risk phenomenon itself. This is also where critical evaluation of the events would inhere. Risk, therefore, as an emergent property resulting from the interaction between a hazard and our knowledge of it, may include a social constructionist element, but this can be accommodated from within a critical realist perspective.

The second face of risk is to be understood as constituting a *worldview*, which changes the meanings of the framework within which the experience of, for example, employment, makes sense. On this understanding, risk as a worldview was incubated within the insurance industry, and subsequently extended to many spheres of social life in order to address them as uncertainties and complexities. This face of risk involves a different sense of the term 'social construction', since it describes what occurs at a different ontological level of society, namely the interactive process through which individuals constitute themselves relative to the prevailing cultural expectations. Ian Hacking (1999, p. 11) provides a useful summation of this sense of the term. For him, the term social construction is applicable to meanings that have the following attributes: First, the meaning is socially accepted; that is, stable and uncontested to the degree that we take its 'naturalness' (but not necessarily its universality) for granted, and where 'natural' has the vernacular meaning of being unquestioned or obvious, rather than being possessed of any scientifically valid status, or indeed true (which it often is not).[8] Second, the socially accepted meaning is, in fact, an outcome of historical courses that could have been entirely different and have yielded entirely different meanings. Third, the socially accepted meaning presents high levels of resistance to alteration even in the face of acceptance of its contingency. This is a result, Hacking argues, of a fourth feature, which he calls 'looping effects' (p. 34). This refers to the fact that, once a socially meaningful role, concept or structure has taken hold, it becomes reproducible via individual role-taking, identity formation and labelling. Prime examples of socially constructed meanings considered by Hacking include gender, disempowered social roles (such as 'refugee') and 'race', as well as less politically charged concepts. Once these concepts acquire stable, 'natural', and often emotionally charged meanings in people's minds, they are reproduced through their self-conceptions and consequent actions. It is worth also noting the sixth characteristic that Hacking identifies, namely that usually the term social construction carries a negative normative valence. To say something (say, gender) is socially constructed is to suggest not only that it might have been otherwise than it is, but also that it *should* be (which is often the purpose of pointing out its socially constructed status). No doubt this is often the case, and *critical* realists have often taken this route in exposing social constructions for what they are, but it is not central to the meaning of social construction itself. A social construction may be meaningful not only for those who do not take into account the contingent history that produced it, but also for those who do, but – for reasons to do with its salience for their identity, for consciousness raising, or for the preservation of existing social solidarities – continue to find it meaningful. Social construction is therefore not 'irrational' but an unavoidable consequence of the importance of people's socially embedded identities, whatever contingent forms these may take.

The second 'face' of risk can therefore be understood as a social construction along these lines. It refers to a worldview that is taken for granted as 'natural' and 'common sense' by large sectors of the populations of late modern societies, but it is in fact a contingent historical outcome. It has been brought about by the development of structures of the 'second modernity', including such elements as a global financial system, the transformation of labour markets (leading to a decline of traditional occupations) and the diminished role of the 'welfare state'. These changes bring about various looping effects, but paramount among these is the growth of 'risk consciousness'; that is, the increasing consciousness, on the part of the individuals, that they live 'a life of one's own' (Beck & Beck-Gernsheim, 2001, p. 22), or – in Beck's terms – are subject to individualization. I discuss this further below, but it is worth noting that individualization – like racialization – is a social construction with the high potential for looping effects. It is also worth noting that risk-consciousness can be a factor in the social construction of risks as emergent properties.

Once we refine the concept of risk in these terms, it can be seen that there is no contradiction between the two 'faces' referred to above; they refer to rather different areas of inquiry, corresponding to different ontological levels. Risk is an emergent property of certain macro-level features of society that derives from their relationship to the future and human beings' attempts to grapple with this. The generalization of a worldview based on risk – as Beck is at pains to point out – is a relatively recent phenomenon that has *followed* the emergence of institutionalized risks. It has developed, through looping effects, into a generalized (but by no means, universal) attitude, which its bearers regard as natural (in the qualified sense noted above).

Finally, it is worth noting that Beck himself was entirely comfortable with leaving the meaning of risk poised between the alternatives of social fact and social construction. Indeed, it is the very plasticity of his conception of risk that has allowed it to move freely through and between disciplines and sub-disciplines. But the ambivalence of the concept has led some commentators to worry that this leads to a too-easy dismissal on the part of commentators like Joas, and that the undoubtedly prolific character of Beck's theorizing needs to be augmented by more conceptual precision.

RISK AND MODERNITIES

The idea that phenomena defined by risk and its futurity form a distinct class is at the root of Beck's risk society thesis in its earliest forms. This distinctness is also the basis for his sharp contrast between 'first' and 'second' modernity, which he emphasizes in *World Risk Society* and *World at Risk*. In contrast to 'postmodernity', which originated in an aesthetic context,[9] and retained many of the original associations of its provenance, 'second modernity' was launched as a self-consciously sociological term intended to capture structural change in the economic, political and cultural organization of European and North American societies in the 1980s and '90s. In the debates about the modernity/postmodernity distinction that proliferated in the 1990s, Beck worked with Anthony Giddens to try to shift the debate onto the sociological institutional ground. While Giddens preferred the term 'radicalized modernity', there was a shared ambition to redefine the abstractions of 'postmodernity' in the *institutional* terms of the first and second modernity.

Nevertheless – and although Giddens also addresses the centrality of risk to understanding the present (1991, 2000) – there is something of a tension between Giddens and Beck with respect to their frameworks. Giddens (1990) attempted to condense modernization into a four-fold 'dimensional' distinction between industrialism, capitalism, the nation-state system and the technologization of war, understood as sectors (not dissimilar from Parsonian systems) around which institutions tend to congregate, and conceived of radicalized modernity as an amplification of these same dimensions. But the 'radicalized modernity' thesis does not sit well with the concept of a risk society, for reasons already stated. 'Risk' cannot be usefully contrasted with industrialism, nor to the other three 'dimensions' of modernity. So this model does not fit well with understanding the shift from modern society to a risk society.

If risk is the pervasive feature of second modernity, then first modernity must be understood in parallel terms – as designating institutions that exhibit a distinctive relationship to knowledge, and the risk society of the second modernity as overthrowing or transforming that relationship. In *World at Risk* (2009), Beck gets closest to a consistent definition of both modernities by emphasizing the shift in the role of *planning*. As Karl Mannheim (1951) was arguably the first to point out, the emphasis on planning was a distinctive feature of governance and institutional development in the 20th century, especially following World War II. The idea that institutional systems, including the national welfare state, the financial, scientific and industrial systems at the national level, as well as, supra-nationally, the United Nations and the other Bretton Woods organizations, could be instituted to control and anticipate the development of human societies was an article of faith for much of the 20th century. As Beck argues, 'technocracy' was the lynchpin of these planning institutionalizations, and planning depended, above all, on the assumptions of prediction and control. The institutions of the second modernity are, in turn, premised on the recognition of the failure of planning, and the acceptance of uncertainty and the unprojectability of future events. Giddens used the term the 'colonisation of the future' (1991, p. 114) to capture the common theme of institutionalized modernity (including radicalized modernity), but the concept of the risk society is premised precisely on the uncolonizability of the future.

The major features of second modernity undermine the entire perspective of planning that defined first modernity. The Chernobyl Disaster of 1986 came to be a kind of an exemplar of the intersection of knowledge and the risk society,[10] exemplifying many of the central features of the risk society thesis: The effects of the disaster could not be contained through the actions of any single state or private actor; it affected populations far distant both in space and time; was uncosted, uncostable and therefore uninsurable; and was both unpredicted and unpredictable. Finally, Chernobyl brought home the realities of the 'societalization of science', demonstrating how the testing of new knowledge and technologies were increasingly displaced from the laboratory to society at large. The manner in which perception of risk is itself a casualty of the societalization of science is visible in the emergence of the coining of the term 'pro-actionary principle' to counteract what had been considered an overwhelming consensus of conventional wisdom up until the 1990s – the precautionary principle (Fuller, 2007).

INEQUALITY, CLASS AND THE ECOLOGICAL CRISIS

Beck's early focus on ecological risk entailed a perspective on class-based inequality. Again, this was premised on a sharp contrast between first and second modernity, and summed up in Beck's rather glib summation 'poverty is hierarchic, smog is democratic' (1992, p. 36). By this, Beck was calling attention to the fact that hazards, perils and hardship in previous societies, whether 'natural' or 'manufactured', are not experienced in the same way by all portions of the population. Those with capital – educational, cultural or economic – are able to insulate themselves to varying degrees from the shocks and harms of economic ups and downs, as well as more existential threats such as disease or war. But ecological problems, such as atmospheric pollution or radioactive contamination, cannot be evaded by powerful elites; since they are uncontainable, they are likely to enforce the forging of new forms of solidarity in order to address them. Thus, a key insight of the early risk society thesis is that confronting ecological risks will produce new political formations that will challenge those forged throughout the first modernity along class lines.

These developments interact with the social changes brought about by the process of individualization. As Beck notes, individualization

> does not mean individualism. It does *not* mean individuation – how to become a unique person. It is not Thatcherism, not market individualism, not atomization. On the contrary, individualization is a structural concept, related to the welfare state; it means '*institutionalized* individualism'. Most of the rights and entitlements of the welfare state, for example, are designed for individuals rather than for families. In many cases, they presuppose employment. Employment in turn implies education, and both of these presuppose mobility. By all these requirements, people are invited to constitute themselves as individuals: to plan, understand, design themselves as individuals and, should they fail, to blame themselves. Individualization thus implies, paradoxically, a collective lifestyle. (1999, p. 9)

The 'downloading' of risk – made possible by shifts in the structure of economic opportunity – onto people's individual life decisions is an aspect of risk consciousness, discussed in more detail below. But individualization understood as a structural concept (a process) has, as Beck argued in the original *Risk Society*, momentous consequences for the re-constitution of the class societies of the first modernity. In *Risk Society*, Beck discussed the effects of individualization on class through an engagement with Marx and Weber.

The Marxist account of the development of classes assumes a relatively simple mechanism by which the class of employees (it seems hopelessly anachronistic to refer to the diverse mass of people today across multiple economic and geographical sectors whose assets comprise primarily only their labour power as 'proletariat') transform themselves from a class-in-itself to a class-for-itself; that is, ongoing immiseration. This account has been supplemented, more recently, by arguments that take into consideration the globalization of capital and the phenomenon of 'modernization without growth' (cf. Wallerstein, 2007). But for Beck, this mechanism is far too linear, and also depends on the other key, but simplistic, Marxist mechanism, the tendency of the rate of profit to fall. Since neither immiseration nor declining profits materialized in the course of the first modernity, Beck suggests that Marx's explanation for the emergence of class solidarity provides no viable mechanism. Beck was therefore more persuaded by Max Weber's account of social class, insofar as he used the concept of 'market position', which was compatible with a theory of status groups and allowed historical analysis of differentiated, cross-cutting inequalities based on class, status and power (1992, p. 96). Moreover, market position, as an analytical tool, is much more compatible with one of the major features of the second modernity, which is the expansion of the market system into areas of social life hitherto determined by tradition or custom. Education, social networks surrounding occupations and the means of social mobility generally increasingly become 'opened up' to internal competition and quasi-capitalist accumulation processes.[11]

However, Beck suggests that Weber's framework relies on assumptions of continuity. The expansion of mobility, education and the proliferations of professions are structural processes, but at the level of the individual they enable greater choice, premised on personal reflexivity, and the emergence of the individual life course. These point, in fact, to fundamental changes in the constitution of the self (discussed below), but at the level of society they undermine the bases of traditional class and status solidarities, whether conceived of in Marxist or Weberian terms.

Beck mobilizes a similar logic to argue, in *World at Risk*, for the overcoming of ethnically based forms of national solidarity in modern nation-states. He argued that the acceleration of global migration, from global South to North – partly as a result of ecological collapse and military conflict in these areas – would induce a *forced* cosmopolitanism in the host countries. The forced cosmopolitanism thesis does not mean that all are equally affected by the consequences of global migration, but that no group can evade the consciousness of and consequences of it. Similarly – at least over the long term – no one will be in a position to prevent it, which will lead, ultimately, to re-integration and new multi-ethnic or post-ethnic solidarities.

These three theses deriving from Beck's risk trilogy – the 'democratizing' effects of ecological crises, the recomposition of classes through individualization, and the forced cosmopolitanism of global migration – are key insights, and Beck's analysis of them has an enduring value. They have, of course, also been subjected to a range of criticisms. The first two theses were discussed extensively in the 2000 collection, *The Risk Society and Beyond*. The forced cosmopolitanism thesis has inspired less commentary, but its significance has been magnified by the surge in migration globally that has followed the Syrian civil war, and the ongoing political instability in the global South more generally.

Nevertheless, it is difficult to know how to evaluate either thesis, for a number of reasons. Alan Scott and Ruth Levitas (Adam et al., 2004) both sharply criticized Beck's assumption that class-based forms of solidarity would be displaced by the intensification of ecological risks, and the surging levels of inequality based on the capital–labour divide that have proliferated since the 1990s (Piketty, 2014) would tend to support their criticisms. On the other hand, as Beck himself pointed out, inequalities are not necessarily impacted by the idea that 'smog is democratic'. An obvious way to interpret this thesis is that class-based forms of inequality are likely to be overlaid by a conditional solidarity, in the face of shared risk. The emergence of the SPD–Green alliance of Gerhard Schroeder in the late 1990s and early 2000s in Germany appeared to herald this, but in no country since has a Green political party attained anything even close to a political majority. However, the advance of environmental consciousness in unlikely places – for example, among the New French Right (Lilla, 2018) – suggests that environmental politics looks set to sweep away some elements of the Left–Right structure that emerged from the class (capital/labour)-based inequality of the 'first modernity'. This points to another ambiguity that besets both theses, namely the time scale on which Beck thought they would play out. It was only in 2016, for example, that migration from Central America to the United States became sufficiently prominent a topic of national consciousness to figure as a key election issue. The fact that this resulted in the election of Donald Trump, who specifically mobilized anti-cosmopolitan sentiment, in order to oppose it, is not the decisive fact, according to Beck's thesis. On the contrary, cosmopolitanism can only be 'forced' in the face of opposition to it. Beck argues that South–North global migration on a scale that will undermine the basis of ethnic nationalism is – in the longer term, perhaps – inevitable. But the history of ethnic conflict and of the phenomenon of statelessness in the 20th century, provides few clues as to how to evaluate this claim.

THE INEQUALITIES OF EXPERTISE

I now turn to another theme that has emerged from understanding the risk society thesis as an account of social forces deriving from new relations of knowledge, which also bears on the issue of inequality. This concerns what has come to be known as the 'knowledge society' thesis and is strongly associated with the work of the German–Canadian sociologist Nico Stehr (Böhme and Stehr, 1986) and his associates. Stehr argues that knowledge-work – that is, work that produces knowledge as a distinct value-input in economic productivity (Adolf and Stehr, 2004) – has become an increasingly indispensable component of modern capitalist economies. The obvious importance of knowledge in the growth of the digital economy is not an integral feature of this shift because knowledge is as important in the production of, for example, cars, as it is for apps. According to Stehr, the growth of the knowledge economy produces a work-force whose comfort with the logic of decision-making in accordance with standard operating procedures concerning project timelines, projected futures, various forms of social forecasting and other complex knowledge forms dealing with the future – comprises an increasingly large segment. Polling, surveying, marketing, data analysis, quality control, management, and other jobs, as well as growth areas such as medicine, healthcare, teaching, finance and IT, are all part of the knowledge economy and employ upwards of 40% of the workforce in OECD countries (Stehr and Grundmann, 2011, p. 23).[12] Such professions are increasingly bound to scientific criteria and much of knowledge society theory is concerned with the growth of this sector, from an economic and social point of view.

Within the more general category of knowledge professions, however, there are specific 'experts', and the growth of expertise in particular areas of social life is a widely acknowl-edged phenomenon. Questions as to whether experts constitute a new class, how they establish legitimacy, set priorities, shape decision-making or define situations are important areas of social inquiry. They presuppose, however, the fundamental insight that experts exercise *power*, albeit of a particular kind. The adage that knowledge is power is not particularly revealing, nor true in any useful sense.[13] Nevertheless, it is true that knowledge, risk and power are intertwined in complex and often counter-intuitive ways. This point is magnified once we consider that the concept of expertise becomes increasingly extended into professions con-cerned with human relations. Thus, in the same way that expert systems have grown up around instrumental institutions (that is, institutions that are oriented to action), we have seen expert growth around institutions oriented to meaning. The emergence of therapy and counselling as essentially public services accessed by a mass public produces a parallel growth in expertise for the management of meaning and intimacy as that associated with action.

The power of expertise in the risk society is in a dynamic relationship with reflexivity. This can be understood in terms of what Beck calls primary scientization (1992, p. 155), which is characterized by a sharp demarcation of lay from expert knowledge, together with a rapid and extensive differentiation of the types of expertise. This cleavage, while producing the condi-tions for new forms of inequality based on access to knowledge, also reproduces existing ones, because knowledge at this stage behaves in a manner analogous to capital and in tandem with it (Bourdieu's major insights into the structures of inequality in French society in the 1970s were achieved by equating knowledge with capital).[14] It corresponds roughly to the period from 1945 to 1977, and consists in a heightened 'capacity to act'. In this respect scientific knowledge *is* power, in the sense of being able to 'get things done', and is authoritarian and technocratic. But, as Daniel Bell pointed out in his 1999 *The Coming of Post-Industrial Society* (p. 191), which masterly captured the key elements of this shift, the growth of scientific expertise greatly complicates class-based forms of inequality, by reducing the importance of labour power as an independent input.

With the advent of the risk society (again, Chernobyl is a useful hinge event), however, the relationship of expert to other forms of knowledge and to inequality changes fundamentally. According to Beck, this corresponds to a 'demonopolization of scientific knowledge claims' (1992, p. 156), and to the dissolution of the asymmetries of scientific authority. Partly, this is due to the societalization of science. This means the effects and outcomes of scientific thinking and innovation are less and less containable within the laboratories, industrial centres and quality control regulations that bounded the traditional scientific-industrial complexes. Increasingly, scientific expertise is eroded because it is *impossible to know* the effects of new technologies on groups of people independently of their actual usage of them. Expertise therefore becomes more unreliable as more and more areas are opened up to uncertainty. As Beck points out, 'it is not their failures, but their successes that have dethroned the sciences' (p. 163). But this 'dethronement' does not result in fewer experts or less expertise. On the contrary, the proliferation and availability of expert knowledge (mostly through degree programmes in the increasingly complex and differentiated higher education sector) leads to an oversupply of technical and scientific professionals. Stehr and Grundmann (2011), indeed, argue that it is the supply, rather than the demand, that explains the ongoing growth of the scientific and technical professions (p. 100).

To see the implications of this in the sphere of individual lives (the second 'face' of the risk society theory), consider, for example, the contemporary experience of pregnancy and childbirth. In societies of the first modernity, pregnancy and childbirth were processes shadowed by health professionals but – as it was and is in traditional societies – was subject to the accidents and dangers stemming from lack of control. Today, it is thoroughly penetrated by technology and expertise, and the potential for control is far greater, including the increasingly personal and deliberative control over insemination and implantation. This leads to the emergence of expert professions such as birth psychologists, genetic counsellors, obstetric technical specialists and other cadres of reproductive medicine, all charged with maximizing the amount of knowledge that can be brought to the process. This has not reduced the degree of uncertainty involved in pregnancy and childbirth – although it may have decreased mortality and morbidity – but, on the contrary, increases it by expanding the scope of what can be known or not known. Testing – from preimplantation genetic diagnosis to amniocentesis to periodic monitoring of fetal development – introduces a forest of decision points, both about whether to undergo the test and what to do in the case of an undesired result.[15]

This points to the reality that, under the conditions of reflexive scientization, it is not simply 'professionals', directly exposed to scientific norms, who are implicated in the structures of expertise, but also consumers, clients and patients, who have to acknowledge and deal with the expert knowledge they are now privy to, in determining, to a great extent, their own bodily and social fate. Given the high degree of uncertainty that pervades all the systems for which there are experts, *how to take expert advice becomes itself a kind of expertise*, of an everyday kind. Thus, the prevalence of expertise and growth in the knowledge sector workforce becomes itself a major source of lay forms of expertise about expertise, in which managing uncertainty becomes a key feature.

INDIVIDUALIZATION, MEANING AND IDENTITY

'A Life of One's Own in a Runaway Word' – the title of the key essay (co-authored with Elisabeth Beck-Gensheim) in *Individualization: Institutionalized Individualism and Its Social and Political Consequences* – refers to both the enhancement of individual agency *and* to the devolvement of responsibility and risk away from collectivities that individualization presages. According to Beck, individualization advances hand in hand with detraditionalization, the latter being understood in a broad sense that includes kinship structures, traditional communities and welfare states. Detraditionalization and individualization are therefore two sides of the same coin – or, perhaps, dialectically related social transformations. Yet, although individualization is a 'structural concept', its effects are best understood through the social construction of 'risk consciousness'. It has also given birth to a whole literature of its own, which is concerned with the transformations of the self that individualization brings about. This has generated a welcome re-examination of such concepts as character, personality, self and habitus, understood as attributes of individuals subject to sociological understanding, and which had tended to be sidelined by the postmodernist programme of 'de-centering the subject'.

Understanding the effects of individualization at the level of risk-consciousness, as a social construction, entails a focus on the phenomenon of personal reflexivity, since it is a key component of individualization that heightens people's consciousness of themselves as individuals and opens up their projected life-courses as objects of inquiry and intervention in a historically unprecedented manner. This entails, as Beck first argued in the second half of *Risk Society*, the growth of risk-consciousness, uncertainty and deliberation in people's approach to their everyday relationships. Institutions like religion, family, marriage, love, friendship, as well as gender, sexuality and ethnicity are increasingly opened up to self-monitoring and re-alignment of priorities in terms of means, ends, opportunities, deficits and risks. This has an array of effects on inequality.

First, growing personal reflexivity involves a changed relationship with time. Risk and insurance are built up around conceptions of what the future will be like. The insurance principle is that x is probable, but y is possible. Only if a possible/probable bifurcation can be imagined is it possible for insurance to function. Growing personal reflexivity means the increasing awareness of such distinctions and the recognition of their operating in the course of individual lives. Understood as temporal self-experience then, risk – as Giddens (1991) argues – is something like the opposite of fate. Whereas fatalistic consciousness looks backwards, not attempting to engage with the future, risk consciousness manages the future actively in a way that enables calculation of possible outcomes. But the possibility of correct calculation of future outcomes is heavily impacted by structural inequality. The decline of long-term employee–employer relationships (analysed by Beck in terms of the 'destandardization of labour' (1992, p. 142)) means that longer-term uncertainty in terms of life-course is decreasing at the same time as the importance of longer-term planning is increasing.

Second, reflexivity increases the sense of personal responsibility. A 'life of one's own' is one in which blame (and esteem) are focused heavily on the individual irrespective of the conditions under which 'success' or 'failure' occur. This 'downloading' of responsibility – not least for reinventing oneself as a 'unique individual' (Bauman, 2005, p. 56) is arguably one of the more pernicious effects of individualization. At the same time, as Beck and Giddens argue, this heightening of personal responsibility is the condition for all kinds of innovations in relationships, including the emergence of 'pure relationships' – in which partners confront each other as individual selves, consciously 'bracketing out' the social markers such as class, race and family in how they define their relationship. In *Distant Love* (2014) Beck and Gernsheim-Beck present a picture markedly at odds with Bauman, who emphasizes the more negative consequences of individualization – narcissism, hyper-consumerism and social atomization. Beck and Gernsheim-Beck present a more measured analysis, noting the emancipatory as well as the corrosive effects of mass individualization. *Distant Love* explores the myriad ways in which individualization has pulled intimate relations apart – geographically, temporally, normatively – but also how people adapt to these challenges through technology, initiative, sharing resources and redefining relationships.

One way to think about the manner in which individualization and the growth of personal reflexivity impacts traditional institutions is to see the growth of the phenomenon of 'Platonic partnered parenting' as an index of more fundamental changes. Here, two (or potentially more) people choose to birth and rear a child together, but to forego the sexual and romantic attachment that was seen to be the central dyadic bond in the 'nuclear' (conjugal) family, or even in the failed conjugal relationship in the case of divorced or separated parents. The practice is indicative of the uncoupling of sexual/romantic relationships from child-rearing, and the emergence of each as distinct differentiated intentional 'projects', which are planned and ordered in accordance with the rational management of risks. Rachel Hope's book, *Family By Choice: Platonic Partnered Parenting* (2014) is an interesting reflection on the perceived advantages of the practice. Since raising a child is both a practical and an ethical project, a central element is the choice of partner with whom to rear. But the person best 'qualified' to be a parent (given the complex and diverse criteria that might be advanced to define this) is not necessarily the person best qualified to be a life partner. In other words, the standards of 'rationality' that tend to prevail in romantic and sexual love are different from those involved in child-rearing. This points to the extent to which intentionality and temporality have been introduced into the 'project' of child-rearing. Indeed, redefining these spheres of life in terms of 'projects' differentiates them sharply from each other and redefines the meaning of each. The practice has the potential to further 'purify' pure relationships, by removing the need to take into account possible future parenting roles.

How might the growth of 'parenting by choice', 'pure relationships' and 'distant love' impact inequalities? Obviously, there are no straightforward answers to this question, but we can speculate on some possibilities. Although 'pure relationships' are premised on egalitarian relations, and represent a challenge to hierarchized kinship relations, they are also fragile. As Arlie Hochschild (2003) has argued, the individualization of marriage has the effect of removing the protective screen that extended family and neighbourhood child-rearing were formerly able to provide. Similarly, platonic parenting has the effect of foregrounding the bonds between the individuals involved in the relationship, rather than the family unit as a whole. This likely allows for greater mutual negotiation in how parental and child roles are constructed, introducing a more 'democratic' element into these relationships. However, it potentially also increases the fragility of the bonds, making these more subject to individual choice. Finally, distant love both subverts traditional bonds – for example, Filippino nannies whose relationships with the children they essentially rear feel more real to them than those with their own distant children – at the same time as it opens doors to new equalities.

CONCLUSION

This article has explored the consequences of understanding Beck's risk society thesis from a critical realist perspective. Understanding risk both as an emergent feature of certain macro-level phenomena and – as risk-consciousness – as a feature of how people confront uncertainty in the institutions of everyday life, has been seen to involve elements of social con-struction that are not, however, inconsistent with a critical realist perspective. Distinguishing between the different ontological levels of society at which the element of risk is operating was also shown to be a central component of this understanding. The risk society thesis was then shown to shape our understanding of inequality in three areas: the effects of the ecolog-ical crisis and forced cosmopolitanism on traditional class- or nation-based solidarities, the inequalities of expertise, and the effects of individualization on intimate relationships. All of these are ongoing areas of research in which risk society theory will likely continue to be a major paradigm. For Beck, risk was something of a key that allowed him to redefine almost any social problem in the manner of a lock. There are limits to the utility of this approach, but the risk society thesis remains a powerful and fertile source of thinking for social scientists.

NOTES

1.   The book was published in German in 1986. Throughout the chapter, I use dates for the English translations of Beck's books.
2.   I use the term 'face' in a similar sense to Steven Lukes' reference to the distinct 'faces' of power (2004). By distinguishing these faces, Lukes brings much-needed clarity to the different ways in which power operates and is understood without conceding the need to understand it as an essen-tially contested concept (Gallie, 1955, p. 167).
3.   The German term carries with it broader and subtler connotations than the English 'worldview', notwithstanding its association with phenomenology. I use it here in a manner similar to Karl Mannheim.
4.   In the Introduction to *World Risk Society*, Beck identifies five 'interlinked processes' (2001, p. 2) that he argues are constitutive of the second modernity. Apart from globalization and individualiza-tion, he cites 'gender revolution, underemployment and global risks' (ibid.). Since these phenomena exist at rather different social ontological levels, it is hard to see them as the last word in defining 'second modernity'.
5.   The critical realist theorist Margaret Archer (1995) has defended the stronger thesis that the division of labour introduced via the factory system counts not only as a distinct social fact, but also pos-sessed *causal powers*, by virtue of its emergent effects, such that it could operate as an independent variable in bringing about the changes described under various versions of 'modernization theory'. Only phenomena that exhibit emergence could, in her view, possess causal powers and count as independent variables. Thus, for example, queuing is explained not by powers existing at the col-lective level but by the intentions and meanings in individual people's minds. The sharp distinction between various human 'ontological levels' is compatible with the view of risk being argued here, notwithstanding Archer's consistent and often strident critique of the risk society thesis.
6.   Beck's insistence that many of the costs of contemporary risk phenomena are incalculable sets his analysis apart from more economic accounts, which contrast risk with uncertainty. For example, as Helga Nowotny (2016) writes, 'Risk is calculable a priori and can be treated as a cost .... Uncertainty, in contrast, is uninsurable, because it depends on the exercise of human judgment'

(p. 70). But part of Beck's *critical* account of the risk society is that this distinction between risk and uncertainty cannot be upheld because of the catastrophic and unpredictable potential of many contemporary risk phenomena, together with the continuing willingness to insure against their effects.

7. As Roy Bhaskar argues (1993, p. 393), absences have to be understood as real entities that exercise causal powers in certain situations.
8. This distinction could be made by any competent language user without consequence for the stability of the meaning.
9. The term is reputed to have been first coined to describe the design of the Hotel Bonaventure in Los Angeles (Jameson, 1991).
10. It occurred during the copy-editing process of the publication of *Risk Society*, according to Beck (1987, p. 154).
11. Pierre Bourdieu (1984) tried to capture the quasi-capitalist character of these areas of social life by coining the term 'cultural capital'. The term covers the way social advantage is reproduced over generations not merely through inheritance of financial capital, but also by the transfer of taste, manners, standards of demeanour and deference, and other features that determine people's capacities to negotiate the educational, occupational and cultural system. Insofar as Bourdieu's concepts refer to structural processes, they are, perhaps, compatible with Beck's perspective. However, at the individual level, they break down because they take insufficient account of personal reflexivity.
12. The number is approximate and subject to problems besetting definitions of 'knowledge work', which prevent any final accounting of the knowledge-based professions.
13. This depends, to a very great extent on how power is defined. But if, as Lukes (2004) has argued for example, against Foucault, the concept of power is to have any significance for critical social science, it must be possible to locate it between unequal social positions. Since differences in level of, or access to, knowledge is only one way in which inequality is manifest, power cannot be equated with it.
14. Bourdieu's overextension of the concept of capital to include culture and knowledge ignores the fact that economic capital behaves entirely differently. For example, it can be accumulated, transferred and distributed in the manner of resource; culture and education depend on human agency, application and judgment in a fundamentally different way.
15. The growth of experts in obstetric technical areas is also implicated in the decline of traditional professions such as midwifery, with arguably negative consequences.

REFERENCES

Adam, Barbara, Ulrich Beck and Joost Van Loon (2004) *The Risk Society and Beyond: Critical Issues in Social Theory*. London and Thousand Oaks, CA: Sage.
Adolf, Marian and Nico Stehr (2004) *Knowledge*. Abingdon, Oxon: Routledge.
Archer, Margaret (1995) *Realist Social Theory: The Morphogenetic Approach*. Cambridge: Cambridge University Press.
Bauman, Zygmunt (2005) *Liquid Life*. Cambridge: Polity.
Beck, Ulrich (1987) 'The Anthropological Shock: Chernobyl and the Contours of the Risk Society', *Berkeley Journal of Sociology*, Vol. 32, pp. 153–165.
Beck, Ulrich (1992) *Risk Society: Towards a New Modernity*. London and Thousand Oaks, CA: Sage.
Beck, Ulrich (1999) *World Risk Society*. Cambridge: Polity.
Beck, Ulrich (2009) *World at Risk*. Cambridge: Polity.
Beck, Ulrich and Elisabeth Beck-Gensheim (2001) *Individualization: Institutionalized Individualism and Its Social and Political Consequences*. London and Thousand Oaks, CA: Sage.
Beck, Ulrich and Elisabeth Gensheim-Beck (1995) *The Normal Chaos of Love*. Cambridge: Polity.
Beck, Ulrich and Elisabeth Beck-Gensheim (2014) *Distant Love*. Cambridge: Polity.
Bell, Daniel (1999) *The Coming of Post-Industrial Society*. New York: Basic Books.
Bhaskar, Roy (1993) *Dialectics: The Pulse of Freedom*. London: Verso.

Böhme, Gerhard and Nico Stehr (1986) *The Knowledge Society: The Growing Impact of Knowledge on Social Relations*. Norwell, MA: Kluwer.

Bourdieu, Pierre (1979) *Distinction: A Social Critique of the Judgement of Taste*. London: Routledge.

Bourdieu, Pierre (1984) *Distinction: A Social Critique of the Judgment of Taste*. Cambridge, MA: Harvard University Press.

Curran, Dean (2016) *Risk, Power and Inequality in the 21st Century*. London: Palgrave.

Douglas, Mary (1982) *Risk and Blame: Essays in Cultural Theory*. London and New York: Routledge.

Douglas, Mary (1996) *Purity and Danger: An Analysis of Concepts of Pollution and Taboo*. London: Routledge.

Douglas, Mary and Aaron Wildavsky (1982) *Risk and Culture: An Essay on the Selection of Technological and Environmental Dangers*. Berkeley, CA: University of California Press.

Fuller, Steve (2007) *New Frontiers in Science and Technology Studies*. Cambridge: Cambridge University Press.

Gallie, W.B. (1955) 'Essentially Contested Concepts', *Proceedings of the Aristotelian Society*, Vol. 66, pp. 167–198.

Giddens, Anthony (1971) *Capitalism and Modern Social Theory*. Cambridge: Cambridge University Press.

Giddens, Anthony (1990) *The Consequences of Modernity*. Stanford, CA: Stanford University Press.

Giddens, Anthony (1991) *Modernity and Self-Identity: Self and Society in the Late Modern Age*. Cambridge, UK: Polity Press.

Giddens, Anthony (1992) *The Transformation of Intimacy: Sexuality, Love and Eroticism in Modern Societies*. Stanford, CA: Stanford University Press.

Giddens, Anthony (2000) *Runaway World: How Globalization is Reshaping Our Lives*. London: Routledge.

Hacking, Ian (1999) *The Social Construction of What?* Cambridge, MA: Harvard University Press.

Hochschild, Arlie (2003) *The Commercialization of Intimate Life*. Berkeley, CA: University of California Press.

Hope, Rachel (2014) *Family By Choice: Platonic Partnered Parenting*. [No location]: Family By Choice Publishers.

Jameson, Frederic (1991) *Postmodernism, or the Cultural Logic of Late Capitalism*. Durham, NC: Duke University Press.

Joas, Hans (2003) *War and Modernity*. London: Polity.

Lilla, Mark (2018) 'Two Roads for the New French Right', *The New York Review of Books*, December 20.

Lukes, Steven (1972) *Durkheim: His Life and Works*. New York: Harper and Row.

Lukes, Steven (2004) *Power: A Radical View*, 2nd edn. Basingstoke, UK: Palgrave Macmillan.

Mannheim, Karl (1951) *Freedom, Power and Democratic Planning*. London: Routledge & Kegan Paul ([1929] 1993).

Mannheim, Karl ([1929] 1993) 'Competition as a Cultural Phenomenon', in *From Karl Mannheim*, edited and translated by Kurt Wolff, pp. 399–437. New Brunswick, NJ: Transaction Book.

Nowotny, Helga (2016) *The Cunning of Uncertainty*. London: Polity.

Piketty, Thomas (2014) *Capital in the 21st Century*. Cambridge, MA: Harvard University Press.

Sawyer, Keith (2002) 'Durkheim's Dilemma: Toward a Sociology of Emergence', *Sociological Theory*, 20:2, 227–247.

Smith, Christian (2015) *What is a Person? Rethinking Humanity, Social Life and the Moral Good from the Ground Up*. Chicago, IL: Chicago University Press.

Stehr, Nico and Reiner Grundman (2011) *Experts: The Knowledge and Power of Expertise*. Abingdon, Oxon: Routledge.

Strydom, Piet (2002) *Risk, Environment and Society*. Buckingham, UK and Philadelphia, PA: Open University Press.

Wallerstein, Immanuel (2007) *World Systems Analysis: An Introduction*. Durham, NC: Duke University Press.

9. Corporations, class and the normalization of risk

Laureen Snider and Steven Bittle

INTRODUCTION

The language of risk permeates academic, political, economic and cultural discussions of virtually every event in modern capitalist societies. Public policies and private sector innovations are conceptualized and understood through risk discourse. For example, what is the risk of an oil spill from a pipeline vs. transportation by rail or tanker truck? Are we at greater risk of catching colds if we avoid crowds or stop kissing people? What is the risk of a terrorist attack in a particular city? The result has been a tendency by analysts to present "riskiness" as universally distributed and experienced, with minimal attention to the vast differences in the ability of differently situated individuals, institutions and social classes to generate and protect themselves from risks. In this chapter we examine the "science of risk" and unpack the complex relationship between risk, class and inequality.

The concept of "risk" probably originated in games of chance that were commonly played in both the Greek and Roman empires. It referred to the probability of winning a particular match in the near or distant future. It was, in other words, a way to introduce a knowable level of certainty/uncertainty into a game. In addition, both societies identified objects likely to cause harm and acted accordingly. The Roman writer Vitruvius noted that workers exposed to molten lead fumes fell sick, thus water should not be carried in lead pipes or containers (British Medical Association 1987, p.1). After these empires lost power, medieval Europe went through ten centuries of dominance by religious orders who believed "the will of God", not man, would – and should – determine future events. Attempting to control or predict the future could be seen as pre-empting or disrupting God's will, arrogant if not sacrilegious. People should seek to find Him through rituals, sacrifices, prophets and prayers. Passive acceptance, not management of "opportunities", was the cultural norm. Sacrifices and rituals, however, can be seen in hindsight as attempts to control the future – to lessen the risk of adverse events, ensure good crops or lessen the chances of falling victim to whatever plague was then sweeping the area (Sandoval 2016).

As trade and commerce became more important in the city-states of Europe, the concept of risk was revived. Elites in prosperous 14th-century towns such as Venice and Genoa in Italy needed a concept that reflected the chances that the products they were sending to foreign places would arrive at their destination intact, in order to decide whether or not to insure the cargoes, and at what cost. The word "risk" derives from the Italian *risc(h)io* and spread to other European languages as commercial trade increased. As "risk" became more widely used, terms such as "risk taker" (coined in 1892) and "risk factor(s)" (1906), became widespread (RiskNet n.d.).

Commerce, even in the earliest days of capitalism, had begun what would prove to be an unending series of triumphs over competing cultural norms.

With the development of mathematics and statistics it became possible to distil risk into an equation: risk equals "the frequency of hazard occurrence and magnitude of its outcomes/consequences" or R=M×F (magnitude times frequency), and this became the standard way administrators and "experts" of all kinds referred to future events.[1] National population statistics (and only states had the resources to collect comprehensive statistics of births, deaths, imports vs. exports, harvest yields, etc.) promised objective, scientific "evidence-based policy". As scientific knowledge of various risks expanded throughout the 19th and 20th centuries governments began passing laws delineating particular risks their citizens might encounter in their daily lives and assigning liability (blame) for risk events. While definitions of risk today abound, that adopted by the European Commission – "the likelihood of an occurrence and the likely magnitude, given a certain time, of the biological and economic consequences of an adverse effect" – incorporates the most common components and this is the definition we shall employ in this chapter (Liuzzo et al. 2014). Modern nation-states have a multitude of adjectival concepts of risk, such as current, emerging, inherent, acceptable, perceived, residual, baseline and reduced (!). "Risk management" was coined in 1963, followed by "risk aversion" in 1992. German jurisprudence divides risk into three types: *certain* – unacceptable risks, which are scientifically proven and the relevant issue is when, not whether, they will happen; *residual acceptable risks* – risks associated with everyday life but not scientifically proven; and *uncertain risks*, whose existence can't be ruled out but are not (yet) scientifically established (Liuzzo et al. 2014).

Through most of the 20th century, the natural sciences, bolstered by the legitimacy conferred by their ability to translate risk claims into *numbers*, were accepted as the only legitimate arbiters of risk. Technical, positivist studies assessed risks by weighing the costs of "accidents" against the costs of preventing them. "Risk management" and "risk communication", on the other hand, were the jobs of the social scientist. In the early days, the former meant persuading the hypothetical uninformed and uneducated "average citizen" to accept the claims of the experts and act accordingly, while risk communication conveyed purely technical fact claims. Managing risks, enabling growth and encouraging innovation were the dominant mantras of governments and their policy wonks. However, as various "innovations" in workplaces, corporations and state enterprises began unleashing disaster after disaster on unsuspecting citizens: the nuclear accident at Chernobyl; the poisoning of soil and water in Love Canal, New York; Minimata disease caused by dumping mercury into waterways or mesothelioma from breathing asbestos – the risk claims of experts were trusted less and less. In response, government and corporate elites funded risk communication studies to study public perception and discover how it could be managed and shaped to fit whatever interests were at play. With social media playing an ever-larger role, we see today an explosion of activists and protest groups disputing expert claims on everything from pipelines to the environmental and health implications of eating red meat, vaccines and water fluoridation. Activists were forced to hire their own experts to counter those paid by states or corporations, leading to duelling experts, truth claims and risk assessments. Not to be outdone, corporations sponsored their own industry-friendly "public interest" groups to peddle the industry line. And populist politicians have both exacerbated public cynicism and stoked public fears to serve their own interests.

Sociology has variously embraced, explored, employed and critiqued the concept of risk. Risk communication studies have measured differences in risk perception by class, gender, ethnicity and age. Social constructionist scholars have studied the creation of "risks", arguing that an event only becomes a risk when it has been calculated, publicized and negotiated, thereby becoming an accepted cultural fact (Douglas 1992; Douglas and Wildavsky 1982; Zinn 2010). When, how and whether this happens depends on the cultural, political and economic power of the group making the claim. "Understanding who will be affected, who might gain and who defines a risk is central to understanding how risks are defined and managed" (Zinn 2010, p.111). This explains why decades of struggle are necessary to get a dangerous but profit-maximizing substance in the workplace defined as a risk, or to convince governments that certain chemicals kill bees or cause climate change.

However, sociologists, particularly Ulrich Beck (1992, 2000), have also made claims that the technological developments of modernity have made it necessary to replace class analysis with risk analysis. In what Beck calls "the risk society", the side effects of our inventions, our manufacturing processes, our attempts to control the future, inevitably spawn unpredictable and uncontrollable side effects (Beck 1999). He argues, first, that risks today are distributed in an egalitarian fashion – that is, that the momentous changes wrought by technological achievements have created a world where innovation ("progress") inevitably brings with it complications that are unforeseen, unpredictable and often life-destroying for all humankind (nuclear disaster or climate change are good examples of this).

His second claim is that class and class identity have been replaced by individualism due to changes in the labour market. In neoliberal societies, education, mobility and competition, increasingly necessary to secure and keep a job, undermine collective class identity by setting individuals against each other. Not only that, Beck claims that individualism is now baked right into socialization processes, so class distinctions and inequality (which he acknowledges are still very real) have lost their social identity' (Beck 1992, p.100; Curran 2017, p.41). Ethnic, gender, racial and sexual identities are now the primary badges of identity.

Beck's third argument is that class analysis is inextricably linked to the nation-state, to the rights of citizens in a particular society or nation, but capitalism has gone global and the nation-state has basically collapsed. People now socialize, work, interact, identify and inter-marry in global, not national spaces. Beck claims all social science disciplines are guilty of "methodological nationalism" (Beck 2007), the assumption that certain forms of organization such as nation and social class are the basic tools for social analysis. In Beck's view we have entered a "second modernity" with a new kind of capitalism, a new kind of global order, a new kind of politics and economy. To understand this, a new kind of analysis employing different categories and language is required.

These three arguments have been extensively debated in the ensuing two decades (for an excellent overview, see Curran 2017). Beck's revised position on the egalitarian distribution of risk is: 'The greater the planetary threat, the less the possibility that even the wealthiest and most powerful will avoid it' (Beck 2010, p.175). His claim that 'poverty is hierarchic, smog is democratic' has been narrowed. Thus "[c]limate change is both hierarchical and democratic" (Beck 2010, p.175). Catastrophic risk and universal vulnerability generate what Beck calls the "cosmopolitan imperative: cooperate or fail" (Beck 2011, p.23). As risks grow, he argues, it becomes more and more difficult for any group to avoid or evade them (Curran 2017, p.40). Thus, risk rather than class remain the primary determinants of inequality for Beck – his emphasis is on *risk* class rather than risk *class*.

DECONSTRUCTING RISK, RECLAIMING CLASS

Using the modern corporation as our empirical focus, we take issue with the downplaying of the significance of class in the risk literature. In this sense, while risk scholars such as Curran (2017) argue Beck's notion of risk has spawned important debates about the link between risk and class, we argue the ways in which class is addressed (or not) in the risk literature is both unfortunate and misguided. We argue below that risks have not been democratized and that, in fact, the growing inequality in modern capitalist society requires that we situate risk within class processes. While Beck's (2010) claim that there is a hierarchy to poverty but that pollution negates class boundaries rings true in some senses – the environmental crisis does, ultimately, threaten the entire planet – it is also important to recognize the profound and growing inequalities affecting the distribution of risks in the environment and beyond. It is no accident that the most marginalized individuals and groups in society bear the greatest costs from (corporate-generated) pollution. The environmental racism literature, for instance, points out that impoverished and racialized communities around the globe – e.g., indigenous peoples in Canada and African–Americans who live next to giant refineries or on toxic lands left behind by multinational corporations – face the greatest risks from environmental degradation (Bullard 1999; Paludo 2017). What is more, as we expand upon below, increased financial-ization in recent decades demonstrates how risks associated with the so-called free-markets are anything but democratized, particularly as governments throughout the Global North pursued austerity measures in the wake of the 2007/08 global financial crisis and passed the costs to those who were already economically marginalized – a crisis that was itself a result of (under)regulated risk-taking by corporations. We also point out later in this chapter the countless deaths produced by corporations taking massive risks with the lives of workers and consumers – the thousands of workers who die annually on the job, or the untold number of consumers who are sickened or killed annually from adulterated or faulty products that are rushed to market – as evidence that the pain and suffering inflicted by risks flows down the social hierarchy, not up. As we will show, the only risks that are mitigated are those compati-ble with capitalist class interests. Similarly, they are addressed only to a degree congruent with these interests. In our view, too many risk scholars, persuaded by Beck's influential work, have adopted a democratized notion of risk at the precise historical moment when class-based analyses of risk are essential. As Curran (2013, p.78) points out: "by rejecting class without providing an alternative basis of power that structures the social production and distribution of goods *and* risks, the nature of these inequalities is elided, not exposed".

To demarcate our theoretical position on the class/risk dilemma, we highlight three inter-related points on the marginalization of class (or certain interpretations of class) in the risk literature. First, we submit that an unnecessarily narrow and humanist interpretation of class has dominated the risk literature; particularly the debates around whether and how class inequalities are disappearing as risks (supposedly) become ubiquitous and democratic (for examples, see Curran 2017). Beck equates class largely with class consciousness, but most academics using class analysis, from Marx to Bourdieu, now conceptualize class as a resource, a source of cultural, political and economic capital. Yet Beck maintains that individualism has fatally undermined class struggle – political struggle no longer consists of class against class, workers against capitalists, but of one-issue coalitions based on a temporary and fleeting alignment of interests.[2] This position is consistent with Beck's contention that individualism has destroyed the solidarity upon which class analysis depends, a claim that has been adjusted but not fundamentally changed in response to critiques.

From our perspective, class has not so much been transformed but re-formed within global capitalism. Adopting this position entails transcending dominant understandings of class as a position that individuals occupy – such as the risks associated with an individual's social location – in favour of exploring class relations, the reproduction of class and the resulting risks therein. This requires moving beyond traditional views of the (re)production of the capitalist system as the "laws of motion" requiring the ongoing exploitation of the working class by those who own the means of production (Gibson-Graham, Resnick and Wolff 2001, pp.1–2). While not denying the significance of this exploitation, we argue, with Resnick and Wolff (2006, p.129), that Marx's reference to class is not about two opposing groups, the proletariat versus the bourgeoisie. "Class", in this analysis, refers to the "process of producing surplus labour" (Resnick and Wolff 1987, p.110), which is essential for generating corporate profits. Take, for instance, the gig or Uber economy in which zero-hours contracts and 'flexible' employment relationships (dubbed in official rhetoric as 'wins' for employees who can choose their own working hours) help to ensure the steady flow of corporate profits at the expense of workers who ultimately bear all the risks and all the costs (Snider 2018). In these situations, individuals are only "personifications of economic categories, embodiments of particular class-relations and class interests", not people who occupy a particular class position within society. We must therefore seek to examine the ways in which class processes – not just property and power – are constitutive of various non-class processes (e.g., political, cultural and economic factors) in the (re)production of capitalism; class thereby becomes an "adjective, not a noun" (Resnick and Wolff 1987, p.159; also see Marx 1977, vol. 2, pp.129–152, as cited in Resnick and Wolff 1981, p.3). For us, this approach is essential for understanding how class is integral to the production of risk in modern, globalized capitalism.

Second, and relatedly, the risk literature too readily "airbrushes out" the state (Coleman et al., 2009). Beck's argument that the social sciences are guilty of "methodological nationalism" has re-invigorated debates about the continued existence of nation-states and the role of social class within them (Curran 2017, p.32). Beck himself, while still prioritizing the theoretical importance of risk over class, argues that we now live in a world risk society where social inequalities have been intensified and globalized (Beck 2010) but also, particularly with regard to climate change, social inequalities have been "dissolved" (Beck 2010, p.175; Curran 2017, p.32). For Beck, risk, particularly environmental risk, now spans the globe, reaching beyond the bailiwick of the nation-state to take on truly global proportions. As Beck (2010, p.173) argues, the "production of risk and being subject to risk are being spatially and temporally decoupled".

Yes, Beck and other risk scholars are correct in pointing out that risk is now global – the fallout from the 2007/08 global financial crisis is one of the most recent cases in point – but this does not mean any of this happened despite the state. Instead, as Tombs (2012) argues, the reconfiguring of corporate capitalism was only possible because of decisions (or non-decisions) by states to open up free markets globally through trade agreements and related policy measures aimed at advancing corporate interests around the world (also see Michalowski and Kramer 1987; Whyte 2014). The same is true of state inaction on the home front, embracing anti-regulatory measures that weakened social protections concerning the environment, economy, and worker and consumer health and safety but freed up capital essentially to operate beyond democratic control (Pearce and Snider 1995, p.26). Key for us here is the need to understand, not ignore, how states have propped up and strengthened the multinational corporation and its interests, furthering and normalizing their risk-taking activities, intervening only when the risks they take are judged to endanger the capitalist status quo (Whyte 2014). As Tombs and Whyte (2013, p.12) argue in their critique of the globalization literature,

> there remains little or no theoretical or empirical evidence that globalization or the 'globalisation of risk' *per se* autonomously places constraints on states and thus governments. A much more plausible explanation is that those governments and nation-states that have most enthusiastically pursued neo-liberal policies ... have been pivotal actors in producing risk, illegality and harm.

As such, the complex relations between states and corporations, and the risks stemming from those increasingly symbiotic relations (Tombs 2012), cannot be "wished away" by failing to make sense of them – a position we find "theoretically untenable and politically dangerous, conservative at best, highly reactionary at worst" (Pearce and Tombs 1998, p.570).

Returning to Beck's argument that risk has been "spatially and temporally decoupled", we would instead argue, via our neo-Marxist interpretation of class, that risk is simply moved around spatially and temporally under global capitalism, and this movement is vital for understanding the risks generated by the expansion of capitalism. It is certainly *not* an indication of the decreasing relevance of class. Capitalism constantly searches for ways to maximize its return on investment and generate surplus value. There is no evidence that risks to the community, to their employees or to society at large are first and foremost in their search (Harvey 2010; Lebowitz 2010; Marx 1977). However, this search is complex and contested as capital confronts and then tries to thwart barriers or disruptions (cultural, political or economic) that limit realizing this goal. Crises in the production process emerge when surplus values can no longer be reabsorbed into the system to ensure its renewal – referred to as a problem of over-accumulation (Harvey 2010). As Harvey (2014, p.4) notes, when capital faces a problem of over-accumulation, the problem is not resolved, but moved, spatially and temporally, averting a full-on crisis and, in the process, creating new contradictions with the potential to generate new dilemmas. This is what happened in the early 1970s, as Western states faced growing fears over stagflation and increased global competition, which in turn produced neoliberal economic reasoning and brought about the death of state socialism (Barry, Osborne and Rose 1996). The subsequent advancement of neoliberal political and economic reasoning aided capital as it scoured the planet in search of new profit-making opportunities (Harvey 2005; Resnick and Wolff 2010; Soederberg 2010). It is a scenario that, in part, begins to explain the massive risks that followed increased financialization, most notably the 2007/08 global financial crisis wherein credit soared to unsustainable levels and massive corporate frauds followed the creation of various financial products (Sayer 2016; Tombs 2016). Once again, it bears repeating that this process of renewing capitalism by moving it around spatially and temporally was only possible because of, not despite, the (capitalist) state. If capitalism lionizes greed and inequality, underpinned by (erroneous) beliefs that this produces the greatest economic efficiency whereby everyone gets what he or she "deserves" based on their individual contributions to the market (Glasbeek 2002, p.19), we would do well to keep in mind that states play a vital role in creating the architecture – what Whyte (2014) refers to as "state regimes of permission" – for this greed, and all of its attendant risks.

This takes us to our third issue: that any examination of risk must also seriously consider the unprecedented power of the modern corporation and its increasingly symbiotic relationship with the state (Tombs 2012). Yet another consequence of the democratization of risk thesis is that it undermines questions of corporate power. The modern corporation has become ubiquitous, occupying almost every aspect of our lives, tracking our consumption preferences and focusing advertising accordingly, providing us with much-needed jobs at a time when good paying employment is hard(er) to come by, and dominating political and economic discussions about the inherent benefits of private enterprise (Bittle et al. 2018). It has become nearly impossible to imagine a world without corporations – they are seen as a vital component of modern capitalist economies. As Tombs and Whyte (2015, p.3) argue, "the corporate presence in our lives ... significantly shapes how we think about corporations and makes the corporation appear to us as 'natural' and a permanent social institution". This dominance of the modern corporation has normalized the risks they take as a necessary and yet largely unavoidable aspect of modern capitalism.

Underpinning the unprecedented influence and power of corporations is its architecture – its very *modus operandi* is the embodiment of risk-taking. As many critical corporate crime scholars have argued, the modern corporation's incessant quest for profit maximization makes it an inherently risky enterprise (Glasbeek 2002, 2017; Snider 2015; Tombs and Whyte 2015). Important for our purposes is that what these scholars call the corporation's criminogenic tendencies are facilitated by the corporation's constitution as a "creature of statute" with its own "legal existence" separate from those who invest in it. In legal terms, it is a natural, independent person, regardless of whether one or thousands of individuals own shares in the company (Glasbeek 2002). A vital aspect of this arrangement is limited liability whereby the primary risk for the individual investor is solely the money that he or she provides to the venture (Snider 1993, 2015). In short, risk embodies what the corporation is – it is a legally created part of the corporation's existence – and the modern corporation is lionized for its ability to take risks in the name of maximal profits. The corporation's architecture also means that risk is passed from those who benefit the most from the corporation's risk-taking (i.e., the shareholders, board and senior executives) to governments and taxpayers who are left holding the bag when those risks result in destruction of the environment, harms to the economy, or the death of workers and/or the public. The risks that corporations routinely take, the serious harms and damage caused by this risk-taking, is baked into the very essence of what the modern corporation stands for, what it is wired to do. The unending growth of global capitalism and its incessant production of ever-greater risks therefore demands that we interrogate the very essence of the corporation and the massive power it has achieved at this moment in history.

We elaborate on each of these points in the next section, drawing empirical insight from our respective work on financial corporate crimes and corporate killing. We will demonstrate how the concept of risk has been appropriated by powerful corporations and moulded to their interests in financial markets and the workplace. In essence, the modern (increasingly transnational) corporation has variously used the risk concept to increase profits and remove itself from legal and economic responsibility for its acts. However, this appropriation has not come about simply as a result of corporations imposing their will on the rest of us, but also, as noted above, through the (in)action of the state. As such, we will explore the legal mechanisms though which this has been done and show how class relations have been deepened and extended in ways that validate and normalize the risk-taking of corporations.

When considering risk, law and the corporation it is first necessary to acknowledge the contradictory position of the state in regulating and controlling the modern corporation. On one hand, the state bears responsibility for enabling the capitalist social order through the passage of laws to ensure the smooth flow of capital, prioritize private property and stabilize so-called 'free' markets. On the other hand, it is charged with managing a highly unequal social order, one in which the benefits of capitalist accumulation predominantly flow up the social hierarchy, while the harms flow downwards, leaving society's most marginalized individuals and groups to bear the costs of capitalist greed (Glasbeek 2002; Mahon 1979; Whyte 2018). Law therefore plays an important role in balancing this contradictory position, effectively establishing what constitutes tolerable levels of risk as corporations seek maximal profits. As Rianne Mahon (1979, p.163) argues, the pro-capitalist "bias" of the social formation is "produced in a complex way – through the unequal structure of representations inside the state, a structure expressive of inter- and intra-class relations of power". This means that, while the state will enact laws that support and maintain the capitalist status quo, such as laws protecting private property and securing limited liability for corporations, it also imposes certain limits that are not always in the interests of business, even if these limits are intended to preserve rather than upset the status quo.

This brings us to a final theoretical point: it is impossible to understand the role of risk in modern capitalist society without some accounting of the impact of neoliberalism. While we are careful not to suggest that neoliberalism is *one* thing – that it has uniformly affected (and infected) the entire Global North – it is nevertheless important to understand the massive risks that corporations have taken since neoliberalism's ascent starting in the 1970s (Hall 2011). Of particular note, neoliberalism ushered in an unprecedented period of re- and de-regulation, during which states reconfigured their responsibilities in pro-business, market-friendly ways. Laws governing the economic realm were increasingly deemed unnecessary because competition through the "free" marketplace was seen as the best way to separate out irresponsible corporations. Governments readily accepted this anti-regulatory rhetoric, corporate power increased and self-regulation dominated (Snider 2015; Tombs 2016). However, the state, as the chief cheerleader and enabler of the neoliberal revolution, found itself in a difficult position when faced with sobering evidence corporate capitalism was running wild – that corporations were taking massive risks with peoples' lives, the economy and the environment, all in the name of progress and profits. By the turn of the century the contradictions between neoliberal promises and global realities were too obvious, the risks and inequalities too stark, for the state to ignore. Within this context, the state was forced to introduce new rules and laws that, at least theoretically, aimed to control the very entity it helped catapult to such prominence. It is on this basis that we argue class, key nation-states, and corporations remain pivotal to any analysis of risk today. The next section provides empirical evidence to support our claims by analysing the regulation of stock markets and workplaces.

STOCK MARKET REGULATION IN CANADA

As we shall see in the next section, while workplace safety laws have reduced some of the risks employees confront, the primary decisions about which risks are "acceptable" are made by those at the top of corporate hierarchies and endured by those at the bottom. Capital and the state have responded to changing political, economic and technological conditions by redistributing risks rather than eliminating them. "The responsibility to refuse unsafe work", for example, ignores the fact that most workers have neither the knowledge nor the power to refuse an order from their employer. Nonetheless employees, employers and government share a basic assumption (however differently realized), that killing and injuring employees is a bad thing. Thus, an important and very public aim of workplace safety law is to minimize risk. Risk-taking in the buying and selling of stocks in a public marketplace stock market, on the other hand, is assumed to be a good thing. It encourages growth, innovation, progress! Stock market regulation, therefore, is always two-faced and inherently contradictory: the regulators' task is both to encourage/facilitate trading *and* to discover, prevent and sanction fraud. Achieving the latter goal almost inevitably threatens the former one.

Another factor complicating risk and class in this sector is that, unlike workers, those cheated by stock market traders are the relatively privileged. Homeless people and those living paycheck to paycheck (or gig job to gig job) are unlikely to own stocks and bonds. Even so, four decades of neoliberal government in capitalist democracies has made this generalization much less true than it once was (Harvey 2007). The destruction of universal entitlement to state pension programmes, for example, has forced both wage and business owners into stock markets to provide for themselves in old age. The pension funds of those lucky enough to still have pensions rise and fall with stock market prices. Moreover, those who have the least suffer the most when welfare and employment funds are cut and the costs of other public services such as education rise to pay for bank bailouts. As noted earlier, governments used public funds to rescue the banks, mortgage brokers and insurance companies responsible for the 2008 financial meltdown, then cut services for the non-rich to compensate.

Stock market regulation in Canada faces problems regulators in other capitalist democracies do not. Canada is the only developed country in the world without an overarching central agency responsible for stock market regulation nationwide.[3] It has, instead, 13 provincial and territorial agencies, one wannabe national regulator, and a federal police force tasked with pursuing those offences covered by the Criminal Code. Regulation occurs in a highly contested political terrain where regional specificities, turf wars, historical differences and inter-provincial rivalries compound the already enormous challenges of governing powerful economic actors. Its many competing provincial, territorial and federal regulators vary in size and power – the largest and most powerful (and thus most fiercely resented) is the Ontario Securities Commission (OSC), followed by commissions in Quebec, Alberta (a key oil producer) and British Columbia. As one venerable participant in the (many) task forces and commissions established to "fix" Canadian securities lamented: "Ontario domination of securities regulation is feared by other provinces almost as much as they fear federal regulation" (Baillie 2004, p.440, ftnote 10).

Canada's stock market regulators all employ the language of risk and "riskiness" to decide which traders and transactions merit intense scrutiny (surveillance) and which do not. Those deemed most risky are typically the "rogue traders", the smallest and least powerful actors; those deemed least risky are the large, established multinational corporations (Snider 1993, 2015). That said, generalizations are impossible across this potpourri of systems, each with its own regional economic issues, market quirks and languages (one operating entirely in French and several in both French and English), each with its unique set of competing interests and histories. To our knowledge, no one has done the intensive empirical studies of thirteen agencies plus two sets of laws, prohibitions, warning and regulatory sanctions – plus separate studies of the federal police squads (Integrated Market Enforcement Teams, IMETs) with their own mandate and legal powers – that would be necessary to allow definitive conclusions on how risk is deployed. Where there is agreement, however, is that stock market regulation in Canada is inadequate. Canada has an unenviable reputation as a haven for financial criminals and trading is seen as "riskier" here, thus capital costs disproportionately more than elsewhere, producing what is known as "the Canada Discount" (Halpern and Puri 2008). Without a central coordinating agency with statutory power over all stock markets in the country, ample scope for rogue operators is virtually guaranteed since those denied trading privileges in one province can merely shift operations to the one next door. Indeed, statistics show that the largest and most prestigious agency, the Ontario Securities Commission (OSC), with jurisdiction over most of the major international firms trading in Canada, prosecutes ten times fewer securities law violations and twenty times fewer insider trading violations per firm than its American counterpart, the Securities and Exchange Commission (SEC). And its average fines per insider trading case are seventeen times smaller (Gray 2013).

To understand how Canadian stock market regulation became so "risky" for would-be investors and the general public, we must look at the complicated, many-faceted history of the regulatory agency. Getting the state to pass laws regulating the activities of powerful actors in a capitalist society is *always* difficult (Tombs and Whyte 2015). Predictably, government regulation of stock markets and the financial sector developed slowly, reluctantly, and only in response to financial scams and disasters. National governments in the 19th and 20th centuries saw themselves as facing conflicting realities: "nation-building" required them to attract investment, seen as essential to develop natural resources and ensure growth and prosperity, but the primary industries involved in this quest, particularly the pivotal mining industry, showed a lamentable, repeated susceptibility to fraud. This threatened investor confidence and thus the very basis of the system.

The first Canadian securities legislation, passed in Manitoba in 1912, required the registration and licensing of brokers and securities salesmen (there were no women). In 1928 the government of Ontario passed the Securities Fraud Prevention Act[4] prohibiting any person from trading in securities unless registered as a broker or salesman, and gave the Attorney-General of Ontario power to deny registration "for any reason which he may deem sufficient" (Emerson 1972, p.9). The Securities Fraud Prevention Board was established in 1933, four years after the 1929 stock market crash in the depths of the Great Depression, but it could only act after fraud was discovered (and presumably the damage was done) (Condon 1998; Stenning et al. 1990). The dawn of modern regulation in Ontario came in 1945, when the 1944 Royal Commission on Mining recommended the establishment of an agency that could prevent as well as sanction fraud. The Ontario Securities Commission became responsible for ensuring that those selling stocks in Ontario filed a prospectus disclosing "all material facts" and "the integrity of the applicant" (Condon 1998, p.19), and enforcing "more rigorous prosecution" with sanctions including "possible cancellation of registration" (Condon 1998, p.20). It is no accident that mining was the industry that necessitated the establishment of Canada's largest and most powerful stock market regulator. As noted earlier, raising capital to develop and promote Canada's natural resources – coal, potash, gold, uranium, oil, copper – has long been a/the major function of all provincial stock exchanges. Canada's major banks (e.g., BMO Nesbitt Burns, the Royal Bank of Canada) have made their fortunes and reputations as funders of choice for the mining industry. And while Ontario has the most diversified economy in the country, and has been Canada's manufacturing and industrial hub since Confederation, mining and oil stocks still occupy a strategic position. The Toronto Stock Exchange (TSX) has the most mining company listings in the world – 1612, *vs.* Australia with 860 and London with 181 (Younglai 2014, p.B1, 9).

The major factors shaping stock market regulation today are the changes introduced by neoliberalism and the explosion of new technologies, new ways to buy and sell stocks. Both have increased risk levels for the majority of investors while enriching elites. Under the sway of neoliberal doctrines, government institutions were pressured to "free" markets by cutting regulations to enhance "prosperity" and "efficiency". Through the last decades of the 20th century the United States, Canada's biggest trading partner, passed a series of laws loosening or removing restrictions on banks and insurance companies – the products they could sell, the interest rates they could levy and the capital cushion financial institutions had to maintain, thus eroding the distinction between commercial and investment banks. In 1999 the US Congress repealed the Glass–Steagall Act of 1933, which prevented commercial banks from selling securities, replacing it with the Gramm–Leach–Biley Act (a.k.a. the Financial Services Modernization Act) (Braithwaite and Drahos 2000, p.93).

The Canadian government reacted to these changes in 1987 by abolishing laws meant to prevent any single sector from dominating the financial stability of the country. The traditional "four pillars" of economic regulation forced the banking, insurance, trust companies and securities sectors into separate silos. Demolishing the pillars allowed banks to sell stocks and own brokerage houses, insurance companies to lend money and/or own banks. Stock markets boomed and share volumes, trading venues and investment "opportunities" dramatically increased. And as governments privatized and shrunk public services and pensions, Canadians began putting more of their savings in investments rather than bank accounts. The number of shareowners in Canada increased from 23% of all Canadian adults owning publicly listed securities in 1989 to 46% by 2003 (Wise Persons' Committee 2003; *Report on Business Magazine*, June 2004). The federal government perceived that this increased dependence on stock and investment income would create more need for an effective national regulator and made dozens of attempts to establish one, none of them successful. The final blow came in a Supreme Court decision on December 22, 2011, which ruled such efforts unconstitutional (Financial Post 2011). However, a decision on November 9, 2018 did confirm the legality of the rather toothless national agency, the Cooperative Capital Markets Regulatory System, which currently has five members. Quebec and Alberta are two of the most significant holdouts.

Technological changes have both increased "riskiness" for all investors *except* the top tier of investors and further decreased regulatory effectiveness. The first "modern" stock markets were meeting places where those with capital could "nation-build" by finding worthy entrepreneurs looking for capital to make "things" – battleships, steam engines, automobiles, refrigerators. Stock markets were geographically fixed institutions, located in and centred on a particular nation-state, where human traders shouted buy-and-sell bids. Traditional stock exchanges were mutual, not-for-profit entities owned by their members, who typically enjoyed exclusive trading rights on the exchange and in that region or state. Record-keeping was pen and paper based. Sectoral regulatory agencies made some sense in this reality.

All the major exchanges today have been converted into for-profit commercial companies, open to outside investors and frequently selling their own shares on the stock market they operate (a process called "demutualization"). They now compete with new players and venues for new listings and the fees they generate (Snider 2014). Trading itself has become an almost entirely electronic process, deterritorialized, abstract and virtual, dominated by Electronic Communication Networks (ECNs), algorithmic trading and spin-offs such as High Frequency Trading (HFT), Special Investment Vehicles and hedge funds. Today, trading is more about the making and selling of specialized financial products than the making of "things": profits from the financial sector were only 16% of total profits in the US economy in 1975, but by 2007 this had risen to 41% (McNally 2011, pp.85–86). In this new "virtual economy" profits, it was said, would be made through the trading of knowledge, information and symbolic assets such as brands. However, in fact they were made from the invention of thousands of new ways to package and sell debt. Thus, consumer debt in the US, fed by relentless marketing and easy credit access, doubled from 1980 to 2007. But debt in the financial sector quintupled, from 25% of the American GDP in 1982 to 121% in 2008 (McNally 2011, p.86).

While the main goal of those who developed, adapted and adopted these instruments was (and is) to make it cheaper to buy and sell stocks, thereby increasing the number of transactions (the volume of sales) and maximize profits (in the language of financiers this is known as optimizing "liquidity" and "price discovery"), the consequences of this uncontrolled social experiment are immense, leaving people at the mercy of private market forces (Harvey 2007). No regulatory agency had the power to prevent economic elites from creating these very risky debt instruments; this would have meant "stifling innovation". Indeed such "innovators" were and are richly rewarded, both socially and economically. Creating new risks has been extremely profitable for the capitalist class.

Thus technological "innovation" and the removal of social security supports under neoliberalism have made citizens and institutions around the globe more dependent on world financial markets, more vulnerable to theft, misrepresentation and market collapse than ever before. And those who pay the price for this "casino capitalism" are not the banks and large-scale investors who caused the problems in the first place. Risk was successfully transferred down the class scale – these were the people who lost their houses, jobs, pensions and hopes. And regulatory agencies are not equipped, economically, technologically or politically, to prevent, remedy or sanction the perpetrators.

WORKPLACE SAFETY: REGULATING RISK

As with the regulation of stock markets, interrogating risk in relation to workplace safety demands we understand the system of regulating injury and death at work. The history of capitalism is one in which corporations have routinely risked workers' health and safety for the sake of profits. The industrial revolution witnessed incredibly dangerous working conditions – child labour was commonplace, women worked from morning until night, factories lacked even basic safety practices (Snider 1993, p.95) – that seriously sickened and killed workers. The extent of the problem was so great that it eventually posed a threat to capitalism's legitimacy – factory owners were literally working people to death. States were forced to act, if only to save capitalism from itself. Britain, for example, passed a series of Factory Acts beginning in the first half of the 19th century that, among other things, limited the length of the working day and introduced mandatory breaks and safety standards. However, even though these laws were criminal offences, factory owners vigorously (and effectively) resisted enforcement efforts and many inspectors and magistrates identified with owners and their interests, which resulted in insignificant fines or none at all (Carson 1979; Whyte 2018). Carson chronicles how these offences were gradually "conventionalized" as "accidents" and dealt with through a separate category of law – strict liability rather than criminal offences – which meant they were deemed less serious than "real" crimes. Through this process, risk in the workplace was normalized and harms that happened along the way were deemed accidental or aberrant, not the result of factory owners taking massive risks with workers' lives.

Using the Canadian province of Ontario as a case study, Eric Tucker notes how a first wave of health and safety regulations (1830–1880) was premised on the belief that workers and employers entered freely into contractual arrangements, and that any negotiation of the terms and conditions of employment, including safety measures, was to be decided between the two parties. Within this framework, workers were assumed to understand and accept certain levels of risk in the workplace (Tucker 1995, p.246). A second wave of regulations (1880–1970) witnessed the introduction of government standards and regulations that attempted to balance workplace risks. Although workers were provided with minimum safety protections, the prevailing assumption was that workers were only entitled to measures that were "reasonably practicable in the circumstances" for all the remaining risks (Tucker 1995, p.246). A third wave of regulation (beginning in the 1970s) gave workers legal rights to participate in occupational health and safety decisions. Internal responsibility systems gave workers the right to participate in decisions related to health and safety, most notably through joint health and safety committees. Unfortunately, these processes were deeply flawed by the unequal distribution of power between employers and workers (Tucker 1995, p.256). Meanwhile, external responsibility systems, which involved regulatory oversight of workplace safety, remained weak and under-funded, and government enforcement typically favoured education and persuasion over enforcement (Tucker 1995, pp.262–263). While Tucker's research focuses on the Canadian context, his conclusions nevertheless provide important insights about the overall nature and impact of health and safety regulation within capitalist societies.

Instructive for our purposes is that, in each instance, regulations effectively managed risks in the interests of owners at the expense of workers' health and safety. *Risks were mitigated and normalized through law, not significantly reduced, or eliminated.* "Tolerable" risk levels were those that reflected the interests of the owners of capital and ensured the (re)production of the capitalist status quo. The underlying assumption was that workplaces are always "risky" (for employees, not owners) and that both parties agreed on what constitutes acceptable risk levels (Tucker 1995, p.246). There was also – and always – resistance from corporate owners and managers who argued that even these modest safety measures cost too much, interfered with management's right to develop effective production strategies ("most effective" is not necessarily synonymous with "safest"), and gave workers and unions too much power and control over working conditions (Noble 1995, p.268). This does not suggest that all corporate owners resisted all legal reforms, but that they supported such efforts only to the extent that they served their (economic) interests (McMullan 1992).

The current period of neoliberal self-regulation only exacerbates the problems. Since the early 1980s, the dominant response to corporate offending across most of the Global North has been regulation based on a cooperative model, meaning regulators endeavour to educate and work with corporations to ensure they operate in a safe manner. As a result, self-regulation replaced state regulation, which was thought to be ineffective and overly intrusive (Snider 2000, p.173). Fuelled by neo-liberal beliefs that the market was the most efficient means of dealing with corporate wrongdoing – that "reputation" and market forces would prevent misdeeds (Tillman and Indergaard 2005, pp.15–16; also see Bakan 2004, p.143) – there was a gradual and pronounced erosion of "formal rules of law and regulation" (Tillman and Indergaard 2005, p.28). The result was a clawing-back of regulations deemed overly intrusive, coupled with the introduction of new laws essentially allowing businesses to self-determine how they would adhere to health and safety standards (Snider 2000). In the meantime, many regulatory agencies were cut to the bone, leaving them severely under-resourced when it came to inspecting companies and enforcing already weak laws. As Tombs and Whyte (2013, p.758) note, the "removal of surveillance sends a message to employers that they might endanger the worker's lives and livelihoods with greater impunity".

For many observers (Bittle et al. 2018; Snider 2015; Tombs 2016; Tombs and Whyte 2015), the *de facto* system of self-regulation is at the heart of many corporate disasters that cost workers their lives. The death of 26 workers in an underground explosion in 1992 at the Westray mine in Canada – a disaster caused by unsafe and illegal working conditions (Bittle 2012; Glasbeek 2002); the sinking of the sea ferry *Herald of Free Enterprise* in 1987, killing more than 200 passengers and crew (Slapper and Tombs 1999); the *Piper Alpha* oil platform disaster in the British North Sea, which killed 170 workers (Whyte 1999); and a runaway 74-carriage freight train – transporting crude oil and with no staff on board – exploding in southern Québec, killing close to 50 residents of the municipality of Lac-Mégantic (Campbell 2018), are just a few examples of the harms caused by under-regulated corporations. In essence, as corporations were left increasingly to their own devices, the profit imperative took precedence, with devastating effects.

Governments' response to these disasters reveals a further (re)production of class interests through law and the associated belief that certain levels of risk in the workplace are regrettable but largely unavoidable. With state regulation drastically weakened by neoliberalism, government responses to the many voices demanding meaningful reform was, in Canada and the UK, to pass laws criminalizing the negligent killing of workers and/or members of the public. The UK's law, the *Corporate Manslaughter and Corporate Homicide Act* (CMCHAct), enacted in 2007, holds organizations criminally liable in cases where the company had a duty of care to deceased individual(s). For a CMCHAct conviction the organization must have been managed or organized in a manner that was "far below what can reasonably be expected" (2004). In Canada, the introduction of corporate criminal liability legislation in 2004, commonly referred to as the Westray law, created a legal duty for "all persons directing work to take reasonable steps to ensure the safety of workers and the public" and attributed criminal liability to an "organisation" if a senior officer knew or ought to have known about the offence.

While a full account of these laws is beyond the scope of this chapter (see Almond 2013; Bittle 2012; Glasbeek 2013; Gobert 2008; Slapper 2013; Tombs 2016), we must nevertheless discuss how they (re)normalize risk in the workplace and downplay the seriousness of workplace injury and death. Three points are instructive in this regard. First, in addition to the fact that governments in both countries were less than keen about the idea of criminalizing corporations – it took 13 years for the UK government to introduce the CMCHAct and Canada's law was 10 years in the making – neither law has effectively reined in corporate power. In the UK, for instance, there were only 26 convictions in the law's first decade of existence (Hébert et al., 2019); in Canada there have only been approximately six convictions/guilty pleas since the law took effect in 2004 (Bittle and Stinson 2018; Glasbeek 2013). This enforcement record raises questions about the "real" purpose of these laws given the deaths of thousands of workers in both jurisdictions during the intervening years (Hébert et al. 2019; Tombs 2018).

Second, when contemplating the introduction of corporate killing laws, it was readily apparent that legislators in both countries were uncomfortable with cracking down on corporate violence. Whether it was organized business expressing concerns with the idea of criminal prosecution for workplace fatalities (Tombs and Whyte 2013), or legislators not wanting to be or be seen as harsh in their treatment of corporations (Bittle 2012), there was widespread reluctance to criminalize corporations. The message in both jurisdictions was (and is) that laws must not seriously jeopardize corporate profits and that risk-taking was and would remain a necessary and inescapable component of production (Bittle 2012; Bittle and Snider 2006; Tombs 2018). Relatedly, in both countries initial demands to change the law to hold senior executives and boards to account for workplace fatalities were removed due to concerns about the difficulties of proving intent (*mens rea*) of individuals who were not "directly" involved in an incident. This meant that the laws in both countries ultimately criminalized only the corporation (i.e., the corporate person) (Tombs 2016; Bittle 2012). Thus, those who own, control and profit from the business – the ultimate risk-takers in major corporations – still cannot be held liable for risking workers' health and safety.

Third, as history repeatedly demonstrates (Slapper and Tombs 1999; Snider 1993, 2000, 2015), when states hold corporations to account for their crimes, they target the smallest and weakest. In the UK, for instance, of the 26 CMCHAct convictions to date, almost all have been against "micro- or small companies" (Hébert et al. 2019), with a similar situation unfolding in the Canadian context (Alvesalo-Kuusi et al. 2017). This enforcement record gives the impression that risks in the workplace are confined to mainly small, rogue companies that are unwilling or unable to adhere to the law, a situation that belies the fact that large, multinational companies routinely sicken, injure, and kill workers with relative impunity.

Overall, when it comes to regulating and controlling workplace safety, we can see the state's efforts to intervene, particularly in Canada and the UK, provide at best an illusion of protecting workers from the risks that employers take with their lives. This does not suggest that law offers no measure of protection – workers have won some concessions through law – but that the ways in which these laws are developed and enforced sends the erroneous message that the corporate sector, generally speaking, does everything it can to avoid harming employees and the public, effectively obscuring the truth that corporate profit maximizing routinely generates risks that can and do lead to workers' injury and death. As Whyte (2003, p.144) reminds us, "regulation in capitalist societies is as much about social order maintenance as it is about control efforts *per se*". Risk is therefore not something that can be understood outside of the conditions of existence that make certain forms of regulation possible and which, in the end, help preserve capitalist class interests.

CONCLUSION: RISK, CLASS AND (RE)CEMENTING THE STATUS QUO

This chapter has challenged the idea that risk can be understood outside of capitalist class relations. Our primary concern was that Beck's revised position on risk – the recognition that risk has not been completely democratized – still relies on a narrow interpretation of class as being related to positions that individuals occupy in the social hierarchy. While inequalities between classes abound in capitalist society, we argued that class is about much more than two opposing groups, the bourgeoisie and proletariat; instead, it is a "process of producing surplus labour" (Resnick and Wolff 1987, p.110). From this perspective individuals are only "personifications of economic categories, embodiments of particular class-relations and class interests", not people who occupy a particular class position within society. Using the regulation (or lack thereof) of financial crimes and workplace safety, we have shown that risk remains highly asymmetrical, benefiting those at the higher end of the social hierarchy (especially the 1%), while leaving the majority of people, particularly those already in precarious economic circumstances, to deal with its deleterious effects. More importantly, however, we demonstrated that states have passed various laws giving the impression that risks associated with the financial markets and workplace safety are being addressed when in fact they are being mitigated only to an extent that does not undermine capitalist class interests. Law in this context does little to resolve the fact that corporations, particularly large companies that operate globally, are legally wired to take massive risks with the economy and workers' health and safety in order to secure maximal profits.

These "state regimes of permission" (Whyte 2014) that both permit and perpetuate corporate risk-taking require constant renewal. A case in point is the surge in popularity of various corporate social responsibility (CSR) initiatives aimed at conveying what is expected of corporations both normatively and ethically (Livesey and Kearins 2002). Today, almost every major corporation employs the language of transparency, trustworthiness, learning from their mistakes and caring for workers, consumers and the environment as routine elements of their public pronouncements to social responsibility. However, as a form of self-regulation, CSR is only possible because of the hegemonic and culturally created belief that most corporations are law-abiding and socially responsible, and likely to comply when offered a combination of market incentives and persuasion (Tombs and Whyte 2013, p.67). In other words, and once again, corporations are believed to be rational entities with the capacity and desire to manage and avoid unnecessary risks to their employees, communities and the general public.

We therefore conclude by arguing that risk and class are inherently interconnected – that we cannot understand the production of risk without interrogating the class relations that generate and perpetuate these risks in their current forms. This means we need to critically question the "increasingly symbiotic" relationship between states and corporations" (Tombs and Whyte 2015), particularly how this relationship allows corporations to take massive risks and commit serious crimes with relative impunity, and the ways in which the state's legal interventions (or lack thereof) normalize the risks that corporations are hardwired to take. We cannot abandon class as an analytical focal point in our interrogation of risk – class cannot be wished away by ignoring it or downplaying its relevance in understanding the risk society. From our perspective, it is only by engaging in questions of *class* risk, as opposed to *risk* class, that we can begin to struggle for different outcomes.

NOTES

1.   For public audiences the accepted formula is H × O (hazard times outrage)! https://www.ncbi.nlm
     .nih.gov/pmc/articles/PMC5076675/
2.   Indeed, the number of job actions in the US has surged as teachers, GM workers and others
     have declared, "Enough is enough!" Support for unions stands at 64.9%, up 16 points from
     2009 and a mere 2% shy of all-time highs (Woodyard 2019). https://www.usatoday.com/story/
     news/education/2019/10/18/gm-strike-uaw-contract-vote-cps-chicago-public-schools-teachers/
     4013610002/
3.   Many, like the USA and Australia, have provincial or state agencies as well as a national agency.
4.   Since Ontario tends to be copied by the other English-speaking provinces, and its regulatory commission is the largest, the primary focus in this chapter will be on the historical development and subsequent battles over government regulation here. Although specifics differ, it is typical of, at the very least, the largest of the regulatory bodies.

REFERENCES

Almond, P. (2013), *Corporate Manslaughter and Regulatory Reform*, London: Palgrave Macmillan.
Alvesalo-Kuusi, A., S. Bittle and L. Lähteenmäki (2017), 'Repositioning the Corporate Criminal: Comparing and Contrasting Corporate Criminal Liability in Canada and Finland', *International Journal of Comparative and Applied Criminal Justice*, 42(2–3): 215–231.
Baillie, J. (2004), 'The Wise Persons' Committee Report: Another Attempt to Revolutionize Canadian Securities Regulation', *Canadian Business Law Journal*, 40: 434–449.
Bakan, J. (2004), *The Corporation: The Pathological Pursuit of Profit and Power*, Toronto, ON: Penguin Canada.
Barry, A., T. Osborne and N. Rose (1996), *Foucault and Political Reason: Liberalism, Neo-Liberalism and Rationalities of Government*, Chicago, IL: The University of Chicago Press.
Beck, U. (1992), *Risk Society: Towards a New Modernity*, London: Sage.
Beck, U. (1999), *World Risk Society*, Malden, MA: Polity.
Beck, U. (2000), 'The Cosmopolitan Perspective: Sociology of the Second Age of Modernity', *British Journal of Sociology*, 51(1): 79–105.
Beck, U. (2007), 'The Cosmopolitan Condition: Why Methodological Nationalism Fails', *Theory, Culture & Society*, 24(7–8): 286–290.
Beck, U. (2010), 'Remapping Social Inequalities in an Age of Climate Change', *Global Networks*, 10(2): 165–181.
Beck, U. (2011), 'We Do Not Live in an Age of Cosmopolitanism but in an Age of Cosmopolitanisation: The "Global Other" is in Our Midst', *Irish Journal of Sociology*, 19(1): 16–34.
Bittle, S. (2012), *Still Dying for a Living: Corporate Criminal Liability After the Westray Mine Disaster*, Vancouver, BC: UBC Press.
Bittle, S. and L. Snider (2006), 'From Manslaughter to Preventable Accident: Shaping Corporate Criminal Liability', *Law and Policy*, 28(4): 470–496.
Bittle, S., L. Snider, S. Tombs and D. Whyte (eds) (2018), *Revisiting Crimes of the Powerful: Marxism, Crime and Deviance*, London: Routledge.
Bittle, S. and L. Stinson (2018), 'Corporate Killing Law Reform: A Spatio-Temporal Fix to a Crisis of Capitalism?', *Capital & Class*, 43(2): 251–270.
Braithwaite, J. and P. Drahos (2000), *Global Business Regulation*, Cambridge, UK: Cambridge University Press.
British Medical Association (1987), *Living with Risk*, Toronto, ON: John Wiley & Sons.
Bullard, R. (1999), 'Dismantling Environmental Racism in the USA', *The International Journal of Justice and Sustainability*, 4(1): 5–19.
Campbell, B. (2018), *The Lac-Mégantic Rail Disaster: Public Betrayal, Justice Denied*, Toronto, ON: Lorimer.
Carson, W.G. (1979), 'The Conventionalization of Early Factory Crime', *International Journal of the Sociology of Law*, 7: 37–60.
Coleman, R., J. Sim, S. Tombs and D. Whyte (eds) (2009), *State Power Crime*, London, UK: Sage Publications.
Condon, M. (1998), *Making Disclosure: Ideas and Interests in Ontario Securities Regulation*, University of Toronto Press.
Curran, D. (2013), 'What is a Critical Theory of the Risk Society? A Reply to Beck', *British Journal of Sociology*, 64(1): 75–80.
Curran, D. (2017), 'Beck's Creative Challenge to Class Analysis: from the Rejection of Class to the Discovery of Risk-Class', *Journal of Risk Research*, 21(1): 29–40.
Douglas, M. (1992), *Risk and Blame: Essays in Cultural Theory*, London: Routledge.
Douglas, M. and A. Wildavsky (1982), *Risk and Culture*, Berkeley, CA: University of California Press.
Emerson, G. (1972), 'Towards an Integrated Disclosure System for Ontario Securities Legislation', *Osgood Hall Law Journal*, 10(1): 1–11.
Financial Post (2011), 'Supreme Court Moves against Ottawa's Single-Regulator Move', *Financial Post*, accessed 20 September 2019 at https://financialpost.com/legal-post/supreme-court-rejects-national-securities-regulator-plan.

Gibson-Graham, J.K., S. Resnick and R. Wolff (eds) (2001), *Re/Presenting Class: Essays in Postmodern Marxism*, Durham, NC: Duke University Press.

Glasbeek, H. (2002), *Wealth by Stealth: Corporate Crime, Corporate Law, and the Perversion of Democracy*, Toronto, ON: Between the Lines.

Glasbeek, H. (2013), 'Missing the Targets – Bill C-45: Reforming the Status Quo to Maintain the Status Quo', *Policy and Practice in Health and Safety*, 11(2): 10–23.

Glasbeek, H. (2017), *Class Privilege: How Law Shelters Shareholders and Coddles Capitalism*. Toronto, ON: Between the Lines.

Gobert, J. (2008). 'The Corporate Manslaughter and Corporate Homicide Act 2007: Thirteen Years in the Making, but Was it Worth the Wait?' *The Modern Law Review*, 71(3): 413–463.

Gray, J. (2013), 'After Nortel Verdict, RCMP Fraud Unit Racks Up Dismal Conviction Record', *Globe and Mail*, accessed 20 September 2019 at https://www.theglobeandmail.com/report-on-business/industry-news/the-law-page/after-nortel-verdict-rcmps-fraud-unit-racks-up-dismal-conviction-record/article7344652/.

Hall, S. (2011), 'The Neo-Liberal Revolution', *Cultural Studies* 25(6): 705–728.

Halpern, P. and P. Puri (2008), 'Reflections on the Recommendations of the Task Force to Modernize Securities Legislation in Canada', *Canadian Business Law Journal*, 46: 199–212.

Harvey, D. (2005), *A Brief History of Neoliberalism*, Oxford: Oxford University Press.

Harvey, D. (2007), 'Neoliberalism as Creative Destruction', *The Annals of the American Academy of Political and Social Science*, 610: 22–44.

Harvey, D. (2010), *The Enigma of Capital and the Crisis of Capitalism*, Oxford: Oxford University Press.

Harvey, D. (2014), *Seventeen Contradictions and the End of Capitalism*, Oxford: Oxford University Press.

Hébert, J., S. Bittle and S. Tombs (2019), 'Obscuring Corporate Violence: Corporate Manslaughter in Action', *The Howard Journal of Crime and Justice*, 58(4): 554–579.

Lebowitz, M. (2010), 'Change the System, Not Its Barriers', *Socialism and Democracy*, 24(3): 46–59.

Liuzzo, G., S. Bently, F. Giacometti, E. Bonfante and A. Serranio (2014), 'The Term Risk: Etymology, Legal Definition and Various Traits', *Italian Journal of Food Safety*, 3(1): 2269. 10.4081/ijfs.2014.2269.

Livesey, S.M. and K. Kearins (2002), 'Transparent and Caring Corporations? A Study of Sustainability Reports by the Body Shop and Royal Dutch/Shell', *Organization & Environment*, 15(3): 233–258.

Mahon R. (1979), 'Regulatory Agencies: Captive Agents or Hegemonic Apparatuses?', *Studies in Political Economy*, 1: 162–200.

Marx, K. (1977), *Capital, Volume 1*, New York: Penguin Books.

Marx, K. (1972), *Capital, Volume 2*, New York: Penguin Books.

McMullan, J. (1992), *Beyond the Limits of the Law: Corporate Crime and Law and Order*, Halifax: Fernwood Publishing.

McNally, D. (2011), *Global Slump: The Economics and Politics of Crisis and Resistance*, Oakland, CA: PM Press.

Michalowski, R. and R. Kramer (1987), 'The Space between Laws: The Problem of Corporate Crime in a Transnational Context', *Social Problems*, 34(1): 34–53.

Noble, C. (1995), 'Regulating Work in a Capitalist Society', in F. Pearce and L. Snider (eds), *Corporate Crime: Contemporary Debates*, Toronto, ON: University of Toronto Press, pp. 268–283.

Paludo, L. (2017), 'Geographies of Race and Ethnicity II: Environmental Racism, Racial Capitalism and State-Sanctioned Violence', *Progress in Human Geography*, 41(4): 524–533.

Pearce, F. and S. Snider (eds) (1995), *Corporate Crime: Contemporary Debates*, Toronto, ON: University of Toronto Press.

Pearce, F. and S. Tombs (1998), *Toxic Capitalism: Corporate Crime and the Chemical Industry*, Toronto, ON: Canadian Scholars' Press.

Resnick, S.A. and R.D. Wolff (1981), 'Classes in Marxian Theory', *Review of Radical Political Economics*, 13(4): 1–18.

Resnick, S.A. and R.D. Wolff (1985), 'Introduction: Solution and Problems', in S.A. Resnick and R.D. Wolff (eds), *Rethinking Marxism: Struggles in Marxist Theory*, New York, NY: Autonomedia Incorporated, pp. 1–9.

Resnick, S.A. and R.D. Wolff (1987), *Knowledge and Class: A Marxian Critique of Political Economy*, Chicago, IL: The University of Chicago Press.

Resnick, S.A. and R.D. Wolff (eds) (2006), *New Departures in Marxian Theory*, London: Routledge.

Resnick, S.A. and R.D. Wolff (2010), 'The Economic Crisis: A Marxian Interpretation', *Rethinking Marxism*, 22: 170–186.

Sandoval, V. (2016), *The Origins of the Word Risk (etymology)*, accessed 20 December 2020 at https://vicentesandoval.wordpress.com/2016/02/23/the-origins-of-the-word-risk-etymology/.

Sayer, A. (2016), 'Moral Economy, Unearned Income, and Legalized Corruption', in D. Whyte and J. Wiegratz (eds), *Neoliberalism and the Moral Economy of Fraud*, London: Routledge, pp. 44–56.

Slapper, G. (2013). 'Justice Is Mocked if an Important Law is Unenforced', *The Journal of Criminal Law*, 77: 91–94.

Slapper, G. and S. Tombs (1999), *Corporate Crime*, Essex, UK: Pearson Education Limited.

Snider, L. (1993), *Bad Business: Corporate Crime in Canada*, Toronto, ON: Nelson Canada.

Snider, L. (2000), 'The Sociology of Corporate Crime: An Obituary (or: Whose Knowledge Claims Have Legs?)', *Theoretical Criminology*, 4(2): 196–206.

Snider, L. (2014), 'Interrogating the Algorithm: Debt, Derivatives and the Social Reconstruction of Stock Market Trading', *Critical Sociology*, 40(5): 689–709.

Snider, L. (2015), *About Canada: Corporate Crime*, Halifax, NS: Fernwood Publishing.

Snider, L. (2018), 'Enabling Exploitation: Law in the Gig Economy', *Critical Criminology*, 26(5): 563–577.

Soederberg, S. (2010), *Corporate Power and Ownership in Contemporary Capitalism: The Politics of Resistance and Domination*, London: Routledge.

Stenning, P., C. Shearing, S. Addario and M. Condon (1990), 'Controlling Interests: Two Conceptions of Order in Regulating a Financial Market', in Martin Friedland (ed.), *Securing Compliance*, Toronto, ON: University of Toronto Press, pp. 88–119.

Tillman, R.H. and M.L. Indergaard (2005), *Pump and Dump: The Rancid Rules of the New Economy*, New Brunswick, NJ: Rutgers University Press.

Tombs, S. (2012), 'State–Corporate Symbiosis in the Production of Crime and Harm', *State Crime*, 1(2): 170–195.

Tombs, S. (2016), *Social Protection after the Crisis: Regulation without Enforcement*, Bristol: Policy Press.

Tombs, S. (2018), 'The UK's Corporate Killing Law: Un/fit for Purpose?' *Criminology & Criminal Justice*, 18(4): 488–507.

Tombs, S. and D. Whyte (2013), 'Transcending the Deregulation Debate? Regulation, Risk and the Enforcement of Health and Safety Law in the UK', *Regulation & Governance*, 7(1): 61–79.

Tombs, S. and D. Whyte (2015), *The Corporation as Criminal: Why Corporations Must Be Abolished*, London: Routledge.

Tucker, E. (1995), 'And Defeat Goes On: An Assessment of Third-Wave Health and Safety Regulation', in F. Pearce and S. Snider (eds), *Corporate Crime: Contemporary Debates*, Toronto, ON: University of Toronto Press, pp. 245–267.

RiskNet (n.d.), accessed 20 September 2019 at https://www.risknet.de/en/knowledge/etymology/

Whyte, D. (1999), 'Learning the Lessons of Piper Alpha?', in E. Coles, D. Smith and S. Tombs (eds), *Risk Management and Society*. London: Springer Nature, pp. 263–281.

Whyte, D. (2003), 'Regulation and Corporate Crime', in J. Muncie and D. Wilson (eds), *Student Handbook of Criminal Justice and Criminology*, London: Cavendish Publishing Limited, pp. 133–152.

Whyte, D. (2014), 'Regimes of Permission and State-Corporate Crime', *State Crime*, 3(2): 237–246.

Whyte, D. (2018), 'The Autonomous Corporation: The Acceptable Mask of Capitalism', *King's Law Journal*, 29(1): 88–110.

Wise Persons' Committee to Review the Structure of Securities Regulation in Canada (2003), *It's Time: Report of the Committee to Review the Structure of Securities Regulation in Canada*, Ottawa, ON: Department of Finance.

Woodyard, C. (2019), 'Are Unions Back? GM, Chicago Teachers Strike Show How Unions Can Start Winning Again', *USA Today*, accessed 20 December 2020, at https://www.usatoday.com/story/news/education/2019/10/18/gm-strike-uaw-contract-vote-cps-chicago-public-schools-teachers/4013610002/.

Younglai, R. (2014), 'Global Bourses Challenge TSX's Junior Mining Supremacy', *Globe and Mail*, accessed 20 September 2019 at https://www.theglobeandmail.com/report-on-business/industry-news/energy-and-resources/global-bourses-challenge-tsxs-junior-mining-supremacy/article17389335/.

Zinn, J. (2010), 'Risk as Discourse: Interdisciplinary Perspectives', *Critical Approaches to Discourse Analysis across Disciplines*, 4(2): 106–124.

Zinn, J. and P. Taylor-Gooby (2006), 'Introduction: *Learning about Risk*', *Forum: Qualitative Social Research*, 7(1): 1–6.

10. Risk and trust: ethnomethodological orientations to risk theorizing

Patrick G. Watson

INTRODUCTION

With few exceptions, ethnomethodologists have not actively engaged the risk theorizing of Beck (1995) or Giddens (1991) explicitly, although there has been a common interest in the linkage between *risk* and *trust* represented in the risk theorists' models (i.e. Lidskog & Sundqvist, 2012; Luhmann, 1979). The renewed interest among ethnomethodologists in Garfinkel's (1963) "trust" paper presents an interesting angle from which to look at notions of *risk*, and the mitigation of *risk* through situated reasoning in interaction. The ethnomethodological critique of risk theory has noted a failure of theory to sufficiently explain empirically grounded derivations from the risk thesis (i.e. Dingwall, 1999), or a lack of suitable attention to how *risk* is conceived and used according to actors (members) in practice (Horlick-Jones, 2005). But the (renewed) connection between *risk* and *trust* does provide some occasion for cross-pollination of ideas and is worthy of consideration.

Of particular interest to readers of this volume, Turowetz and Rawls (2021) have recently argued a tightly coupled connection between *trust* and inequality. Using the trajectory of Garfinkel's PhD dissertation through the various stages of committee review, from initial proposal to acceptance, they argue that Garfinkel's fundamental and guiding concern had been matters of racial or ethnic inequality, and how equality is contingent on *trust* for the achievement of self in social interaction (*ibid.*, p. 5). Indeed, Rawls has actively pursued a programme of reframing Garfinkel's studies as primarily attending to the production of inequality through interaction (2000, 2008; Rawls and David, 2005; Rawls and Duck, 2017). This chapter takes up this discussion and analyzes the relationship between *risks*, variously conceived, *trust* and *inequality* with reference to three other ethnomethodological studies of self-evidently *risky* situations – rock climbing and changing multi-piece truck wheels.

My objectives here are restrained, as there are a great number of pitfalls around the notions of *risk* and *trust*. These are astoundingly difficult phenomena to find "in the wild", and in scenarios that are, *prima facie*, *risky*, or *trust*-imbued, it is not necessarily common to see talk of *risks* or *trust*. These are often assumed by participants to these settings, and the discourse may migrate from issues of *risk* to issues of safety or otherwise, as we will see below. There is also the matter of the local orientation to *risk* as distinct from *risk* in the abstract; that is, what is a *risky* activity for some can and will be, dare I say, mundane for others. One of the great promises of the risk theory agenda was a close examination of the professional practices in assessing *risk* in the abstract – i.e. actuarial and public safety professions that go about calculating *risks* across an abstract population – a proposal that, as Horlick-Jones (2005) points out, sadly did not come to fruition. Nevertheless, existing studies in ethnomethodology can be used to demonstrate the relevance of these notions, and I will conclude this chapter by problematizing some assumptions in the "deficit model" of *trust* in public policy making introduced by

Collins and Evans (2017; Collins 2014), contrasting that with an ethnomethodological notion of *risk* and *trust* to a recent public policy discussion on *risk*, *trust* and vaccine hesitancy.

THE ETHNOMETHODOLOGICAL CRITIQUE OF RISK THEORY

Starting in the 1990s, *risk* rose to remarkable prominence in sociological theorizing, as Beck (1995) and Giddens (1991) along with Coleman (1990), Lash (i.e. Lash, Szerszynki, & Wynne, 1996), and Ericson and Haggerty (1997) engaged in conceptual studies of orientations to *risk* as foundational to social and political action. There were and are some profoundly interesting aspects to the risk theory agenda for ethnomethodologists, not the least of which is how *risks* are mobilized in interaction to achieve some political end. However, for the most part, ethnomethodologists remained removed from discussions of *risk* on the grounds that accompanying studies to risk theorizing remained largely conceptual and did not explicitly engage with the use of *risk* as a member's phenomenon (with some notable exceptions, i.e. Vaughan 1996; Wynne 1996). A great deal of the risk-theorists' work centred on the distribution of *risk* – that due to the progress of technology and the expanded adoption of *risky* technologies (i.e. nuclear power) the wealthy would no longer be insulated from *risk* – and while there is acknowledgment by the risk-theorists that a good deal of the conceptualization of *risks* is tied to contentious matters of occupation and expertise, there is little focus on the situated work of analyzing the *production* of these risk-figures (a contrast to the "audit cultures" theorizing in anthropology that emerged contemporaneously, i.e. Power, 1997; Strathern, 2000).[1]

The ethnomethodological case against risk-theory was presented most vociferously by Dingwall (1999), who, aside from taking exception to the ethnocentrism of Beck's treatise, notes that the critical tradition in German sociology, through the impact of Jurgen Habermas and the Frankfurt School, has led to a tendency to shy from empirical evidence for theoretical claims (see p. 476). Dingwall's objection to Beck's assertion that *risk* distribution would replace income distribution as a core issue for sociological theorizing has borne out in hindsight, as global income disparities in the 21st century have grown to astronomical levels (Lindert & Williamson, 2012). Further, the extreme measures the billionaire class are taking to avoid the exact *risks* Beck and Giddens mention (global climate change, radioactive fallout), such as underground bunkers[2] or colonizing outer space,[3] put the predictions of the risk theorists in doubt. Ultimately, Dingwall identifies that Beck (alongside other risk theorists) uses a broadly constructionist paradigm when conceptualizing *risk* as a core feature of late capitalist social organization, but does not subject his (Beck's) own assumptions about notions of scarcity and poverty to a similar treatment (p. 480; see also Curran, 2013; Mythen, 2005; Scott, 2002). As such, Beck's thesis, that late stage capitalism has/will resolve the issue of scarcity, not only fails in empirical hindsight (as Dingwall predicted) but also falls prey to a failure to critically interrogate how scarcity is commonly conceived in whatever cultures were meant to be included in the risk theorists' models.

Horlick-Jones (2005) made a valiant effort to reproach risk theory from an ethnomethodological perspective, focusing on the conduct of *risk* analysis as a situated and organizationally relevant phenomenon – risk assessment as work. He instructs readers to attend to "the everyday use of resources to accomplish organizational tasks in efficient ways, and with the creation of an audit trail for decision-making which provides a cover against possible blame or liability should something go wrong" (*ibid.*, p. 295). The ethnomethodological reframing or *risk* involves attending to how *risk* is used as a tool in the accomplishment of administrative or practical action. One may wonder, if the sociological community took more notice of Dingwall and Horlick-Jones, might we not have, by this point, acquired a deep trove of empirical ethnographic studies of the actuarial practices that undergird risk assessment such that we could better aid in resolving the questions of expertise that pervade the contemporary political and social discourse?

Studies of Risky Activities from Ethnomethodologists

Despite the scepticism of risk-theory, ethnomethodologists do produce studies of what we might call inherently *risky* situations, although these studies expend almost no effort conceptualizing *risk* independently of the actor's own vernacular uses of the term. For example, Baccus's (1986) study of the profoundly *risky* activity of installing multi-piece truck wheels (*risky* on the grounds that the wheel installation had a significant failure rate that would lead high-pressure tires to explode, potentially killing or maiming installers) only mentions the word "risk" six times across thirty-eight pages. Baccus's incorporation or *risk* in her description of regulatory efforts to prevent injury and/or death from exploding wheels examined the exact types of practices Horlick-Jones would advocate nearly twenty years later, summarizing the actuarial practices that the United States Insurance Institute for Highway Safety (IIHS), the National Highway Traffic Safety Administration (NHTSA), and other regulators or industry bodies who sought to counter the claims of the IIHS (i.e. representatives from auto manufacturers) employed to articulate the population of individuals at *risk* and the probability of injury occurring. Of interest to readers of this volume, the NHTSA's decision-making around the acceptability of *risk* in multi-piece truck wheels is (or was) partially based on the type of people exposed to *risk*. The NHTSA prioritized *risks* to "the driving public" placing lesser importance on mechanics and technicians working on the wheels (*ibid.*, p. 34). It is important to note here that, while this study preceded the works of Beck or Giddens and the risk-theorists, the actuarial/expert articulation of *risk* guided the decision-making of officials on the acceptability of a *risk*, and far from *risk* being distributed equally across a population, presumably lower-wage, lower-status shop mechanics were explicitly deemed to be less worthy of *risk* mitigation than the broader public. For the discussion of this chapter, the programme the IIHS and NHTSA agreed upon to mitigate *risk* for these workers was an instructional diagram/poster illustrating the proper steps for handling multi-piece truck wheels to be displayed in the shops where this work was being done. Rather than regulating the wheels completely out of existence (something they have since done) the NHTSA effectively *trusted* employers to properly inform and train their employees about the *risk* and safe handling of the wheels. Here we see how the constitutive practice of "safely [i.e. injury free] handling of multi-piece truck wheels" was premised on a *trust* relationship between regulators and employers to mitigate potential *risks* to lower-status employees.

Along another line, both Jenkings (2013) and Smith (2020) look at the inherently *risky* activity of rock-climbing, Jenkings from a recreational perspective and Smith in the service of mountain rescue training exercises. Again, explicit references to *risk* are limited; Jenkings introduces the subject noting that part of the attraction to recreational rock-climbing is the *risk* associated with the activity, although no further articulation about the prevalence of *risk* (i.e. some actuarially derived figures on the prevalence of injury or harm) is presented. The ethnographic description instead attends to the means by which climbers, either to themselves or with partners, go about preparing to undertake what they know to be a *risky* activity without explicitly articulating such *risks*. Jenkings's description does show the reader the preparation activities, again as either an individual exercise by the climber of "psyching themself up" or a collaborative exercise between partners. Although Jenkings does not make explicit reference to *trust* or *inequality*, the reader may conclude that such glosses are relevant to his descriptions of the activities. Climbers go to some lengths to know and understand each other's capabilities and demeanours before any given climb in efforts to avoid harm (i.e. *risk* avoidance), and it is hard to imagine how an activity like rock-climbing in pairs could be constituted without a *trust* between partners. The constitution of *equality* within a setting such as this would, presumably, not be based on identical climbing ability, but rather a familiarity and openness about ability and demeanour on any given day/climb, such that *trust* that mitigates *risk* is achieved through an equal sharing of capacities on the day.

Smith's analysis is also tangential to risk theorizing, although an interesting element of his discussion revolves around how a potentially unsafe alignment of rescue equipment represented in a photograph of a mountain rescue rope-and-carabiner configuration was addressed by senior leaders of the mountain rescue team not present at the training exercise itself. Photos shared through a private Facebook group were flagged by those senior team members, who asked trainee members not to post the pictures publicly. Upon consultation, Smith (as a participant himself in the team) was informed that the picture might have depicted an unsafe crossing between carabiners. Again, there is limited reference to *risk* or *trust* in the text, although both seem a reasonable (Garfinkel & Sacks, 1970; Sacks, 1992) *gloss* for several of the practices and/or concerns in the scene – *risk* of rig failure through poor alignment, *trust* (or lack thereof) in social media to accurately represent the scene, *trust* between trainers and trainees on proper procedure, etc.). This issue of *glosses* is one to which I will refer later, as Smith's attention to situated practices of seeing and interpreting *risk* and *trust* points us toward a matter that, from my perspective, contemporary efforts to embrace Garfinkel's *trust* paper are not adequately addressing.

What I want to stress from the above is, despite some rather obvious errors in Beck's risk theorizing, errors that have become even more evident with the benefit of nearly thirty years of hindsight, there are still lessons for interactionally inclined sociologists to take from the risk theory agenda. The ethnomethodological *incommensurable, asymmetrically alternate* (Garfinkel & Weider, 1992) is to attend to the grammatical practices of conceptualizing, accounting for, and working through *risk* as a situated phenomenon. As such, risk theory can stand as a *sensitizing concept* (Charmaz, 2003) that draws our attention to some social phenomenon and yet remains held in abeyance waiting further in-depth consideration. We might attend to the importance of *risk* with a nod to Beck, Giddens, Lash, et al., but seeing how *risk* is formulated through a course of work (i.e. Baccus, 1986; Horlick-Jones, 2005; Vaughan, 1996) or how *risks* are produced or mitigated through *trust* conditions (i.e. Jenkings 2013; Smith 2020) gives us greater understanding of the position of *risk* in social life. The significance of *trust* to *risk* is important for these relationships, and it is to the matter of *trust* we now turn.

RISK AND *TRUST* AS CONSTITUTIVE TO MEANINGFUL INTERACTION

Giddens, Beck, Lash, Luhmann (1979), and Coleman (1990) each draw upon the notion of *trust* as a candidate means for *risk* mitigation. However, as Rod Watson (2009) notes, *trust* is never given a fully situated exegesis, either conceptually or idiosyncratically to lived circumstances of individuals. For Watson, formal analytic approaches undertaken by the above trust theorists have,

> signally failed to capture that first-order phenomenon, and particularly its contextual nature .... Indeed, their approach to the issue of trust shows the ways in which the very design features of these research technologies lead them to change the subject, to present trust in terms of something else – trust as choice, as attitude, as risk, as a game, and so on. (*ibid.*, p. 477)

This stands in marked contrast to Garfinkel's handling of *trust* through the "trust paper" (1963) and chapter two of *Studies in Ethnomethodology* (1967). Rather than treating *trust* as attitudinal or functional, Garfinkel proposes it is *constitutive* of social interaction. Watson also brings our attention to the fact that *trust* as a first-order phenomenon has proved elusive, which perhaps gives some explanation for why the risk theorists have found it so difficult to conceptualize (Garfinkel, 1963, pp. 477–478). What Watson means is people rarely articulate that they are (inter)acting on the basis of *trust*, announcing, "I will climb this rock face because I *trust* my belaying partner!" or "I fully *trust* this procedure for changing a truck tire!" *Trust* is presumed to be present, or is sociologically theorized to be present, but remains an object of minds unavailable to empirical scrutiny (i.e. how much *trust* must one have in a partner or a procedure before undertaking some *risky* task?). This was anticipated by Garfinkel, who saw the now-infamous "breaching experiments" (which arguably remain the least understood exercise in sociologically inquiry's history, and which he would later rename "tutorial problems" (2002) as an opportunity to disrupt social norms as a means of interrogating the constitutive practices necessary for *trusting* social interaction.

The breaching experiments served as an opportunity to correct what Garfinkel perceived as an inadequacy with Parsons' theory of action (1937), wherein Parsons presumed that a shared common culture, incorporated into the superego, resulted in an absence on the part of actors (members) to perform the interpretative and judgmental work to manage their navigation of the social structural world. For Parsons, the social structure is used to produce what Garfinkel described as a "cultural dope" who would react mechanically to any abutment with societal restraints – a rule governed or rule following model of individual activity. The tutorial problems were a means of pulling back the curtain on the work individuals were doing to maintain the social structure, that social structure was determinative of, but also determined by, a mutual commitment by actors to reconcile the stable features of the society with any discrepancies between expected and actual events. That members are *rule using* in order to resolve any such discrepancies is an indication of the efficacy of tutorial problems to illustrate that mutual commitment to the social structure by members in their ongoing production of social order (*ibid.*, pp. 187–189).

Games, and the misplay thereof, were a useful pedagogic technique for Garfinkel's directions to his students. In the "trust paper", he sets out his instructions for understanding games as bounded occasions that give purchase on disrupting expectancies such that the social ordering of *trust* would reveal itself:

> In our terms, a game is defined by listing its basic rules to which constitutive expectancies are attached. In addition to basic rules, there are at least three other features which are necessary to describe the game as a normative order of discipline: (a) an "et cetera" provision, (b) an enumerated set of rules of *preferred* play, and (c) an enumerated set of "game-finished" conditions. Beyond these, there are two further features which describe a game as people actually play it: (a) the "validity" of this discipline, i.e., the likelihood that persons will act in motivated compliance with the discipline, and (b) the non-game conditions which, whatsoever they consist of, determine the likelihood of motivated compliance. (*Ibid.*, p. 191)

Thus, games inhabit a territory of possibilities that furnish both the explicit rules of play or game-furnished conditions for appropriate conduct constitutive to play. The breaches to this territory of possibilities were quite simple at first: playing tic-tac-toe and putting pieces between squares while insisting this was a legitimate play, or removing an opponent's pieces, or swapping about one's own pieces, on a chess board without explanation. Games function such that the shared mutual commitment to some structural elements (the rules of games) are enacted through the play, and the meaning of any given game action gains its sense in reflection of those structural elements. When an unexpected novel move was made, Garfinkel and his students found ways in which players attempted to resolve the indeterminacy of the action in light of the game ("Don't be sloppy. Put your mark in the square" or "What game are you playing?" as examples, *ibid.*, p. 197) such that the contingent mutuality to achieving the game's play was leveraged as a corrective for the deviant player. The player who was the subject of the experiment *trusted* that both they and the experimenter–player were mutually committed to the same action. Garfinkel instructed 67 of his undergraduate students to replicate this procedure, and they gathered 253 instances of play, which were statistically analyzed according to a coding procedure presented on pages 201–205, leading to the finding that,

> a behavior that was at variance with the constitutive order of the game immediately motivated attempts to normalize the discrepancy ... under the condition of a breach of legal play the discrepant event seemed to best produce a senseless situation if the player attempted to normalize the discrepancy while attempting to retain the constitutive order without alteration ... [results] were filled *with expressions of distrust*. (*Ibid.*, p. 206, italics added)

Garfinkel has a reputation for being exceedingly careful with his wording, which leads me to believe there is profound significance to his use of "expressions of distrust" emphasized above. I take it we should not assume that experimented-upon players came out and annunciated their *distrust*, but rather some correlation was drawn between what was said or done in play and the conclusion that this conveyed *distrust*. The *senselessness* Garfinkel identified indicated that, for all intents and purposes, game play was no longer possible until the errant move was resolved. The game was halted until such time as sense could be restored. This is important to note given some of what I will propose below. Leaving this note aside for the time being, let us consider how this is important to discussions of *risk* and *inequality*.

Garfinkel's ambitions extended beyond games. It was his intention to show how *trust* underwrites the constitutive order of any number of events in everyday life. The advantage of games was their relatively simple demonstrations of order that were constituted through the interaction and unexpected events thereto. Extending this into everyday life involved creating scenarios for his students where their actions would produce the same conditions of *senselessness* experienced in the order of games. There were numerous breaching experiments/tutorial problems, including: instructing students continually asking an interlocutor for further clarification on statements; returning to a parent's home for a holiday and treating it as if it were a bed-and-breakfast (i.e. asking permission to go into the fridge or kitchen, etc.); and from his dissertation research, sharing an "interview" of a boorish medical school applicant and informing research subjects, who were also prospective medical school applicants, that this "interviewee" was a strong candidate to see how they resolved the boorish behaviour with the "medical school admissions officer" (i.e. the experimenter's) assessment of "good conduct". And indeed, there were *risks* involved in these experiments! Several of Garfinkel's students reported being verbally berated or even threatened with harm by the subjects of their experiments after the senselessness of the breaches set in. As the *trust* constitutive to collaborative action diminished, the reaction from interlocutors could be quite severe.

A Contemporary Revisiting of Garfinkel's "Trust" Paper

Following the 1963 paper, Garfinkel did not return to *trust* in his published works. Elements of the *trust* paper show up in chapters two and three of *Studies*, but not framed around matters of constitutive expectancies and their relationship to *trust*. Rather Garfinkel changes his focus to matters of commonsense reasoning through the breaching experiments. In a lecture delivered in 1992–1993, Garfinkel said he was reluctant to publish anything related to the trust paper in *Studies* and viewed that work as not related to ethnomethodology. Erving Goffman pressured Garfinkel to include the chapter, insisting it was the "high-water mark" of his scholarship, but Garfinkel was able to resist (Eisenmann & Lynch, 2021, pp. 4–6; Garfinkel, 2021).

This did not stop ethnomethodologists from returning to the "trust" paper in the mid-to-late 2000s, including contributions by Rawls and David (2005), Rawls (2008), Rod Watson (2009), and Gonzalez-Martinez and Mlynar (2019). Of particular interest to readers of this volume, Duck (2017) and Turowetz and Rawls (2021) adapt Garfinkel's trust argument to address issues of inequality. Duck synthesizes Garfinkel's trust paper with Du Bois' (1903) *double consciousness* to provide new insights into the racial and identity dynamics at work in interactions between the citizens of an American, predominately Black, economically depressed neighbourhood and the law enforcement personnel who patrol the area. Duck introduces the notion of *submissive civility* to denote an over-subscription to, or over-demonstration of, social norms in order to indicate deference to authorities. He argues that this in turn degrades *trust*, particularly in combination with other breaches of constitutive expectancies, i.e. when police use lethal force against citizens and face no repercussions. Duck uses a vignette from his fieldwork to illustrate this. When a young Black man is shot in the back by police, but no action is taken by the police against the offending officer despite a *prima facie* breach of a citizen's Fourth Amendment rights, Duck's respondent articulates how the lack of public accountability for the killing creates and/or perpetuates conditions where background expectancies go unfulfilled (i.e. justice and protection of the individual from abuses by the State). Duck's accompanying notion of *nonrecognition* is likely instructive here: by failing to recognize basic elements of a victim's humanity and identity *as a citizen with rights to freedom of the person*, Duck argues the conditions for *trust* are lost and this creates *risks* to the perceived legitimacy of State authority (see Rawls & Duck, 2017 for a similar discussion of the experience of high-status Black men in non-violent scenarios).

Turowetz and Rawls (2021) argue that Garfinkel was focused on issues of inequality throughout at least the first twenty years his career, from the time he started his PhD studies in 1939 until he published the trust paper. At this time, Garfinkel believed that interactional problems were ascribable to a lack of *trust* between parties due to status differences. Inequality creates conditions for *mistrust* as individuals' identities are either not fully embraced or understood through interaction, and marginalized, status-based "interaction orders" (a concept of Goffman's (1983) that Rawls has often attempted to incorporate into ethnomethodological research (i.e. 1987, 2000) prevent fair and open exchange between interactants. They support their argument by using Garfinkel's PhD research proposals as evidence, noting that he progressed from initially proposing to look explicitly at the experience of Jewish students attending medical school, and ultimately being told to study the experiences of all medical students. This, for Turowetz and Rawls, stood as a formative matter for Garfinkel, who more-or-less covertly included sections into the final thesis that did examine the experience of Jews as distinct from non-marginalized groups. From their analysis of Garfinkel's early writings, they assert that the trust paper was largely oriented on matters of,

> how outsiders could learn a group's rules well enough to claim membership despite not "really" being a member and thereby sustain the appearance of compliance with Trust Conditions: an obvious extension of his own experience. [Garfinkel] wanted to know how marginal identities could sustain the sense that they share the same constitutive expectancies, commitments and object-orientations as other participants, when they are forced to "guess" what the rules are. (Turowetz and Rawls, 2021, p. 10)

There are some issues that require resolution from Turowetz and Rawls' initial efforts to link the trust paper to issues of inequality. First, they deliberately do not provide any explanation of what *inequality* comprises. Importantly for ethnomethodologists, inequality would fundamentally be a member's phenomenon. While political and sociological indexes exist to formally define unequal relations on, say, economic terms (i.e. the Gini coefficient) or access to education (i.e. UNESCO-quality learning indicators), inequality as experienced by individuals in interaction is decided by parties to those interactions (members of a (sub-)culture). This leads to a situated and locally accountable formulation of inequality that reflects an individual's interpretation of unequal conditions based on race, class, gender, or whatever other axes, rather than a sociologically affirmed and formalized status. An analyst could not independently attest to some interaction being imbued with interactional inequalities and resultant *mistrust* based on the identities of those involved alone. Instead, there would need to be some locally organized vernacular of inequality that is made available to both the interactants and observers. Turowetz and Rawls repeatedly indicate that these features are "hidden and taken for granted" or "tacit", which begs the question how these hidden features become observable to analysts. Their answer is that Garfinkel's position, as a marginalized person himself, made him acutely attentive to such concerns in a way that members of a dominant status could not be. They state,

> Critics like to say that equality cannot be a prerequistite for using constitutive practices because there is a great deal of inequality and yet "things work just fine". But this entirely misses the point. Garfinkel demonstrates that *things are not working fine at all*. They only appear to be working if we either (1) do not interact across groups (excluding minorities from majority interactions), which is all too common, or (2) deny the validity of the minority viewpoint when interaction across groups does occur. In other words, the claim that things are working fine in spite of inequality is itself a racist claim that is only supportable from a majority perspective, which denies the legitimacy of the minority experience. (Turowetz and Rawls, 2021, p. 6)

Readers will note similarities with standpoint epistemology (i.e. Smith, 1987, 1990), where membership of a certain group or status gives unique perspective of social circumstance. Garfinkel's notion of *unique adequacy* (2002) would play an important role here; not only does the marginalized individual gain unique adequacy[4] of the dominant group's constitutive order, which they replicate although they are not a part of it, but the sociological analyst would, at least potentially, use studies to develop a marginalized individual's perspective on what is or is not unequal in the interaction. Thus, familiarity with expressions of inequality members of marginalized groups experience make an alternate interaction order apparent, one that is largely governed by expressions of inequality that escape members of the dominant group (i.e. having one's dissertation subject matter changed in a manner that would mask racial/ethnic *inequalities* for the sake of "equally" representing some greater sum of individuals).

Following this procedure seems to set up conditions for a synthesis of Goffmanian role descriptions and performance (1956) with a close attention to racial identity politics in congruence with some versions of critical race theories (i.e. Kerrison, Cobbina, & Bender, 2018). Nonrecognition of identity produces an *untrusting* circumstance by either the marginalized or dominant party to an interaction (compensatory by the marginalized individual, exclusionary by the dominant). The connection becomes even more apparent in Rawls' co-authored work with Duck (2020). There may be some cause to question the degree to which studies of this form can correspond to the tenets of ethnomethodology – for example, ethnomethodologists would generally bristle at the claim that these interaction processes are "hidden" or "tacit" on the grounds doing so privileges an analyst's account of events over a member's. Garfinkel's concerns about the "trust" paper being formally analytic as opposed to ethnomethodological rear their head in that regard. What we might agree upon is that, at the very least, ethnomethodological sensibilities are useful for forcing an analyst to more closely attend to their own underlying presumptions about social life, and here it seems that there is significant overlap between the concerns of critical race theories and ethnomethodology, both of which are interested in how *seen but unnoticed* social structural features both produce and are produced by social interaction. The biggest problem, following Garfinkel, is finding real-world scenarios where such breaches make such structures evident for sociological analysis.

From here, it is worth reconsidering some elements of *trust* and *risk* in contemporary discussions in the sociology of expertise, namely the programme of "elective modernism" advocated by Harry Collins and Robert Evans (2017). What I find so compelling in the work of Duck, Rawls, and Turowetz is the maleability of their discussion of inequality for inequalities not explicitly tied to race but that nevertheless will have impacts on racialized peoples. This draws into question some of the assertions made by Collins and Evans in their advocacy for more "scientific" reasoning into public policy making. Collins and Evans write with reference to some astoundingly acute *risks* facing the entire human species – risks that have certainly been made more salient through the tragedy of the global COVID-19 pandemic or the ever-increasing number of weather catastrophes explicitly linked to global climate change. Where Collins and Evans differ from an ethnomethodological orientation would be the attention they are willing to grant those who refuse to *trust* the pronoucements of scientists demanding public-policy changes to address these *risks*.

RISK, TRUST, AND INEQUALITY, *ETHNOMETHODOLOGICALLY*

I would like to propose here that ethnomethodological inquiries in *trust* relationships are a tool that compliments other approaches to the confluence of *risk* and inequality. Ethnomethodology cannot replace, for example, critical theories more engaged in analyses of power distribution and the effects of authority on marginalized classes (although ethnomethodologists would take great interest in the conduct and reasoning exhibited in those analyses as a field site unto themselves). What ethnomethodology can add is an analysis of members' own accounts of risk-calculating activities, following in the vein of both Horlick-Jones and Baccus. That is, ethnomethodologists would take a distinct ethnographic interest in how members themselves evaluate *risk* and account for reasoned decisions in *risk*-imbued circumstances.

This deviates from the deficit model Collins and Evans have been arguing for nearly twenty years (2002, 2009, 2017; Collins, 2014). Space precludes a thorough discussion of their contributions, or the critiques thereof (see Coopmans & Button, 2014; Jasanoff, 2003; Wynne, 2003), and instead I reserve comment to the programme of "elective modernism" proposed in their 2017 treatise *Why Democracies Need Science* (WDNS). In the book, Collins and Evans note a lack of *trust* in the appointed experts that advise government officials. They argue that the process of expert appointments has become too politicized and as such expert advice is tainted for a sceptical public. Their answer to the deficit model is specially appointed counsels of natural science experts who also "properly understand the social analysis of science" – they call these "owls" (p. 78) – to advise governments, a distinct group from current science advisors employed by government. Collins and Evans are painfully cognizant that they may be accused of slipping from democracy into technocracy, although to my eye, their solution to this problem is to appoint more technocrats, just ones who are better at communicating the apparent "social analysis of science" (see pp. 70–78).

Collins and Evans do point to a problem that is prevalent in sociological analyses of the intersection between science and politics – why are politicians so reluctant to heed the warnings and impending *risks* their science advisors keep enunciating? – and these matters, and their disproportionate impact on the most marginalized communities in our societies, are becoming increasingly evident (against the predictions of Giddens (1991) and Beck (1995)). However, they studiously avoid close studies of sceptical communities, leaning heavily on caricatures of science denialism through their many writings on the subject. This leads them to the conclusion that a solution lies in creating a more "publicly accountable" means of appointing government science advisors. For example, they assert:

> The Owls would, essentially, do the job of the Chief Scientific Advisor, advising on the substance and degree of consensus about some technical issue. But they would be a statutory committee appointed in a politically neutral way with full scrutiny of the appoint procedure – and their reports and conclusions would need to be a matter of public record. (*Ibid.*, p. 91)

Garfinkel instructed his students that, in real life, unlike games, "there are no time-outs" (Maynard, 1991, p. 279), which I have always interpreted as meaning there is nothing that can be absolved of the claim of "politics" – that, adapted to something like Latour's famous idiom that "science is politics by other means" (1988, 2007), there can be no place from which we escape the consequences of our actions, no place from which we operate as purely disinterested and "unpolitical beings" as Collins and Evans propose. Collins and Evans provide no example of how "politics" can be removed from the appointment process other than deploying facile buzzwords like "scrutiny" and "transparency", and there is no suggestion of how those whose scrutiny is appreciated are appointed, or who it is that determines the relevant information to be included in the public record the owls are to create. If, as I assert, there is nothing in this social world that can be absolved of "politics" because there is no time out from scarcity and decision-making, the very phenomena that comprise "politics", and make all of our decisions – appropriately wearing a face mask during a global pandemic, choosing an electric over petroleum-powered vehicle, replacing appliances with high-efficiency alternates, etc. – fall subject to "political" scrutiny.

Collins and Evans overplay the issue of knowledge and defer on more nefarious issues of *trust*: if people, maybe especially policy makers, were merely better informed about their *risks*, they would act differently. However, the global COVID-19 pandemic, and especially its reception among certain communities thought to be sceptical of vaccines, has highlighted that problems of knowledge, while existent, are secondary to problems of *trust*. One highly publicized example was the case of indigenous communities in Canada who were anticipated to be vaccine hesitant, not on the grounds of any lack of knowledge, but rather because of a long-standing history of medical malpractice, unauthorized experimentation, and other forms of abuse of Indigenous peoples by medical practitioners (Griffith, Marani, & Monkman, 2021; Mosby & Swidrovich, 2021). In terms of knowledge bases for making decisions around vaccine hesitancy, Collins and Evans produce little by way of guidance for how to overcome two conflicting knowledge-domains – the lived experience of Indigenous peoples versus the science community's insistence that, this time, they are getting it right. Thankfully, the fears of vaccine scepticism among Canada's Indigenous peoples have not come to fruition, and further, claims of scepticism among Indigenous people are perhaps better understood as lazy media tropes blown well out of proportion (Coburn, 2021). This adds to the complications of legitimate knowledge claims and overlapping "political" concerns that may be made of any given technical policy area; Collins and Evans overplay the significance of employing Owls to navigate the science of policy decisions for the citizenry or public officials, when the Owls are drawn from ostensibly the same group that was responsible for such abuses, or who erroneously (at least in Coburn's estimation) even produced a concern for the Indigenous' populations willingness to accept COVID-19 vaccines.

This speaks to the matter of establishing knowledge claims in the first instance. Perhaps it is unfair to insert Collins and Evans into an active and rapidly evolving scientific and political debate, although the case does illustrate the complications of simply replacing one set of experts with another and presuming this resolves the matter of *trust*. Instead, what we can learn from ethnomethodology, and in particular the contemporary revisiting of Garfinkel's "trust" paper, is that the constitution of *mistrust* can be put at the feet of a failure to engage marginalized groups on their own terms. While Griffith et al. (2021) and Mosby and Swidrovich (2021) are presumably operating in good faith on a matter of urgent public concern, Coburn's (2021) assertions (supported by survey data from Health Canada as well as his own research experience) draw their assumptions into question, indeed mark them as based on a set of prejudiced stereotypes from a bygone era.

What we should draw from this is the very nature of the scientific task when it comes to policy formation eludes expertise: public policy is not predicting and communicating the stable features of a scientifically theorized world, but rather the inherently stochastic and unpredictable responses of (groups of) individuals to dense, rapidly changing, and complex information and the associated perceived *risks*. Science communication may be an asset in this regard, but it is not a vehicle of *trust* unto itself. Earning that *trust*, at least according to Turowetz and Rawls, relies on understanding the perception of *risks* according to members, and when marginalization and difference are at play, the *trust* relationship can be further complicated. Absent mutual intelligibility of the circumstances leading to the *mistrust*, the advice of experts cannot be expected to resolve with individual experience.

CONCLUSION: *RISK* AND *TRUST* IN ETHNOMETHODOLOGICAL AND SOCIOLOGICAL INQUIRY

This chapter discussed the ethnomethodological response to risk theory and briefly introduced some incommensurate, asymmetrical ethnomethodological alternates. It then built on the connection between *risk* and *trust* identified by Luhmann, Giddens, and others using a recent revisiting of Garfinkel's trust paper by ethnomethodologists. Particular attention was granted to Turowetz and Rawls' discussion of the connection between *trust* and inequality. This discussion was leveraged to analyze the conditions of *mistrust* exhibited through a recent speculation and response on vaccine hesitancy in a marginalized population, Canada's Indigenous peoples. The example confronted an assumption presented in the "deficit model" proposed by Collins and Evans (2017), in that their model presumes that replacing one expert for another, and providing greater "transparency" and "accountability" in a "political neutral" process would resolve discrepancies of *trust* or *mistrust* between experts and the citizenry. Leveraging the thesis of Turowetz and Rawls, I suggest that a more productive approach would involve attending to the nature of the apparent *mistrust* (or lack thereof) itself as experienced by the marginalized community, instead of trying to convince the marginalized that the new slate of experts resolves all the objections.

NOTES

1.   There is a more contemporary literature falling under the rubric of Foucault's theory of *governmentality*, stemming from Francois Ewald's ethnography of insurance (1991), and taken up by Dean (2010, ch. 9), and applied to a broader "ethnographic turn" (Brady 2014) in neo-Foucauldian studies that intersects with risk-theorizing. The ethnomethodological critique of these ethnographies, were one to be produced, would likely note that the imposition of the "neoliberal frame" dominant in the neo-Foucauldian is an analyst's import that has little by way of situated manifestations. Nevertheless, there are lessons to be taken from this literature on the production of *risk* as a situated practice, regardless of the governmentality theorizing that may accompany them.
2.   https://www.forbes.com/sites/jimdobson/2020/03/27/billionaire-bunker-owners-are-preparing-for -the-ultimate-underground-escape/?sh=a7f7bcf4e12a
3.   https://www.businessinsider.com/jeff-bezos-reveals-blue-origin-future-space-plans-2019-5
4.   Garfinkel defines unique adequacy as such: "In its weak use, the unique adequacy requirement of methods is identical with the requirement that for the analyst to recognize, or identify, or follow the development of, or describe phenomenon of order* in local production of coherent detail the analyst must be *vulgarly* competent to the local production and reflexively natural accountability of the phenomenon of order* [s/he] is 'studying'" (2002, pp. 175–176). There is a strong use of the unique adequacy criteria that Garfinkel goes on to articulate (*ibid.*, p. 176), which might be paraphrased as, the methods for sociological inquiry cannot be different than the methods for everyday inquiry, although this is more complex and less relevant to this discussion. In brief, the 'weak use' would amount to an adoption of Weber's *verstehen* sociology taken to its extreme, where the sociologist becomes fluent in the practices of a member of a culture to such a degree that they could partake in

that culture themselves, unproblematically. Traditionally this has been applied to the ethnomethodological studies of work programme (Garfinkel 1986), where unique adequacy is achieved when the analyst can seamlessly see things from the perspective, even undertake the tasks, of the member/worker. Applied here, it is more akin to seeing the parameters of an unequal relationship from the perspective of the marginalized individual.

REFERENCES

Baccus, Melinda D. (1986), "Multipiece Truck Wheel Accidents and their Regulation", in Harold Garfinkel (ed.), *Ethnomethodological Studies of Work*, London, UK: Routledge & Kegan Paul, 21–58.
Beck, Ulrich (1995), *Risk Society: Towards a New Modernity*, London, UK: Sage.
Brady, Michelle (2014), "Ethnographies of Neoliberal Governmentalities: from the Neoliberal Apparatus to Neoliberalism and Governmental Assemblages", *Foucault Studies*, 18, 11–33.
Charmaz, Kathy (2003), "Grounded Theory: Objectivist and Constructivist Methods", in Norman K. Denzin and Yvonna S. Lincoln (eds), *Strategies for Qualitative Inquiry 2nd Ed.*, Thousand Oaks, CA: Sage, 249–291.
Coburn, Veldon (2021), "Contrary to Sensational Reporting, Indigenous People Aren't Scared of a COVID-19 Vaccine", *The Conversation*, March 14th, accessed May 3rd 2021 at https://theconversation.com/contrary-to-sensational-reporting-indigenous-people-arent-scared-of-a-covid-19-vaccine-156444.
Coleman, James S. (1990), *Foundations of Social Theory*, Cambridge, MA: The Belknap Press of Harvard University.
Collins, Harry (2014), *Are We All Scientific Experts Now?* Cambridge, UK: Polity.
Collins, Harry and Robert Evans (2002), "The Third Wave of Sciences Studies: Studies of Expertise and Experience", *Social Studies of Science*, 32(2), 235–296.
Collins, Harry and Robert Evans (2009), *Rethinking Expertise*, Chicago, IL: University of Chicago Press.
Collins, Harry and Robert Evans (2017), *Why Democracies Need Science*, Cambridge, UK: Polity.
Coopmans, Catelijne and Graham Button (2014), "Eyeballing Expertise", *Social Studies of Science*, 44(5), 758–785.
Curran, Dean (2013), "Risk Society and the Distribution of Bads: Theorizing Class in the Risk Society", *The British Journal of Sociology*, 64(1), 44–62.
Dean, Mitchell (2010), *Governmentality: Power and Rule in Modern Society 2nd ed.*, Los Angeles, CA: Sage.
Dingwall, Robert (1999), "'Risk Society': The Cult of Theory and the Millenium?', *Social Policy & Administration*, 33(4), 474–491.
Du Bois, William Edward Burghardt (1903), *The Souls of Black Folk*, New York, NY: Penguin.
Duck, Waverly (2017), "The Complex Dynamics of Trust and Legitimacy", *The Annals of the American Academy of Political and Social Science*, 673, 132–149.
Eisenmann, Clemens and Michael Lynch (2021), "Introduction to Harold Garfinkel's Ethnomethodological Misreading of Aron Gurwitsch on the Phenomenal Field", *Human Studies*, 44(1), 1–17.
Ericson, R. V. and K. D. Haggerty (1997) *Policing the Risk Society*, Toronto, ON: University of Toronto Press.
Ewald, Francois (1991), "Insurance and Risk", in Graham Burchell, Colin Gordon, and Peter Miller (eds), *The Foucault Effect: Studies in Governmentality*, Hemel Hepstead, UK: Harvester Wheatsheaf, 197–210.
Garfinkel, Harold (1963), "A Conception of, and Experiments with, 'Trust' as a Condition of Stable Concerted Actions", in O. J. Harvey (ed.), *Motivation and Social Interaction*, New York: Ronald Press, 187–238.
Garfinkel, Harold (1967), *Studies in Ethnomethodology*, Englewood Cliffs, NJ: Prentice-Hall.
Garfinkel, Harold (1986), *Ethnomethodological Studies of Work*, London, UK: Routledge.
Garfinkel, Harold (2002), *Ethnomethodology's Program: Working Out Durkheim's Aphorism*, Lanham, MD: Rowman & Littlefield.

Garfinkel, Harold (2021), "Ethnomethodological Misreading of Aron Gurwitsch on the Phenomenal Field", *Human Studies*, 44(1), 19–42.

Garfinkel, Harold and Harvey Sacks (1970), "On Formal Structures of Practical Actions", in J. C. McKinney and E. A. Tiryakian (eds), *Theoretical Sociology: Perspectives and Developments*, New York, NY: Appleton-Crofts, 337–366.

Garfinkel, Harold and D. Lawrence Weider (1992), "Two Incommensurable, Asymmetrically Alternate Technologies of Social Analysis", in Graham Watson and R. M. Seiler (eds), *Text in Context: Contributions to Ethnomethodology*, London, UK: Sage, 175–206.

Giddens, Anthony (1991), *Modernity and Self-Identity*, Cambridge, UK: Polity.

Goffman, Erving (1956), *The Presentation of Self in Everyday Life*, Edinburgh, UK: University of Edinburgh Social Science Research Centre.

Goffman, Erving (1983), "The Interaction Order", *American Sociological Review*, 48(1), 1–17.

Gonzalez-Martinez, Esther and Jakub Mlynar (2019), "Practical Trust", *Social Science Information*, 58(4), 608–630.

Griffith, Janessa, Husayn Marani, and Helen Monkman (2021), "COVID-19 Vaccine Hesitancy in Canada: Content Analysis of Tweets using the Theoretical Domains Framework", *Journal of Medical Internet Research*, 23(4). doi:10.2196/26874

Haggerty, Kevin D. and Richard V. Ericson (1997), *Policing the Risk Society*, Toronto, ON: University of Toronto Press.

Horlick-Jones, Tom (2005), "On 'Risk Work': Professional Discourse, Accountability, and Everyday Action", *Health, Risk & Society*, 7(3), 293–307.

Jasanoff, Sheila (2003), "Breaking the Waves in Science Studies: Comment on H. M. Collins and Robert Evans, 'The Third Wave of Science Studies'", *Social Studies of Science*, 33(3), 389–400.

Jenkings, K. Neil (2013), "Playing Dangerously: An Ethnomethodological View upon Rock-Climbing", in Peter Tolmie and Mark Rouncefield (eds), *Ethnomethodology at Play*, Farnham, UK: Ashgate, 191–210.

Kerrison, Erin M., Jennifer Cobbina, and Kimberly Bender (2018), "'Your Pants Won't Save You': Why Black Youth Challenge Race-Based Police Surveillance and the Demands of Black Respectability Politics", *Race and Justice*, 8(1), 7–26.

Lash, Scott, Bronislaw Szerszynski, and Brian Wynne (1996), *Risk, Environment and Modernity: Towards a New Ecology*, London, UK: Sage.

Latour, Bruno (1988), *The Pasteurization of France*, Cambridge, MA: Harvard University Press.

Latour, Bruno (2007), "Turning Around Politics: A Note on Gerard de Vries' Paper", *Social Studies of Science*, 37(5), 811–820.

Lidskog, Rolf and Goran Sundqvuist (2012), "Sociology of Risk", in Sabine Roeser, Rafaela Hillerbrand, Per Sandin, and Martin Peterson (eds), *Handbook of Risk Theory: Epistemology, Decision Theory, Ethics, and Social Implications of Risk*, Dordrecht, NL: Springer, 1002–1027.

Lindert, Peter H. and Jeffrey G. Williamson (2021), *American Incomes 1774–1860*, Cambridge, MA: National Bureau of Economic Research, accessed January 27, 2021 at https://www.nber.org/system/files/working_papers/w18396/w18396.pdf.

Luhmann, Niklas (1979), *Trust and Power*, Chichester, UK: Wiley.

Maynard, Douglas W. (1991), "Goffman, Garfinkel, and Games", *Sociological Theory* 9(2), 277–279.

Mosby, Ian and Jaris Swidrovich (2021), "Medical Experimentation and the Roots of COVID-19 Vaccine Hesitancy among Indigenous Peoples in Canada", *Canadian Medical Association Journal*, 193(15). DOI: 10.1503/cmaj.210112

Mythen, Gabe (2005), "Employment, Individualization and Insecurity: Rethinking the Risk Society Perspective", *The Sociological Review*, 53(1), 129–149.

Parsons, Talcott (1937), *The Structure of Social Action: A Study in Social Theory with Special Reference to a Group of Recent European Writers*, New York, NY: The Free Press.

Power, Michael (1997), *The Audit Society: Rituals of Verification*, Oxford, UK: Oxford University Press.

Rawls, Anne Warfield (1987), "The Interaction Order Sui Generis: Goffman's Contribution to Social Theory", *Sociological Theory*, 5(2), 136–149.

Rawls, Anne Warfield (2000), "'Race' as an Interaction Order Phenomenon: WEB Du Bois's 'Double Consciousness' Thesis Revisited", *Sociological Theory*, 18(2), 241–274.

Rawls, Anne Warfield (2008), "Harold Garfinkel, Ethnomethodology and Workplace Studies", *Organization Studies*, 29(5), 701–732.

Rawls, Anne Warfield (2009), "An Essay on Two Conceptions of Social Order: Constitutive Orders of Action, Objects and Identities vs Aggregated Orders of Individual Action", *Journal of Classical Sociology*, 9(4), 500–520.

Rawls, Anne Warfield and Gary David (2005), "Trust, Reciprocity and Exclusion in a Context of Situated Practice", *Human Studies*, 28(4), 469–497.

Rawls, Anne Warfield and Waverly Duck (2017), "Fractured Reflections of High Status Black Male Presentations of Self: Non-Recognition of Identity as a Barrier to Exercising Legitimate Authority", *Sociological Focus*, 50(1), 36–51.

Rawls, Anne Warfield and Waverly Duck (2020), *Tacit Racism*, Chicago, IL: University of Chicago Press.

Sacks, Harvey (1992), *Lectures on Conversation*, Oxford, UK: Blackwell.

Scott, John (2002), "Social Class and Stratification in Late Modernity", *Acta Sociological*, 45(1), 23–35.

Smith, Dorothy E. (1987), *The Everyday World as Problematic: A Feminist Sociology*, Toronto, ON: University of Toronto Press.

Smith, Dorothy E. (1990), *The Conceptual Practices of Power: A Feminist Sociology of Knowledge*, Toronto, ON: University of Toronto Press.

Smith, Robin (2020), "Seeing the Trouble: A Mountain Rescue Training Scenario in its Circumstantial and Situated Detail in Three Frames", *Ethnographic Studies*, 17 (2020): 41–59.

Strathern, Marilyn (2000), *Audit Cultures: Anthropological Studies in Accountability, Ethics and the Academy*, London, UK: Routledge.

Turowetz, Jason and Anne Warfield Rawls (2021), "The Development of Garfinkel's 'Trust' Argument from 1947 to 1967: Demonstrating How Inequality Disrupts Sense and Self-Making", *Journal of Classical Sociology*, 21(1), 3–37.

Vaughan, Diane (1996), *The Challenger Launch Decision: Risky Technology, Culture, and Deviance at NASA*, Chicago, IL: Univeristy of Chicago Press.

Watson, Rod (2009), "Constitutive Practices and Garfinkel's Notion of Trust: Revisited", *Journal of Classical Sociology*, 9(4), 475–499.

Wynne, Brian (1996), "May the Sheep Safely Graze?", in Scott Lash, Bronislaw Szerszynsky, and Brian Wynne (eds), *Risk, Environment and Modernity: Towards a New Ecology*, London, UK: Sage, 27–43.

Wynne, Brian (2003), "Seasick on the Third Wave? Subverting the Hegemony of Propositionalism", *Social Studies of Science*, 33(3), 401–417.

PART III

SPECIAL TOPICS AND NEW AREAS OF RESEARCH

11. Inequality rising: the gendered impacts of precarious labor and financialization

Ghazal Mir Zulfiqar and Aleena Shafique

INTRODUCTION

In the last few decades a new global economy has emerged that is characterized by an 'increasing extension, interpenetration and interdependence of production systems, corporations, markets and networks' (Martin et al. 2018, p. 5). This has been actively promoted by neoliberal governments, transnational corporations, and global institutions, including the International Monetary Fund (IMF) and the World Bank, driven by their free market and free trade agendas. Operating in an unpredictable transnational environment with intense competitive pressures and high levels of financial risk for local and transnational corporations, the proliferation of Global Production Networks (GPNs) has led to uneven territorial development and precarious labor regimes (Coe and Yeung 2015, 2019). This has become dramatically clear during the COVID-19 pandemic, as people across the globe experience unexpected and severe disruptions in global supply chains (Yeung, 2021). In doing so it has exposed not only the fault lines of the new global economy but also the deep vulnerabilities built into its functionings (Alamgir et al. 2021).

The present chapter describes how the new political and economic reality has re-crafted the lived realities of people across the Global South through two simultaneously occurring processes. The first has to do with the rapid informalization and feminization of the global labor force (Standing 1999), which has led to lower incomes and precarious labor contracts. The second is the increasing proliferation of credit channels in places never before mapped by the financial centers of the world (Aitken 2013). The fact that these two processes have ensued at the same time is no coincidence. The informalization and feminization of labor does not just overlap the rising formalization of credit, in fact both purposefully feed off of each other. With the eclipse of the male breadwinner model (Elson 2002), women are increasingly shouldering primary income-bearing responsibilities, even as they continue with their care work, which subsidizes the productive economy (Bakker 2007). In this new informalized labor market, women face lower incomes and their contracts are much more precarious than men had previously enjoyed.

At the same time, women across the Global South have found themselves at the frontiers of risk, for being labelled as more creditworthy than their men by global finance (Roy 2012). Development interventions such as microfinance, assimilate laboring women in the informal economies of the world into mainstream finance, for the clients of microfinance are the operators of informal enterprises and homebased work (Elyachar 2002). In so doing, a new poverty capital has emerged that rests on the idea of 'bottom billion capitalism' (Prahalad 2005) and the new riskscapes that animate it (Roy 2012).

The redirecting of work and credit away from poor men and towards poor women is lauded as an important win for gender equality and a fulfilment of the World Bank's (2012) 'smart economics agenda', that what is good for women is good for growth. In reality, these processes have led to increasingly insecure livelihoods and a greater burden on women to fund social reproduction, often at high rates of interest. There is evidence that the disenfranchisement of men has also led to higher levels of domestic violence for women. All of this has meant higher levels of poverty, inequality, and risk for women and their households.

INFORMALIZATION AND FEMINIZATION OF THE GLOBAL LABOR FORCE

The Rise of the New Informal Economy

Spatially dispersed and organizationally fragmented GPNs are the backbone of the new global economy. Their driving factors are cost, flexibility, and speed (Coe and Yeung 2015). The proliferation of flexible production systems is a strategy for sustaining competitive advantage, and depends crucially on sub-contracted work. The advantage of subcontracting work to people in the Global South is not only that wages here are low, but also that there is little danger of legislation promoting unionization, wage increases, and regulating working conditions.

There is a further sub-division between core workers and a peripheral workforce, which is utilized during peak seasons and laid off during slack periods, termed the 'permanent temporary workforce' (Chen 2012). This brings up the notion of informalization, which until recently was considered a temporary and atypical process in Western economies (Benería 2001; Breman and Linden 2014). Until the 1970s, it was assumed that the informal economy would eventually be absorbed into the 'modern' formal economy, but instead the formal economy has displayed a propensity to encourage precarious forms of work (Razavi 2008). Informal activities were previously viewed as the lingering remnants of backwardness or as a residual feature of developing economies, confined to select urban poor and immigrant groups. In the new global economy, what is termed 'non-standard employment' in the Global North and 'informal employment' in the Global South has become increasingly difficult to disentangle from the formal economy due to its close linkages with it and the increasing involvement of formal firms in the informal sector (Benería 2001; Benería and Floro 2004; Khan 2018). The informal economy is, therefore, no longer regarded as an anomaly and the modern economy is no longer exclusively identified with formal activities (Benería 2001; Khan 2018). As a result, there is a growing need to define labor informality in less ambiguous terms, with a shift from an enterprise-based understanding to one rooted in precarious labor relations. Informal employment thus captures various forms of work, from wage work and piece-rate contracts, to survivalist strategies with limited returns (Razavi 2008).

The trend in the rise of informal work, reduction of public sector employment, closure of factories, falling wages, and a marked increase in the number of households reliant on unregulated and informal work arrangements in the new global economy is unprecedented and uneven. This has created spatial divisions of labor (Massey [1984] 1995), regional investment and disinvestment, and socio-spatial fragmentation. The processes of inclusion and exclusion have led to growing differentiation between regions included in global production networks and those that are not (Werner 2016).

While the informal economy was initially considered a consequence of the incapacity of the formal economy to absorb labor, a fundamental reappraisal indicates that the informal economy is not the problem; instead, it is a solution that facilitates the new global economy's race for ever-higher rates of return and growth (Benería 2001; Khan 2018), or what is euphemistically referred to in the mainstream literature as GPN 'upgrading' (Werner 2016). In order to achieve higher net margins, firms cut down on formal workers while increasingly leaning on the informal sector (Elgin and Elveren 2019). Alongside this unchecked pace of globalization and market deregulation, governments have rolled back their public welfare provisions, which has led to an erosion of workers' rights and unionized labor (Benería 2001). Thus, the flexibilization of employment has resulted in a reconceptualization of worker identities and decreased expenditure on social welfare and security (Peterson 2012).

Although the informal economy might foster innovative capacities and generate wealth for a minority, the majority of informal workers are left vulnerable in terms of socio-economic constraints, such as fewer resources, lower skill levels, smaller enterprises, as well as limited access to capital, technology, and networks that could facilitate growth (Coe and Yeung 2015). Market conditions continue to be steered by the formal economy, while the informally employed are for the most part unable to exert their influence on either the market of the goods and services they produce or the labor market. Small or informal firms lack the knowledge, skills, and resources to compete with formal firms for both import and export markets. Additionally, formal firms increasingly hire workers under informal work arrangements, or they simply outsource production to other firms and contractors that are spatially dispersed (Chen 2012).

The informal labor regime consists of several key features (Breman 2011; Breman and Linden 2014). The most prominent is the substitution of regular, full-time jobs by casual or part-time work arrangements, with a constant rotation of the workforce based on the principle of 'hire and fire' at little to no notice. Time-rated wages are replaced by task work or piece-rated employment, accompanied by a sharp decline in overall wages and little to no compensation for increased costs of living. Poor working conditions, lack of a fixed workplace, and long and irregular working hours are common characteristics of the informal economy (Zulfiqar and Khan 2020). Informal work is primarily driven by subcontracting, outsourcing, and lack of transparency in order to drive down the cost of labor and avoid the provision of fringe benefits. The replacement of waged work by self-employment is another significant element, which appears to be the modus operandi of a large proportion of the informal economy, such as homebased work (Breman 2011). The informal economy is further marked by an insistence on self-reliance and self-representation in the name of petty entrepreneurialism. Overhead allowances and benefits such as minimum wage, regulated working conditions, social protection, and job security are put on the back burner. There is a stark absence of control by state authorities in matters of compliance with legal requirements in terms of working conditions and terms of employment. Additionally, informal activities are typically identified by precarious labor regimes, coupled with a lack of collective representation or agency (Breman 2011; Breman and Linden 2014).

The informal sector can be divided into two broad categories: informal self-employment, consisting of employers in informal enterprises, contributing family workers, and own-account operators; and informal wage employment, such as contract workers, domestic workers, employees in informal enterprises, casual laborers, unregistered workers, or industrial workers (Chen 2012). Benería (2001) similarly classifies informal activities into either some form of industrial or service work, or survival activities taking place at the household level. While the former is linked to profit-oriented operations and formal production processes, the latter represents even more precarious types of work with little or no links to formal processes or any possibility of capital accumulation. Another division can be made in informal work on the basis of the legal/illegal divide, as much of the informal sector lacks legal status and is filling the vacuum left by the formal economy. This is referred to as 'nomad labor' or 'labor exclusion', typically associated with constant unemployment, poverty, and marginality (Benería 2001).

While globalization in the Global North has produced inequalities of economic power that threaten democratic processes, there still exist established political structures that seek to guarantee workers' rights and the enforcement of labor contracts, to an extent. In the South, however, where the welfare state was already struggling to form, globalization has led to the emergence of contradictory forces as transnational corporations feed off of the existing vacuum in workers' rights. While informality and economic insecurity are not new phenomena in the South, due to increased flexibilization and deregulation they have reached unprecedented heights (Benería 2001). The informal economy appears to have become a permanent feature of capitalist development – it makes up the primary source of income in the South, and gives shape to the resource accumulation and social reproduction strategies of households across the globe (Coe and Yeung 2015). More than two billion people are currently engaged in informal employment, most of whom are in the Global South. The sector with the highest level of employment is agriculture, estimated at over 90 percent. Out of the two billion informal workers, over 740 million are women (ILO 2018).

Feminization of the Labor Force

Since the 1970s, there has been a steady convergence in male and female labor participation rates. British economist Guy Standing (1999) was the first to call this trend the 'feminization of the labor force', arguing that jobs such as factory work were rapidly becoming feminized so that, even if they were held by men, they would find themselves in a 'feminized position'. In other words, the characteristics of certain jobs have been transformed in a way that aligns with women's historical workforce participation, which has meant considerable deterioration in working conditions for labor-intensive positions previously held by men (Elgin and Elveren 2019). Alongside, there has been an overall decline in jobs previously performed by men, so that women are pushed into the workforce to make up for the loss of men's wages, also known as the distress sale of women's labor (Mahmud 2003; Kabeer 2012). Keeping women workers as a reserve army also serves as a threat to men, putting downward pressure on the wages of both (Elgin and Elveren 2019).

The feminization of the workforce is related to its informalization. The informal economy is closely linked with racialized, feminized work, power imbalances, histories of colonization, geopolitical and economic hierarchies, and migration flows. Feminized labor and informal work are both characterized by economic and cultural devaluation, with little economic compensation of feminized or female workers (Coe and Yeung 2015).

Although global informal employment figures for men are slightly higher than for women, at 63 percent and 58 percent respectively, across the Global South the same ratios are 87 percent for men to 92 percent for women (ILO 2019). This means that the growth in women's labor force participation is highly uneven. First, this growth is only witnessed in certain sectors, such as in the garment and sporting goods industries. Second, the growth of the export-oriented economy has triggered an increase in subcontracting and homebased employment for women in the Global South since the production of export industries is labor intensive. Statistically speaking, there has not been a marked increase in female participation in formal employment; in fact, there has been a real decline at absolute levels (Prasad 2018).

Employers along the GPN are attracted by women's 'suitability' to new forms of low-wage factory or homebased contractual work, thanks to traditional stereotypes of women being 'cheap labor' with 'nimble fingers', 'non-political' attitudes, and an obedient nature that makes them less likely to unionize as compared to men (Munir et al. 2017; Prasad 2018). Additionally, employers' perceptions about the costs of a female workforce, such as absenteeism and turnover due to marriage, pregnancy, and childbirth discourages them from investing in upgrading their skills (Mahmud 2003).

This leads to greater marginalization, invisibility, and denial of labor rights for poor, working women (Prasad 2018). While the informal economy is a larger source of income for women than for men across the Global South, men tend to be concentrated in relatively higher-paying jobs within the informal economy, with women taking up jobs with lower wages (Razavi 2008). Men also occupy more authoritarian positions while women are unpaid or underpaid as homeworkers or helpers in family enterprises (Prieto-Carron 2008). Not only do women workers in the informal economy earn less than men, they also earn less than women in the formal economy. Benefits such as health and disability insurance, and maternity leave are absent in such non-standard work. Due to an influx of unpaid and part-time workers, the overall market for women's labor has deteriorated and segmentation has increased at a much faster rate than in the male labor market (Mahmud 2003).

Adolescent women are also at risk of having their education cut off as they are required to look after their siblings while their mothers work. This in turn affects their chances of acquiring the necessary skills and education for earning a decent wage, perpetuating the cycle of inequality and poverty (Mahmud 2003). In other words, the gendered division of labor has not changed with women's economic participation, and women may even experience a loss in welfare due to reductions in their leisure time.

Nevertheless, the remarkable expansion of women's participation in the labor force in the last few decades does carry with it certain empowering benefits, such as an improvement in their bargaining power, a chance for skill development, and increasing their social networks. In some cases, women are even able to extend their influence into the public sphere and work towards the broader advancement of their interests and agendas (Peterson 2012). Paid employment offers women a way to renegotiate existing power structures. For instance, the migration of rural women to urban areas for industrial and other kinds of work may expand their autonomy and offer an opportunity to escape from oppressive forms of rural patriarchy, even though this may also expose them to exploitative and discriminatory working conditions (Bennería 2001; Zulfiqar 2019). Nevertheless, as women's contribution to household finances increases, evidence suggests that they begin to have more of a say in household decision making (Bennería and Floro 2004; Duflo 2012).

Despite some emancipatory benefits, the 'squeeze on care', that is, rollbacks in public welfare, exacerbate the double burden of paid and unpaid work for women (Gideon 2007). More recently, this has been referred to as a 'triple burden', as forced participation in the informal economy constitutes a third burden on women's time, after their reproductive labor and waged work in the formal economy (Lyon et al. 2017). Whether a woman is able to transform her earnings into capability functioning is contingent upon a variety of factors, such as the nature of household decision-making processes and relations, as well as the terms of employment (Bennería and Floro 2004). Research has highlighted that the contradictory processes of globalization have increased the vulnerability of poor households, exposing them to greater shocks and risks, which are primarily absorbed by women (Gideon 2007).

During the COVID-19 pandemic, research on homebased women workers uncovered their disposability and vulnerability against the large-scale disruption of domestic and global supply chains, alongside equally meager male incomes. The casual, sub-contracted nature of work along the GPN, amplified exposure to the risks of the massive shock that was the pandemic and its subsequent lockdowns. Workers were 'to live or be left to die', since neither the state nor the owners of capital took responsibility for their sustenance or survival (Alamgir et al. 2021, p. 1; Zulfiqar 2021).

Feminist political economists point out that the pandemic has been a crisis of social reproduction as much as it is a crisis of work, especially for women laboring in the informal economy (Mezzadri et al. 2021; Stevano et al. 2021). Women continue to bear primary responsibility for care work, which forces them to take on casual low-paying work to make up for falling real incomes, for both male and female household members, and shrinking social protections (Elson 2010). The crisis of social reproduction continues as households struggle to survive and ensure their daily and generational continuity. This is largely invisible due to the hidden nature of household relations, with its embeddedness in underlying patriarchal contexts.

FINANCIALIZATION AT THE BOTTOM OF THE PYRAMID

As mentioned earlier, social reproduction relates to the biological reproduction of the labor force and the provisioning of care work (Bakker 2007; Roberts 2013). Since the emergence of industrial capitalism, social reproduction has been relegated to the domain of the domestic, segregated from the productive economy, even as the latter depends on the former. The nurturing of the human race or care work has come to be associated with motherhood and the home, making gender a social relation that comprises material practices, processes, and control over resources (Adkins 2018). This has restricted women's access to finance to small loans for petty informal enterprises or to meet their domestic needs (Roberts and Zulfiqar 2019). De Goede (2000, p. 60) argues that 'the historical notion of credit carries a gendered dimension: the reputation and authority that underlies credibility distinctly belong to the *gentleman* – the only recognized autonomous subject'.

In the past three decades, however, with the stagnation of wages, the increasing informalization of the economy, and the decline in state provisioning of social welfare services, on the one hand, and a loosening of restrictions on lending and a demand for access to finance, on the other, households have become sites of financial accumulation (Roberts 2018). This is because several regulatory and cultural transformations have enabled the expansion and deepening of financial relations into more and more spaces of everyday life, as growing numbers are forced to rely on credit to finance the costs of living (Lazzarato 2012; Roberts 2018). Across OECD countries, the reduction of public subsidies, social protections for rental housing, and the proliferation of sub-prime mortgage credit, has led to a proliferation of mortgage debt (Roberts 2013, p. 18).

At the same time, there continues to be a male institutional bias in state policies and mainstream economic modeling that is assumed to be gender neutral (Acker 1990). For instance, state policies continue to operate on employment patterns constructed around the 'male breadwinner' model, which perpetuates the assumption that the survival of women and children ultimately depends on the incomes of husbands and fathers (Elson 2002). Additionally, it is assumed that 'typical' workers have limited domestic responsibilities (Acker 1990). In reality, the majority of poor and near-poor households depend on multiple livelihood strategies, including women being involved in the formal and informal economy while simultaneously undertaking unpaid care work. But women's paid and unpaid work is ignored as is their economic participation in informal, low-paid, homebased, or part-time work. Due to this structural male bias, women are relegated to the status of secondary workers with restricted labor rights, while public policies continue to prioritize ruminative employment for men instead of women (Elson 2002). Although in recent years, family policies in the Global North have been moving away from the male breadwinner model towards the dual-earner household model, the speed and nature of this transformation varies significantly according to national and socio-cultural contexts (Von Gleichen and Seeleib-Kaiser 2017).

Simultaneously, neoliberal economies operate on a privatisation bias for public provisioning of goods and services is considered less efficient than private provisioning. The sharing of risks and resources is, thus, effectively replaced by individualized, market-based insurance alternatives (Elson 2002). Women continue to find themselves as dependents for insurable risks, such as against old age and disease, which are constructed around male norms of labor market status. Many women have also lost formal jobs in the textile industries due to 'rationalization' and restructuring policies, and as a result now engage in street trading and other forms of survival activities in the informal sector such as homebased work. In China, both men and women face employment insecurity due to the processes of industrial restructuring (UNRISD 2005). Many workers were laid off from public enterprises, and were absorbed into small businesses in the private sector, often termed as 'laid-off worker's enterprises'. These workers predominantly belong to vulnerable groups for they are hired on a temporary, part-time, and flexible basis (ILO 2018).

Across the Global South, poor women have been using their meagre earnings and savings to meet their households' social reproduction. Their earnings are used up in paying rent, grocery bills, and school fees, while their savings are liquidated in times of family crises, religious ceremonies, and to continue their children's education (Boeri 2018). In the past three decades, however, formal finance has made inroads into the lives of poor women across the Global South, primarily through microcredit, which gives them access to tiny amounts of formal credit.

The Gendered Agenda of Microfinance

Microfinance as an intervention was first introduced in the late 1970s and early 1980s, as a means to assist the subsistence businesses of the poor. The loans are to be repaid with interest, which is usually higher than the market rate. Despite this, repayment rates have always been high, well into the 1990s, so that microfinance has come to be symbolized by the catchphrase 'the poor always pay back' (Dowla and Barua 2006). Since the late 1980s, microfinance has been dubbed the *ideal* development intervention. Early studies indicated that it effectively alleviated poverty, while empowering poor women (Khandker 1998; Pitt, Khandker, and Cartwright 2006), and facilitating community engagement through group lending (Osmani 2007).

Access to finance has been the post-millennium mantra of development since at least the 1990s. With respect to women, the World Bank and others assert that, if women are to have access to high-quality financial services, they will achieve greater gender equity (John Isaac 2014). In the era of financial deregulation, there is a call to 'democratize finance' (Shiller 2003). Roy (2010) describes this as part of a broader transformation in development that aims to project capitalism's softer side by reaching out to the bottom of the pyramid to seek both profits and poverty alleviation (Prahalad 2005). Women play a particularly important role in this transformation (Roy 2012). The movement of financial and corporate interests to the bottom of the pyramid claims to reduce gender inequalities, while transforming economies through women's income (Roy 2010).

The World Bank has drawn on these claims to articulate a 'smart economics' agenda, that is, a win–win synergy between gender equality and efficient economic development, contending that investing in women and girls results in more effective development outcomes. Women are seen not only as responsible borrowers but also entrepreneurs with acumen (Assassi 2009). The smart economics agenda is supported by research such as Pitt et al.'s (2003) famous study of women borrowers in Bangladesh. They showed that, when women are provided with micro-credit, the measures of nutrition and health for both girls and boys improve significantly, while credit provided to men has no significant results. These findings support other literature that show a mother's control over resources significantly alters the human capital of her children for the better (Pitt et al. 2006). Research, however, shows that the small amounts of credit microfinance provides to poor women are used primarily for consumption smoothening rather than to fund their entrepreneurial pursuits (Rankin 2013; Zulfiqar 2019).

Microfinance and Vulnerability to Risks

The provision of credit can no doubt be beneficial for poor women and their households, particularly when it is the only source of credit available to them (Assassi 2009). However, as levels of debt rise, household vulnerability to risks also rises. For cash-strapped, income-poor households, an economic or non-economic shock, such as death or marriage, can result in disastrous consequences because of the paucity of resources to fall back upon. Additionally, since much of this credit is used to supplement immediate income generation, the credit rarely helps lift them out of poverty and instead leads to rising indebtedness, and the making of extreme choices such as the farmer suicides at the behest of microfinance officers in India (Kinetz 2012).

Microfinance makes individuals the subjects of risk by enacting self-responsibility and financial discipline (Roy 2012: 139). This is in line with the overarching neoliberal ideology of finance capitalism, which seeks to individualize risk by conceptualizing citizens as entre-preneurs, moving away from all forms of social security or socialization of risk (Aitken 2013). Commercialized microcredit erodes social capital among the very poor, while transforming it into profits for MicroFinance Institutions (MFIs) and Return On Equity (ROE) for its inves-tors. As many as 75 percent of MFIs are reported to charge rates in what is termed the 'red zone'. Roy (2012) argues that the poor across the Global South, who were once left out of the circuits of formal finance, are now its 'risk frontiers'. This exposes them to 'speculative instability, over-extended (and oversold) credit, unpredictable chains of financial fragility at both micro and macro levels' (Aitken 2013, p. 495).

Roy (2012, p. 140) argues that such 'riskscapes' are deeply gendered, as the 'Third World woman transforms risks into responsibility'. Casting women as 'heroic entrepreneurs' and 'selfless altruists', and advancing microfinance as a development program serves to further entrench the domestication of care work, with poor women disproportionately carrying the burden of social reproduction. By producing female borrowers as financially responsible moral women, microfinance produces new technologies of gender (Roy 2012). Relations of dependency, control, and gender ascription are downplayed as the empowered, entrepreneurial subject is promoted, which imposes heavy costs in terms of household risks, that are borne largely by women who become even more economically vulnerable (Assassi 2009). This is supported in no small part by smart economics-type discourses. Feminists argue that the World Bank 'aims to increase women's participation in land, labor, products, and financial markets – while privatizing them as much as possible – which benefits corporations the most' (Zuckerman 2007, p. 2). These include microfinance investment funds, which have led the way for the globalization of microfinance, and increasing interest in it as an asset class. From modest NGO beginnings microfinance has evolved into a profit-based intervention, entering the domain of commercial finance and investment vehicles. This is the domain of poverty capital, that is, 'the conversion of the social world of the poor into monetized, profitable finance' (Roy 2012, p. 142), similar in process and structure to North American payday lending (Barth, Hilliard and Jahera 2015; Zulfiqar 2018).

Women's assets have long been known to be the first to go in times of crises. Amirthalingam and Lakshman (2010) detail how internally displaced Tamils in Sri Lanka have had to pawn and sell their jewellery to dampen the impact of displacement. Similarly, the conflicts in Palestine and Iraq forced women to sell off their gold ornaments to protect their families from the effects of economic and political sanctions (Cainkar 1993; World Bank 2004). Quisumbing et al. (2011) find that in Bangladesh and India women's assets are sold off before any other household assets, when families face shocks such as illnesses or deaths. This further skews the already unequal gender asset gap, impacting women's investments inter-generationally. But more recent research shows that commercialized microfinance is also becoming involved in the pawning and sale of women's investments in gold, the only asset poor women in regions such as South Asia are able to own (Zulfiqar 2018; Roberts and Zulfiqar 2019).

However, even in the case of non-collateralized microcredit studies show that a significant proportion of women lack control or even knowledge of how microfinance loans taken in their names are used (Goetz and Gupta 1994; Chowdhury 2009; Zulfiqar 2017). These women have been referred to as 'postboxes', for their entire role in the process is limited to passing the proceeds onto male members of the household (Hunt and Kasynathan 2001). In Pakistan, for example, over half of microfinance's clients are women, and between 50 to 70 percent are known to transfer their loans to male family members who might have been unsuccessful in accessing loans themselves. These studies also show that there is no significant correlation between microfinance participation and female autonomy (Safavian and Haq 2013; Zulfiqar 2017). A similar study from Bangladesh indicates that, in over 60 percent of the households surveyed, women have drawn out loans in their names while male relatives have consumed the cash to meet their own needs (Staveren 2001).

In such cases, it is the women who bear the transaction costs and risks associated with the loan, while male household members benefit from the proceeds of the loan (Safavian and Haq 2013). These studies show that most MFIs are aware about household dynamics and understand that women will not control the loans disbursed in their names (Zulfiqar 2017). In general, commercial lending institutions are reluctant to lend to women-owned businesses for on average they earn lower returns than male-led businesses (Duflo 2012). In heavily patriarchal regions, even when women do take loans for their businesses, they are required to have male guarantors. In microcredit arrangements, women are primarily relegated to group rather than higher-denomination individual loans, which are reserved for men (Zulfiqar 2017).

There is also some evidence of a correlation between microfinance participation and increased intimate partner violence (IPV). The transformation in traditional gender norms that comes with women's access to finance through MFIs that lend primarily to women rather than men, is thought to lead to an escalation in violence. A husband's perceived loss of authority as well as greater financial independence and autonomy for women has been shown to cause increased marital conflict (Bajracharya and Amin 2013; Christian 2015). Goetz and Gupta (1994) find that violence against women can escalate when women either delay or fail to access credit. Other studies from Bangladesh have corroborated this by indicating that there is an associated increase in the incidence of domestic violence among beneficiary households (Rahman 2001; Ahmed 2005). But a South African study finds that intimate partner violence reduces by more than half after a two-year microfinance intervention (Kim et al. 2007).

There is also a possibility that a selection bias shows a higher rate of domestic violence among female microcredit clients (Bajracharya and Amin 2013). Microcredit borrowers may be more susceptible to violence than non-members due to their higher rates of poverty and prior experience of violence. This is because microcredit programs primarily target poor women, and poverty is positively correlated with domestic violence. Households who live in poverty experience higher rates of stress, and women in poor households have fewer resources to combat domestic violence, making them more prone to it. Secondly, debt in general is associated with domestic abuse and violence (Littwin 2012).

Studies have shown that microfinance, because of the group-lending model of shared risk, increases women's susceptibility to other forms of violence and abuse as well. In her ethnographic account of women debtors in Bangladesh, Karim (2014) provides a detailed account of community-level violence against women debtors. Here loan officers threaten delinquents with public humiliation, flogging, breaking into their homes with other community members to confiscate beds, pots, pans, and other household items. Zulfiqar's (2017) study of microlending in Pakistan corroborates this account, with loan officers admitting that the violence that women who were unable to repay their loans experienced, and the shame and humiliation that came with that, ended up destroying the community's social capital. The Andhra Pradesh suicides in 2009 and 2010 also exposed the coercive practices of Indian microfinance institutions. Overindebted borrowers were driven to take their lives by drinking pesticides, jumping into a pool, or by other means when told by loan officers that only in death would debts be forgiven (Kinetz 2012). Several officers were implicated for the aggressive and threatening ways in which they tried to exact repayment (Biswas, 2010). This is a major reason why, while women are almost always able to repay their microcredit loans, for fear of social sanction, the credit rarely lifts them or their households out of poverty, for it is at best only partially used to support immediate income generation (Armendariz and Morduch 2010; Karim 2014).

CONCLUSION

The twenty-first century brought hope that more inclusive social and cultural change would accompany economic development, particularly in terms of gender relations and economic equality (Prasad 2018). However, this essay has shown that the lived experiences of laboring women at the bottom of global production networks (GPNS) are very different from the gender equity wins that the smart economics development agenda proclaims. In the new globalized economy, with its dependence on outsourcing, piece-rate work, and flexible labor contracts, women are the focus of neoliberalism's efficiency-driven strategies of competitive advantage and the structural problems created in its wake. Women's reproductive and productive labor is expected to pick up the slack that loss of stable employment for men, welfare rollbacks, and austerity measures bring, requiring extraordinary sacrifices from them in terms of their labor, energy, time, and other resources (Chant and Sweetman 2012). As Peterson argues, women's income-generating capacity cannot be considered a feminist triumph if it does nothing to disrupt capitalism and only intensifies the amount of work they end up doing.

The notion that women's marginalization and subordination results from a lack of participation in the workforce is, therefore, misguided, for the provision of employment opportunities alone is not a solution as this chapter has shown. Rather it is *how* women are integrated into development processes that is the real concern (Elson and Pearson 1981). What needs to be paid attention to are the relations through which women are included into the labor force – which for poor women is mainly through informal, casual contracts – and the reproduction of the sexual division of labor in world markets, even as men lose their foothold in formal employment (Peterson 2012).

It is clear now that the informal economy is not a temporary feature of a changing global economy. In fact, it has become the primary source of employment for the majority of the world's poor and near poor (Chen 2012; ILO 2018). As GPNs enjoy the benefits of informality, their informal workforce pays the price with job insecurity, falling real wages, and precarious working conditions (Vanamala 2001). Unionization is rendered near impossible due to the heterogeneous and dispersed nature of labor. This hurts women the most, for as many as 92 percent of women are employed in the informal economy in certain regions of the Global South (Elgin and Elveren 2019). The regulatory environment continues to disregard entire sections of this informal labor force, including street traders, rag pickers, and homebased workers who are not granted traditional employment benefits such as social security, pensions, or access to labor courts.

As the liberalized global economic order increases household vulnerabilities, the architecture of finance forges new relations between personal finance, household survival, and women (Adkins 2018). Mainstream economics' preoccupation with waged labor marginalizes accounts of the reproductive economy (Peterson 2002), and it is to meet the social reproduction needs of their households that women are drawn into circuits of debt. These needs have traditionally been met by informal moneylenders and by the pawning and sale of household or personal assets, but increasingly formal financial institutions such as MFIs and microfinance banks have entered the market for low finance (Assassi 2009; Roberts and Zulfiqar 2019). The research cited in this chapter establishes that the exuberance with which microfinance was first greeted by global development institutions, states, and philanthropists was misguided as microfinance became commercialized and lost its development mission (Rahman 2001; Karim 2014; Zulfiqar 2017, 2018). But even without commercialization, the promise of microfinance did not ring true for those scholars who had pointed out that such interventions were shifting the blame and responsibility of poverty onto individuals, removing its structural dimensions from view, while placing women at the risk frontiers of bottom billion capitalism (Rahman 2001; Roy 2012; Aitken 2013; Rankin 2013).

REFERENCES

Acker, J. (1990), 'Hierarchies, jobs, bodies: A theory of gendered organizations', *Gender & Society*, 4(2), 139–158.

Adkins, L. (2018), 'Work in the shadow of finance: Rethinking Joan Acker's materialist feminist sociology', *Gender, Work & Organization*, 26(12), 1776–1785.

Ahmed, S. M. (2005), 'Intimate partner violence against women: experiences from a woman-focused development programme in Matlab, Bangladesh', *Journal of Health, Population and Nutrition*, 23(1), 95–101.

Aitken, R. (2013), 'The financialization of micro-credit', *Development and Change*, 44(3), 473–499.

Alamgir, F., F. Alamgir, and F. I. Alamgir (2021), Live or be left to die? Deregulated bodies and the global production network: Expendable workers of the Bangladeshi apparel industry in the time of Covid, *Organization*, 1–24. https://doi.org/10.1177/13505084211028528

Amirthalingam, K. and R. W. D. Lakshman (2010), 'Financing of internal displacement: Excerpts from the Sri Lankan experience', *Disasters*, 34(2), 402–425.

Armendariz, B. and J. Morduch (2010), *The Economics of Microfinance: Second Edition*, Cambridge, Massachusetts and London, England: The MIT Press.

Assassi, L. (2009), *The Gendering of Global Finance*, Basingstoke, UK: Palgrave Macmillan.

Bajracharya, A. and S. Amin (2013), 'Microcredit and domestic violence in Bangladesh: An exploration of selection bias influences', *Demography*, 50(5), 1819–1843.

Bakker, I. (2007), 'Social reproduction and the constitution of a gendered political economy', *New Political Economy*, 12(4), 541–556.

Barth, J. R., J. Hilliard and J. S. Jahera (2015), 'Bankers and payday lenders: Friends or foes?', *International Advances in Economic Research*, 21, 139–153.

Benería, L. (2001), 'Shifting the risk: New employment patterns, informalization, and women's work', *International Journal of Politics, Culture, and Society*, 15(1), 27–53.

Benería, L. and M. S. Floro (2004), 'Labor market informalization and social policy: Distributional links and the case of homebased workers', Economics Working Paper No. 60, Vassar College.

Biswas, S. (2010), 'India's micro-finance suicide epidemic', BBC News, 16 December, accessed at https://www.bbc.com/news/world-south-asia-11997571.

Boeri, N. (2018), 'Challenging the gendered entrepreneurial subject', *Gender and Society*, 32(2), 157–179.

Breman, J. (2011), 'The informal sector economy as a global trend', presented at the Cape Town Conference on Research on the Informal Economy, March, WIEGO.

Breman, J. and M. Linden (2014), 'Informalizing the economy: The return of the social question at a global level', *Development and Change*, 45, 920–940.

Cainkar, L. (1993), 'The Gulf war, sanctions and the lives of Iraqi women', *Arab Studies Quarterly*, 15(2), 15–51.

Chant, S. and C. Sweetman (2012), 'Fixing women or fixing the world? "Smart economics", efficiency approaches, and gender equality in development', *Gender & Development*, 20(3), 517–529.

Chen, M. A. (2012), 'The informal economy: Definitions, theories and policies. women in informal economy globalizing and organizing', Working Paper No. 1, WIEGO.

Chowdhury, M. J. (2009), 'Microcredit, micro-enterprises, and self-employment of women: Experience from the Grameen Bank in Bangladesh', paper presented at the FAO-IFAD-ILO Workshop on Gaps, trends and current research in gender dimensions of agricultural and rural employment: differentiated pathways out of poverty, Rome, 31 March to 2 April.

Christian, A. (2015), 'Microfinance as a determinant of domestic violence in Bangladesh: Who is at risk?', CUNY Academic Works.

Coe, N. M. and H. W. Yeung (2015), *Global Production Networks: Theorizing Economic Development in an Interconnected World*, Oxford, UK: Oxford University Press.

Coe, N. M. and H. W. Yeung (2019), 'Global production networks: Mapping recent conceptual developments', *Journal of Economic Geography*, 19(4), 775–801.

De Goede, M. (2000), 'Mastering "Lady Credit"', *International Feminist Journal of Politics*, 2(1), 58–81.

Dowla, A. and D. Barua (2006), *The Poor Always Pay Back: The Grameen II Story*, Bloomfield, CT: Kumarian Press.

Duflo, E. (2012), 'Women empowerment and economic development', *Journal of Economic Literature*, 50(4), 1051–1079.

Elgin, C. and A. Elveren (2019), 'Informality, inequality, and feminization of labor', Working Paper no. 483, University of Massachusetts, Political Economy Research Institute.

Elson, D. (2002), 'International financial architecture: A view from the kitchen', *Femina Politica: Zeitschrift für Feminstische Politik-wissenschaft 1–21.*

Elson, D. (2010), 'Gender and the global economic crisis in developing countries: A framework for analysis', *Gender and Development*, 18(2), 201–12.

Elson, D. and R. Pearson (1981), 'Nimble fingers make cheap workers: An analysis of women's employment in third world export manufacturing', *Feminist Review*, 7, 87–107.

Elyachar, J. (2002), 'Empowerment money: The World Bank, non-governmental organizations, and the value of culture in Egypt', *Public Culture*, 14, 493-513.

Gideon, J. (2007), 'A gendered analysis of labour market informalization and access to health in Chile', *Global Social Policy*, 7(1), 75–94.

Goetz, A. and S. R. Gupta (1994), 'Who takes the credit? Gender, power and control over loan use in rural credit programmes in Bangladesh', *World Development*, 24(1), 45–63.

Hunt, J. and N. Kasynathan (2001), 'Pathways to empowerment? Reflections on microfinance and transformation in gender relations in South Asia', *Gender and Development*, 9(1), 42–52.

ILO (2018), 'Women and men in the informal economy: A statistical picture (third edition)', International Labor Organization, Geneva.

ILO (2019), 'World employment and social outlook: Trends 2019', International Labor Organization, Geneva.

Isaac, J. (2014), 'Expanding Women's Access to Financial Services: The World Bank, Project and Operations', http://www.worldbank.org/en/results/2013/04/01/banking-on-women-extending -womens-access-to-financial-services.

Kabeer, N. (2012), 'Women's economic empowerment and inclusive growth: Labour markets and enterprise development', SIG Working Paper 2012/1.

Karim, L. (2014), 'Analyzing women's empowerment: Microfinance and garment labor in Bangladesh', *The Fletcher Forum of World Affairs*, 38(2), 153–166.

Khan, F.C. (2018), 'Women's employment in the informal sector in developing countries', in Kirsten Madden and Robert W. Dimand (eds), *The Routledge Handbook of the History of Women's Economic Thought*, Abingdon: Routledge. https://www.taylorfrancis.com/books/edit/10.4324/9781315723570/ routledge-handbook-history-women-economic-thought-kirsten-madden-robert-dimand

Khandker, S. R. (1998), *Fighting Poverty with Microcredit: Experience in Bangladesh*, New York: Oxford University Press.

Kim, J. C., C. H. Watts, J. R. Hargreaves, L. X. Ndhlovu, G. Phleta, L. A. Morison, J. Busza, J. D. H. Porter, and P. Pronyk (2007), 'Understanding the impact of a microfinance-based intervention on women's empowerment and the reduction of intimate partner violence in South Africa', *American Journal of Public Health*, 97(10), 1794–1802.

Kinetz, E. (2012), 'Lender's own probe links it to suicides', *Boston Globe*, 24 February.

Lazzarato, Maurizio (2012), *The Making of the Indebted Man: An Essay on the Neoliberal Condition* (trans. J.D. Jordan), London, England: Semiotext(e)/The MIT Press.

Littwin, A. (2012), 'Coerced debt: the role of consumer credit in domestic violence', *California Law Review*, 100, 1–74.

Lyon, S., T. Mutersbaugh and H. Worthe (2017), 'The triple burden: The impact of time poverty on women's participation in coffee producer organizational governance in Mexico', *Agriculture Human Values*, 34, 317–331.

Mahmud, S. (2003), 'Is Bangladesh experiencing a "feminization" of the labor force?', *The Bangladesh Development Studies*, 29(1/2), 1–37.

Martin, R., P. Tyler, M. Storper, E. Evenhuis, and A. Glasmeier (2018), 'Globalisation at a critical conjuncture?', *Cambridge Journal of Regions, Economy and Society*, 11(1), 3–16.

Massey, D. (1984), *Spatial Divisions of Labour: Social Structures and the Geography of Production*, reprinted in D. Massey (1995), *Second edition*, New York: Routledge.

Mezzadri, A., S. Newman, and S. Stevano (2021), 'Feminist global political economies of work and social reproduction', *Review of International Political Economy*, 1–21. https://www.tandfonline.com/doi/full/10.1080/09692290.2021.1957977

Munir, K., M. Ayaz, D. Levy, and H. Willmott (2017), 'The role of intermediaries in governance of global production networks: Restructuring work relations in Pakistan's apparel industry', *Human Relations*, 71(4), 1–24.

Osmani, L. (2007), 'A breakthrough in women's bargaining power: The impact of microcredit', *Journal of International Development*, 19, 695–716.

Peterson, V. S. (2002), 'Rewriting (global) political economy as reproductive, productive, and virtual (foucauldian) economies', *International Feminist Journal of Politics*, 4(1), 1–30.

Peterson, V. S. (2012), 'Rethinking theory', *International Feminist Journal of Politics*, 14(1), 5–35.

Pitt, M., S. Khandker, O. H. Chowdhury, and D. Millimet (2003), 'Credit programs for the poor and the health status of children in rural Bangladesh', *International Economic Review*, 44(1), 87–118.

Pitt, M., S. Khandker, and J. Cartwright (2006), 'Empowering women with micro finance: Evidence from Bangladesh', *Economic Development and Cultural Change*, 54(4), 791–831.

Prahalad, C.K. (2005), *The Fortune at the Bottom of the Pyramid: Eradicating Poverty through Profits*, Upper Saddle River, New Jersey: Wharton School Publishing.

Prasad, A. (2018), 'De-feminization and (dis)empowerment of women workers in garment factories', *Indian Journal of Women and Social Change*, 3(1), 12–23.

Prieto-Carron, M. (2008), 'Women workers, industrialization, global supply chains and corporate codes of conduct', *Journal of Business Ethics*, 83, 5–7.

Quisumbing, A. R., N. Kumar, and J. Behrman (2011), 'Do shocks affect men's and women's assets differently? A review of literature and new evidence from Bangladesh and Uganda', Discussion Paper 1113, Washington D.C. IFPRI.

Rahman, A. (2001), *Women and Microcredit in Rural Bangladesh: An Anthropological Study of Grameen Bank Lending*, Boulder, CO: Westview Press.

Rankin, K. (2013), 'A critical geography of poverty finance', *Third World Quarterly*, 34(4), 547–568.

Razavi, S. (2008), *The Gendered Impacts of Liberalization: Towards 'Embedded Liberalization'?*, London, UK: Routledge.

Roberts, A. (2013), 'Financing social reproduction: The gendered relations of debt and mortgage finance in 21st century America', *New Political Economy*, 18(1), 21–42.

Roberts, A. (2018), 'Financialization and the production of gender and class relations', in Alexandra Scheele and Stefanie Wöhl (eds), *Feminismus and Marxismus: Beltz Juventa in der Verlagsgruppe Beltz*, Basel: Weinheim, pp. 187–201.

Roberts, A. and G. Zulfiqar (2019), 'Social reproduction, finance and the gendered dimensions of pawn-broking', *Capital & Class*, 43(4), 581–597.

Roy, A. (2010), *Poverty Capital: Microfinance and the Making of Development*, New York, USA: Routledge.

Roy, A. (2012), 'Subjects of risk: Technologies of gender in the making of millennial modernity', *Public Culture*, 24(1), 131–155.

Safavian, M. and A. Haq (2013), 'Are Pakistan's women entrepreneurs being served by the microfinance sector? Directions in Development—Finance', Washington, DC: World Bank.

Standing, G. (1999), 'Global feminization through flexible labor: A theme revisited', *World Development*, 27(3), 583–602.

Staveren, I. (2001), 'Gender biases in finance', *Gender and Development*, 9(1), 9–17.

Stevano, S., A. Mezzadri, L. Lombardozzi, and H. Bargawi (2021), 'Hidden abodes in plain sight: The social reproduction of households and labor in the COVID-19 pandemic', *Feminist Economics*, 27(1–2), 271–287.

UNRISD (2005), 'The feminization and informalization of labour', in *Gender Equality: Striving for Justice in an Unequal World*, Geneva: UNRISD/UN Publications, pp. 63–88.

Vanamala, M. (2001), 'Informalisation and feminisation of a formal sector industry: A case study', *Economic and Political Weekly*, 36(26), 2378–2389.

Von Gleichen, R. D. and M. Seeleib-Kaiser (2018), 'Family policies and the weakening of the male-breadwinner model', in Sheila Shaver (ed.), *Handbook on Gender and Social Policy*, Cheltenham, UK and Northampton, MA, USA: Edward Elgar Publishing, pp. 153–178.

Werner, M. (2016), 'Global production networks and uneven development: Exploring geographies of devaluation, disinvestment and exclusion', *Geography Compass*, 10(11), 457–469.

World Bank (2004), 'Disengagement, the Palestinian Economy and the Settlements', Middle East and North Africa Discussion Papers, Washington, DC.

World Bank (2012), 'World Development Report 2012: Gender equality and development', World Bank, accessed at https://openknowledge.worldbank.org/handle/10986/4391.

Yeung, H. W. (2021), 'The trouble with global production networks', *Economy and Space*, 53(2), 428–438.

Zuckerman, E. (2007), 'Critique: Gender equality as smart economics: A World Bank Group Gender Action Plan (GAP) (fiscal years 2007–10)', Gender Action, January, accessed at http://www.genderaction.org/images/04.22.08_EZ-GAPlan%20Critique.pdf

Zulfiqar, G. M. (2017), 'Does microfinance enhance gender equity in access to finance? Evidence from Pakistan', *Feminist Economics*, 23(1), 160–185.

Zulfiqar, G. M. (2018), 'Financializing the poor: "dead capital", women's gold and microfinance in Pakistan', *Economy and Society*, 46(3–4), 476–498.

Zulfiqar, G. M (2019), 'Dirt, foreignness and surveillance: The shifting relations of domestic work in Pakistan', *Organization*, 26(3), 321–336.

Zulfiqar, G. M. and M. Khan (2020), 'NGO-led organizing of Pakistan's homeworkers: A materialist feminist analysis of collective agency', *Journal of Business Ethics*, 162(1), 1–14.

Zulfiqar, G. M. (2021), 'Global production networks and the social reproduction of homebased worker households in the COVID-19 pandemic: Gendered vulnerabilities in the Global South', working paper, Suleman Dawood School of Business, Lahore University of Management Sciences (LUMS), Lahore, Pakistan.

12. Beyond the spirit of the new urban crisis: risk-class and resonance

David Tyfield

1.   INTRODUCTION

It does not seem hyperbole, overestimating the importance of one's own time, to talk of the present moment globally as one of great disruption. In these circumstances, this chapter addresses a key question: How can we best understand and practically explore the contemporary new urban crisis (NUC) as a singular lens on the Four Challenges of the age in order to mitigate and overcome them? I argue here that the combined contributions of two concepts promise to be particularly illuminating in this regard: risk-class and resonance. Specifically, they offer strategic illumination regarding both means and plausible but surprising ends for better futures.

Let us first define some terms in this question. Three longer-term trends spell increasingly insistent political challenges that are unprecedented in both profundity and scale. These are (Tyfield 2018): first, the crisis of the environment and the transgressing of so-called 'planetary boundaries', most obviously regarding climate change and biodiversity loss, in a new planetary age of the 'Anthropocene' (e.g. Bonneuil and Fressoz 2016); secondly, the emergence of digital technologies and artificial intelligence and their increasing penetration into social life (e.g. Harari 2016); and thirdly, the unprecedented interconnection and mixing of humanity, across cultural, national and ethnic categories (e.g. Beck 2006, 2009). Each of these on its own would pose serious challenges to societies. Together, they amount to an extraordinary qualitative paradigm shift, and one that may be summarized in terms of a fourth, and 'meta', problem of learning how to govern complex systems well. Meeting these Four Challenges thus demands commensurately significant conceptual innovation and upgrading.

So pervasive, ubiquitous and profound are these Four Challenges that they are manifest in, and could be studied through, innumerable concrete issues of concern regarding habitable futures: e.g. of food and agriculture; energy and heating/cooling; or health and wellbeing. Yet one issue arguably incorporates and sits above all of these issues and is thus an acme of this emergent social condition: the city.

The urban is a key manifestation of the Four Challenges in two respects. First, because it brings out so clearly and immediately the important issues of contemporary social injustices and inequalities, being a site of an existing and acute system crisis. This 'new urban crisis' (henceforth, NUC) is 'much more than a crisis of cities'; rather, it is 'the central crisis of our time' (Florida 2017: xxvi).

Secondly, as humanity becomes an ever-more urbanized species, it will be in the resilience of cities that our successes (or failures) in responding to the Four Challenges are likely to be most vividly evidenced. In particular, urban infrastructure is a key practical, and so political, arena of the profound rethinking that is needed. For infrastructure is not only a matter of significant (if recently neglected) public concern with disproportionate effect on the quality of social life, rendering it highly important in its own right. It is also an exemplary site of current conceptual confusion, being widely conceptualized as the supposed archetype of enduring stability and technical mastery but now in a new age of 'normal disruption' (Graham 2010) that directly upends such expectations. Building urban infrastructures fit for the future thus quickly confronts numerous intense challenges: of system complexity, uncertainty, non-linear unpredictability etc., or just that there are no simple, universal answers.

Settled common-senses regarding the very meanings of these key terms (i.e. 'city', 'urban', 'infrastructure') are thus now in play over the medium term. The questions being raised about the future of city centres and the urban form due to the Covid-19 pandemic (e.g. KPMG 2021) are simply early foretastes in this regard. And precisely as sites of so many lives and livelihoods, and significant contemporary inequalities, what these keywords come to mean will continue to be fiercely contested for the foreseeable future.

With significant and qualitative social change underway, however, it follows that new concepts adequate to, and illuminating of, these still-emerging realities are needed. Here we explore the separate and combined contribution of two major conceptual innovations to these crucial issues.

First, there is 'risk-class'. This denotes a new and emergent form of social stratification amidst global risk-society that is shaped by differential positioning regarding both system goods *and system bads*, old and new. Moreover, the term incorporates both: (a) an emerging dynamic and productive *system* of social stratification; and (b) the *particular* risk-class most actively driving that system emergence, namely the rising/emerging 'global middle risk-class' (Tyfield 2018; cf. Kharas 2010, 2017; Ravallion 2010).

Contemporary studies of inequality have largely taken the place of what was previously explored in terms of class. The latter is now widely understood not to capture new and egregious inequalities. Instead, focus has shifted to quantitative measurement of inequalities, understandably seeking to bring them to public attention. Yet this largely empirical approach generally lacks any theoretical framework that replaces and upgrades prior understandings of 'class'.

Understanding, however, abhors a vacuum. In the absence of explicit attention to new conceptualization, the vacancy is filled by default with explanation in terms of mechanisms that are taken to be already well understood. Such explanations range across a political (economic) spectrum, from a focus on specific circuits of economic activity for more (small 'c') conservative analyses, to (now often 'racialized') 'capitalism' per se in more radical ones. In all cases, though, the still-emerging novelty and system complexity of key dynamics regarding (new) inequalities tend not to be either acknowledged or explored. The result is a range of explanations that tend to reaffirm, and so entrench and polarize, existing political positions.

Conversely, by specifically tackling the need for new theoretical understanding, a risk-class lens offers a much more informative analysis, and in at least two key respects. First, regarding how we have got to the NUC in the first place; and, secondly, regarding where this could yet lead, in particular regarding *how much worse it could get*. This thus motivates even greater political response and urgency.

Yet a risk-class perspective also thereby enables a critique of dominant, including critical, perspectives on (urban) inequality. In particular, it situates such arguments and consequent policy/political responses themselves within the system dynamics that continue to drive and exacerbate the grinding inequality and urban system dysfunctions characteristic of the NUC. It may at first seem unfair to include implacable critics of contemporary capitalism in the dynamics producing current system crisis. Yet this seemingly simple move is of the greatest significance, as we shall see, transforming the normative tenor of the whole analytic enterprise.

In particular, against the polarization of positioning one generally finds at present, a risk-class analysis is quintessentially ambivalent – or, rather, constitutively open-minded – in its normative stance, not least regarding its own key issue of appraisal of risk-class as emergent system (and global middle risk-class as particular ascendant social agency). For risk-class is, on the one hand, singularly dynamic and productive, not least regarding mass cultivation of the crucial 21st-century competence of complexity adeptness; while, on the other it is driving and driven by increasing polarization of societal 'winners' and 'losers'. The former is societally necessary; the latter is ethically unacceptable and societally ruinous. And yet, it seems, for the time being they come together as a single package.

The picture thus painted of humanity's global predicament is one of essential and constitutive political turbulence and ethical questioning, with no clear options that simultaneously tackle all the multiple complex and wicked challenges besetting cities, regions and their populations. Confronting us with this situation, a risk-class perspective thus immediately dispenses with ideological proposals that seek influence via populist and reassuring promises manifesting binary worldviews of 'good' vs 'evil'. Yet such extreme and polarized political stances are now dominating and fracturing democratic political settlements, even in the most stable polities. Accordingly, by challenging this cultural trend head-on, the concept 'risk-class' has already, at this stage, earned our concerted attention and even gratitude.

However, we may go much further. So far, 'risk-class' has emerged as a necessary but not sufficient step to show how our current seemingly bleak predicament grounds plausible visions of much more positive, if unfamiliar, futures. For this second step, though, we need the contribution of a second conceptual innovation: the sociology of resonance (Rosa 2019). Specifically, 'risk-class' and 'resonance' together open up entirely uncharted conceptual territory for exploration of key challenges and paradoxes, conceptual and strategic, of the present. This exploration is simultaneously constructive, sobering and inspiring; and here, focuses on city life, urbanization and infrastructure.

In particular, immanent dynamics may be identified that are otherwise missed and/or neglected through which the rising global middle risk-class will likely, in the medium term, birth a new relatively stabilized yet highly productive regime of 'green', digital capitalism; and/via the associated cities and infrastructures. That system will most likely remain egregiously unequal, even as it advances sustainability. In the longer term, though, further extrapolation of the same dynamics would likely push, for the first time in history, beyond a system built on socially stratified material distribution, possibly challenging the class-capitalism dyad itself and at global scale.

In short, armed with the new concepts – the missing jigsaw pieces – of 'risk-class' and 'resonance', a whole new, updated and enabling strategic vision for 21st-century society, and sociology, can begin to emerge. This will be able to work with the unquestionably profound socio-technical and planetary/environmental transformations (Clark & Szerszynski 2020) still ongoing without being defeated, bewildered or silenced by them. Indeed, we could even say that only with risk-class and resonance can we move towards a new sociological understanding that keeps and renews what was most valuable in classical 19/20th-century sociology, not least of Marxian inspiration – in terms of its perspicacity and efficacy of strategic vision regarding the live and productive social dynamics of its time (the proverbial 'baby') – while abandoning, updating and so transcending its substantive conceptual understanding (the 'bath-water'), formulated for a world that no longer obtains.

In short, together 'risk-class' and 'resonance' enable an updating of the foundational sociological concepts of 'class' and 'emancipation' respectively. And, likewise, they enable both critical engaged understanding of a new and still-emerging digital, green capitalism, just as the cognate concepts did for Marx in his strategic aetiology of the then-emerging industrial capitalism; *and* a longer-term vision of trans-capitalist planetary resonance, rather than industrial communism/socialism.

In what follows, tracing this conceptual journey, we first consider the concept of risk-class in more detail (section 2), before applying it to the New Urban Crisis (section 3), showing how risk-class illuminates the NUC better than does its original formulation by Florida (2017). Extending this critique further, in section 4 we then use a risk-class analysis to explore how much worse the NUC could yet get. As this argument depends on several elements that are generally overlooked, including in critical inequality studies, this also effects a preliminary critique of those approaches. Further exploring these neglected dimensions – which we may collectively label as issues of 'spirit' – in section 5, then opens up an entry point with which to engage with the paradigm-shifting sociology of resonance, proposed by Rosa.

In section 6, therefore, we introduce this perspective and use it to elaborate a scheme of sociological understanding for, inter alia, contemporary urban inequalities. Finally, then, with the paradigm shift taken, we can return to complete our investigation: first, by finalizing the critique of inequality studies from this resituated perspective; and secondly by illustrating how risk-class and resonance together illuminate productive, if anti-utopian, dynamics of urban inequalities to better futures that are otherwise missed but must be first imagined and recognized if probabilities of their realization are to be optimized. We conclude with final considerations, summarizing the crucial contribution of risk-class to understanding and tackling the singular challenges of the age, and as part of a broader project of rebasing sociological thought for the 21st century.

2.   WHAT IS RISK-CLASS?

Our journey starts with the work of Ulrich Beck (2009, 2013) regarding critical exposition of the emergence of global risk-society and increasingly profound evidence of new and egregious inequalities, inter- and intra-nationally. These include new *forms* of inequality, and thence injustice, such as regarding issues of networks and mobilities (Sheller 2018). In the emerging Anthropocene, it also includes exposures to new systemic bads, e.g. environmental and financial risk (Curran 2016), almost in perfect inverse relation to one's responsibility for causing them and one's opportunity to benefit from their creation.

In such circumstances, class, as understood from 150 years of (critical) sociology, is not only increasingly redundant as a social category (Beck 2013), but harmfully misinforming. In the first instance, this is because the settled gradations and definitions of class society, institutionalized in the socio-political bargains of the post-war welfare state, themselves broke down. As the UK's Deputy Prime Minister and former union shop steward, John Prescott, allegedly put it at the turn of the millennium, 'We're all middle class now.'

More seriously, though, was how such class analysis was also increasingly unable to see, much less explain, what was becoming most striking, new and egregious about the novel forms and yawning gaps of inequality. For Beck, then, global risk-society demands the abandoning of critical sociological analysis using the now outdated categories of the settled class stratifications of industrial capitalism and their well-documented dynamics of reproduction.

It is into this debate that Curran (2013) suggested the conceptual innovation of 'risk-class'. This aims precisely to identify and name this new process and system of social stratification, with the new social conditions of global risk-society front and centre, not awkwardly dealt with on the side. Up to this point, class is explored as a system of the (necessarily unequal and asymmetric) distribution of the goods or benefits produced by contemporary social processes, quintessentially of capitalism, in whatever is its current regime manifestation. Think, for instance, of the various forms of capital identified in Bourdieu's (2001) classic class analysis of mid/late 20th-century France (viz. economic, cultural and social). The key insight of 'risk-class' is to explore class in the early 21st century in terms of distribution not only of these system goods but also of the system bads.

There is no shortage of these system bads to consider today. However described and explained – whether in terms of global risk-society (Beck 2009), acceleration (Rosa 2013) and overflowing complexity (Urry 2003), or neoliberal financialized globalization (Harvey 2005) – what is unarguably striking of the past four decades is the dynamism and fecundity with which innovations (technological, cultural, legal and political economic) have constantly created ever more numerous and more existentially challenging risks, hazards and dangers.[1] (Clearly, this has profoundly shaped parallel processes of urbanization too.)

These 'bads', created by the system as a whole in its particular dominant trajectory of social change, clearly benefit and/or enrich some, usually those most active in creating them, for obvious reasons. Yet they also land as new burdens and costs too; and, almost inevitably, asymmetrically and unequally so. Indeed, bearing the costs of these new system bads is strongly indicative of the extent to which one is not (also) benefitting from them.

Any comprehensive analysis of contemporary society, inequality and injustice, therefore, must pay significant (if not greater) attention to the distribution of these constantly proliferating system bads as it does to that of the familiar system goods. For one's actual situation and comparative enablement to thrive is at least as conditioned by one's specific societally positioned exposure to the system bads as it is by access to the system goods, and with these inseparable and mutually compounding. Hence 'risk-class': a new and emergent form of social stratification amidst global risk-society that is shaped by differential positioning regarding both system goods *and system bads*, old and new.

It is, in fact, quite remarkable how profound a transformation in conceptualization is contained in this seemingly simple addition to our definition of class. As this handbook demonstrates, in fact, there is therein an entire research programme of theoretical development and empirical insight to unfold. For our purposes, though, we focus on a few key corollaries of particular pertinence to the argument of this chapter.

First and foremost, by incorporating system bads into our analysis of social stratification, we are always and inevitably confronted by the systemic production of factors and system outputs that no one will want to bear. While familiar class analysis in terms of goods may admit that there is intrinsic contestation over those scarce goods, it is also possible to reach a conceptualization – and, indeed, a relatively enduring institutionalized reality, as history attests – in which all classes are more-or-less satisfied with their share. Class-as-goods is thus conceivable as a system that can settle into relative stability, even though this is built on dynamics of constant haggling, 'struggle' and manoeuvre.

As soon as system bads are added to the equation, though, this settlement is fundamentally upended. For the individualized acceptance of a system bad, the benefits of which also likely go elsewhere, is simply unthinkable. Risk-class, thus, is inevitably a system of even greater dynamism and turbulence than the fiercely contested class politics of industrial capitalism.

Secondly, though, it is also a system of extraordinarily (system-)productive dynamism, including of its own emergence as a system of social stratification. Consider how these novel risks, dangers and system bads emerge at such pace and intensity. On the one hand, they have an upside for some that is intoxicatingly motivating and will continue to be so insofar as the costs can (continue to be) 'outsourced' or 'offshored' (Urry 2014) to others. Meanwhile, on the other, such displaced risks will tend to strengthen those enabled and weaken those emburdened, generating further rounds of enabling and emburdening. Finally, this very dynamic incubates a broader culture of both celebration of and avid, existential flight from systemic risks in the form of ever more rounds of self-serving 'organized irresponsibility' (Curran 2015, citing Beck 2009).

Moreover, in this prevailing and deepening politico-cultural context, this complex system dynamic takes on a particularly intense and objectionable form. For here not only are system bads relentlessly innovated and unleashed. There is also increasing and mutual reinforcement between, on the one hand, benefitting from the associated goods while escaping from exposure to the system bads (almost, i.e. short of planetary catastrophe), and, on the other, enjoying no such benefits but carrying disproportionate costs and exposures to the harms. Moreover, this dynamic pertains no matter how trivial or gratuitous the supposed benefit and how serious the harms thereby externalized.

It follows that risk-class has emerged as (and as a primary expression of) a massive multiplier of inequality and polarization of life chances, *permanently* diverging life courses even over generations. Class as *risk*-class is thus now the manifestation of not just (perhaps dramatically) unequal distribution of system goods (wealth, health, meaningful work, education) but also compounded and intensified by unequal exposure to new and increasingly profound (if possibly invisible, unfamiliar and/or undocumented) dangers. Of course, the latter also accumulate into global and/or planetary threats that likewise have uneven and localized effects.

We have here, therefore, a classic positive feedback loop characteristic of complex systems, and hence a ratchet of proliferating complexity and runaway acceleration.[2] From the perspective of sociological analysis, then, risk-class is also strikingly different to class(-as-goods) in that it must be investigated not as a system of enduring reproduction of existing structures, but one of ever-deeper systemic transformation and (destructive) (re)construction of new social worlds. In this respect, risk-class in the early 21st century, as an emergent and powerful force of social change, much more resembles the emergent construction of industrial class-based society of the 19th century than the subsequent settlement and reproduction of that form of class in the 20th, even as the latter is now reflected in sociological orthodoxy, not the former.

The concept of 'risk-class' thus presents a new resource with which to illuminate and hold to account novel dynamics of quantitatively and qualitatively new inequalities, precisely as Beck demanded. Yet it has not abandoned 'class' (and, by association, 'capitalism') as a key category, but updated it. And here too, therefore, we have the concepts with which we can begin to explain and hold up for critical political scrutiny the empirical dynamics through which the current global 'epidemic' of inequality actually manifests. These novel system dynamics, however, are not reducible to more populist, but also simplistic and misdirected, explanations (of Right or Left) in terms of personalized and/or structural moralistic blame.

As such, detailed research becomes possible, discerning the diverse socio-technical and spatio-temporal processes and mechanisms through which risk-class emergence and yawning inequality are currently feeding each other in specific times/places.

3.　THE NEW URBAN CRISIS AND RISK-CLASS

Perhaps the most graphic illustration of this risk-class dynamic today is that key manifestation of the Four Great Challenges, as mentioned above: the 21st-century city and associated challenges of urban inequality, infrastructure and resilience. Underpinning and exacerbating these diverse urban issues in recent years is the 'new urban crisis' (NUC). This manifests a model of 'winner-takes-all urbanism' that exemplifies the more general dysfunctions of late neoliberal capitalism with its strikingly 'winner takes all' (WTA) economy and model of (digitalized) innovation (Tyfield 2013).

The NUC consists of five primary dimensions (Florida 2017: 6–9):

1. The deep and growing gap between a few global 'superstar' cities and the rest (i.e. both inter- and intra-nationally);
2. the crisis of these superstar cities themselves, as the fragmentation into polarized 'haves' and 'have nots' reaches levels of inequality and unaffordability that threaten their very dynamism;
3. the growing inequality, segregation and 'disappearing middle' across cities and societies more generally;
4. a crisis of the suburbs too, as growth assumes spatially concentrating, not spreading and dispersing, forms, and the 'cheap land' for such sprawling growth is exhausted; and
5. emergence of an unprecedented phenomenon across the global South of 'urbanization without growth' (Jedwab and Vollrath 2015).

Altogether, then, these factors illustrate a new *geographical* inequality – i.e. with inequality taking on new, fundamentally place-based forms, no longer explicable in the abstracted non-space of a quasi-universalistic, purely 'social' theory – and *a new geography* of inequality – i.e. with novel, complex, fragmented and fractal spatial distribution of inequality (cf. Graham & Marvin 2001).

As Florida comprehensively documents, the central driver of this crisis concerns the dynamics of socio-economic clustering of innovative, 'high-skilled' knowledge-based or 'creative' activity. The twin result is both global competitiveness and localized economic growth, and demographic sorting, segregation and inequality. Placed atop pre-existing asymmetric distribution of socio-economic profiles (itself a time-honoured, foundational characteristic of capitalist development (e.g. Harvey 2005, Smith 2010)), then, this process has acted as a ratchet for the constant 'amplification of economic and geographic divides' (Florida 2017: 11). Indeed, these dynamics thereby overlay and compound pre-existing inequalities of diverse social forms, including along racial, ethnic and/or religious lines; worsening demographic disparities across multiple metrics even, perhaps, amidst significant improvements in tackling explicit and intentional discrimination and prejudice on such grounds, both legally and in everyday lived social norms.

Florida's book-length analysis stands out for the clarity and comprehensiveness of its exposition regarding this key system-level dynamic and the multiple social pathologies to which it leads. The account, though, is told as something of a mea culpa for his prior work as arch-evangelist of the 'creative class' who are now identifiable as leading protagonists, and system winners, of this crisis. The focus of the explanation is thus on how seemingly positive dynamics of innovation generate the unintended consequences characterizing the NUC. Moreover, his analysis focuses on the global North (and the US in particular) regarding both the mechanisms that have got us to where we are now and, relatedly, his key case studies, in both major global cities and failing ones.[3]

The result is certainly an illuminating and extremely valuable analysis, yet key issues are also missed or downplayed regarding possible futures of urbanism, or the ongoing process of mass urbanization and its future-perfect characterizability as comedy or tragedy. So too are the regions of the world that are already utterly dominating the 21st century's story of the city, namely China and the global South. These issues, however, come readily into view when the NUC is explored and explained not in terms of the (unintended consequences of) economic geography of innovation and knowledge-based globalizing economies – how this 'good' ends up doing 'bad' – but in terms of risk-class. And Florida's insights can indeed be fully and comfortably incorporated and situated in such an approach, while also illuminating aspects that are otherwise missed.

For instance, in both the general descriptions of his argument and the more detailed illustrations thereof, Florida is explicitly describing the emergence of a new polarized stratification of society, not captured in conventional categories of inequality. This is precisely 'risk-class', even as he never uses the term. Hence, 'the process of economic sorting is even more vexing than inequality per se, as it compounds the advantages to those at the top while also compounding the adverse circumstances of the less advantaged' (p.104). The result is that the 'nub of the NUC is increased economic isolation and insecurity of far less advantaged urbanites' (p.40). Elaborating on these dynamics, he notes (citing Wilson 1987) how the deleterious effects of the spatial concentration of poverty generates vicious cycles, in which fewer and lower-quality jobs, worse social networks (e.g. for work and/or marriage and/or role models), poorer schools, higher crime rates and prevalence of criminal cultures in peer networks (e.g. gangs), and worse health care and wellbeing constantly reinforce each other.

Arguably such dynamics have long been in evidence. But what is remarkable and new is how, in parallel, the clustering and segregation of the wealthy has become so much stronger, and in ways that '*reinforce* one another [such that today] they are [both] consistently a feature of large, dense knowledge-based metros' (p.113, emphasis added). In other words, 'in advanced nations and great global cities today, economic inequality is also spatial inequality: rich and poor increasingly occupy entirely different spaces and worlds' (p.110) albeit still in the same 'cities' and possibly cheek-by-jowl in complex, fractal 'splintered' (Graham & Marvin 2001) patterns not large, demarcated blocks of streets.

Indeed, so inadequate is conventional understanding of inequality, in the key form of urban inequalities, that 'our traditional measures of income and wage inequality understate the true extent of the economic divide because they fail to take account of this devastating combination' of 'economic inequality and economic segregation' (p.125), a combination that is 'deadly'. Moreover, chiming precisely with the argument of risk-class that this is the construction of new forms of inequality that endure and compound over time, Florida notes how 'class and location combine to reinforce one another, not just in the present moment but over generations', thereby generating 'a more permanent and dysfunctional inequality of opportunity' (p.125).

In short, there can be no doubt that the phenomenon Florida wants to bring to public attention is new and especially troubling, and that it involves the synthesis of the unequal distribution of social goods and wealth and of social bads, in their asymmetric geographical concentration. This is risk-class. Yet, 'risk-class' does more than just give a theoretical name to the empirical phenomena identified by Florida. Rather, the recasting of Florida's account is itself stronger when the concept risk-class is used explicitly, and indeed is placed at the heart of the analysis, rather than just as its peripheral output.

First, on its own terms, risk-class illuminates and rectifies several key gaps or weaknesses in Florida's argument. For instance, he insightfully argues, drawing on the work of Lance Freeman (2009), that the heated issue of urban gentrification of neighbourhoods is both sometimes overstated as an issue and not the real challenge. It can be overstated in that gentrification actually tends actively to displace far fewer than thought, with most erstwhile middle and working class areas 'riding' the increase in moneyed interest in their neighbourhoods (Florida 2017: ch.4). The real challenge, meanwhile, is almost a matter of the *limits* of the gentrification model of urban improvement (if we could call it such) in that poor areas are permanently excluded from the dynamic and tend, rather, to get ever worse. The destructive dynamic at work, thus, is how those displaced out of gentrifying areas and those never in them in the first place are moved to ever-worse and ever-worsening neighbourhoods. Such 'chronic, concentrated poverty is a far bigger problem than gentrification', Florida concludes (p.85), 'and remains the most troubling issue facing our cities'.

This argument is compelling as far as it goes, but there are key missing pieces to its explanation. The relatively sanguine interpretation of gentrification per se emerges from the structure of Florida's argument throughout, i.e. conducted in terms of the economic geography of knowledge-based globalizing capitalism, while retaining a generally positive (or at least resigned or unquestioned) view on this specific political economic model. As such, he argues, 'gentrification is the product of the very attributes that define knowledge hubs and superstar cities .... Acute gentrification is more a symptom of urban success than it is a general characteristic of cities and metro areas across the board' (p.75). In other words, insofar as we cannot be against urban success, we cannot be against gentrification.

Yet what is missing in this argument is the enthymeme – or tacit, presupposed premise – that by 'urban success' we understand this condition per se, rather than a particular historical form of it. By foregrounding considerations of risk-class, however – i.e. the new and newly egregious form of inequality that Florida himself ends up highlighting, rather than the economic geography of clustering – we can readily see that just such a specific and contingent form of political economy is indeed being presumed here. In other words, gentrification may be considerably less concerning and more benign than its bitterest opponents argue. And yet it is also the case that it is a particular manifestation of urban success – and an undeniably exclusive one, as part of 'winner takes all' urbanism – in the context of a broader 'winner takes all' political economy.

Moreover, once this first step is taken, we can also then situate, within the same explanation, both gentrification's corollary of concentrated urban poverty (not least in 'superstar cities') *and* the persistent political currency of arguments regarding gentrification's essential malignity, notwithstanding careful evidence to the contrary.

Regarding the former, it is the persistence and parallel reproduction of this underlying winner-takes-all risk-class economy that underpins both 'urban success' taking the particular form of gentrification together with the deepening and permanent exclusion from any such 'win' for 'loser' districts. While, regarding the latter, as precisely a manifestation of this more fundamental challenge, gentrification will understandably continue to generate resentment and ire so long as this root cause is not itself named and tackled directly. And that, in turn, would be evident in changed dynamics in which urban success no longer has to manifest as gentrification specifically. Demanding that political effort should be focused on alleviating concentrated urban poverty but not gentrification thus makes no sense from this broader perspective, since they are two sides of the same risk-class coin – losers and winners, respectively.

Similarly, while he offers useful, constructive and sometimes even radical policy suggestions about how to go from the current crisis to an 'urbanism for all' (ch. 10), there is a certain implausibility in these prescriptions, and particularly insofar as they are to be applied in the burgeoning cities of the global South. Indeed, there is a marked and jarring disconnect between some of his conclusions regarding the deep state of dysfunction of urbanization in the majority world and his upbeat conclusions that, with appropriate policies, all could yet be well (see Pieterse 2013).

For instance, he writes that, 'in the midst of the greatest urban migration in human history [i.e. in the global South, over recent decades and still continuing], urbanization has ceased to be a reliable engine of progress' (p.188). Indeed, for billions of these urbanites, 'urbanization has been a *near total failure'* (p.186, emphasis added), as a model of 'urbanization without growth' has increasingly taken hold. One would need strong evidence indeed to counteract such unequivocal statements with hopes that readily available policy interventions could generate better outcomes.

Yet the suggested interventions almost entirely presume functioning liberal polities and governmental apparatuses, with significant budgets available to spend on the public good (see Bigger & Webber 2021); or even a political context that agrees what that 'public good' is and can deliver on that goal (e.g. Jaglin 2008). This, however, is to underestimate radically the challenges of such policy across many areas of the global South, in ways that underline the general preference of the analysis for the global North. In doing so, Florida's argument also neglects the intricate systemic interweaving of issues of economic geography, his explicit focus, with those of political contexts and associated capacities of governmental administration. In short, what is manifestly lacking in Florida's account is explicit examination of the implicit presupposition of the specific regime of capitalism (and hence, inseparably, class) and the differential position within it of different cities around the world, which together massively over-determine the potential for a city to be a 'winner' or not.

Similarly, any attempt to address this manifest and 'near total failure' of urbanization in the majority world (and hence the majority of contemporary urbanization) must grapple with the cycles between specific dominant form of political economy and the power relations and social persons constructed in different places over time (e.g. Pieterse 2013). The latter, of course, is precisely the agenda of risk-class. Indeed, from a risk-class perspective, questions may even be raised regarding how credible, politically or strategically, some of Florida's policy recommendations are in the global North too, notwithstanding their reasonableness; and perhaps especially in the superstar cities.

For instance, while both London and New York have centre-left mayors at present, and both tend to lean that way politically, it would seem particularly hard to imagine such cities adopting land value taxes in ways that could dramatically harm their global economic competitiveness – and this precisely because of the issue of the concentration of power in these cities, and the supreme significance there of property asset prices in recent decades. These factors are then manifest in the risk-class profile of their respective demographies that would veto any such move.

Overlooking the crucial underpinning of the negative form of urbanism by a specific 'winner-takes-all' capitalism, however, Florida also opens his argument up to further critique and unpicking. In particular, he argues, 'inequality is not just an occasional bug of urban economies; it is a fundamental feature of them', but 'clustering is necessary for economic growth, inequality is not' (p.103). However, it becomes hard to sustain this distinction, at least as an insight capable of supporting a rationale for equality-boosting policy action, as soon as this wider perspective is taken.

Once we admit the underlying driver of this inequality is the specific political economy, it becomes clear that any initiative to mitigate particular inequalities is necessarily but a sticking plaster that allows the continued growth and intensification of the system as a whole. In other words, without addressing the engine of inequality, efforts to boost equality will end up only exacerbating the problem in the slightly longer term; and the distinction between 'clustering, good' and 'inequality, bad' becomes transparently untenable.

Placing risk-class at the heart of the analysis, however, situates the insights of Florida's account while going beyond this failing. First, in this way, we can bear witness to the emergence of a new urban condition that becomes itself a key factor in the ongoing evolution of global urban inequality, rather than as mere output; and in terms that provide a unified, yet geographically differentiated, explanation across the world, including the global South.

Secondly, for Florida equality/inequality is an external variable open to policy intervention. From a risk-class perspective, though, we see instead a complex system feedback loop. This is certainly mediated through 'winner-takes-all urbanism' and economic clustering, but it is primarily the relation between the propagation of the particular regime of WTA capitalism and the emergence and polarization of risk-classes (see Figure 12.1).

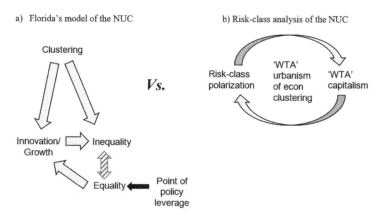

a) Florida's model of the NUC

Clustering

Vs.

Innovation/
Growth

Inequality

Equality

Point of
policy
leverage

b) Risk-class analysis of the NUC

Risk-class
polarization

'WTA'
urbanism
of econ
clustering

'WTA'
capitalism

Note: Clear arrows indicate positive impacts and striped arrows indicate negative impacts

Figure 12.1   Comparing explanations of the new urban crisis

Lastly, but by no means least, with risk-class as our lens we can incorporate – and as increasingly central – the dynamics of global risks in all their diversity (e.g. environmental, financial, health) and their differential impacts on urbanites; and with the efflorescence of such global-risks themselves endogenous to the explanation in a complex system that may be characterized as a totality specifically as that WTA political economy. By contrast, such global-risks feature in Florida's account only as background and external problems – no doubt shaping a 'perfect storm' of problems for 21st-century urbanization, but without their featuring in an explanation of how one could respond.

What makes this difference in explanation so important, though, is that this form of political economy – overlooked in an account of the NUC without risk-class – is still emerging. As such, the specific dominant regime of capitalism emerging from and through the 'winner-takes-all' urbanism that Florida illustrates remains uncertain and inchoate. The tendencies highlighted by a risk-class account thus leave open and put in question the future of these trajectories of social change: whether to even greater exacerbation of existing inequalities and/or potentially positive dynamics (see below).

Both possibilities, though, point to a third key issue regarding risk-class for our particular purposes. This concerns how risk-class matters not just as a system of social stratification and its dynamics. For it also relates to the ongoing formation of the specific class within that risk-class system that is the primary agent and beneficiary of that system's construction: the global middle risk-class. There is much excited commentary at present regarding a new global middle class (e.g. Kharas 2017, Ncube & Lufumpa 2015). Yet it must be immediately admitted, as our starting point, that this incipient but mushrooming socio-political constituency is not 'middle class' on any meaningful and recognizable definition that can withstand comparison with the settled sociological sense of this term regarding the post-WW2 global North (e.g. Goodman 2015; Milanovic 2013).

Conversely, it is credibly characterized as a 'middle *risk*-class'. This group is both sufficiently privileged to have meaningful access to the opportunities and (novel system) benefits of 'global risk society' *and yet* unable to secure themselves totally and lastingly from the risks of being disproportionately burdened with the associated system bads. Both the carrots and sticks of global risk-society thus present themselves most compellingly to this ascendant 'global middle class', vis-à-vis all other strata (Figure 12.2).

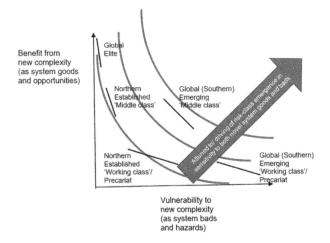

Figure 12.2   *Comparative orientation to risk-class amongst emerging risk-classes*

The global middle risk-class is aspiring, personally ambitious, inchoate, fluid and ill-defined, and potentially massively influential at global scale, given the combined effect of their huge numbers and significant economic wealth and dynamism. The result is thus that this demographic is the most significant agent in the ongoing emergence and shaping of the system of risk-class – and its associated transformation of capitalism.

In short, if we want to understand 'whither the NUC?' we cannot limit ourselves to the retrospective story of innovation clustering (in the US and UK) told by Florida and must instead invert the lens. Instead, we must look at the issue prospectively and from the perspective of risk-class and the epochal momentum of its ongoing emergence (and hence the global middle risk-class in particular). Doing this reveals, first, an even darker prospect as default future in the short term. But also, by identifying immanent, embryonic social systemic mechanisms, new visions and medium/long-term futures in which sustainable, resilient 'urbanism for all' is indeed a realizable possibility.

4.   HOW BAD THINGS COULD YET GET (EVEN AS WE GO 'GREEN'): A RISK-CLASS PERSPECTIVE

It may appear that, in foregrounding the importance of the political economic context, the argument so far resembles a relatively standard approach of critical inequality studies. But this, in fact, is not the case, and the differences are of utmost significance.

The former generally proceeds on the basis of spelling out the entrenched social mechanisms, springing ultimately from the structures of capitalism, that condition a relentless and one-way process of the reproduction of class distinction and growing inequality. As such, the conclusions of such analysis tend to be calls – to a greater or lesser extent, depending on the 'radicalism' of the argument (e.g. compare Piketty 2018 and Klein 2015) – for the wholesale transformation of that foundational structure, as the root problem. Absent such structural revolution, the alternative will be the continued status quo, with continued growth in inequality: the rich getting richer and accruing increasing shares of aggregated wealth; the poor facing ever-worse grinding poverty and carrying ever-worse global risks.

Conversely, a risk-class perspective disagrees with this argument on every one of these crucial points. First, placing the emergent social relations of risk-class at the centre (but not the foundation, given complex systems reasoning) of the argument shows that contemporary inequalities are a new and unfamiliar condition. Risk-class is a productive and dynamic social phenomenon, not reproductive and stabilizing. It is also, therefore, both unpredictable in its longer-term trajectories, and capable of historically rapid change – given its localized and positive feedback dynamics – not just steady incremental accretion. While agreeing with and accepting arguments regarding the inescapable tendencies of capitalism per se to asymmetric distribution of social goods, and indeed to class-based society, it also does not place the 'structure' of capitalism as the foundation and well-spring of all that follows. Rather, a risk-class perspective sets up a systemic-relational conceptualization of contemporary social realities that admits no such foundations at all.

The empirical focus is thus on the parallel and mutual construction of the specific social power relations and subjectivities of risk-class and the specific regime of capitalism, there being no capitalism in the abstract. Altogether, then, the conclusion and purpose of this form of analysis is also entirely different: not to show the urgent (yet timeless) need to overthrow capitalism per se, but to explore and illuminate existing powerful dynamics and to identify strategic openings and points of leverage here and now.

This more strategic and pragmatic approach will surely be rejected as being insufficiently radical, too accommodating of the outrageous inequalities of the present. But the exact opposite is actually the case. For, in the first instance, a risk-class perspective enables new ways of thinking about contemporary inequalities that show how much worse inequalities could yet become; and even as there is meaningful global action on environmental challenges, which is widely (mis-)interpreted as being necessarily 'win–win' for environment and social injustice. In other words, admitting only a reproductive (if incrementally worsening) logic, and perhaps also premised on a totalizing critique of capitalism, the broadly realist endeavour of mainstream critical inequality studies actually underestimates the dangers of contemporary inequalities.

Key to this difference in analysis are the emergent system dynamics of positive feedback amongst a network of three key issues; a network that places real, living, vulnerable social beings as central to the empirical trajectories of change. This triad is particularly apparent from a perspective of risk-class, and at this moment of neoliberal global system crisis, namely:

$$\text{complexity/acceleration} \leftrightarrow \text{alienation/polarization} \leftrightarrow \text{fear}$$

This system dynamic is intimately associated with risk-class. On the one hand, it is feeding the emergence of the risk-class system, in its proliferating production of uncontrollable system bads. On the other, it is then fed by the emergence of risk-class, through dynamics of system 'winners' having particular determination to separate, distinguish and secure themselves from (becoming) 'losers'.

In the first case, it is in the context of this dynamic of complexity–alienation–fear specifically that system bads are produced and then responded to in ways that attempt to contain and mitigate them through deliberately skewed distribution and externalization to the extent this is possible. And there is a huge amount that can indeed be externalized in this way, or at least sufficiently to keep that promise alive, thereby driving risk-class system construction. Such a process of successful externalization in risk-class formation, however, then underpins a further round of 'organized irresponsibility', driving yet more production of system bads.

In other words, while risk-class emerges as a system compelled, pushed and prodded by proliferating system bads, it is propelled, pulled and shaped by the specific dynamic of complexity–alienation–fear. This may be more easily understood by zooming in on the mechanisms of risk-class construction regarding the primary agents of this process, the global middle risk-class.

Taking each of the triad in turn, first, the global middle risk-class, as winners, are major beneficiaries and key creators of further complexity and acceleration, like global elites (e.g. Birchnell and Caletrío 2011). Yet, unlike those elites, they embrace complexity with full understanding of its costs and the personal dangers of falling instead into positive feedback loops of alienation/runaway acceleration that would catapult them into reinforcing cycles as system losers. Such enduring pressure and precarity thereby keeps fear on steady simmer. That fear in turn then keeps elbows sharp, conditioning the tendential reaction to the proliferating, uncontrollable, ill-understood and confounding – i.e. frightening – complexity of the world to be its most pitiless and self-serving.

This, in turn, ensures primary responses will be attempts at externalization and only personal mitigation,[4] hence driving further complexity and destructive acceleration and high-stakes alienation... and so on. In this way, then, risk-class is constructed at its most polarizing, system bads continue to accumulate and each feeds the other; hence complexity, alienation and fear intensify in reinforcing cycles.

Once we have identified these dynamics, though, it would seem they will be more or less prevalent for so long as such challenging global risks and system bads endure, i.e. for the long haul, not least since this process itself feeds production and exacerbation of system bads. Indeed, they will be at work even in brighter scenarios where there is significant climate action, and especially amongst that most populous and powerful rising global social force. Specifically, given the (entirely understandable) determination to build on their current but precarious status as system winners so as to remain such, a sustainable transition dominated by the global middle risk-class will inevitably drive incremental system bad mitigation only where externalization is seen as a failed or insufficient strategy; and then most likely in ways that disproportionately accrue benefits to the winners and costs to system losers.

Here, in other words, we have a powerful social dynamic that is constitutively normatively ambivalent. There are positive feedback loops (e.g. of green innovation and complexity adeptness) that are both highly dynamic and system productive, and at the crucial global scale needed for meaningful global transition, but that also remain no less polarizing of social (technical, environmental, economic, political) inequalities.

Moreover, this constituency is likely to take increasing hold of the machinery of state power in their respective countries and cities, arguably including even the massively powerful and globally significant apparatus of the Chinese state, and to turn its activities to prioritize their interests. This will, in turn, tend to legitimize their interests as the universalized 'public good', not least as this group do indeed observably lead the individualized adoption of (potentially expensive) 'green technologies'. It thus becomes even more likely that this group will be increasingly enabled in its self-advancing agenda, enjoying both ever-greater levers of power and ever greater public acclamation and moral approbation.

But the underlying dynamics of complexity–alienation–fear will persist. And in these circumstances especially, the combination of growing power *and* moral standing is ripe for the emergence of its dark side too. This would involve ever-greater conviction that those who are not so successful or enabled *deserve* their situation through personal fault and must be policed 'for their own' and/or 'society's' benefit. This, in turn, tends to generate a growing blindness to their suffering and to the ways in which this is greatly compounded by precisely such action.

In short, even if/as this middle risk-class demand significant action to mitigate such global risks as climate crisis, given the underlying sociological dynamics of this process as primarily those of self-preservation in a context of generalized fear, it is likely that this will exacerbate, not diminish, levels of inequality. The continued emergence of the system of risk-class and restratification of societies into risk-classes is then itself a key outcome and driver of this process of green transition.

So, this is what may well come to pass in the 'best case' scenario for climate change. But things would be no better, and likely a great deal worse still, if no such concerted climate action emerges. For all that would then be changed is the generally perceived hostility vs. hospitality of the environment, while the same underlying sociological dynamic of risk-class will remain in place. Given a world that is increasingly unpredictable and dangerous and societies already primed to sensitivity in this regard, though, this latter dynamic would most likely drive even more pitiless demands for self-preservation, and with the most powerful constituencies obviously the most influential regarding who is thereby prioritized.

In such circumstances, the most credible outcome, and especially across the more fragile and exposed polities of the global South (including China), would surely be a growing determination amongst those states that can do so to securitize responses to climate emergency in ways that privilege their powerful middle risk-classes (cf. Wainwright and Mann 2013). In turn, by default if not design, this would increasingly penalize poorer, if more populous, sections of society (including, for instance, 'climate refugees', internal and external: Bettini 2017).

Here, in other words, we have exactly the same dynamic of complexity, alienation and fear, and of accumulation of power for self-preservation of the middle risk-class at the expense of those below them. Yet there is also the added bleakness of nobody (nor the world as a whole) benefitting from significant mitigation of global climate risk, even sharper antagonism between the classes and a pervading zeitgeist of apocalyptic emergency, exhausting tension and cut-throat 'life-boat' politics.

Bringing this back to the NUC, it is obvious how this could play out specifically through issues of urbanization and infrastructure, and especially given the redefinition of the latter term immanent in the ongoing emergence of the digital condition. Regarding the worst futures of continued utterly inadequate climate action, harbingers of such cities are, in fact, already there for us to see in the highly securitized, paranoid urban forms of major Latin American and/or African cities, of razor-wire-enclosed compounds and ubiquitous surveillance.

In such futures, this would spread to other countries that have so far escaped it (e.g. across north/west Europe), and with security measures, forms of mobility and associated infrastructures 'upgraded' through digital technologies in ways that enable the 'more perfect' (cf. 'punish better' per Foucault 1979: 82) sorting of haves and have-nots. Moreover, movements towards that urban form in the global North may be triggered simply by growing unrest over inequality more generally (e.g. the proliferating urban racial unrest in the US in 2020), without any need for such protests to be specifically identified by those involved with issues of global risks.

Even in 'green' futures, though, infrastructures and urban configurations may well exacerbate inequalities, and even as they appear to be much more inclusive. Again, examples of this process are already clearly in evidence regarding, for instance, seemingly progressive programmes of bike-lane construction and/or bike-sharing schemes. For such initiatives, when simply placed atop the severe but fractal existing geographies of inequality, tend overwhelmingly to benefit demographics who are already comparatively privileged, while compounding pressures upon those who are not in ways that, for instance, actually intensify dynamics of gentrification and neighbourhood sorting (Fishman et al. 2014). The result is the surprising vehemence of negative reaction, or 'bikelash' (Wild et al. 2018), to such policies, not least from those who are supposedly thereby included and enabled by the downgrading of the car.

Similarly, the building of clean, efficient and dependable public transport infrastructures (and especially underground rail systems), serving city centres in particular, have been shown to benefit those living and working in these central and desirable districts disproportionately (Smith et al. 2020). Hence, even making such means of travel affordable is very likely to subsidize primarily the mobility of those who are already comparatively well-off. Here, in other words, we have perfect examples of how existing urban inequalities – and the political economic system dynamics that have produced them – are currently so great that even attempts to mitigate them may very likely actually just change their form, or even make them worse in the first instance.

So a risk-class perspective illuminates system dynamics that augur futures that could well be considerably worse than the present and that, even in best-case scenarios, are strikingly sub-optimal. In both respects, this offers a marked contrast to the arguments of mainstream inequality studies, which tend to miss the dangers of the former and, regarding the latter, proffer, or at least tacitly presuppose, optimal alternatives. What is crucial, though, is how a risk-class perspective highlights not just the key driving role of global risks in the ongoing restratification of society but also sets up insights into the qualitative and intersubjective dynamics (i.e. complexity–alienation–fear) that are, in parallel, profoundly shaping of actual outcomes. The significance of this subtle shift in perspective can hardly be overstated. For we have thereby been led, by risk-class, not just to different and novel substantive concerns but also to different methodological and ontological stances.

Specifically, faced with such flagrant injustices and dysfunctional social mechanisms it is tempting – obvious! – to conclude that we must tackle them at root. But what is this root? The answer from a risk-class perspective is likely to be unwelcome: there is no 'root cause' and hence no fundamental and 'really-existing' 'structure' to resist or oppose.

The 'structural' causes certainly matter, but they are not real qua foundational. Instead, we find that system dynamics can adopt a particular 'hue' or 'mood' that then pervades, conditions and colours the specific way in which the system evolves, and across scales of micro-, meso- and macro- levels. Regarding the NUC, WTA capitalism and risk-class, then, it is the 'mood' of fear that both characterizes, or expresses, *and* shapes, or rather poisons, the trajectory of system evolution. While in no way a foundation, such a mood is also then a key point of leverage and a key locus of responsibility for any analysis of the problems seriously committed to tackling them. Certainly, it cannot be ignored.

The strategic imperative is thus for forms of analysis that directly counter this mood of fear and anxiety, whether by providing insights that deflate fears with a bracing realism or by illuminating openings and courses of action that offer convincing, substantiated grounds for hope and inspired response. In short, what is needed in this case is analysis that both explicates contemporary inequality in ways that embrace the dynamics of the system as a whole, and shed light on the *positive* opportunities therein while concealing nothing of its negative tendencies. In this way, it also thereby takes responsibility for its *own* tendential effect on the system's evolution as a potentially influential perspective on these issues, and at the key level of the general 'mood' that it is itself committed to support and/or weaken. Here, in other words, we have an approach that is both critical and yet (re-)constructive. In the case of global inequality amidst existential global risks, risk-class is a key building block of just such an approach.

By contrast, structural and/or realist 'inequality studies' not only completely miss the key issue of contemporary inequality, namely the 'productive' dynamism of the system and hence the unfamiliar novelty of the new inequality. They also completely misdiagnose how best to combat it, namely by forlorn attempts to tackle, and indeed overthrow, the 'structure' at its strongest, i.e. having already conceded its enduring reality and, moreover, mischaracterized it.

Every element of this approach thus further weakens its strategic efficacy: determining to depose, not just develop and direct, …a supposedly solid structure, not just a productive and dispersed dynamic, …that is misunderstood, not strategically apprehended. What it does achieve, therefore, is largely the feeding of the alienation/polarization and fear that is the 'key' to the entire dysfunctional system dynamic as set out here. In other words, we can also now see how inequality studies does not just confuse understanding of its indubitably crucial subject matter. But it is itself part of the system dynamic that creates and compounds the very outcomes it deplores, a point to which we shall return below once we have done some ground-work on our second theory, to which we now turn.

5. DIGGING DEEPER: THE DANGERS OF FEAR AND THE IMPORTANCE OF SPIRIT

The problem before us has now been clarified: a dynamic system logic between the ongoing emergence and construction of a global risk-class system of social stratification and the con-tinued proliferation of unchecked global system bads through spiralling feedback loops of complexity/acceleration-alienation-fear. From this point, though, we are led (it turns out) in two complementary directions for deeper understanding.

First, if such complexity is the problem, it follows immediately that what is needed is some rebalancing simplicity – even if this is itself emergent rather than retrogressive. Let us call this a 'vertical' expansion (see Fig 12.3). What this emergent simplicity is and where it comes from, though, is almost by definition impossible to answer in advance and in the abstract. And it is even harder to envisage given the deeply entrenched social and material dynamics that condition accelerating complexity, or what Rosa (2019) calls 'dynamic stabilization', as matters of system functioning. While it is a useful starting point to have enunciated emergent simplicity as the goal, therefore, it is hard to do more with this realization alone, and so we will have to return to it below.

In this first step, though, we have already admitted the need for a different and new approach to the NUC. Inequality is not to be addressed primarily and directly by any levelling up of distribution of system goods, teleologically to 'equal' distribution. Instead, focus shifts to a system (and subjects therein) oriented primarily towards conceptions of the good life and ways of relating to the world that are not premised only and always on 'more is better', and particularly more material social goods. For this prevailing common-sense necessarily drives the relentless – and now manifestly dysfunctional, as planetary limit-transgressing – ratchet of complexity and acceleration and hence inequality, that is birthing risk-class society.

In opening up this agenda, of the conception of the good life/good society and concern with the presupposed and 'normal' relation to the world, and a social science thereof, however, we also thereby open up a second line of enquiry and expansion of our framework. This concerns the 'horizontal' expansion of the framework; in the first instance, through deeper exposition of the system dynamics of complexity ↔ alienation ↔ fear. Put together with the vertical expansion above, however, we also find ourselves able to expand horizontally regarding their respective opposites, i.e. expanding both vertically and horizontally (see Fig 12.3).

The resulting framework not only now offers other promising ways into the otherwise suggestive but opaque (almost noumenal) goal of 'simplicity'. It also sets out a much fuller and richer system logic that situates, opposes and so opens up the clear, present and daunting prospect of the complexity ↔ alienation ↔ fear dynamics taken on their own. In both these respects, the work of Hartmut Rosa is of unrivalled assistance.

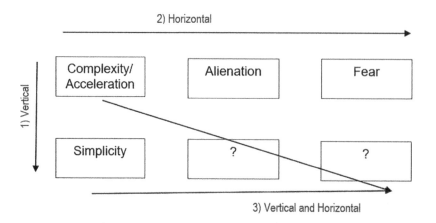

Figure 12.3   *Expanding the understanding of contemporary social system dynamics*

First, regarding elaboration of our understanding of the negative system dynamics, a focus on complexity and acceleration not only signals the otherwise neglected importance of their opposites (respectively, simplicity and stabilization, if not necessarily deceleration) in any effort to redress current dynamics of growing inequality. It also signals the ways in which, absent the countervailing balance of the respective opposites, the particular dynamics today of complexity/acceleration are singularly troubling, and in ways not fully captured or spelt out by these terms alone. For they are conditioning positive feedback loops of deepening burdening and lack of control, mediated through the generalized adoption across populations of a specific and (self-)harmful relation to the world, i.e. of deepening and even catastrophic alienation.

In other words, the terrible irony of contemporary, radicalized forms of modernity and 'progress' is that such 'advancement' actually spells worsening of human wellbeing, both for the majority especially, and for all to some extent (e.g. climate change or planetary boundaries) in a classic negative-sum game that is the very definition of madness. And it is precisely this dynamic that is driving risk-class emergence. Ever-greater system bads are cultivating and feeding a generalized alienation from the world and each other, and a determination to survive by being amongst the few lucky (but not so lucky) comparative 'winners', which thereby shapes socio-technical change in turn. In short, so emerges the logic of the 'race to lose last' (Wackernagel 2016).

Moreover, we may go one step further still. These global risks have, slowly but surely, percolated ineluctably into public consciousness, and so too the continued failure to mitigate them; indeed, with growing awareness that system dynamics actually have continued, all but unabated, to worsen the global risks. This has subsequently given rise not just to a generalized alienation, but also to the specific zeitgeist and habit(us) of fear. And fear multiplies, not least because – whether personal or collective – it massively further complicates and undermines practical action to address challenges. The systemic context of risk-class emergence is thus the systemic dynamics of positive feedback of this constellation as a whole. The ratchet of complexity/acceleration is in mutual reinforcement with the relation-to-the-world of alienation, which, in turn, is in mutual reinforcement (now to climactic peak) with the zeitgeist of fear. And it is on this basis that inequality could yet get much worse, beyond the gloomiest imaginations of largely reproductivist sociology of inequality.

For amidst not just normalized alienation, ennui and bleakness or 'muteness' in relation to the world, but actually unleashed fear that things will, relentlessly but perhaps suddenly, get dramatically worse, system dynamics of risk-class take on even more aggressively self-preserving characteristics. Yet this very stance and expectation thereby sets up even more dynamically dysfunctional and actively stratifying trajectories of socio-technical change. In short, a zeitgeist of fear not only feeds itself but also feeds specific responses, at both collective/state and individual/private levels, of intense self-preservation that then feed and legitimize that existential insecurity and fear yet further.

Finally, today this whole process is compounded and mediated by the exceptional mega-phones and deliberately targeted messaging of social media, post-truth and conspiracy theory. In a further hyperloop, therefore, fear hypertrophies and metastasizes through the associated disintegration, disorientation and polarization of public discourse; that key locus of accounta-bility, democratic oversight and public unification.

At its worst, then, and in places where the division between 21st-century global risk-society winners and losers is particularly acute and transparent, this will be actively shaping the built environment and urban forms and practices (and associated socio-technical innovations) in ways that are entrenching and cementing this 'normal' way of relating to the world. The massive building and reshaping ongoing in cities of the global South are striking 'concrete' manifestations of such zeitgeists, locking in dynamics of sociological stratification and ine-quality of the very worst kind. Yet even in cities of the global North, where the exposure to global risks is arguably less intense, we see here too an attenuated version of this dynamic – in the form of the NUC as documented by Florida, and as a canary in the coal mine regarding the more broadly dysfunctional and society-destroying dynamics of contemporary digital knowledge capitalism.

In other words, we can now understand the 'new urban crisis' as not just the outcome of the success of a particular form of innovation-clustering economic geography, but, set in this wider context, indicative of an entirely new and emergent challenge for global society as a whole; precisely the challenge of emergent risk-class stratification. Moreover, it is clearly a crisis, not just a new 'normal', because of the vertiginous and, indeed, genuinely terrifying self-propelling logic of the zeitgeist of fear that is both its product and its super-charger. In short, attending to the NUC in these terms we come to a rather surprising – and certainly social scientifically unfashionable – conclusion that the key socio-political challenge and point of primary leverage is a prevailing zeitgeist, not any specific socio-material mechanisms. Echoing FDR's famous dictum, it is imperative, in fact, that we learn to fear nothing but fear itself.

Such reasoning suggests the essential importance of cultivating an attitude and zeitgeist that directly counters such fear and its perilous self-propagation. Moreover, it suggests the importance of forms of analysis that are capable of supporting such a stance. This could be in terms of a deflationary puncturing of the worst fears and/or illuminating openings for more positive future developments, even spotting positive trends already in play but otherwise occluded. Acknowledging the importance of the 'mood' or 'spirit' of such research itself to its actual or potential contribution regarding the social issue at hand, though, is actually to call for a transformation in the foundational self-understanding of the social sciences per se. For it is manifestly not the concern of the vast majority of contemporary social science – and studies of inequality and class included – to take into account what effect its own relation to the world will tend to have, or is capable of having, in the world. Indeed, issues of psychophysical orientation or habitual affective stance, such as fear, feature rarely in such work.

That such issues really do matter, however, is simply a direct corollary of admitting that understanding complex social systems necessarily embeds the analyst as always already included in the dynamics under investigation (e.g. Fazey et al. 2020: 6 on 'second order science') – and so *how* one researches and/or relates to the system will itself inescapably both colour the findings and shape the potential impact thereof back on the system dynamics. In other words, we are confronted by the need for a paradigm shift in approach for sciences in and of and *for* (the better governance of) complex systems. This may be summarized as a move to a 'post-objective' science and a reorientation from perspectives grounded in the primacy of what Schweitzer (1923/1955) called 'worldview' – or one's sense of the real, objective constitution of the world 'out there' – to perspectives grounded in the primacy of 'lifeview'. This key term denotes the all-important sense of efficacy of one's stance regarding, and living relation to, the world, as a self-conscious will-to-live.

This is thus to propose a significant shift in the foundations of (a still critically illuminating) social science. It is therefore, perhaps, little wonder that it has proven so hard to abandon these prevailing standard ways of thinking – e.g. about inequality – notwithstanding their multiple frustrations and manifest shortcomings. In Rosa's ingenious development of a sociology of resonance, however, it is arguable that we now have the grounds on which to break with this outdated and sterile approach.

In particular, for our purposes, tooled up with the insights from Rosa's explorations of resonance, we are also now capable of a full statement of the horizontal expansion of the positive contraries to the fearsome system dynamics of complexity/acceleration ↔ alienation ↔ fear. And from there, we can begin to map out the full implications of a new sociology of risk-class: i.e. not just in terms of new and productive substantive concepts for thinking about the egregious new global inequalities, and the dynamics that are producing them; but also, and crucially, concerning new ways of thinking about these issues and of conducting research on them, with the potential to illuminate, and even to contribute directly to the construction of, brighter futures.

6.   'RESONANCE, SIMPLICITY, LIBERALITY' VS. 'ALIENATION, ACCELERATION/COMPLEXITY, FEAR'

This is not the place to spell out in detail what is, without exaggeration, the paradigm shift in sociological thinking manifest in Rosa's (2019) magisterial and seminal explorations of resonance and the 'sociology of our relationship to the world'. With our focus firmly on global inequality and risk-class, though, we can make the following key points.

What Is Resonance?

First, let us define 'resonance' and its importance in a critical, but engaged, assessment of contemporary societies. Working with the physical metaphor of actual resonance between two tuning forks (such that striking one, and then holding it close to a second, will make the latter also 'resonate' and 'resound'), Rosa progressively unfolds a usable meaning of 'resonance' for sociological thought. At base, this involves two closely inter-related meanings of the term.

On the one hand, and more abstractly, 'resonance' connotes a 'specific mode of relation – a specific way of being-related-to-the-world' (p.169). In this respect, Rosa builds on arguments concerning the most productive way of conceptualizing social phenomena as in terms of (perhaps dynamic, systemic) relations. In contrast to conceptions of social ontologies in terms of individuals and social structures, this posits instead systems that are constitutively relational (e.g. Bhaskar 1998). It is thus the specific forms of relating that give rise to both the seemingly 'macro' social entities (or 'wholes') and the specific subjects (or relata) that constitute it. Humans (and indeed, arguably, all non-humans too) are thus constitutively social in the specific sense of being constitutively relational, and hence characterised by their particular modes of relating to other beings, whether human or not.

In this context, resonance becomes a foundational concern of sociology – or a 'science' of understanding social systems – in that resonance is a *relational phenomenon* and a specific *quality of relating*. Indeed, it is a particular and singularly important one, being the 'relation of relatedness' (p. 178). Rosa's insight regarding resonance and its sociological importance is thus arguably just a spelling out of the reflexive logic of acknowledging the importance of a relational perspective, insofar as we admit a key element of consciousness and subjectivity to such distinctly human social relations.

More specifically, on the other hand, 'resonance' is also used to refer to the fact that this importance of resonance is not merely a theoretical posit but is a (perhaps, singularly) profound and felt need of the human person. In other words, the actual experience of resonance is one that is singularly significant and motivating to people, and hence can be seen (as Rosa shows exhaustively with myriad and wonderfully imaginative examples) to condition social behaviour and decision-making, whether everyday or of biographical significance. People actively seek out resonance – or resonant experience – even if/where they have no sense of articulating what they are doing in these terms. As Rosa puts it, resonance is thus

> a specifically cognitive, affective and bodily relationship to the world in which subjects are touched and occasionally even 'shaken' down to the neural level by certain segments of the world, but at the same time are also themselves 'responsively', actively and influentially related to the world and experience themselves as effective in it. (p. 163)

Taken together, then, Rosa's theory presents clearly and for the first time the need of human persons to experience resonance – both as the 'resonated' and 'resonator', the second *and the first* tuning fork – and the ways in which such experiences, and (perhaps habitual) failure or absence thereof, offer singular insights into the shaping of current societies and the trajectories of social change. Moreover, and of immediate relevance to our concern here of global inequalities, Rosa is also unequivocal in arguing that resonance too thereby elucidates not just the self-experienced 'success' or 'failure' of a particular life; it also and inseparably illuminates the social conditions for further resonant experience, and the extent of one's efficacy (both actual or 'objective' and self-experienced) in shaping these to one's advantage.

As such, one's capacity for resonant relation to the world is thereby understood as to some irreducible extent a matter of personal psychophysical disposition or character, but also and crucially (and, in practice, inseparably) a profoundly sociological matter; indeed, arguably the key sociological issue. For different social conditions will necessarily shape *both* the extent to which resonant experience is potentially available (e.g. consider, at limit, the chain-gang prisoner or hostage, as against the successful artist, or the rich man or lady of leisure) *and* one's capacity and power to shape one's conditions in order to improve the prevailing potentials thereof.

Moreover, we see in Rosa's analysis clear potential for dynamics of self-reinforcement and positive feedback via what Rosa calls 'self-efficacy', i.e. being able to feel in resonant relation with the world in ways that affirm one's capacities. Ripe conditions for experience of personal self-efficacy engender stronger openness and active, effective pursuit of resonance, which are then experienced by others with whom one successfully resonates, and so thereby compounding and strengthening those conditions etc. And equally, worse circumstances condition failure to resonate, which begets worse conditions. One might even say it is no longer just 'who you know, not what you know' that matters, but '*how*, in what relation and ways, you know them'.

It should thus also be immediately evident that such an analysis resonates(!) strongly with the analysis of risk-class and its dynamics of compounding 'Matthew Effect' social stratification described above. Risk-society 'winners' will tend to build on their initial advantages in ways that elicit more effective interventions for their reproduction and expansion *as well as* greater enthusiasm and active energy in support of established trajectories of change (if not the status quo itself) that supports them personally in turn. Meanwhile, system 'losers' juggle greater obstacles and in ways that are less effective and tend to be more disposed to the self-confirming disappointment of the failure or absence of resonant experience, thus sapping senses of self-efficacy yet further.

Here, in other words, is furnished a crucial and compelling characterization of the subjective counterpart to 'objective' iterative dynamics of risk-class: 'compelling' as phenomenologically persuasive; 'crucial' as offering insights for optimized strategic intervention as and amongst such resonance-seeking subjects with the objective and subjective processes only analytically separable.

Resonance and Alienation

Secondly, resonance theory offers a compelling account of the nature of alienation and its relation to resonance, in ways that serve to illuminate both of these concepts/phenomena, and hence the broader dynamics of risk-class. Specifically, alienation is the 'other' of resonance (and vice versa) (p.178), but not its opposite. Regarding the former point, whereas resonance is the relation of relatedness, and the experience of a mutually responsive and affirming relation between self and world, alienation is the 'relation of relationlessness' (p.175), and the experience of a 'mute' relation to the world. Alienation is thus precisely the absence or failure of resonance, or, as habitual disposition, of a felt capacity or potential for resonant experience.

As such, though, alienation is itself illuminated and in intrinsic relation with resonance, and vice versa. Hence they are like dialectical sub-contraries, not binary opposites. But this specific relation between the two may be clarified further. In particular, on the one hand, while persons may be more or less self-conscious, and more or less skilled, in their pursuit of resonance, it is never the case that any particular instance of attempted resonant experience can be guaranteed. Even someone's favourite song may grow tired, or fall flat in the context of a particular mood. Any such attempt thus risks resulting not in resonance but in disappointment and alienation. And, indeed, this risk is itself a prerequisite for the arising, as and when it does, of genuine resonance, without which the crucial specialness of the experience would be lost.

On the other hand, alienation is given renewed and compelling meaning through its inter-relational definition vis-à-vis resonance. The concept of alienation has fallen dramatically out of favour in (critical) sociological analysis in recent decades (Rosa 2019: 174 et seq.), despite having been a foundational concept of critique from Marx onwards. For all this august lineage, though, attempts to spell out more clearly and persuasively exactly what it means – and what it is alienation from – have proven forlorn, again and again, while the term itself has slipped into lay, and hence lazier, usage. In such circumstances, abandoning the concept altogether, as simply a loose arm-waving, appears the only option for rigorous social analysis. Yet, here, defined in terms of resonance and its absence, we finally have such a clear and precise definition: that alienation (of all its various forms) is at root alienation from (the capacity and possibility of) resonance.

The importance and usefulness of this revived concept of alienation, however, is particularly apparent and marked today, as Rosa's earlier work (2013) on acceleration shows and the centrality of the acceleration–alienation–fear dynamics above further attests. Specifically, with this concept we can understand the dynamics of the current manifestation of modernity as a particularly intense positive feedback loop between continual acceleration of socio-technical change and deepening muteness in relations to the world, or deepening incapacity for resonance. In particular, Rosa (p.17 et seq.) enumerates four key structural elements of contemporary modernity, namely:

1. understanding of ethical horizons of a human life as fundamentally open;
2. privatization or personalization of the ethical problematic (viz. 'how do I live a good life?') with the result that it is effectively insoluble;
3. a socio-political and political economic system that must constantly grow and innovate or collapse ('dynamic stabilization'); and
4. the resulting normality of constant competition between increasingly individualistic and materialistic persons, to drive that systemic growth and secure one's place within it.

Again, we may immediately note the 'resonance' of such analysis with that of risk-class.

Built on these conditions, though, positive feedback dynamics emerge of deepening mass alienation. Humans continue – given the insupportable but unshiftable burden of 'ethical privatization' and relentless competition – to search unstintingly and desperately for resonance. But this is systemically conditioned so as to be manifest usually in displaced and even impossible forms,[5] especially those of greater accumulation and appropriation of the world, not least in the form of the supposed promise and security of greater personal resources. Regardless of the passing success or disappointment of such attempts, this tends to cultivate the specific mode of relating to the world that treats it (ex ante) as mute, and hence primed for deeper alienation.

Moreover, in pursuing the 'jam tomorrow' promise of resonance in material(ist) accumulation (of experience), such action directly contributes to the further socio-technical acceleration and destabilization that further condition the likelihood of relationlessness, and hence deeper alienation. The dysfunctional dynamic of the present, thus, is fundamentally that of the self-defeating pursuit of resonance in ways that serve only to make it increasingly difficult and remote. Hence '*[r]esonance is [today] the momentary appearance, the flash of a connection to a source of strong evaluations in a predominantly silent and often repulsive world*' (p.185, emphasis in original).

Crucially, though, this dialectical relationship between resonance and alienation also illuminates a twist in this tale of the present. For the intimate connection between the two means that 'sensitivity to resonance directly and necessarily implies [sensitivity to alienation]' (p.186), and *so too vice versa*. The present is characterized by the mushrooming search and appetite for self-affirming experience by the insatiable and demanding individualists produced by this dynamic, *and* the growing inability of a world *deliberately created* mute to afford such.

It follows that this deepening alienation has within it the seeds of unprecedented sensitivity to and demand for resonance. In this way, the relation between resonance and alienation is seen to be 'highly complex and genuinely dialectical' (p.174), and we see how the current age – of unprecedented complexity, acceleration and, inseparably, deepening alienation – is also one of unique potential in terms of a new, and newly explicit, reorientation to resonance.

Expanding 'Horizontally'

Returning to the system logic outlined above, we see now more clearly how resonance theory illuminates and resurrects the crucial concept of alienation, and so enables the key 'horizontal' elaboration of the negative dynamics of the present, i.e. as complexity ↔ alienation ↔ fear, with alienation the key bridge concept, unlocking the whole. What is most important for our current purposes, though, is how this, in turn, also enables the horizontal elaboration of their respective contraries in the all-important specification of the associated *positive* dynamics (or, at least, possibilities thereof). Resonance theory is thus the all-important missing piece in a constructive yet still critical social theory fit for a world of complex systems. Or, to put it more concretely, if opening up just how bad global inequalities could yet become unpacked the key dynamic of complexity ↔ alienation ↔ fear, we may, with resonance theory, move to a fuller system logic that opens other, better possibilities.

Here, first, the contrary of complexity, i.e. simplicity, is connected to and illuminated in terms of resonance, enabling the fleshing out of what and how this otherwise supremely 'simple', and hence contentless, term. For instance, simplicity may be more clearly specified in terms of how it is a condition that optimally enables relations of relatedness, as against the constant and exhausting readjusting needed in contexts of proliferating complexity and runaway acceleration. Note also how this understanding of 'simplicity' also remains perfectly compatible with it being a specific and geo-historically contingent emergent quality of a socio-technical system, not a timeless and transcendent purity. Such simplicity is also, therefore, potentially uncertain and unforeseeable, …until it spontaneously and unpredictably manifests.

However, just as alienation provides a crucial bridge between complexity and the zeitgeist and/or affective disposition of fear, so too does resonance connect simplicity to the contrary of fear, enabling its specification. Tessellating and constellating between 'resonance' and 'fear', as presupposition and opposite respectively, identifies the key missing piece as (what may be called) 'liberality' (Murray 1938). This is an affective disposition of positivity and generosity towards the world, an active and practical celebration of one's freedom and efficacy as an agent in the world, and with an explicit rejuvenated *ethical* (not political) orientation that sees ethics and value(s) as of crucial *practical* importance, not just as constraints and/or pieties. Liberality thus connotes embracing and skilfully cultivating the opportunities for successful (i.e. resonant) participation in the constant making of the world, and in arguably the most important respect of being *free of fear* (Moffatt and Tyfield 2021).

More specifically still, whereas fear is the default effective stance of the subject confronted by a world understood to be potentially hostile but certainly given, liberality is that of the subject able to see the world as (potentially) responsive to their attempts to remake it. In other words, fear characterizes the person who takes worldview as primary, while liberality the person who sees lifeview as primary. And a resonance perspective shows not only that the former is, per se, alienation, while the latter is in resonance, but also that adopting a resonance perspective allows one to *see this* and thereby to *choose* to think in terms of that more strategically enabling framing.

In short, just as a zeitgeist of fear is identified as a key obstacle – but also, as subjective, an important site of agential leverage – to the emergence of more positive system dynamics and positive feedback loops, resonance theory thus enables the identification of liberality as the specific orientation needed to take up this agenda. In other words, with resonance theory at our disposal, we can identify that the crucial positive corollary to complexity/acceleration ↔ alienation ↔ fear is (emergent) simplicity/stabilization ↔ resonance ↔ liberality.

Once alerted to this, however, it also becomes possible to begin to look for and observe how this latter is not merely posited as the idealized opposite but is in fact evident and manifest already in various ways. To start with, this perspective immediately resituates the ratchet of inequality/risk-class emergence. Framed by resonance theory, we can see this is driven not just – or, arguably, even primarily, at least in terms of its specific form and shaping – by a purely negative social logic of existential flight and self-preservation, of misanthropic malevolence, malice and selfish disregard. Just as, if not more, important is the active and positive search – albeit often misconceived – for human flourishing of those who find themselves, for the first time, precarious but definite system winners and so determined to pursue their advantages and opportunities with all the energy at their disposal. Both negative *and positive* dynamics are thus at play, albeit asymmetrically and, at present, only embryonically.

Resonance and Risk-class

Finally, there is significant mutual conceptual enrichment in placing resonance theory and risk-class in conjunction. First, as Rosa notes, the 'root of this incapacity' (i.e. for resonance, as in habitual feelings of alienation) lies 'in either rigid fixedness or chaotic openness of either subject or world to which it relates' (p.179), both of which have clear risk-class sociological allusions, along the lines noted above (see p.209). There are also two specific important ways in which this is the case.

First, the increasing sensitivity to resonance that is the corollary of increasing experience of alienation is arguably a particularly productive dynamic amongst precisely that social constituency that is also at the vanguard of the construction of the risk-class system, i.e. the emerging global middle risk-class. In short, this powerful emerging global constituency is arguably uniquely primed for a rapid emergent self-consciousness of a conception of the good life (and good society) explicitly conceived in post-materialist terms of the optimal pursuit of resonance.

Poised most precariously, but promisingly, between futures characterized by self-confirming cycles of resonance or alienation, the intensity of attraction and repulsion respectively is uniquely strong for this group. The novelty of the enjoyment of opportunities for experiences of resonance afforded by middling prosperity is still great (in ways it is still absent for the global precariat and has grown stale for established classes in the global North), while, conversely, exposure to global risks is a live and threatening possibility (in ways it is not for the established middle classes of the global North, for instance). Moreover, in these circumstances, experiences, and hence positive feedback loops, of self-efficacy are likely particularly vibrant amongst the global middle risk-class (even as they are likely regularly thwarted). This is evident, for instance, in their broader (and palpable) mood of cautious but unquestionable optimism and liberality; a mood that is all the more striking for the contrast it presents to the doom and gloom prevailing in the global North.

For example, so dynamic and positive is this constituency that one may speculate that it is capable of an unprecedentedly rapid education and development of its consumer tastes. In this way, the all-but-inevitable surge, in the first instance, of materialist consumerism may quite quickly be overtaken by a move to post-materialist aspiration of the sort identifiable in the global North (e.g. Inglehart and Abramson 1999), but taking just years rather than decades. The rapid evolution of sophistication in consumer tastes in China, for instance, already evidences such a process (Yu 2014).

One must also surely add here that not being Western, Euro-centric cultures could well assist this further. For these groups are not burdened with a deeply entrenched and endogenous fetishism of the autonomous individualist consumer as corollary of the mute world of secular materialism and the enduring scars of the 'Death of God'. Even to the extent such societies may themselves have become extremely materialist (potentially even more so than the contemporary post-materialist West), longstanding cultural dispositions regarding a greater appreciation of collectivism and interdependence and/or an enduring pragmatism of thought, as opposed to Western literalism, are also potentially significant advantages.

Moreover, it is surely germane that it will simply be too difficult, expensive, 'wickedly' challenging and even environmentally impossible for the emerging global middle risk-class to attain the secured high levels of materialist and consumerist lifestyle they may see in the late 20th- and/or early 21st-century global North even if they aspire to this. Consider, for example, developments over recent decades regarding traffic congestion and/or traffic-related air quality across East and South Asia and Africa (The Economist 2018). It is already evidently the case that the obvious and default pursuit by such constituencies of such a class-as-goods standard of living very quickly emerges as, not only a zero-, but a negative-sum game.

Secondly, resonance theory enables the identification of the *full system* dynamics of contemporary global inequalities and the emergence of risk-class:

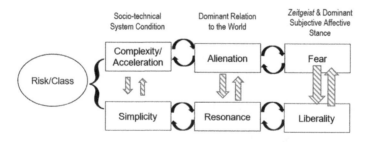

Note: Black circular arrows indicate positive feedback and light grey striped arrows indicate negative feedback

Figure 12.4   Complex system dynamics of resonance/alienation and risk-class emergence

As such, resonance theory not only allows the specification of the second, positive row, but also a sense of how the whole fits together and is in dynamic inter-relation, with upper and lower rows mutually informing and inter-related. Crucially, with the whole system thus specified, we can see that it is the *integrated effect of both rows* that will shape the effects, and hence the specific forms, of risk-class. Consequently, an analysis of risk-class alone points to how much worse global inequalities could get and to the system dynamic of the upper row. In synthesis with resonance theory, however, we also now have the theoretical outlines for exploration of the opportunities for better futures emergent with the rise of the system of risk-class (to which we will shortly turn).

With the system dynamic as a whole before us, not only can we see the dangerous positive feedback loops of the destructive dynamics; we can also begin to conceptualize and explore how these could generate their contraries and especially to the extent there is conscious acknowledgement and effort. This would thereby set up productive positive feedback loops that directly counter, dampen and/or mitigate dynamics of frenzied disintegration and extreme inequality. This applies not just to the contrast between the two rows as a whole, but also to the complex dialectical ('and/vs.') relations between each element thereof, viz. alienation and/vs. resonance in the first instance, but also fear and/vs. (perhaps deliberately cultivated cultures of) liberality and, ultimately, complexity and/vs. simplicity.

Indeed, the emergent 'lower' re-constructive system dynamic, in fact, only makes sense and earns its dynamism and, ultimately, stability through and in contrast to the lived experience and understanding of the upper. As we have seen, resonance presupposes the experience and understood possibility of alienation. So too, liberality emerges as a deliberate stance precisely as one witnesses unmistakably the clear and present dangers of a zeitgeist of fear and becomes determined to reject it in defence of things one values and/or perhaps thereby comes self-consciously to value.

Finally, even the great imponderable of an emergent simplicity is illuminated, at least in abstract, by this schema: not as a totalized wiping of the slate, a revolutionary clear-out, to some supposedly pure, prelapsarian state, but always and necessarily an *emergent* state out of the level of complexity – i.e. *life* – that has evolved to that point. In each case, therefore, we also see slightly, but interestingly, different relations between the dialectical pairs, furnishing a richly qualitative picture.

7.   CRITIQUE OF INEQUALITY STUDIES: REPRISE

We will shortly turn to our final issue, seeking to illustrate the arguments regarding more constructive dynamics and brighter futures potentially immanent in risk-class emergence. Before we do so, though, let us conclude our critique of mainstream critical sociology of inequality, now building on arguments that Rosa himself (2019, ch.1) also makes explicitly in his exposition of resonance theory. As already stated, resonance offers the crucial missing piece – for a compelling critical social theory in this new age of complex, global system challenges – of a credible positive counterpart and conception of the 'good life' that is capacious enough to be non-specific and so pluralist and inclusive of diverse cosmo-political conceptions, and yet also specific enough to be analytically usable and useful.

More specifically, resonance theory offers an account of the positive goals of sociological enquiry that is compatible with a complex systems perspective. Complex systems, however, demand the admission that one is always already situated within the dynamics one is seeking to illuminate and divert. Social investigation aims to assist in, or itself to deliver, the realization of social futures that are better than those currently tendentially in play. It follows that it is a matter of the utmost importance not only to have a clear and compelling account of what that 'better' looks like, but also to embody and exemplify it. This marks a significant break with a critical social science formulated in an age of relatively enduring social structures. For this latter project could justifiably legitimize its enterprise – both epistemically, in terms of requisite modesty, and politically, in terms of openness to democratic process – in purely negative terms, allowing the 'better alternative' to emerge in the course of time as society responded to its criticisms.

Today, however, where the *spirit* of the research itself sets the limit to what it can contribute or not in terms of positive change, a positive enunciation of that goal (however abstract) is now inescapable. In resonance theory, we have one that fits the bill perfectly. Indeed, what is needed is precisely a programme of research (e.g. on global inequalities) that itself manifests and supports the key stance of liberality. And the conjunction of risk-class analysis and resonance theory (captured in Figure 12.4) enables exactly that: for instance, in terms of combined exploration of both the negative system dynamics of risk-class emergence, and the positive possibilities and opportunities associated with the emergence of the global middle risk-class (in particular) as a new and unfamiliar social phenomenon.

In other words, risk-class and resonance together make clear that the former is precisely *not* another manifestation, at grander, global scale, of the emergence of the Western bourgeoisie, thereby spelling only an even more catastrophic and violent rerun at global scale of its rise over the last two centuries. Rather the global middle risk-class is *both* a class and *yet also something else and as-yet-unknown*, poised between intense fear and liberality. What is needed is thus to explore it in ways that channel and manifest that same spirit of liberality, or direct opposition to the zeitgeist of fear, so that the potential for positive impact of the investigation itself may be optimized.

Framed thus, however, it is not just the substantive conceptualization of inequality studies that is problematic. This work is characterized by a 'normative abstinence' specifically regarding a positive conception of the good life and a 'psychophysical scepticism' (p.23) regarding the importance of personal affective stances to the trajectories of social change. The former is today mostly premised on pluralistic and relativistic, rather than positivist, grounds; the latter on a sociological realism that seeks to eliminate personal characteristics from causal relevance on normatively egalitarian grounds. Yet such positions systematically neglect what is amongst the most important of considerations; namely the importance of the spirit of the investigation to its potential impact in the world. Indeed, from a resonance theory perspective, we can see this contemporary common-sense perspective is doubly flawed.

On the one hand, it is an intrinsically imbalanced and one-sided exercise. For absent any explicit, defensible and credibly realistic formulation of the better world to which it is aiming in its criticism of how things actually are, it, at best, tacitly presumes the possibility of effectively total equalization of distribution of material and social goods (e.g. at least as an implicit benchmark against which to measure and critique what is in fact the case). At worst, it has no alternative at all, hence making it a thoroughly negative enterprise of unreasonable and insatiable indignation.

The latter is easily dismissed, but the former also needs rational defence. And in the context of climate change, it is, if anything palpably false that inequality could be 'fixed' if everyone's standard of living was raised to that to which all aspire, i.e. of a relatively comfortable, 'normal' middle-class family in the global North in 2020. Given current conditions, this would only ensure planetary environmental catastrophe. Indeed, from the crucial perspective of one-planet living, it is currently the case that even environmentally 'best practice' forms of crucial elements to a high-quality living standard (e.g. regarding education, democratic politics, vibrant public sphere etc.) would not yet be capable of achieving this goal (O'Neill et al. 2018).

This approach thus lacks grounding in terms of the all-important implicit contrast – viz. 'Well, what instead then? "Bad" *compared to what?*' – that it cannot but draw on in its criticisms of the present actuality. Yet, with no justified or mobilized sense of what good outcomes look like, its gaze is unilaterally focused on the endless spotting of the unequal distribution of resources and goods – of which, of course, there is limitless, and genuinely troubling, evidence. In other words, thus framed, such studies can and will only ever find, and so spread, more reasons to be discouraged – and, indeed, cannot fail but to find such evidence of terrible inequalities, which, after all, abounds – and never with any findings that might signal glimmers of hope in the opposite direction.

On the other hand, though, we have seen that the spirit in which knowledgeable engagement with complex systems takes place matters profoundly – maybe even pre-eminently – in colouring its actual and potential impact on the issue in question. In this case, the one-sidedness of its epistemic project means that such approaches are 'capable of constantly mobilizing social outrage' (p.24) regarding what are, unarguably, grievous harms, but *only* this. Indeed, since such perspectives offer no grounds for identification of cycles of improvement – do not even have a credible conception of what 'better' means so as to be able to look for it – and conversely, cannot fail but to find inequality wherever they look, they tendentially develop but one affective response to the world: righteous anger, grievance and alienation from a world increasingly confirmed to be constitutively hostile.

The result is that the research programme as a whole is premised on categorically unreasonable and insupportable demands: that unless and until the (not just improbable, but) impossible outcome of a (non-specified) 'fully equal' society is realized, they will adopt the unbending posture of decrying the injustice of society and deliberately inciting social antagonism about such issues, regardless of whether such an approach itself is helpful or harmful (in any particular instance) to efforts to tackle those very problems.

The terrible irony, thus, is that, once we acknowledge that the contribution of a research programme to the zeitgeist is itself a key element of its potential impact in society and that a mood of fear and outrage is the worst possible context for the tackling of new and challenging complex system problems, it emerges that such studies actually serve to feed and compound the very dynamics that are generating the outcomes they rightly deplore and are determined to expose. Certainly, the more self-consciously 'radical' they are, the more they are incapable of insights that could make a meaningful and positive change in the opposite direction, could offer findings that cultivate the opposite zeitgeist, and hence could drive positive feedback loops of societal flourishing.

And, with Rosa, we may note that the root of this weakness is precisely their continued adherence to the objectivist and materialist perspective, which manifests in the focus on inequality as an issue of unequal distribution of (material) resources, thereby excluding from view any concern with issues of resonance. Such work is thus an exercise in reification of the world it rejects, and hence also of the broader condition of social alienation that underpins the whole dynamic array of negative social outcomes.[6]

In sum, orientation to resonance illuminates how the goal is to stimulate new experiments and subjectivities capable of resonance – and *thence* unpredictable emergent simplicity – in and through expanding liberality; and that mainstream, critical social science simply does not engage with this process. But what could such a process look like regarding our concern here of global risk-society inequalities? In other words, is there any evidence and/or traceable dynamic that could mean the ongoing emergence of risk-class could – has the potential to – lead to better futures than we currently tend to imagine, not just worse? To this final and crucial issue we next turn.

8.   MORE POSITIVE URBAN/INFRASTRUCTURAL FUTURES?

We have seen how a resonance theory perspective illuminates a whole and still-emerging system dynamic, in which the ongoing construction of a new system of social stratification, i.e. risk-class, could yet be productive, not just a ratchet of deepening alienation and inequality. The key question that emerges, though, is arguably a surprising one, namely: 'How does, or could, emergence of risk-class system affect and/or effect a mass self-conscious reorientation of social aspiration to resonance?' Or: 'How does the rise of (the global middle) risk-class (and through the challenges of urban infrastructure) condition the shift from the primacy of worldview to lifeview, and then with what potential impacts (via cycles/feedback) on urban infrastructure and risk-class *itself*?'

To explore this question, then, let us return to our issue of urban inequalities and infrastructures and the potential interaction with risk-class system emergence, with the global middle risk-class as the vanguard. From this new and broader theoretical perspective, we find that such issues are in fact ripe for such analysis, and potentially perfect examples of these more positive dynamics. On the one hand, the global middle risk-class likely has acute sensitivity to issues of inadequate infrastructure (i.e. 'for me and my middle risk-class life and aspirations'); that is, what is not addressed even when one can afford individualist technologies and avail oneself of contemporary socio-technical opportunities and complexity. Specifically, infrastructure is such a political bellwether today precisely because of the current inadequacies of the systems bequeathed by a generation of neoliberalism for construction of such infrastructures. Indeed, over four decades of global free market fundamentalism and associated digital technological change have problematized the very common-sense definitions of 'infrastructure' itself.

These prevailing definitions of infrastructure, legacies of the understanding of the 19th and 20th century, see it as a matter of top-down public bequest of single-best, all-but-permanent and massive physical structures. 'Infrastructure' is thus widely understood as: standardized, often grandiose in scale, concrete and built once-and-for-all; managed, governed and provided by 'others', namely publicly credentialled bodies of technocratic experts, and with little or no need for citizen involvement, beyond the passive role of user; and enabling primarily materialist forms of 'good life' (for a presumed 'majority') and associated cultures and ways of life (not least regarding a settled stratification of class-as-goods) (cf. Graham & Marvin 2001).

By contrast, it is increasingly clear that the agenda for the building of the resilient, inclusive cities needed today militates against almost every element of this understanding, in terms of the importance of public participation, experimentation, pluralism and personalization, adaptability, and update-ability of infrastructures. The global middle-risk class, as the constituency of powerful denizens of these 21st-century cities, are thus particularly attuned to these challenges.

Yet, on the other hand, it is precisely this group that is most likely to be motivated and able to build, design and govern these new infrastructures and to work out precisely and in detail how, pragmatically and phlegmatically, to juggle these myriad new and intense challenges in the specific ways relevant to specific places. They will not only act as a significant power bloc, thereby demanding the state resources and powers needed for many of these projects. But as both 'middling' in prosperity, relatively highly educated and aspiring in outlook – i.e. embodying precisely such an aspirational liberality, determined to grab the opportunities for a better life notwithstanding the evident challenges and system risks to which they are also exposed – they will also be well placed actually to do something about it. And to do it en masse, as a large, diverse and global group concentrated in the burgeoning cities and megacities of the global South (including the crucial case of a rising China).

Moreover, turning specifically to the system dynamics above, it is not just this liberality that could promise positive developments in this regard. The potential for such outcomes seems even more compelling when viewed through the lens of resonance theory. It is precisely the visceral concern about and experience of alienation – in exposure to global risks – that acts as motivating 'stick' in this case. While conversely, with little-to-no guarantee regarding the eventual realization of the secured material prosperity of the late 20th-century global North, there is a strong external forcing towards the *self-conscious* acknowledgement of resonance (likely only in occasional, but precious, moments) as the real goal (or 'carrot') of the good life to which they are aspiring.

In this context, while inadequate infrastructures and urban environments are a particularly arresting experience of deleterious acceleration and alienation for the global middle-risk class, the emerging self-consciousness of resonance as life goal could offer ever-clearer – i.e. as realizable and increasingly realized – re-orientation, including not least in their grappling with the challenges of urban infrastructure. As such, this search for, and precious experience of, resonance in leisure *and working life* could well incubate a slow but relentless reorientation of the presumed lives and life-goals that infrastructures and urban forms are meant to serve and enable. Moreover, it could incubate this in and through jobs and careers – and for this group especially – that themselves manifest singular experiences of satisfaction in the resonance of the burst of collective creativity such a framing to urban problems may unleash; and especially in vivid contrast to the pervasive background and life experience of enduring conditions of alienation.

Together, then, a global middle risk-class that is encouraged to embrace its tendential optimism may – through the resulting liberality and progressive, even self-conscious, orientation to resonance – embrace the otherwise seemingly intractable challenges of global risk-society as opportunities for their self-advancement. But this would still likely be a world that is being made increasingly hospitable for a lucky minority – albeit a bigger and more geographically spread group than the elites of contemporary late neoliberalism – who are able to live fearlessly and occasionally meaningfully amidst hostile conditions of global risk-society. What is needed to *change these conditions themselves*, and in ways that are to the benefit of all, with the concomitant mitigation of yawning inequalities, however, is precisely a significant rebalancing of the dynamics of social life from the one-sided production of the overflowing complexity to a new and higher-order simplicity.

This is likely to be a longer-term development. But in basing the specific efforts of the global middle risk-class, e.g. regarding the challenges of 21st-century infrastructure, in orientations to liberality and resonance, the likelihood of such emergence is at least optimized, if still unpredictable. Thus oriented to conceptions of the good life that celebrate both human ingenuity (i.e. liberality) and interdependence and relational connection (i.e. resonance), it does not stretch credulity to imagine how this could even result – from here, with the present as the inescapable starting point – in a new and valued simplicity in the designs and practices of everyday urban life and the infrastructures on which they depend, and even in the iterative processes of their development, maintenance and upgrade.

Over time, and perhaps with startling rapidity given the exponential feedback loops and pent-up energy thereby released, this could then realize a more generalized emergence of system simplicity that is otherwise hard to conceive. Indeed, such dynamics are arguably already in embryonic evidence, for instance in the arguments for cities and infrastructures that are 'smart' not in the sense of being overlain with digital technologies so as simply to increase the efficiency of existing dynamics of complexity and social acceleration (Kitchen 2015), but as newly human centred, place-based and even 'dumb' (Fleming 2020). Alternatively, for a striking example, consider the work of Kongjian Yu and his Turenscape consultancy (https:// www.turenscape.com/en/home/index.html) regarding low-cost, 'nature-based' urban flood defences.[7]

We may even specify this dynamic yet further, by returning to the key dynamics outlined by Florida in his analysis of the new urban crisis, but now from the perspective of our synthesis of risk-class and resonance theories. Florida's account insightfully identifies the key dynamic and tension at the heart of the NUC and its crisis of inequality. This concerns the contradictory relations amongst, on the one hand, a 'knowledge-based' growth model premised on accelerating innovation and its geography of clustering that generates inequalities, and, on the other, the presupposition of some level of equality for continued economic growth and sufficient social cohesion. The result is thus an asymmetric but dynamically tense relation between constantly worsening inequalities and (greater or lesser, but always superficial) attempts to mitigate them to preserve system integrity and keep the growth model ticking.

To this aetiology of the current predicament, our analysis of risk-class in terms of the importance of alienation/resonance and the current zeitgeist of fear adds further crucial variables. These identify how such dynamics of economic geography also: (1) mediate through a deepening zeitgeist of righteous and spiky individualism and alienated materialist acquisitiveness that colours the dynamics of the whole in ways that tend to bring about the worst possible exacerbations of urban inequalities and self-preserving short-sightedness; and (2) crystallize in the parallel and ongoing emergence of the most dynamic social force of the moment, the middle risk-class and the risk-class system of social stratification per se (see Fig. 12.5).

Once we expand the perspective further, to incorporate the full system dynamic outlined above, though, three further elements of the system become apparent, thereby capturing and conveying at least the potential for trajectories of change that are entirely different, as being both hopeful and qualitatively productive. These are:

1. the recognition of the constitutively ambivalent politics of the emerging middle risk-class as potentially self-serving in the meanest of senses; but also, precisely as exposed to global risks, capable both of compassionate empathy – and regarding the most pressing of new

social issues specifically – with those not lucky enough to be in their position, and hence of profound concern regarding issues of equality;[8]

2. the countervailing spirit of liberality, not fearful self-preservation, and the growing orientation to adaptive and resonant relationality and inter-dependence; and

3. arising from that, the progressive design and construction of new urban infrastructures that serve to enable such resonance-prioritizing lives and for as many as possible, hence with dispersive political economic effect and effectively common access (see Fig. 12.5).

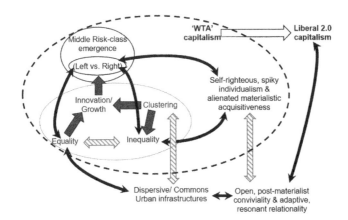

Note: Thin black arrows indicate positive feedback, thick dark grey arrows indicate positive feedback regarding Florida's account of the NUC re risk-class, light grey striped arrows indicates negative feedback, thin dotted inner oval indicate Florida's analysis and thick dotted outer oval indicates risk-class analysis lacking concepts of resonance

Figure 12.5   Resituating the NUC within risk-class and resonance

Altogether, then, we see how the key question of 21st-century urbanism is, '*Which global middle risk-class prevails and comes to dominate?*', amidst the systemic tensions between the benefits of clustering for innovative digital capitalist economies and the drive to significant rebalancing of urban areas towards more egalitarian outcomes through the construction of infrastructures supportive of such goals. Such an analysis, however, not only sheds some light on the possibility of things actually getting better; and while accepting, illuminating and explicitly building on the distressing and entrenched dynamics underpinning contemporary inequalities, not seeking to deny them. It also offers insight into *how* this could happen, and with the possibility that the eventual outcomes could yet be qualitatively better than we could otherwise even conceive.

Indeed, surely the most radical implication of this dynamic is the traceable potential of the emergent risk-class system as an immanent driver to futures of resilient cities in which constitutive socio-economic processes are relentlessly pushing *beyond capitalism per se*, and in two key senses.

First, the global middle risk-class 'winners' of risk-class emergence will certainly drive, benefit from and enjoy disproportionate shielding from continued production of system bads in the short term, and even likely enjoy public moral approbation for their individualized efforts at their mitigation. Yet the sheer impossibility of externalizing these system bads will secure from them increasing determination and action to tackle these at system level.

Precisely as *risk*-class, in other words, the emergence of this group is distinct from the historical parallel of the emergence of the middle class(-as-goods) of industrial capitalism. This time they will not be able to avoid internalizing, and so taking responsibility for; (at least a qualitatively greater proportion of) the negative counterparts of their self-advancement (i.e. system bads or 'risks') in ways the latter managed systematically to externalize. For the risks are now global, fractal and inescapable, while, conversely, the subjectivity of this middle risk-class will itself be forged in explicit response to them, not just the sense of personalized materialist opportunity. In this regard, moreover, urban infrastructures will be a key site of this development.

Secondly, though, in their increasing orientation to issues of resonance and explicit 'anti-fear' liberality, this tendential pressure is also to incubate a new and unprecedented relation to the world; i.e. one that is foundationally antithetical to the materialist, objectivist, individualist yet idealistically secular-utopian alienation that both characterizes and is generated by contemporary capitalism. A life and/or society oriented to resonance, rather than utilitarian satisfaction and maximal appropriation of the world, is one that is also tendentially aware of the *impossibility* of guaranteeing resonance and hence the enduring *imperfectability* of reality. This is not a stance that can sustain, nor bootstrap, the great destructive delusion of limitless acceleration and material growth.

Instead, this new pragmatic and anti-utopian spirit will be both mindfully fearful of the omnipresent dangers of system disintegration in an age of perpetual global risks and complex systems; and self-consciously aware of the dispersed responsibility for avoiding the break-out of such destructive panics. And for that reason, it will also be explicitly and deliberately oriented to liberality as the collective spirit dispelling such positive feedback loops of fear, insofar as there is minimal social and/or personal positivity sufficient to sustain it.

In other words, here we find an emergent and revitalized global *liberal* disposition that may yet condition the socio-technical evolution of a new social form and political economy that does indeed deliver a major systemic shift beyond contemporary inequality. Far from auguring only a new and worse form of capitalist polarization, therefore, the emergence of risk-class may yet be the immanent development that bridges from the present – when it is, notoriously, easier to imagine the end of the world than the end of capitalism– to futures in which we have in fact transcended this form of political economy. Rather, as Figure 12.5 sets out, therein are also dynamics towards a qualitative shift in psycho-social arrangements, away from the ratchet of competitive, materialist individualism to open, post-materialist conviviality and adaptive, resonant relationality – simply as a matter of 'enlightened self-interest', that most powerful of social forces.

We will have done so, though, not through direct, anti-capitalist revolution in the name of 'equality' and 'justice'. And the future that thereby arises will not resemble utopian visions being constitutively sub-optimal, given the impossibility of engineering and guaranteeing resonance, and the intimate (perhaps acknowledged) interdependence of simplicity and complexity, resonance and alienation, and even liberality and fear.

9.   CONCLUSION

There is, and can be, no guarantee that the middle risk-class, spread across the 'developing world', and the dynamics of their emergence will forge a world of simplicity, resonance and liberality rather than a continuation of the overflowing complexity, alienation and fear. Rather, compatible with the paradigm-shift-like break with prevailing social scientific norms, the analysis of such complex system problems admits no room for such conclusive and 'scientific' predictions, nor, therefore, any identification of the preordained 'agents of history', as for 19th- or 20th-century Marxian analysis of class struggle.

That has not been the goal of this chapter. Instead, we have sought to set out some of the more important insights available from the synthesis of new sociological conceptual innovations that have grappled seriously with the challenges of thinking and doing global complex systems better (Tyfield 2018), so as to present something of a vision of this different – and quietly, but powerfully, hopeful – prospect.

From this perspective, we can see how dangerous dynamics of division and snobbery currently observable with the emergence of the risk-class system could be compounded with misrecognition to create futures characterized by even more nefarious inequalities, and with the self-preserving efforts of system 'winners' to 'save the world' simply legitimating and driving that inequality yet further, not challenging it (Curran & Tyfield 2020).

As such, there is no alternative to the concerted involvement and responsibility of all persons, including not least the system 'losers' of the global precariat and longstanding 'uber-winners' of the powerful global elites alike, to steer developments and the emerging historic bloc of the global middle risk-class towards the kinds of collective learning processes and reshaping of built environments that could avoid such outcomes. In doing so, though, it is obviously of the utmost consequence that we can begin to envision and understand how powerful and live system dynamics could yet generate more positive futures (if certainly *not* utopias (cf. Levitas 2013, Wright 2010)); and to accept that the *spirit* of attempts to elucidate empirical evidence of such movements is itself of singular significance.

In short, if the goal emerges as a new liberality, with a new ethical rejuvenation in reorientation to lifeview as primary, out of which may yet emerge a new collectively imagined simplicity and stability, then:

- *resonance* grounds the reorientation in social ontology and the proximal, practical goal that is needed, as conceptual rebasing;
- *risk-class* is the already-emergent social force and agency driving its expedited mass adoption; and
- *resilient urban infrastructure* is one of the most pressing and pivotal problems and opportunities that could compel this collective learning process over the medium term, and at sufficient pace and scale.

As such, risk-class is a key building block of a reimagined and retooled sociology and in three key respects:

1. as a concept, it illuminates contemporary system dynamics, how much worse they could get and the self-defeating danger of reproductivist studies of inequality;
2. as a force in the world, it is driving an expedited mass global learning process that is building a transformed, complexity-adept capitalism in positive feedback loops, even as

this also likely deepens social stratification as part of that turbulent process; but potentially as a stepping stone beyond capitalism in the longer term and the building of that global trans-capitalist society in new resilient cities and places; and

3. as both a concept and as a force in the world, it respectively illuminates and drives the mass reorientation from the unquestioned primacy of (realist and increasingly fearful) world-view to (complex, strategic, affirming, and resonating) lifeview as the key and goal of this moment of system transformation; the stance presupposed for any adequate response to the meta-challenge of learning to govern complex systems well.

NOTES

1. For these reasons, with 'innovation' as the positively valued, 'system good' counterpart of the risk, dangers and system bads underlying the emergence of 'risk-class', it may even be more accurate (if less pithy) to talk of 'risk-innovation-class' (Tyfield 2018).
2. We note the potential confusion over the use of the words 'positive' (and, to a lesser extent, 'negative') throughout this discussion, in that 'positive feedback loops' concern specific system dynamics of proliferating reinforcement but may well be strikingly negative in impact. Whether we are referring to genuinely 'positive' developments or 'positive' feedback loops (the desirability of which will depend on the specific case), should be evident from the sense, and sentences ripe for misunderstanding have been carefully reworded accordingly.
3. Hence, for example, the proportion of 4:1 (depending on how you count it) of the 'dimensions' enumerated above regarding the focus on the global North and global South respectively.
4. A preference for climate adaptation vs. mitigation measures, given the private benefits and the public costs of the former vs. public, dispersed benefits and high, private costs of the latter (Harper and Peake 2021), also follows.
5. As argued further below, this potentially includes various forms of critical social science as an unusual, and rather perverse and intellectualized, form thereof, e.g. in the motivating excitement regarding insight into the negative state of the world, flushed with virtuous pride.
6. Hence, regarding note 5 above, we find that such work is itself a key example of the dysfunctional and directly self-defeating positive feedback loops of misplaced attempts to find resonance in ways that only feed deeper alienation; in this case, for self and others.
7. *TuRen* means 'earth' and 'humanity', a classic conjunction of traditional Chinese thought.
8. In the terms of my recent book on the 'liberalism 2.0' or 'complexity liberalism' (Tyfield 2018) associated with this rising power bloc, this would align, respectively, with a concern primarily for economic liberalism (which would lean Right) and political liberalism (which would lean Left).

REFERENCES

Beck, U. (2006), *The Cosmopolitan Vision*, Cambridge: Polity.

Beck, U. (2009), *World at Risk*, Cambridge: Polity.

Beck, U. (2013), 'Why "class" is too soft a category to capture the explosiveness of social inequality at the beginning of the twenty-first century', *British Journal of Sociology*, **64** (1), 63–74.

Bettini, G. (2017), 'Where next? Climate change, migration, and the (bio) politics of adaptation', Global Policy, **8**, 33–39.

Bhaskar, R. (1998), *The Possibility of Naturalism (2nd edition)*, London: Routledge.

Bigger, P. and S. Webber (2021), 'Green structural adjustment in the World Bank's resilient city', *Annals of the American Association of Geographers*, **111** (1), 36–51.

Birchnell, T. and J. Caletrío (eds) (2011), *Elite Mobilities*, London: Routledge.

Bonneuil, C. and J.-B. Fressoz (2016), *The Shock of the Anthropocene: The Earth, History and Us*, London: Verso.

Bourdieu, P. (2001/1983), 'The forms of capital', in M. Granovetter and R. Swedberg (eds), *The Sociology of Economic Life (2nd Edition)*, Boulder, CO: Westview Press, pp. 96–111.

Clark, N. and B. Szerszynski (2020), *Planetary Social Thought*, Cambridge: Polity.

Curran, D. (2013), 'Risk society and the distribution of bads: Theorizing class in the risk society', *British Journal of Sociology*, **64** (1), 44–62.

Curran, D. (2015), 'Risk illusion and organized irresponsibility in contemporary finance: Rethinking class and risk society', *Economy and Society*, **44** (3), 392–417.

Curran, D. (2016), *Risk, Power and Inequality in the 21st Century*, Basingstoke: Palgrave Macmillan.

Curran, D. and D. Tyfield (2020), 'Low-carbon transition as vehicle of new inequalities? Risk-class, the Chinese middle-class and the moral economy of misrecognition', *Theory, Culture & Society*, **37** (2), 131–156.

Fazey, I., N. Schäpke, G. Caniglia, A. Hodgson, I. Kendrick et al. (2020), 'Transforming knowledge systems for life on Earth: Visions of future systems and how to get there', *Energy Research and Social Science*, **70**, 101724.

Fishman, E., S. Washington, N. Haworth and A. Mazzei (2014), 'Barriers to bikesharing: an analysis from Melbourne and Brisbane', *Journal of Transport Geography*, **41**, 325–337.

Fleming, A. (2020), 'The case for making low-tech "dumb" cities instead of "smart" ones', *The Guardian*, 15 January.

Florida, R. (2017), *The New Urban Crisis*, London: Oneworld.

Foucault, M. (1979), *Discipline and Punish*, trans. A. Sheridan, New York: Vintage.

Freeman, L. (2009), 'Neighbourhood diversity, metropolitan segregation, and gentrification: What are the links in the US?', *Urban Studies*, **46** (10), 2079–2101.

Goodman, D. (2015), 'Locating China's middle classes: Social intermediaries and the party-state', *Journal of Contemporary China*, **25** (97), 1–13.

Graham, S. (ed.) (2010), *Disrupted Cities*, London: Routledge.

Graham, S. and S. Marvin (2001), *Splintering Urbanism*, London: Routledge.

Harari, Y. N. (2016), *Homo Deus: A Brief History of Tomorrow*, London: Vintage.

Harper, P. and S. Peake (2020) 'Emergency technocentrism', *Interantional Journal of Sustainability in Higher Education.* Unpublished manuscript available at: http://peterharper.org/education (accessed 11/7/22).

Harvey, D. (2005), *A Brief History of Neoliberalism*, Oxford: Blackwell.

Inglehart, R. and P. R. Abramson (1999), 'Measuring postmaterialism', *American Political Science Review*, **93** (3), 665–677.

Jaglin, S. (2008), 'Differentiating networked services in Cape Town: Echoes of splintering urbanism', *Geoforum*, **39** (6), 1897–1906.

Jedwab, R. and D. Vollrath (2015), 'Urbanization without growth in historical perspective', *Explorations in Economic History*, **58**, 1–21.

Kharas, H. (2010), *The Emerging Middle Class in Developing Countries*, Paris: OECD.

Kharas, H. (2017), *The Unprecedented Expansion of the Global Middle Class: An Update*, New Delhi: Brookings India.

Kitchin, R. (2015), 'Making sense of smart cities: addressing present shortcomings', *Cambridge Journal of Regions, Economy and Society*, **8** (1), 131–136.

Klein, N. (2015), *This Changes Everything: Capitalism vs. the Climate*, New York: Simon & Schuster.

KPMG (2021), *The Future of Towns and Cities post Covid-19*, London: KPMG.

Levitas, R. (2013), *Utopia as Method*, London: Springer.

Milanovic, B. (2013), 'Global income inequality in numbers: In history and now', *Global Policy*, **4** (2), 198–208.

Moffat, L. and D. Tyfield (2021), 'Governing complexity: Interview with David Tyfield', *Global Discourse*, **11** (1–2), 275–283.

Murray, G. (1938), *Liberality and Civilization*, London: Allen & Unwin.

Ncube, M. and C. L. Lufumpa (eds) (2015), *The Emerging Middle Class in Africa*, London: Routledge.

O'Neill, D., A. Fanning, W. Lamb and J. Steinberger (2018), 'A good life for all within planetary boundaries', *Nature Sustainability*, **1**, 88–95.

Pieterse, E. (2013), *City Futures: Confronting the Crisis of Urban Development*, London: Zed.

Piketty, T. (2018), *Capital in the Twenty-First Century*, Cambridge, MA: Harvard University Press.

Ravallion, M. (2010), 'The developing world's bulging (but vulnerable) middle class', *World Development*, **38** (4), 445–454.

Rosa, H. (2013), *Social Acceleration: A New Theory of Modernity*, New York: Columbia University Press.

Rosa, H. (2019), *Resonance: A Sociology of Our Relationship to the World*, Cambridge: Polity.

Schweitzer, A. (1923/1955), *Civilization and Ethics*, London: Adam & Charles Black.

Sheller, M. (2018), *Mobility Justice*, London: Verso.

Smith, D. A., Y. Shen, J. Barros, C. Zhong, M. Batty and M. Giannotti (2020), 'A compact city for the wealthy? Employment accessibility inequalities between occupational classes in the London metropolitan region 2011', *Journal of Transport Geography*, **86**, 102767.

Smith, N. (2010), *Uneven Development: Nature, Capital, and the Production of Space*, Atlanta, GA: University of Georgia Press.

The Economist (2018) 'People say they hate traffic jams, but are oddly tolerant of them', September 6, https://www.economist.com/international/2018/09/06/people-say-they-hate-traffic-jams-but-are-oddly-tolerant-of-them (accessed 31/5/22).

Tyfield, D. (2013), 'Transition to science 2.0: "Remoralizing" the economy of science', *Spontaneous Generations: Special Issue on 'The Economics of Science'*, September.

Tyfield, D. (2018), *Liberalism 2.0 and the Rise of China: Global Crisis, Innovation and Urban Mobility*, London & New York: Routledge.

Urry, J. (2003), *Global Complexity*, Cambridge: Polity.

Urry, J. (2014), *Offshoring*, Cambridge: Polity.

Wackernagel, M. (2016), 'The race to lose last', accessed 2 February 2021 at http://www.2052.info/glimpse6-3/

Wainwright, J. and G. Mann (2013), 'Climate leviathan', *Antipode*, **45** (1), 1–22.

Wild, K., A. Woodward, A. Field and A. Macmillan (2018), 'Beyond "bikelash": Engaging with community opposition to cycle lanes', *Mobilities*, **13** (4), 505–519.

Wilson, W. J. (1987 [2012]). *The Truly Disadvantaged: The Inner City, the Underclass, and Public Policy*. Chicago, IL: University of Chicago Press.

Wright, E. O. (2010), *Envisioning Real Utopias*, London: Verso.

Yu, L. (2014), *Consumption in China*, Cambridge: Polity

13. Science, food, and risk: ecological disasters and social inequality under the GMO regime

Md Saidul Islam

INTRODUCTION

In today's world, one thing we know for sure is that we do not know for sure what we are eating. With the rise of industrial food systems, consumers hardly know whether the foods they are consuming are environmentally sound, socially responsible, and culturally friendly. Industrial food systems have provided wider and easier choices for consumers, yet there remain questions related to the safety, security, and health implications of those foods. Historically, food has always been related to health, culture, and tradition, but today it is also intricately linked to the scientific establishment and sometimes to social inequality and ecological risk and disasters.

Risk and disasters are usually treated as "natural events" caused by "violent forces of nature"; recent studies, however, emphasize the ways in which socio-technological systems create disaster vulnerability (Wisner et al. 2003; Islam and Lim 2015). Social risk and disasters such as violent conflict, illness, and hunger actually lead to more loss of life than "natural" disasters such as earthquakes and cyclones (Wisner et al. 2003). In this chapter, I delve into food-induced social and ecological risk and disasters that are, to a large extent, linked to the "establishment of science" (see section 2 for details); my focus is the bio-tech regime of the global agro-food system.

The emergence of agro-biotechnology allowing the targeted manipulation of genes in living organisms has fundamentally altered agricultural landscapes and operations on a global scale. While this technology has indisputably led to increased agricultural productivity and in the process improved the socio-economic status of nations and individuals, it has its drawbacks, in particular in the social and environmental realms. In addition, the extension of patent rights to the field of agriculture (e.g. seeds) has enabled corporations like Monsanto to exert economic and political dominance over small firms, driving them out of business. This technology, coupled with the patenting of life/seeds, has been a subject of heated debate over the last two decades. One central issue in this debate is a potential ecological risk and social inequality, posing questions for the future of food.

In this chapter, I aim to uncover a critical nexus between the "establishment of science," food regimes, and social and ecological risk and disasters, focusing on the bio-tech regime of the global agro-food system responsible for the development of genetically modified organisms (GMOs). This chapter has three objectives. Drawing on a framework that addresses (a) the logic and establishment of science, and (b) food regimes and the social and ecological risk and disasters (section 2 below), this chapter analyzes the implications of the massive adoption of agro-biotechnology, in particular the potential environmental risk and social inequality. By revealing the negative aspects of such technology, the chapter contests the science-based technological optimism of the proponents of agro-biotechnology. It also highlights the current structure of the global food production system, which is, to a large extent, based on "scientific" rationality and dominated by transnational corporations (TNCs). In the process, it brings to light the contradictory functions of the Intellectual Property Rights system, which facilitates the concentration of market power in the hands of huge corporations, causing agrarian stress and inequality. Finally, it discusses how science itself and various actors along the food production chain can effect a change in food governance and drive the future of food towards sustainability.

For the methodology, the project relies on an extensive review of secondary sources including documentaries, journal articles, and books in order to understand the different propositions put forth by scholars and thereby developing a balanced critique. A conscious effort has been made to juxtapose the information presented in secondary sources against the information in the documentary *The Future of Food* (Garcia 2009), in search of consistencies and contradictions. Here, I have used "intellectual activism" as a methodological tool for my analysis. "Intellectual activism" is a concept developed by sociologist Patricia Hill Collins (2013) that requires sharp thinking and research, honest and dispassionate analysis, and common sense grounded in experience and observation of a subject. Based on this robust search, I will first address the common misunderstanding between the Green Revolution and Gene Revolution. Then I will discuss the social and environmental impacts of the Gene Revolution, focusing on the intersection between risk and inequality. Finally, I analyze the limited role of the government and the promising role of consumers in shaping the future of food.

SCIENCE, FOOD, AND RISK

The "Logic" and "Establishment" of Science

It is undeniable that science has led to improvements in the standard of living. However, though we must appreciate the results of scientific progress, we must also approach it critically, given that it has been responsible for various environmental and social risk and disasters. We therefore need to understand and grapple with both aspects of science: its power and its horror. For ease of conceptualization, Richard York coined the terms the "logic of science" and the "establishment of science" (2009). The logic of science refers to the "philosophy of knowledge that underlies the scientific enterprise"—namely, the use of empiricism, as opposed to philosophy, as a foundation for theories and methods (York 2009, p. 86). The establishment of science, in contrast, deals with how this scientific knowledge is put into practice, keeping in mind the influences of the cultural, economic, political, and social institutions that support it (York 2009, p. 88). It is important to make this distinction, as it highlights the fact that, though the logic of science may be considered "objective," the establishment of science is not always so. Science, in its practical sense, is intrinsically a social phenomenon and is thus entangled within a web of social pressures and biases (Shrader-Frechette 1994). As York argues, given that contemporary scientific institutions are often funded by members of the industrial–capitalist elite, they find themselves pressured to develop "technologies aimed at aiding global economic imperialism" while simultaneously "accelerating the exploitation of natural resources and labourers for profit" (2009, p. 88).

It is necessary to recognize that, historically, the goal of scientific establishment has not always been to understand the world in which we live, but, to quote York (2009, p. 89), it is "intimately linked to existing power structures and typically focused on achieving ends dictated by the ruling class." He further elaborates:

> This link between the scientific establishment and those in power remains clear in the contemporary world .... [I]t is a matter of no small importance that so much of scientific efforts have been directed at developing weapons. A very substantial share of research that took place over the twentieth century in physics, chemistry, and to a lesser extent biology—from the work on rocketry and explosives to work on poison gases and deadly microbes—was done at the behest of, and with funding from, military interests. (York 2009, p. 89)

Aside from military interests, another substantial share of scientific establishment was driven by "raw financial interests" in which "corporations seek to increase profits by developing technologies of production and new products for the market, without particular regard for human well-being, environmental sustainability, or lives of other creatures" (York 2009, p. 89). These military and financial interests of the scientific establishment have historically caused various environmental, social, and ecological risks and disasters. The ruling class and corporations make profits, while society and the environment pay the price when risks and disasters erupt. Chernobyl, Three Mile Island, and Fukushima are among the disasters driven by the establishment of science. Although the topic is barely addressed in the disaster literature, various food regimes driven by the establishment of science have also caused various social and ecological risks and disasters.

Food Regimes and the Social and Ecological Risks and Disasters

While risks and disasters are often attributed to the forces of nature, human-induced disasters are growing with the rise of the establishment of science. Histories of food disasters usually cite incidents such as the London Beer Flood in 1814, when an absurdly large wooden vat filled with English porter beer ruptured, unleashing a torrent that killed eight people and destroyed a number of homes; the Great Boston Molasses Flood in 1919, in which a 50-foot-tall vat of molasses buckled and collapsed, sending a thick sticky wave pounding through the streets of Boston's North End, killing 21 people and injuring 150 more; the Basra Mass Grain Poisoning in 1971–72, which resulted in nearly 500 deaths; the Honolulu Molasses Disaster in 2013, which killed nearly all life in the harbor; the Austrian Antifreeze Wine Scandal in 1985, which ended Austrian wine exports for nearly two decades; and the Wild Turkey Distillery Fire in Lawrenceburg, Kentucky, United States in May 2000, which killed over 220,000 fish, the largest fish die-off in the state's history (LeBlanc 2014). However, the broader ecological and social risks and disasters generated by science-driven food regimes are hardly mentioned in the discourse of disaster studies.

In the last century, the dietary patterns of the world shifted from traditional food to a wheat-based diet (driven largely by the Green Revolution and American Public Law 480) to animal protein and other high-value foods such as meat, fruits, and vegetables (driven by biotechnology, retail power, and the supermarket revolution), and to exotic foods for wealthy buyers such as shrimp, lobster, shark fins, and whale meat (driven largely by the Blue Revolution) (McMichael 2008; Clapp and Fuchs 2009; Islam 2013, 2014). The establishment of science takes a lead in generating new and unbridled appetites for such foods, and thereafter delivering them to the world's middle class; this phenomenon is causing inequality by draining the resources of the planet and taking them away from the planet's poor. Apart from generating a new global class division and inequality—high-end premium food for wealthy consumers and low-end consumer food for the rural and urban poor (Gardner and Halweil 2000)—food regimes, driven largely by the establishment of science, have generated various other forms of ecological and social risks and disasters. In other words, the elite-dominated "establishment of science" largely shape a bulk of global risk and disasters, which in turn condition and intensify social inequalities. Recent outbreaks such as mad cow disease, bird flu virus, Japanese encephalitis (JE) virus, SARS (severe acute respiratory syndrome) virus, and even COVID-19 are examples of food-induced risks and disasters that, along with severe health implications, have deepened social inequality across human societies. Poor and marginalized are usually affected the most when a risk erupts or a disaster strikes, as the former has little capacity to deal with the latter.

Various food regimes, driven largely by the establishment of science, historically intensified social inequality and ecological dislocation. The "hamburger connection" drives deforestation (about 29% of the Amazon forest) and global warming (Rifkin 1992) affecting the global poor and marginalized. The industrial meat export in India causes the "meat disasters" in which one dollar earned from meat costs nine dollars of ecological capital (McMichael 2008). The "Blue Revolution" is now blamed for 60% forest loss in Asia and various forms of social displacements, land-grabs, exploitative labor relations, and income inequality (EJF 2003; Islam 2014). In India, the "supermarket revolution" causes a severe inequality threatening 12 million small shopkeepers, 40 million hawkers, and 200 million small farmers (Sharma 2007; McMichael 2008). The "neoliberal corporate agriculture" is responsible for a massive agrarian stress with severe inequality causing over 100,000 farmer suicides in India between 1993 and 2003, and creating slums in major Indian cities (McMichael 2008; Islam 2013). The recent bio-tech revolution that gave rise to GMOs is, to a large extent, driven by the desire of large corporations to increase their profits, without regard for the potential ecological and social disasters. With the patenting of seeds, the entire GMO technologies are largely controlled by a handful of corporations causing an unequal relation of production. This further intensifies the risk and vulnerabilities for the consumers and inequality for the farmers.

GREEN AND GENE: A TALE OF TWO FOOD REVOLUTIONS

The Green Revolution and the Gene Revolution are essentially two different regimes of the global agro-food system that emerged in different economic, political, and social contexts, i.e. two different modes of the "establishment of science." The historical trajectory of the technological development of the Green Revolution and Gene Revolution does not follow a deterministic and autonomous route; it is a process of social construction and negotiation, involving heterogeneous political, economic, social, and technical factors (Islam 2013). The Green Revolution, a genuine scientific innovation, is the joint effort of an array of international and interdisciplinary agents involving state and non-state actors (e.g. research institutions, charitable organizations, universities, aid agencies). Its key objective was agro-biotechnological development and transference to the so-called Third World as a solution to food shortages. The technology involved revolved around developing disease-resistant, pest-resistant, fertilizer-responsive crops to increase productivity (Binswanger & Ruttan 1978; McMichael 2008; Islam 2013, 2014). Due to agro-biotechnological efforts, countries like India can not only overcome their food shortage problem but also attain self-sufficiency in food production in the first few years.

Modernity theory, and particularly the European/American modernization project, provided an ideological underpinning for the "establishment of science" in the mid-twentieth century, and the impetus of the Green Revolution can be understood in that light. Europe played an instrumental role in shaping the socio-economic development of the colonies that gained independence after the Second World War. Modernity theory posits that Third World countries have to adopt the First World's time-tested and group-licensed technological systems and practices to experience economic growth. Parayil (2003, p. 978) further asserts that the Green Revolution was an "ironic and unexpected" outcome of the United States' Cold War geopolitics that attempted to suppress the spread of communism.

In short, the Green Revolution was driven by a unique "establishment of science" in which Western ideologies were used to modernize the Third World countries. While economic gains were considered, they played a secondary and latent role in technological development (Parayil 2003). The Green Revolution changed the agrarian landscapes not only of the United States, but also of the rest of the world, as the US chemical-based agricultural model was exported to other countries. High-yield varieties of hybrid seeds designed to require chemicals (fungicides, pesticides, and herbicides) increased yields but generated new forms of agrarian risks and disasters. Millions of rural Americans were displaced by corporate farming, while slum dwellers became 50% of the Third World's population. Industrial farming displaced agro-ecological methods of crop-rotation, compromised soil fertility, and ruptured natural regeneration and renewal. Between 1993 and 2003, as stated earlier, over 100,000 farmers committed suicide in India. The Green Revolution also created "development subjectivity," a shift in beliefs in which farmers devalue traditional farming (McMichael 2008; Islam 2013, 2014).

The technological know-how of the Green Revolution led to more extensive and intensive research in genetics in the 1990s. Some of the noteworthy achievements in the field of modern biology are: Gregor Mendel's laws of Mendelian inheritance in the 1860s; Max Delbrück's discovery of DNA as the genetic information carrier in 1938; James Watson and Francis Crick's discovery of the double helical structure of the DNA molecule in 1953; and Stanley Cohen and Herbert Boyer's genetic engineering experiments in 1973 (Ruttan 2001, pp. 370–374). However, it was not until the late 1970s that such technology was transferred from the academic realm to the biotechnology industry. In the 1980s, the Gene Revolution took off and gained commercial significance; in this period, huge corporations invested vast amounts of resources in the research and development of gene technology (Parayil 2003; Falkner 2009), and the US Supreme Court extended Intellectual Property Rights (IPRs) to genetically modified crops (Paarlberg 2000). Since the mid-1990s, the global planting area for genetically modified (GM) crops has grown at an average annual rate of 10 percent. Led by US firm Monsanto, a small number of powerful biotechnology firms have set out to reshape global markets for key commodity crops such as soybeans, corn, and canola, with more GM crops (e.g. rice, potatoes) and fish species in the pipeline (Falkner 2009).

The Green Revolution and Gene Revolution emerged under two sets of "establishments of science," with significant overlaps. While the Green Revolution came about in a period characterized by industrial capitalism, the Gene Revolution emerged under what Castells (2000, p. 375) called "informational capitalism," which emphasizes the production, distribution, and management of knowledge. In addition, while the Green Revolution is largely supported by state and non-state actors (e.g. the World Bank and Rockefeller foundations), the Gene Revolution is driven by multinational corporations (MNCs) (Parayil 2003; Falkner 2009; Williams 2009). The underlying motivation for MNCs is profit accumulation. More succinctly, the technological trajectory of the Gene Revolution is dictated by the overarching economic pragmatism of modern globalization.

The entrance of the international private sector, or MNCs, is facilitated by the new economic regime. A sharp increase in public investment in agro-biotechnology development in the 1980s was met with an exponential increase in private investment (James 2000). This observation is accounted for by neoliberal ideals, which claim that the market is the best mechanism to ensure the optimum distribution of scarce resources and that state intervention disrupts the normal operation of the market system (Islam 2013). The enactment of intellectual property rights to patents under the Trade-Related Aspects of Intellectual Property Rights (TRIPS) Agreement further encouraged MNCs to engage in R&D in genetic technology. With such legislation in place, the free-rider problem and unauthorized utilization and imitation of knowledge, processes, and techniques are overcome, and MNCs are guaranteed that they can financially recuperate their R&D investment.

POTENTIAL CONSEQUENCES OF THE GENE REVOLUTION

Environmental Risks and Disasters

Proponents of biotechnology assert that agro-biotechnology leads to cheaper, healthier, more nutritious, tastier, and safer food. Uzogara (2000) states that GMOs are engineered in ways that make them resistant to unfavorable conditions like pests, diseases, and extreme weather, while being responsive to fertilizer. In addition, agro-biotechnology allows for the alteration of the natural lifecycle of organisms, i.e. the development, maturation, and demise process. For example, crops like tomatoes, raspberries, strawberries, and pineapples have delayed ripening and rotting processes, which effectively strengthens their hardiness and lengthens their shelf-life (Thayer 1994). Furthermore, agro-biotechnology has enabled scientists and engineers to enhance the nutritional values of the crops. The Golden Rice, also known as the "miracle grain," is one example, representing an effort to alleviate vitamin A deficiency (VAD) in developing countries (Wambugu 1999).

Notwithstanding the benefits brought about by agro-biotechnology, there have been debates about its negative aspects. Agro-biotechnology involves incorporating foreign gene segments into the host genome to induce the expression of particular traits. Very often, pathogens (microorganisms that cause diseases in other organisms) are extracted from their natural environment and disrupted from their natural cycle, artificially cultivated in petri dishes in the laboratory, and inserted into the plant genome to function as a natural biological pest and disease control. The most common is the *Bacillus thuringiensis* (Bt) gene; according to Zechendorf (1999), over 20% of the maize cultivated in the US incorporated the Bt strand in 1998. The massive use of Bt crops (including corn and cotton) has sparked intense debate about the quality of soil. Critics argue that residues of transgenic crops tend to be deposited in or on the soil, and consequently contaminate the soil and adversely affect living organisms there (Jack 2001). While the insecticidal function of such transgenic crops is evident, the risks involved are not (and probably will never be) completely understood. Another concern is unintended and undesirable gene transfer in the wild. For example, terminator genes (more commonly known as "suicide genes") intended to inhibit intergenerational growth, i.e. to make the F2 generation (or offspring) sterile, can have a detrimental consequence for the life cycle of non-targeted wild crops (Koch 1998; Richmond 2008). Yet another example is the proliferation of super-weeds, which is the result of cross-pollination between transgenic crops and those in the wild. Super-weeds are strong competitors for space and nutrients, and can wipe out the entire wild population, threatening genetic diversity in the vicinity. Due to super-weeds' strong resistance to chemicals, more toxins are needed to eradicate them (Huang 2002).

Social Risks, Inequality, and Disasters

Biotechnology has in general led to a higher global standard of living for individuals (Bresnehan & Gordon 1997). However, according to the World Bank (2012), such technological advancement has not resulted in poverty reduction: about 20% of the population in developing countries lived on less than US$2 per day in 2008. Undoubtedly, agro-biotechnology has had economic, social, and health benefits, but they are not symmetrically and universally distributed across the globe.

One approach to understanding the social implications of agro-biotechnology is through the study of the relationship between producers (or corporations) and consumers (including farmers). Put differently, the former is the technology-donor while the latter is the technology-receiver. The effectiveness of technological transfer depends on "institutional capacity," "financial capacity," and "human capital" (Graff, Roland-Holst & Zilberman 2005, p. 1431). To avoid painting a rosy picture of the process of technological transfer, we highlight the exploitative relationship between the donor and receiver. The underlying reason is that capitalistic motivation precedes motivations such as alleviating poverty and solving world hunger. Such an allegation is supported by the type of research conducted in the field of agro-biotechnology, which is largely insensitive to the demands of farmers and consumers and oriented towards the wants (profit maximization) of MNCs (e.g. Monsanto and Novartis) (Stolp & Bunders 1989; Williams 2009). A case in point is the development of Terminator seeds by Delta and Pine Land Company (D and PL), a subsidiary of Monsanto. The invention of sterile seeds serves the interest of the corporation (Graff et al. 2005). By limiting the harvest to one per seed, the corporation has essentially secured for itself a steady stream of business, since the farmers must return for more seeds; they find themselves trapped on a genetic treadmill (Grove-White, Macnaghten, Mayer, & Wynne 1997). In such instances, traditional seed-saving techniques and practices are made obsolete. This invention runs counter to the wider goal of attaining social equity and equality, since corporations (and regulatory bodies) have overlooked (or intentionally ignored) farmers' limited financial ability to continually obtain transgenic seeds. The consequence is clear in generating inequality and displacement: those unable to sustain the high production cost of farming will be eliminated from the agricultural scene. In India, such pressure has led to severe agrarian stress, inequality, and disasters: increased occurrences of farmer suicide (Shiva 2001).

Aside from displacing the livelihood of farmers, agro-biotechnology also imposes a social health risk on the population. This problem is evident in the bio-disaster that occurred in 1987 in Russia, when a massive accidental discharge of gaseous protein dust led to the outbreak of bronchial asthma (Remmington 1989). The accident underscores the unpredictability and uncontrollability of agro-biotechnology products if they escape into the open environment. The situation is even more worrisome because some (side) effects often remain dormant for a long while, or even to the point where remedy is impossible. Our incomplete understanding of the full effects of agro-biotechnology means that the world has become susceptible to unprecedented risks, vulnerabilities, and disasters.

As mentioned earlier, benefits are unequally distributed across different actors; there are winners and losers. Benefits are reaped by those who control the "establishment of science" and are endowed with the institutional, financial, and human capital to acquire the material resources and machines of revolutionary agricultural techniques. Those who have successfully adopted these technologies find themselves in a better bargaining position in the economic (and political) arena and enjoy improved social status and health. Nevertheless, this group of individuals is an infinitesimal minority of the population (Hindmarsh 1990; Fuchs and Clapp 2009). While society has experienced a certain degree of improvement, the situation remains bleak. The possibility of the poor being liberated from dependency on corporations remains pathetically low, and the rich are multiplying their wealth at an unprecedented level. This disparity may lead to escalation of other social risks and disasters, such as food riots and peasant resistance.

THE FUTURE OF FOOD

TNC-Dominated Food System

While traditional food systems were based on centuries-old culture and traditions, the current industrial food system largely operates through various modes of the "establishment of science." The current food system is highly integrated across national boundaries and is dominated largely by TNCs. TNCs play a central role in the agricultural scene, dictating global chains of production, processing, and distribution. Market share is concentrated in the hands of a few companies at each stage. According to Wim Pelupessy (2007), four companies hold an enormous 40% of the market share in the international coffee trade. While one may argue that there is international governance of the food system, the irony is that TNCs have significant influence in shaping the rules and regulations that govern their activities. Thus the legitimacy and efficacy of the rules introduced to provide a certain degree of supervision over the food system (Phillips & Wolfe 2001) are called into question. More critically, questions arise about corporate accountability, food security, food safety, and consumer sovereignty.

The Intellectual Property Rights (IPRs) system has played a decisive role in strengthening the market position of the huge corporations. In agro-biotechnology, six companies (Monsanto, DuPont, Syngenta, Dow, Aventis, and Grupo Pulsar) hold 75% of all patents granted in the US (Dutfield 2003). Such market concentration in the hands of a few corporations means that the world food system is controlled by a few. Against the backdrop of food production, there is intense competition between TNCs for the "gene grab," which not only inhibits sharing of resources and knowledge, and hence hampers innovation, but entraps farmers in a mesh of licensing and royalty obligations, complicating their supposedly simple farming practices (Pistorius & van Wijk 1999). Patents serve as an instrument for corporations to withhold data, processes, and techniques and in the process raises a prohibitive cost barrier for prospective competitors. For example, corporations can either refuse to grant others the commercial license to use their inventions or set unreasonable terms and conditions (e.g. royalties) for their use. All in all, actors have to struggle with the complexity of the IPRs system (which favors the rich) and those unable to compete will be eliminated from the scene. Eventually, the global food market will comprise only the huge, wealthy, and powerful corporations.

Roles of State and Non-State Actors

Food governance in the modern context involves international and multilateral coordination and cooperation. As such, governments can no longer act independently; they are no longer at the pinnacle of the hierarchical food governance system. Instead, governments play the role of "collaborative actors" (Oosterveer & Sonnenfeld 2012), mediating between heterogeneous actors (e.g. international, regional, national, private, and public audiences) through social, political, economic, and ecological networks. More importantly, governments must promulgate policies that are aligned with internationally agreed-upon standards and requirements, or risk being excluded or marginalized in the global food chain (Schaeffer 1995). That being said, we are not suggesting that the role of the government is no longer significant; rather, its role has changed from directing to collaborating. To elucidate, governments are instrumental in creating an environment that encourages private corporations' investment and where non-governmental organizations (NGOs) can play an influential role (Sassen 2006).

To understand how different actors can have an impact on food governance, Levy (2008) posits that one must consider the "production network" and the interactions between the various agents along the food production chain. Through such analysis, one can identify the root of conflict and the interests of diverse actors. Put differently, such an approach suggests that there are multiple possible points of intervention by social-political actors (e.g. NGOs), so that alliances can be formed to effect a change in ideals or interests that are not compatible with social norms and expectations.

To put things into perspective, the retailers in the food production chain (e.g. the supermarkets) can greatly influence the types of food produced at the production level (e.g. the industry). A case in point is supermarket chains in Europe, which led the global movement towards food labeling for GM products (Loader & Henson 1998). In 1997, the British tightened their labeling code to provide less ambiguous labeling: the label must state clearly that a product "contains" (rather than "may contain") GM content (Oosterveer & Sonnenfeld 2012). Following Sainsbury's lead, Tesco and Marks & Spencer have vowed that only non-GM crops will enter their house-brand products (Reuters 1999). In 2005, Greenpeace (2005) reported that 27 of 30 top European retailers had adopted an anti-GM policy and eliminated all GM contents from their products. Thus, retailers can play a significant role in amplifying and relaying consumer demands and preferences to farmers and food producers.

Another critical group of actors is farmers. A prime example of how farmers can influence the food production process is Monsanto's withdrawal of GM wheat from the US and Canada in 2004. The attempt to introduce GM wheat in US and Canada was met with intense resistance from farmers who feared Monsanto's Roundup Ready wheat would create super-weeds, which in turn would require more toxic chemicals to eradicate (Garcia 2009). The result would have been an endless cycle of dependency of farmers on corporations for both seeds and chemicals. More importantly, farmers' opposition was premised on economic rationale. They feared that, by cultivating GM wheat, they would lose access to export markets especially in Europe and Asia, which opposed GM products (Oosterveer & Sonnenfeld 2012). Under intense pressure from farmers (and NGOs), Monsanto was forced to withdraw its plan to introduce GM wheat in the US and Canada.

Consumers also have a definitive role in shaping the food production process. They can play a more reflexive and critical role by voluntarily organizing themselves and voicing their interests to others embedded within food production networks. Micheletti (2003) called such activism "political consumerism." This concept leverages consumers' care and concern for the environment and their personal health, translating them into practical action such as activism, lobbying, and mobilization for sustainability (Oosterveer & Sonnenfeld 2012). Organic food consumption is one of the many ways to support sustainable food production. Reasons for choosing organic food can be varied, but, in general, individuals are willing to pay higher prices for such food because of health, safety, and environmental concerns.

Food Justice

The unjust, unsustainable, and inequitable food production system demands an overhaul. Averting impending ecological and social disasters and establishing sustainable and equitable systems necessitates a transformative change at the societal level. There is a need for a mentality shift and structural change for a just, equitable, and sustainable food production system to be possible. We therefore must speak of food justice. Food justice has its epistemological roots in social justice, which is defined aptly by Basok, Ilcan, and Noonan (2006, p. 267) as "an equitable distribution of fundamental resources and respect for human dignity and diversity, such that no minority group's life interests and struggles are undermined and that forms of political interaction enable all groups to voice their concerns for change." It follows that food justice calls for an end to exploitation and greater opportunities for the oppressed to meet their basic needs. Food justice movements have been instrumental in promoting such ideologies, or more precisely, the ethos of democracy in the global food production chain (Alkon & Agyeman 2011).

Food justice activism serves as a galvanizing factor to bring people of different backgrounds together to achieve a common goal: to create a fair and enduring food system (Buttel 2000). The food justice movement equips participants with the experiences and critical thinking skills necessary for meaningful participation in the political realm. It boosts individuals' self-confidence (derived from the enhanced skills and knowledge) and instills a sense of "civic virtue" (Levkoe 2006, p. 90). Put differently, individuals in the food justice movement identify themselves as citizens as opposed to consumers; they think of themselves as partially responsible for what type of food is produced and, more critically, how it is produced. Thus, activism entails continuous learning that focuses on nurturing new strands of thinking and experimenting with novel problem-solving methodologies to create capacity for change. To quote Levkoe (2006, p. 90), the food justice movement can foster "transformative adult learning."

The power of learning in advocating for democracy must not be underestimated in the food justice movement. It is through learning that individuals become aware of issues and informed of their rights and responsibilities. However, the process of learning does not confine itself to the sphere of formal educational institution. No doubt formal social institutions like the family, schools, and mass media play an influential role in shaping individual attitudes. Nonetheless, individuals also acquire information from other informal sectors like NGOs and community organizations, and Schugurensky (2003) asserts that these groups are "powerful socialization agencies for the development of citizenship values and political competencies" (p. 72).

Active participation in the food justice movement has a generative effect. Activism provides an opportunity for a coalition among dispersed individuals who would otherwise not interact with one another. The aggregation of individuals results in a "louder" voice and greater bargaining power. In the process, they begin to have a clearer idea of their roles in the food production system and think critically and reflexively beyond their individualistic interests to consider higher social goals. The food justice movement provides a channel for individuals to develop a shared mental model and pool their capacities and efforts to push for a fair and sustainable food system. For example, activists who partake in alternative farming practices and food retailing are engaging in forms of food justice. By growing organic food and selling (and buying) such food at farmers' markets, these producers and consumers have created a political space for themselves, insulated from the control and pressure of the global food system dictated by the corporations (Starr 2000).

CONCLUSION

As we have seen, current food regimes are science-driven, operating in particular modes of the "establishment of science," causing, aside from some positive benefits, risks and inequality. In other words, it is not a coincidence that industrial food regimes are facilitated by society's overreliance on scientific technocracy, when the "link between the scientific establishment and those in power remains clear" (York 2009, p. 89). Consequently, the "scientized" trajectory of the global agro-food system is oriented towards the interests of the big players. This phenomenon is observable in the growing genetically modified food industry, and scientific innovation is championed as paving the way for improved food production and sustainability. One implication is that, while "establishment of science" is responsible for causing risks and disasters, which in turn galvanize social inequality, the same science needs to be reoriented to avert impending risks and disasters and pave the way for sustainable practices.

To sum up, agro-biotechnology is Janus-faced. It has brought about a new capacity to increase agricultural productivity. However, it has potentially disastrous outcomes, as it can damage the environment and deepen the social gap between the rich and poor (or corporations and farmers). The patent system, intended to incentivize corporations' investment in agro-biotechnology, has turned out to be an instrument for huge corporations to enhance their market position by creating a barrier to entry for prospective competitors. Notwithstanding the dominance of corporations in the global food production chain, various agents situated along the production chain are attempting to change the current system. Retailers, farmers, NGOs, and consumers must now be reflexive and proactive to serve as the check-and-balance mechanism for corporations, to avert impending environmental and social disasters.

One promising solution discussed in this chapter is the food justice movement. This form of food activism will be instrumental in bringing together diverse groups of individuals with a common goal of attaining a fair and sustainable food production system. This activism will also imbue members with the skills, techniques, and knowledge needed to engage effectively and meaningfully with corporations and policy-makers to effect a change in the current distorted system. The food justice movement will harness the greater value of collective, concentrated efforts to create greater impact in the political realm. Corporations, under the pressure of the growing coalition, will not have the liberty to make self-interested decisions but will be required to consider the wellness of society at large.

ACKNOWLEDGEMENT

This research was supported, in part, by a funding from the URECA scheme of Nanyang Technological University Singapore. The author acknowledges the crucial contribution of Poh Yang Ann during the writing phase and the thoughtful comments and suggestions of Dean Curran on the earlier draft.

REFERENCES

Alkon, A. H. & J. Agyeman (eds.) (2011), *Cultivating Food Justice: Race, Class, and Sustainability*, Cambridge, Massachusetts: MIT Press.

Basok, T., S. Ilcan, & J. Noonan (2006), 'Citizenship, human rights, and social justice', *Citizenship Studies*, 10(3), 267–273.

Binswanger, H. & V. W. Ruttan (1978), *Induced Innovation: Technology, Institutions and Development*, Baltimore, Maryland: Johns Hopkins University Press.

Bresnehan, T. & R. Gordon (1997), *The Economics of New Goods*, Chicago, Illinois: University of Chicago Press.

Buttel, F. H. (2000), 'The recombinant BGH controversy in the United States: Toward a new consumption politics of food?' *Agriculture and Human Values*, 17(1), 5–20.

Castells, M. (2000), *The Information Age: Economy, Society and Culture. Volume Three: The End of the Millennium*, Malden, Massachusetts: Blackwell Publishers.

Clapp, J. & D. Fuchs (eds.) (2009), *Corporate Power in Global Agrifood Governance*, Cambridge, Massachusetts: MIT Press.

Collins, P. H. (2013), *On Intellectual Activism*, Philadelphia, Pennsylvania: Temple University Press.

Dutfield, G. (2003), *Intellectual Property Rights and the Life Science Industries*, Aldershot, UK: Ashgate.

EJF (Environmental Justice Foundation) (2003), *Smash and Grab*, London: Environmental Justice Foundation in Partnership with WildAid.

Falkner, R. (2009), 'The troubled birth of the "biotech century": Global corporate power and its limits', in J. Clapp & D. Fuchs (eds.), *Corporate Power in Global Agrifood Governance*, Cambridge, Massachusetts: MIT Press, pp. 225–251.

Fuchs, D., & J. Clapp (2009), 'Corporate power and global agrifood governance: Lessons learned', in J. Clapp & D. Fuchs (eds.), *Corporate Power in Global Agrifood Governance*, Cambridge, Massachusetts: MIT Press, pp. 285–296.

Garcia, D. K. (2009), *The Future of Food*, accessed 27 June 2013 at: http://www.thefutureoffood.com/

Gardner, G., & B. Halweil (2000), 'Underfed and overfed: The global epidemic of malnutrition', *Worldwatch* Paper No. 150, Worldwatch Institute.

Gibbons, M. (1999), 'Science's new social contract with society', *Nature*, 402, c82–c84.

Graff, G. D., D. Roland-Holst, & D. Zilberman (2005), 'Biotechnology and Poverty Reduction in Developing Countries', *WIDER Working Paper Series* RP2005-27, World Institute for Development Economic Research (UNU-WIDER).

Graff, G., D. Roland-Holst, & D. Zilberman (2006), 'Agricultural biotechnology and poverty reduction in low-income countries', *World Development*, 34(8), 1430–1445.

Greenpeace (2005), 'No Market for GM Labelled Food in Europe', accessed 6 January 2012 at http://www.greenpeace.org/eu-unit/Global/eu-unit/reports-briefings/2009/3/no-market-for-gm-labelled-food.pdf.

Grove-White, R., P. Macnaghten, S. Mayer, & B. Wynne (1997), *Uncertain World: Genetically Modified Organisms, Food and Public Attitudes in Britain*, Lancaster, England: Centre for the Study of Environmental Change, Lancaster University.

Hindmarsh, R. (1990), 'The need for effective assessment: Sustainable development and the social impacts of biotechnology in the third world', *Environmental Impact Assessment Review*, 10(1), 195–208.

Huang, P. M. (2002), 'Foreseeable impacts of soil mineral–organic component–microorganism interactions on society: Ecosystem health', *Developments in Soil Science*, 28(A), 1–36.

Islam, M. S. (2013), *Development, Power and the Environment: Neoliberal Paradox in the Age of Vulnerability*, New York: Routledge.

Islam, M. S. (2014), *Confronting the Blue Revolution: Industrial Aquaculture and Sustainability in the Global South*, Toronto, Ontario: University of Toronto Press.

Islam, M. S. & Lim S. H. (2015), 'When 'nature' strikes: A sociology of climate change and disaster vulnerabilities in Asia', *Nature and Culture*, 10(1), 57–80.

Jack, B. (2001), 'Assessing the environmental impacts of transgenic plants', *Trends in Biotechnology*, 19, 371–372.

James, C. (2000), 'Global status of transgenic crops: Challenges and opportunities', *Developments in Plant Genetics and Breeding*, 5(4), 1–16.

Koch, K. (1998), 'Food safety battle organic vs. biotech', *Congressional Quarterly Researcher*, 9(33), 761–784.

LeBlanc, T. (2014), '7 Strange but True Food Disasters', *Modern Farmer*, accessed 5 June 2014 at http://modernfarmer.com/2014/06/strange-true-food-disasters/

Levkoe, C. Z. (2006), 'Learning democracy through food justice movements', *Agriculture and Human Values*, 23, 89–98.

Levy, D. L. (2008), 'Political contestation in global production networks', *The Academy of Management Review*, 33(4): 943–963.

Levy, D. L. & P. J. Newell (2000), 'Oceans apart? Business responses to the environment in Europe and North America', *Environment*, 42(9), 8–20.

Loader, R. & S. Henson (1998), 'A view of GMOs from the UK', *AbBioForum*, 1(1), 31–34.

McMichael, P. (2008), *Development and Social Change: A Global Perspective*, London, Delhi, Singapore: Pine Forge Press.

Micheletti, M. (2003), *Political Virtue and Shopping: Individuals, Consumerism, and Collective Action*, New York: Palgrave MacMillan.

Oosterveer, P. & D. A. Sonnenfeld (2012), *Food, Globalization and Sustainability*, London, New York: Earthscan.

Paarlberg, R. (2000), 'The global food fight', *Foreign Affairs*, 79(3), 24–38.

Parayil, G. (2003), 'Mapping technological trajectories of the Green Revolution and the Gene Revolution from modernization to globalization', *Research Policy*, 32(6), 971–990.

Pelupessy W. (2007), 'The world behind the world coffee market', *Études Rurales*, 2(180), 187–212.

Phillips, P. & R. Wolfe (eds.) (2001), *Governing Food: Science, Safety and Trade*, Montreal: McGill-Queen's University Press.

Pistorius, R. & J. van Wijk (1999), *The Exploitation of Plant Genetic Information: Political Strategies in Crop Development*, New York: CABI Publishing.

Remmington, A. (1989), 'Biotechnology falls foul of the environment in the USSR', *Bio/Technology*, 7, 783–788.

Reuters (1999), 'Sainsbury says own-brand ingredients GM-Free', accessed 19 July 2012 at http://foodsafety.k-state.edu/en/news-details.php?a=3&c=29&sc=220&id=37337.

Richmond, R. H. (2008), 'Environmental protection: Applying the precautionary principle and proactive regulation to biotechnology', *Trends in Biotechnology*, 26(8), 460–467.

Rifkin, J. (1992), *Beyond Beef: The Rise and the Fall of the Cattle Culture*, New York: Penguin.

Ruttan, V. W. (2001), *Technology, Growth, and Development: An Induced Innovation Perspective*, New York: Oxford University Press.

Sassen, S. (2006), *Territory, Authority, Rights: From Medieval to Global Assemblages*, Princeton, New Jersey and Oxford: Princeton University Press.

Schaeffer, R. (1995), 'Free trade agreements: Their impact on agriculture and the environment', in P. McMichael (ed.), *Food and Agrarian Orders in the World-Economy*, Westport: Praeger, pp. 255–275.

Schugurensky, D. (2003), 'Three theses on citizenship learning and participatory democracy', accessed 21 June 2013 at http://legacy.oise.utoronto.ca/research/clpd/lclp_intro.html.

Sharma, D. (2007), 'Big box retail will boost poverty', *India Together*, February 16.

Shiva, V. (2001), *Stolen Harvest: The Hijacking of the Global Food Supply*, London: Zed.

Shrader-Frechette, K. S. (1994), *Ethics of Scientific Research*, New York: Rowman & Littlefield.

Starr, A. (2000), *Naming the Enemy: Anti-Corporate Movements Confronting Globalization*, New York: Zed Books.

Stolp, A. & J. Bunders (1989), 'Biotechnology: Wedge or bridge?' *Trends in Biotechnology*, 7, 2–4.

Thayer, A. M. (1994), 'FDA gives go-ahead to bio-engineered tomato', *Chemical & Eng News*, 72.

Uzogara, S. G. (2000), 'The impact of genetic modification of human foods in the 21st century: A review', *Biotechnology Advances*, 18(3), 179–206.

Wambugu, F. (1999), 'Why Africa needs agricultural biotech', *Nature*, 400, 15–16.

Williams, M. (2009), 'Feeding the world? Transnational corporations and the promotion of genetically modified food', in J. Clapp & D. Fuchs (eds.), *Corporate Power in Global Agrifood Governance*, Cambridge: Massachusetts: MIT Press, pp. 155–185.

Wisner, B., P. Blaikie, T. Cannon, & I. Davis (2003), *At Risk: Natural Hazards, People's Vulnerability and Disasters*, London: Routledge.

World Bank (2012), *The World Bank Annual Report 2012*, Washington, DC: World Bank and Oxford University Press.

York, R. (2009), 'The science of nature and the nature of science', in K. A. Gould & T. L. Lewis (eds.), *Twenty Lessons in Environmental Sociology*, New York, USA: Oxford University Press, pp. 85–94.

Zechendorf, B. (1999), 'Sustainable development: How can biotechnology contribute?' *Trends in Biotechnology*, 17(6), 219–225.

14. Risk society and epistemic inequality: rising voices from the 'Global South' in global governance
Joy Y. Zhang

This chapter examines a type of immaterial inequality that is often indiscernable to the public gaze yet central to our collective prospect in a world risk society: the epistemic inequality within science. Even in a so-called post-truth society in which expert judgments have been stripped of their presumed authority and objectivity, science, as a systematic and methodical social production of knowledge, remains essential in building resilience against natural and social uncertainties (Jasanoff and Simmet 2017). In this sense, broadening our perspectives, widening our technological options and activating a multiplicity of contributions may seem to be a logical way forward. In fact, in his vision of a global future, Ulrich Beck contends a metamorphosis of our world orders is on the horizon. As the notion of risk becomes ever deeply ingrained in our socio-cultural logic, it inevitably nudges the world into becoming simultaneously more diverse and more inclusive. For the consciousness of risks opens up rather than closes down our critical exploration of and engagement with alternative reasonings (Beck 2016).

Yet the *realpolitik* of global science, as in any other field of sub-politics, persists. That is, while we live in a globalised age that purports to celebrate diversity, it also insists that some alternatives 'naturally' should be given more socio-political legitimacy and credibility than others, and some may simply not be worth taking seriously. A Western hegemonic dictation on what a good life is and how it should be pursued has effectively shaped rationality into 'a linear program based on deterministic notions of immutable progress' (Rajao, Duque and De 2014, p. 768). Fundamental issues such as what is a valid scientific question, what counts as evidence and where we should look for them remain defined by Western-dominated discourse, where alternative knowledge-ways in the Global South have been chronically suppressed (Chambers and Gillespie 2000). That echoes the thorny question put forward by Gayatri Chakravorty Spivak (1993) that yes, the subaltern can speak, but who would listen? If we take the idea of a 'multi-centred world' seriously, we must take the impact of epistemic inequality and its mitigation efforts realistically.

As a strategic area for securing future scientific competitiveness for many countries, the expanding field of regenerative medicine in general and experimental stem cell therapy in particular is most informative on Global South scientists' ongoing struggle to be heard. Despite differences in their approach to research, the globally shared professional language and clinical aspiration have made epistemic inequality harder to discern from outside of scientific establishments but more pronounced for members within the scientific community. This chapter draws on the example of the International Association of Neurorestoratology (IANR), an international professional association mainly comprising members from China, India, Iran, and Argentina. The discussion not only demonstrates how epistemic inequality persists in the absence of scientific certainty, which reinforces arguments from many existing studies that the subversive potential of risk on world order cannot be taken for granted. More importantly, by tracing how scientists associated with IANR have evolved from local mavericks to global players, this chapter examines an underlying mechanism that Global South communities could use to mitigate or even overcome epistemic inequality.

This chapter first provides a conceptual review of the relation between risk society and a historically embedded epistemic inequality experienced by the Global South scientific communities. It articulates why rapid scientific development in these regions in particular has aggravated the sense of unfairness and how previous empirical studies have suggested a cosmopolitanisation process may be underway. It then examines the evolution of IANR and its impact on global norms over the past 15 years, including how it insinuates alternative scientific reasoning into contemporary neuroscience debates.

RISK SOCIETY, EPISTEMIC INEQUALITY AND COSMOPOLITANISATION

Most pertinent to this chapter's discussion is a Beckian framing of risk. This is not least because science is arguably the epitomisation of 'manufacturing risks' (Giddens 1999). As our science and technological discoveries expand our collective 'Island of Knowledge' in the sea of unknowns, they also extend the shore of our ignorance (Gleiser 2014). This in turn has activated the era of 'the unbinding of politics' where socio-political boundaries 'can be chosen (and interpreted), but simultaneously also have to be redrawn and legitimated anew' (Beck 1992, p. 231; Beck 2002, p. 19).

More importantly, despite its Euro-centric nature, Beck's 30 years of theorisation on risk have always been closely connected to his concern over *global* equality, especially through his engagement with climate change and environmental politics (Zhang 2015). But this is also where Beck appears to be an ultimate optimist. In his early works, he warned that, in the face of unpredictable and uninsurable risks, the once-supposed positive logic of Western capitalism's distribution of 'goods' had been taken over by a negative logic of the 'social bads' and that, depending on one's 'social risk positions', the ability to exploit and be negatively affected by risk may differ (Beck 1992). In his last book, *The Metamorphosis of the World*, he concluded that eventually it will be the 'positive side effects of the bads' that exert true and lasting impact (Beck 2016, p. 4). That is, the increasing global awareness of risk, such as climate risk, terrorism and nuclear accidents, will inevitably turn a new 'global generation' into 'members of *Homo cosmopoliticus*' (Beck 2016, p. 189). To put it another way, while there will always be disparities at the individual levels, in general, especially from a group or collective perspective, 'risk' almost has an 'equalising' effect. For the distribution of 'bads', the recognition of the limit, fallibility and contingency of human knowledge will both taunt and efface any monopolies of power or social hegemonies. Instead of class discrimination or national prejudice, risk ushers us into a cosmopolitan age of 'global domestic politics' (Beck and Sznaider 2011, p. 418).

This naive inattentiveness to real-world power asymmetry is also where Beck attracts most criticism and curtailed the validity of his theorisation (e.g. Curran 2016; Engel and Strasser 1998; Mythen 2005). Empirical research across finance, environmental and health sectors have all underlined how socio-economic disparities impact social groups' incentive and capacity to manoeuvre risk, which often can reinforce rather than weaken existing hegemonies (Curran 2015; Van Voorst 2015; Zhang 2018).

Take epistemic inequality, for example: as philosopher Miranda Fricker (2007) elucidated, this is an injustice against someone's capacity as a *knower*. This could be due to an unfairly deflated credibility associated to a knower's testimonies, or due to unequal hermeneutical participation, in which the values held by certain groups are marginalised (Fricker 2007, pp. 9–14, pp. 152–161). Similar to most inequality studies, epistemic injustice is also often most easily detectable with in-group/out-group distinction, such as men and women, East and West.

However, can there be epistemic inequality within contemporary science, especially when, at least in the area of neuroscience and regenerative medicine, a majority of scientists, regardless of nationalities, are trained in the Western tradition, if not directly in Western institutions? Let's not forget the British physicist John Ziman's (1978 [1996], p. 3) widely cited definition that science is essentially 'a consensus of rational opinion over the widest possible field'. But let's also not forget that consensus is not a negation of contention, but rather a particular outcome of contention. As Thomas Kuhn (1962 [1996]) elegantly demonstrated, modern science emerged and evolved through an intricate succession of different systematic discrimination of facts and the interpretation of facts. But more importantly, a globally heightened collective consciousness of scientific uncertainties has made the practice and governance of science more contextualised and value-laden (Giddens 1999).

Social studies in genetically modified organisms and biobanking, for example, have all underlined a social fact that, in a globalised yet fragmented world, doing science has become less of an act on 'the representative determination of knowledge', and more a socially mediated choice (Beck 2009, pp. 127–128; Levidow and Carr 1997; Salter and Jones 2005). Therapeutic research in particular, with clinical standards demarcating what is more acceptable than others, 'create[s] new boundaries of inclusion and exclusion among individuals, groups, spaces, practices, values, concepts and things' (Petersen, Tanner and Munsie 2015; Roseman and Chaisinthop 2016, p. 113).

In this context, Global South countries as latecomers of global science are at a disadvantage in vindicating and interposing their views into existing scientific epistemologies dominated by the traditional scientific powers in the Northern hemisphere. In addition, since many emerging economies often have under-developed governance infrastructure, with indigenous social debates and discourses yet to be 'modernised' into 'internationally' recognisable forms, such as bioethics or public engagement, they collectively suffer an 'image problem'. Countries in Northeast Asia have acquired the reputation of 'particularly prone to scientific scandal' (Lee and Schrank 2010). In terms of stem cell therapy, while regulatory grey areas are exploited in countries such as Australia, Germany and the US, and many countries are complicit in encouraging medical tourism towards the East (Einsiedel and Adamson 2012; McMahon 2014; Petersen, Tanner and Munsie 2015; Turner 2007), it is often India and China that constitute 'the geography of blame' (Bharadwaj 2013, p. 33). Empirical studies have repeatedly highlighted a common frustration among Global South scientists that their lab results are often discriminated against by international journals (Bharadwaj 2014; Zhang 2012). Some of the Chinese life scientists I interviewed shared personal experience in which simple tweaking, such as having a Western co-author or submitting through a North American or European institutional email account, have made their previously rejected submissions to be taken seriously by journals. This kind of 'can't be good enough' prejudicial bias aside, there is also often a barrier to hermeneutical participation, in which clinical priorities and therapeutic values pertinent to the Global South often carry limited weight in global discussions. This is demonstrated in the IANR case.

To be sure, one could say that the Global South themselves had a role in reinforcing this epistemic marginalisation. Until very recently, many developing economies have been preoccupied with 'catching up with the West' with little interest in being 'distracted' by global value debates (Zhang 2012). Aggressive development plans are often tinted with a nationalist aspiration which gave rise to cases such as Hwang Woo-suk, Tae-kook Kim, Jiankui He (Cyranoski 2020; Lee and Schrank 2010).

However, it is also true that the old 'developmental state' (Lee and Schrank 2010) lens has increasingly restricted our vision in seeing changing dynamics between the North and South in science. For example, far from trailing the West, China is currently the second-largest investor in research and innovation and overtook the US in 2017 with the highest number of scientific publications. At the time of writing (spring 2020), IANR, the international professional organisation dedicated to promoting the research and clinical application of neurorestorative therapies, constitutes members from 40 countries and has just published the second version of its Clinical Neurorestorative Therapeutic Guidelines for Spinal Cord Injury, and operates two peer-reviewed English journals, with one based in China and the other in the US (www.ianr .org.cn). It also aims to inspire a new generation of talents through establishing the Raisman Young Scholars Awards, established in honour of the late distinguished British neuroscientist, Honorary President of the IANR, Geoffrey Raisman (Li et al. 2018). Yet a little more than 15 years ago, when key members of IANR, such as American scientist Wise Young and his Chinese post-doc Huang Hongyun, started to explore clinical applications of stem cell-based neurorestorative treatments on spinal cord injuries, their small circle of colleagues needed to fight for academic recognition. Of course, as the next section demonstrates, the fight for academic and public audience is still ongoing, as the central debate over what counts as 'efficient' evidence for clinical efficacy in stem cell therapy remains unsettled.

The point here is that, over the last decade, research capacity and its organisation in the Global South countries have drastically changed. This, together with the collapse of absolute scientific authority, has made the chronic epistemic inequality they experience ever more vexing.

Risk society's 'cosmopolitan moment', as proclaimed by Beck in 2002, cannot be taken for granted. As I have argued elsewhere, there is possibility and feasibility for less advantageous countries to acquire effective leverage in (re)shaping the global norms (Zhang 2012). More specifically, the cosmopolitanisation process often consists of four key elements:

1. *Common strivings for future benefits:* The experience of risk is essentially an encounter with 'social voids' where orders and norms, including expectations, are yet to be negotiated and established (Zhang 2015, p. 335). The motivation for defining and promoting a new social norm is not so much about short-term localised problem-solving, but about shaping practices to secure a satisfactory level or form of future benefits. As philosopher Kwane Appiah asserted in *Cosmopolitanism: Ethics in a World of Strangers* (2006 p. 78): most disputes arise not because of 'clashing conceptions of "the good". On the contrary, conflict arises most often when two peoples have identified the same thing as good'.

2. *Passive ethicisation:* To acquire social legitimacy in a globalised yet fragmented world, social actors are often pressured to deliberate and assimilate stakeholders' diverse

socio-ethical demands into their own outlook. Here ethicisation embraces no specific moral objectives, but situates the making of a norm with a particular rhetoric space.

3. *Reflexive negotiation:* While it is a given that, in world risk society, alternatives compete for influence, the ability to articulate and adjust the framings of these alternatives relies on reflexiveness.

4. *Continuous performance*: Cultivating new norms cannot rely on one-off campaigns, but requires sustained and coherent performances over time, as well as coordinated inputs from various assemblages of actors.

As demonstrated in the next section, the evolution of IANR follows the above pattern. There is possibility and feasibility for less advantageous countries to acquire effective leverage in (re) shaping the global norms. But before going into the empirical analysis, three important points need to be clarified:

1. First, any 'scientific' assessment on the clinical efficacy of experimental therapies is *beyond* and *beside* the scope of this chapter: The scientific rigour of IANR's work can only be proved through time, but the mere fact that these professionals are emerging increasingly as serious players itself has *social* significance.

2. Second and relatedly, it is important, however, to categorically distinguish the difference between fraudulent enterprise in the name of science and the exploration of innovative therapy. Given its lucrative prospects, it is true, as widely reported in the media, that there are many private companies, with little or no appropriate professional background, who operate illegal or fraudulent treatments for short-term financial gain. In fact, scientists involved in IANR, such as Wise Young, have openly criticised these ventures (Judson 2006). The example used in this chapter concerns institutionally trained professionals that explore scientifically and ethically contentious areas in clinical intervention with the aim of contributing to a new field of knowledge and exerting long-term influence in global scientific norms.

3. Finally, the term 'Global South' refers to the actors' epistemic position rather than their geographic or national belongings. For example, IANR incorporates an expanding group of scientists in various countries. A French or US scientist affiliated with IANR also belongs to the 'Global South' as they too are contesting existing gold standards for clinical efficacy and are subjected to similar epistemic marginalisation.

IANR: FROM LOCAL MAVERICK TO GLOBAL PLAYER

Drawing on the cosmopolitanisation of science thesis, this section first discusses the epistemic inequality these scientists perceived at the beginning of their clinical experiments. It is not uncommon for scientists involved in the initial spinal cord injury network to be frustrated by a seeming 'paradox' that the *shared recognition* of the promise of stem cell therapies has almost immediately rendered their work (media) 'visibility', while also seeming to have raised the bar for (academic) recognition. It then examines IANR's path in establishing its voice among the global scientific community and how it follows the pattern of *passive ethicisation* and *reflexive negotiation*. The third section evaluates IANR's efforts to consolidate and adapt its role in global governance through *continuous performance* across institutional and national borders.

'Why Do Westerners See It But Not Believe It?'

Arguably the plethora of studies devoted to stem cell research during the first decade of the new millennium was a result of the risk society mentality (Zhang 2012). When Kuhn (1962 [1996] p. 76) analysed paradigm shifts in science, he noted, 'invention of alternates is just what scientists seldom undertake'. The reason for this seemingly 'conservative' attitude was a practical one: 'So long as the tools of a paradigm supplies continue to prove capable of solving the problems it defines, science moves fastest and penetrates most deeply through confident employment of those tools' (Kuhn 1962 [1996], p. 76). Yet a few decades later, opposite to Kuhn's description, there seemed to be a growing enthusiasm in exploring alternative reasoning and in applying plural interpretations to a given set of data. The 'science is becoming human. It is packed with errors and mistakes …. The opposite attracts, it always has opportunities as well. The scene is becoming colorful. If three scientists get together, fifteen opinions clash' (Beck 1992, p. 167). This is not to say that science has sunk to a state of anarchy. This 'greater versatility' (Beck 1992, p. 167) observed in contemporary scientific endeavours is not simply due to factual ambiguity or inadequate information, but has more to do with a social mentality that practitioners are aware of the limit of their (and other's) knowledge. To paraphrase Dr Jonathan Kimmelman's remark at the release of the International Society for Stem Cell Research (ISSCR) 2016 Guidelines for Stem Cell Research and Clinical Translation (EuroStemCell 2016), science moves quickly, and scientists recognise guidelines are not doctrines but 'living documents' that are subject to ongoing review, interpretation and revision as new evidence emerges. With this mindset, scientists do not blindly submit to a set of discourse, but 'shop for' or actively cultivate socio-political environments that can accommodate their research agenda (Russo 2005).

This was how countries with permissive regulations on stem cells, such as the UK, China, India, South Korea and Japan, start to attract stem cell scientists. It was also in this context that Wise Young, an internationally acclaimed neurologist best known for being Christopher Reeve's doctor, came to China. In collaboration with Huang Hongyun and researchers from 22 Chinese centres, he set up the China Spinal Cord Injury Network (ChinaSCINet) in 2004. This therapeutic network carried out diverse clinical trials on traumatic spinal cord injuries, with similar but not uniformed practices.

Until 2007, despite detailed disclosure of research procedure and data and an inviting attitude towards Western colleagues' site visit requests, opinions on ChinaSCINet and clinical trials carried out by its members have been mostly sceptical if not negative (Judson 2006). To begin with, as stem cell therapy was still at an experimental stage, China's chronic deficiency in ethical oversight casted a shadow of doubt on 'exploit[ing] patients with devastating conditions' (Qiu 2007, p. 59). It is pertinent here that such concerns were not simply due to an absence of (ethical) regulations but were complicated by the contentious nature of how risks and benefits should be calculated in novel areas of science. Quite different from fraudulent scandals, such as China's gene-edited baby controversy in 2018, which was a clear case of illegal medical practice with the fabrication of an ethics review (Normile 2019), the case with ChinaSCINet lay in a legislative and bioethical grey area. In fact, China has promulgated ethical guidelines on stem cell research and on somatic cell therapy as early as 2003. But it struggled, as many countries at the time, to devise a blanket regulation that could fully address the diverse clinical situations explored by this new family of therapies. Consequently, as long as such practice is carried out by a licensed medical professional in state-recognised research institutions (as ChinaSCINet's trials were), it only needed to obtain approvals from home institutional or local healthcare authorities (Zhang 2012, pp. 153–154). In other words, ChinaSCINet's experiments were technically not illegal nor were they devoid of ethical deliberations. But there were epistemic discrepancies over what risks and benefits should be recognised and how they should be prioritised.

For example, a key point of dispute was the fact that, instead of the randomised controlled trials (RCTs), a gold standard of global (Western) life sciences, participating centres relied on self-comparing and patients' testimonials. Critics said that this made it difficult to rule out placebo effects; others felt long-term patient observation was required before any clinical conclusion could be drawn (Qiu 2007). For example, Huang Hongyun devised therapies using nasal cells, dubbed olfactory ensheathing cells, from aborted fetuses and injected them into people's spines. The idea was that, given the regenerative nature of these olfactory cells, they will help renew nerve cells and in turn lessen or cure diseases such as amyotrophic lateral sclerosis, Parkinson disease and multiple sclerosis.

According to an early report on such trials in the UK newspaper, *The Guardian*, Huang and his colleagues exhibited prudence in carrying out their treatments. Huang 'promises nothing. He claims no miracle cure. He admits he cannot fully explain his results. All he knows, and all he tells his patients, is that his method often works, that the results speak for themselves' (Watts 2004). But he was also stubborn in defending *his* ethical rationale for refusing double-blind designs. As most of the patients who contacted him suffered from severe illness, Huang insisted that placebo tests in this clinical context 'are unethical because they involve cutting someone open and only pretending to treat them… I wouldn't do it. Double-blind trials only harm the patient' (Huang in Watts 2004). Yet, this did not prevent his work from becoming 'the unconventional cell therapy that's received the most scientific scrutiny' (Enserink 2006, p. 161). Huang used videos, case reports and scored some patients on tests designed by the American Spinal Injury Association (ASIA) and the International Medical Society of Paraplegia. He published nine papers in China-based journals, including one in English. He was identified as one of the few 'People to Watch' by *Nature Medicine*'s special issue on China in 2006. Yet his papers were nonetheless rejected by all the top international journals (Cryanoski 2005).

In other words, while Huang opened his clinic to Western scientists, and was eager to engage in critical discussions with Western peers about his data, apart from being featured in science news, he was effectively denied an academic voice by Western-based academic journals. *Nature Medicine* cited Huang's frustration: 'Why do Westerners see it but not believe it?' (2006, p. 262).

What further highlighted the epistemic inequality between Huang and his Western peers was a 2006 Xinhua News Press' (Zhu and Wu 2006) exposure that one of the experts who denounced Huang's work, James Guest, plagiarised Huang's research data. This allegedly plagiarised paper described the 'rapid partial recovery' of one of Huang's patients, a 18-year-old Japanese boy, and was published in the most distinguished journal in this field, *Spinal Cord*, with Huang's name only noted in acknowledgment (see Guest et al. 2006; also see one of Guest's criticism on Huang's method, Dobkin et al. 2006). Given Xinhua's status as China's official press agency, this media exposure arguably authenticated and accentuated a shared frustration over a power asymmetry in science experienced by Huang and many other non-Western scientists. In a later publication, Huang openly questioned the implicit practice of double-standards when ascribing validity and legitimacy to research findings (Huang 2010).

To recall Huang's exasperation quoted in *Nature Medicine*, of course, as a properly trained neuroscientist, Huang knew that in science, 'seeing' is not 'believing'. So what really frustrated Huang (and peers who were conducting similar exploratory studies), was perhaps the sobering realisation that results didn't 'speak for themselves'. For a 'fact' to have a voice, it needs to be obtained, ordered and narrated in a formula dictated by Western doctrine. It is precisely because there is a global shared recognition of the future benefits of stem cell-based therapy, that heightens the contentions on whom and by what means should these benefits be claimed.

Passive Ethicisation and Reflexive Negotiation

Scientific uncertainties (e.g. the risks and benefits of experimental stem cell therapies) may have provided rationales for the diversification of science explorations, but they did not warrant different research approaches being given equal weight, or even being perceived with equal legitimacy. After a couple of years of global scepticism, scientists associated with the ChinaSCINet soon realised that their approach was still marginalised. For their work to have a fair chance to be critically assessed by their global peers, they would need to be more proactive in making their voice heard.

One of the first changes the network made was to make *visible* effort in observing mainstream norms. It should be recalled that, as ChinaSCINet is a group of professionally trained scientists based in various academic institutions and/or hospitals, global norms are not foreign to them. Thus, the significance of such a move lies not so much in substantial changes to their everyday practice, but, as illustrated below, in getting their setup 'certified', and be seen by 'experts from around the world'. As scientific legitimacy goes hand in hand with social legitimacy, ChinaSCINet felt the pressure accommodating views from both scientific experts and interested public into its clinical protocols (Zhang 2012). Some of the key efforts were detailed in a *Lancet* article:

> To ensure a high standard, all participating centres in ChinaSCINet must be certified with Good Clinical Practice .... As part of the capacity-building initiatives, ChinaSCINet organises regular training workshops, in which experts from around the world gather to teach and standardise the assessment of sensory and motor functions in patients with spinal-cord injury, cell transplantation, and other surgical methods, as well as rehabilitation techniques .... Some centres also have regular open-house days when the investigators meet patients with spinal-cord injury and their friends and relatives to update them and to discuss recent developments in the field and the initiatives of the network. (Qiu 2009, p. 606)

These efforts certainly helped to create a more 'mainstream' image of the network, and without losing its distinct voice. Arguably, this passive ethicisation process, or the demonstrated grip on the mainstream logic of what 'good science' looks like, shows the network to be an accomplished and proficient voice, able to enter and extend the debate on responsible research.

In October 2007, Huang Hongyun established the IANR and defined 'neurorestoratology' as a 'sub-discipline of neuroscience that studies neural regeneration, repair and replacement of damaged components of the nervous system' (ianr.org.cn). While operating in parallel to ChinaSCINet, the founding of the IANR effectively ushered in a much wider range of experimental regenerative medicine at the margins of contemporary life science into one epistemic community. Its 2008 preliminary Charter emphasised an 'inevitable' 'historical' mission for like-minded scientists to come together in 'advocating science and medical ethics, promoting social justice, developing academic democracy and proposing the scientific spirit of "devotion, innovation, precision and cooperation"' (http://www.ianr.org.cn/xhjj).

The Charter's prioritisation of 'ethics' and 'social justice' before 'academic democracy' (the widening of acceptable forms of evidence in contemporary science) was no accident, for one only needs to recall that Huang's resistance to RCT was that he felt it was ruthless to trade severely ill patients' survival chance with scientific data. Such ethical ambivalence was not uncommon among clinicians from developing countries. My previous fieldwork also suggested that clinicians often forgo 'gold standards' in diagnostic and treatment plans and make discretionary decisions so as to prioritise individual health outcomes and alleviate the financial burden of desperate patients (Zhang 2012, pp. 98–100). Thus, in the eyes of practitioners from the Global South, academic democracy is inherently linked with social justice. This echoes with Boaventura de Sousa Santos (2014, p. 1), that 'there is no global social justice without global cognitive justice'.

Consequently, one important departure of IANR from ChinaSCINet was not simply their difference in scientific scope, but that IANR was much more vocal in articulating their perceived epistemic inequality and their appeal to overcome it. For example, in Huang's introduction to the first IANR special section in the journal *Cell Transplantation*, he was firm on the point that 'the randomising double blind control study is a very important tool to assess effect in clinical trials. But it is not the only feasible tool; sometimes it even is unavailable for some treatments or studies, such as organ transplantation' (Huang 2010, p.129). In fact, Huang went on and drew similarities between patients with severe neural injury and neurone disease (which severely damage cognitive and physical capacities and may cause death) and patients with critical organ failures. He argued that, just as a patient's self-comparison was suited for evaluating efficacies of organ transplant treatments, it should also be considered 'the best and simplest tool' to assess the effect of cell transplantation (Huang 2010, p. 130). He then appealed to clinicians to use 'rational, reasonable and practical research methods to do study, but not follow the mechanical, doctrinal or rigid way' (Huang 2010, p. 130). Similarly, a year later, IANR's *Beijing Declaration*, a mission statement signed by scientists from 18 different countries, made a similar epistemic appeal that 'the importance of small functional gains that have significant effects on quality of life' should be respected and recognised, even if the underlying mechanism remains unclear (IANR 2009, 228). This call for more weight to be given to 'practice-based' evidence was a repeated theme in IANR discussions (Alok and Al-Zoubi 2016).

However, this emphatic call for 'academic democracy' in judging scientific validity does not mean that the IANR is bound to obdurate antagonism with Western-dominated scientific norm. In fact, an examination of IANR's annual conference records shows that, over the past decade, IANR as a group has gradually incorporated RCT into its practice. For example, at the time of writing, the focus of IANR's latest annual conference was to 'actively promote multi-country and international cooperation to conduct multi-center randomized controlled clinical trials' (Chen et al. 2019, p. 1). Although the conference presentations, as with IANR's journal publications, were a mixture of double-blind controlled trials and non-randomised trials, and that policy discussions campaigned for 'greater permissiveness for use of cell therapy in incurable conditions … [and] giving importance to practice based evidence and existing published literature' (Chen et al. 2019, p. 5), Huang himself certainly started RCTs with his trials and IANR never shuns from supporting evidence-based medicine originated in Western academia.

In addition to adapting relevant protocols and ethical debates into its operation, IANR has been reflexive in negotiating a space where their practice and findings can be given a fair opportunity to participate in a global conversation on regenerative medicine. Their campaign was not directed by an 'either/or' logic of replacing one approach of conducting science with another, but, as Santos (2014, p. 190) points out, the search of epistemic equality 'is not to ascribe the same validity to every kind of knowledge but rather to allow for a pragmatic discussion among alternative, valid criteria without immediately disqualifying whatever does not fit the epistemological canon of modern science'.

Continuous Performance

As our realms of knowledge and non-knowledge unceasingly evolve, to sustain one's voice in a risk society requires continuous performance across time and space. Soon after its establishment, IANR founded online and offline platforms to render visibility to works carried out by marginalised practitioners. In 2009 alone, the network announced three official publication platforms. This includes a US based journal *Cell Transplantation* (2020 impact factor 3.477, ranked 15 out of 26 in *Cell & Tissue Engineering*), an open-access journal *Frontiers in Neurorestoralogy*, and *American Journal of Neuroprotection and Neuroregeneration* (ceased publication in 2016). In 2013, the latter two platforms seemed to be consolidated into a Beijing-based open access publication, *Journal of Neurorestoralogy* (www.ianr.org.cn).

Offline, IANR's annual conference provides a venue for neuroscientists working on alternative forms of clinical interventions to share results and compare notes that would otherwise be invisible. This serves as a critical knowledge-sharing opportunity, especially before the organisation's official journals had not yet been launched (Roseman and Chaisinthop 2016). Since IANR's first conference in Beijing in May 2018, these annual events have travelled to a number of cities in the Global South – Armann (2011 and 2019), Bucharest (2013), Mumbai (2014), Tehran (2016), Buenos Aires (2017). In 2018, Wise Young hosted IANR's annual conference at the University of Rutgers in New Jersey, so far the only IANR event in the West. The conference's global outreach also helps community building and nurtures a collective voice. Through the years, IANR have joined forces with the UK-based Global College of Neuroprotection and Neuroregeneration (Leng et al. 2012), the Indian Society of Regenerative Science (formerly known as the Stem Cell Society of India), and the American Society for Neural Therapy and Repair (Sharma and Sharma 2011). In addition to extending its outreach across geographic borders, IANR has also founded the Raisman Neurorestoratology Foundation to encourage and support young scientists' participation in this field (Li et al. 2018).

These comprehensive efforts have all contributed to strengthen IANR's position in publicising their alternative view on how good science should and could be conducted. In 2016, IANR first trialled the publication of a 'national guideline' on neurorestoratology in China. Following this, in 2017 it launched its global *Clinical Neurorestorative Therapeutic Guidelines for Spinal Cord Injury* in the *Journal of Orthopaedic Translation*, and published an updated version in 2019 (Huang et al. 2019).

The focus of the two versions of international guidelines echoes the same ethical–negotiation trajectory through which this network has evolved. That is, the 2017 Guideline devoted more room to justifying the socio-ethical legitimacy of the alternative scientific framework it proposes before the 2019 Guideline's further elucidation on how it maintains its scientific legitimacy. The 2017 Guideline covered issues such as patient-informed consent, cell quality control, indications for undergoing cell therapy, contraindications for undergoing cell therapy, documentation of procedure and therapy, safety and efficacy evaluation, and refers to the US and Europe on policies regarding repeated treatments, compensation for clinical trials and publishing responsibility (Huang et al. 2018; Huang et al. 2019). Comparatively, the 2019 Guideline had a clearer ambition in offering a systematic introduction to 'neurorestorative therapeutic standard' for clinical practice from evaluation, diagnosis, to treatments and managing complications (Huang et al. 2019, p. 14).

On a more modest scale, Wise Young continued to push clinical trials for spinal cord injuries. In 2009, Young filed for US FDA approval to undertake a Phase III trial in North America based on studies carried out by ChinaSCINet. At the time, Stephen Minger from King's College London commented that, 'Regardless of the outcome of the clinical trials, it will be a significant achievement to demonstrate that this can be done in China .... To have a stem-cell trial approved by the FDA based on studies in China would be rather extraordinary' (Minger in Qiu 2009, p. 607). To date, based on his China experience, Young has set up SCINetUSA, SCINetIndia and SCINetNorway (https://keck.rutgers.edu/research-clinical -trials/clinical-trials).

The 'risk society' may announce the demise of absolute authority in abstract terms, but it does not eliminate various forms of hegemonies, including epistemic hegemony in *realpolitik*. But it does make the agonising power disparity between the centre and the peripheral more pronounced. Early rejections and scepticisms on their alternative research 'puzzled' and 'confused' core members of ChinaSCINet (Cryanoski 2005, p. 810; Nature Medicine 2006), but they also stimulated their determination to seek and develop similar voices from the epistemic Global South. It is worth reiterating that it is beyond and beside the scope of this chapter to evaluate the scientific value of this network of scientists, for epistemic equality and epistemic influence are two separate things. But sociologically, the path IANR scientists tread has been insightful on how epistemic inequality can be mitigated through reflexive and continuous efforts.

CONCLUDING WORDS

The world is not flat. Even as the idea of a 'risk society' swept across institutions and communities around the world, the world is still tilted towards a Western–Northernly direction. While there is an increasing consensus on seeking scientific solutions to meet global challenges, our collective resilience does not hinge so much on an *equal distribution* of the same set of knowledge as on an ecology in which different knowledge-ways have *equal opportunity* to contribute to our collective wisdom (Santos 2014). Otherwise, we are simply blinding ourselves into a mono-colour vision of our options. In this sense, Ulrich Beck was right in arguing for world risk society to evolve away from an 'either/or' logic premised on the first modernity into a cosmopolitan logic of the 'both/and' (Beck 2009, pp. 173–177). But as the experience of the group of neuroscientists associated with IANR suggests, the awareness of our own limits itself does not translate into unconditional embracement or even endorsement of diversity. In fact, the rising voices from the Global South in the field of regenerative neuroscience indicate that to counter epistemic inequality requires intricate balancing acts between selective conformity with dominate norms and reflexive negotiation of a epistemic rigour, as well as between carving out shared interests and values and empowering a space of difference.

REFERENCES

Alok, S. and Z.M. Al-Zoubi (2016) 'Rethinking on ethics and regulations in cell therapy as part of neurorestoratology', *Journal of Neurorestoratology*, 4, 1–14.

Appiah, K.A. (2006) *Cosmopolitanism: Ethics in a World of Strangers*. London: Penguin Books.

Beck, U. (1992) *Risk Society: Towards a New Modernity*. London: Sage.

Beck, U. (2002) 'The cosmopolitan society and its enemies', *Theory Culture & Society*, 19 (1–2), 17–44.

Beck, U. (2009) *World at Risk*. Cambridge: Polity Press.

Beck, U. (2016) *The Metamorphosis of the World: How Climate Change is Transforming Our Concept of the World*. Cambridge: Polity.

Beck, U. and N. Sznaider (2011) 'Self-limitation of modernity? The theory of reflexive taboos', *Theory and Society*, 40, 417–436.

Bharadwaj, A. (2013) 'Ethic of consensibility, subaltern ethicality: The clinical application of embryonic stem cells in India', *BioSocieties*, 8(1), 25–40.

Bharadwaj, A. (2014) 'Experimental subjectification: The pursuit of human embryonic stem cells in India', *Ethnos*, 79(1), 84–107.

Chambers, D.W. and R. Gillespie (2000) 'Locality in the history of science: Colonial science, technoscience, and indigenous knowledge', *Osiris*, 15, 221–240.

Chen, L., W. Young, G.A. Moviglia and Z.M. Al-Zoubi (2019) 'Summary report of the 11th Annual Conference of International Association of Neurorestoratology (IANR)', *Journal of Neurorestoratology*, 7(1), 1–7.

Curran, D. (2015) 'Risk illusion and organised irresponsibility in contemporary finance: Rethinking class and risk society', *Economy and Society*, 44(3), 392–417.

Curran, D. (2016) *Risk Power and Inequality in the 21st Century*. Basingstoke: Palgrave Macmillan.

Cyranoski, D. (2005) 'Fetal-cell therapy: Paper chase', *Nature*, 437, 810–811.

Cryanoski, D. (2020) 'What CRISPR-baby prison sentences mean for research', *Nature*, 577, 154–155.

Dobkin, B.H., A. Curt and J. Guest (2006) Cellular transplants in China: Observational study from the largest human experiment in chronic spinal cord injury, *Neurorehabil Neural Repair*, 20(1), 5–13.

Einsiedel, E.F. and H. Adamson (2012) 'Stem cell tourism and future stem cell tourists: Policy and ethical implications', *Developing World Bioethics*, 12(1), 35–44.

Engel, U. and H. Strasser (1998) 'Global risks and social inequality: Critical remarks on the risk-society hypothesis', *The Canadian Journal of Sociology*, 23(1), 91–103.

Enserink, M. (2006) 'Selling the stem cell dream', *Science*, 313, 160–163.

EuroStemCell (2016) 'ISSCR releases new global guidelines for stem cell research', accessed 17 October 2021 at https://www.eurostemcell.org/isscr-releases-new-global-guidelines-stem-cell-research

Fricker, M. (2007) *Epistemic Injustice, Power and the Ethics of Knowing*. Oxford: Oxford University Press.

Giddens, A. (1999) 'Risk and responsibility', *The Modern Law Review*, 62, 1–10.

Gleiser, M. (2014) *The Island of Knowledge: The Limits of Science and the Search for Meaning*, New York: Basic Books.

Guest, J., L.P. Herrera and T. Qian (2006) 'Rapid recovery of segmental neurological function in a tetraplegic patient following transplantation of fetal olfactory bulb-derived cells', *Spinal Cord*, 44, 135–142.

Huang, H. (2010) 'Neurorestoratology, a distinct discipline and a new era', *Cell Transplantation*, 19, 129–131.

Huang, H. et al. (2018) '2017 yearbook of neurorestoratology', *Journal of Neurorestoratology*, 6, 67–70.

Huang, H. et al. (2019) 'Clinical neurorestorative therapeutic guidelines for spinal cord injury (IANR/CANR version 2019)', *Journal of Orthopaedic Translation*, 20, 14–24.

IANR (2009) 'Beijing Declaration of International Association of Neurorestoratology (IANR)', *Neuroscience Bulletin*, 25(4), 228.

Jasanoff, S. and H.R. Simmet (2017) 'No funeral bells: Public reason in a "post-truth" age', *Social Studies of Science*, 47(5), 751–770.

Judson, H.F. (2006) 'The problematical Dr. Huang Hongyun', *MIT Technology Review*, 16 February 2006, accessed 17 October 2021 at https://www.technologyreview.com/s/405327/the-problematical-dr-huang-hongyun/

Kuhn, T.S. (1962 [1996]) *The Structure of Scientific Revolutions*. Chicago, IL: The University of Chicago Press.

Lee, C. and A. Schrank (2010) 'Incubating innovation or cultivating corruption? The developmental state and the life sciences in Asia', *Social Forces*, 88(3), 1231–1256.

Leng, Z., L. Guo, H.S. Sharma, H. Huang and X. He (2012) 'IANR V and 9th GCNN Conference with 4th ISCITT Symposium', *CNS & Neurological Disorders – Drug Targets*, 11(6), 643–646.

Levidow L. and S. Carr (1997) 'How biotechnology regulation sets a risk/ethics boundary', *Agriculture and Human Values*, 14, 29–43.

Li, Y., P. Tabakow, D. Li and H. Huang (2018) 'Commemorating Geoffrey Raisman: a great neuroscientist and one of the founders of neurorestoratology and the IANR', *Journal of Neurorestoratology*, 6, 29–39.

McMahon, D.S. (2014) 'The global industry for unproven stem cell interventions and stem cell toursim', *Tissue Engineering and Regenerative Medicine*, 11(1), 1–9.

Mythen, G. (2005) 'From goods to bads? Revisiting the political economy of risk', *Sociological Research Online*, 10(3), accessed 17 October 2021 at http://www.socresonline.org.uk/10/3/mythen.html

Nature Medicine (2006) 'People to watch: Huang Hongyun', *Nature Medicine*, 12, 262.

Normile, D. (2019) 'Chinese scientist who produced genetically altered babies sentenced to 3 years in jail', *Science*, 30 December, accessed 17 October 2021 at https://www.sciencemag.org/news/2019/12/chinese-scientist-who-produced-genetically-altered-babies-sentenced-3-years-jail

Petersen, A., C. Tanner and M. Munsie (2015) 'Between hope and evidence: How community advisors demarcate the boundary between legitimate and illegitimate stem cell treatments', *Health*, 19(2), 188–206.

Qiu, J. (2007) 'To walk again', *New Scientist*, 10 November, 57–59.

Qiu, J. (2009) 'China spinal cord injury network: Changes from within', *Lancet*, 8, 606–607.

Rajão, R., R.B. Duque and R. De (2014). 'Introduction: Voices from within and outside the south— defying STS epistemologies, boundaries, and theories', *Science, Technology, & Human Values*, 39, 767–72.

Roseman, A. and N. Chaisinthop (2016) 'The pluralisation of the international: Resistance and alter-standardisation in regenerative stem cell medicine', *Social Studies of Science*, 46(1), 112–139.

Russo, E. (2005) 'Follow the money: The politics of embryonic stem cell research', *PLoS Biology*, 3(7): e234.

Salter, B. and M. Jones (2005) 'Biobanks and bioethics: The politics of legitimation', *Journal of European Public Policy*, 12(4), 710–732.

Santos, B. de Sousa (2014) *Epistemologies of the South: Justice against Epistemicide*. New York: Routledge.

Sharma, H.S. and A. Sharma (2011) '8th Annual Conference of the Global College of Neuroprotection and Neuroregeneration', *Expert Review of Neurotherapeutics*, 11(8), 1121–1124.

Spivak, G.C. (1993) 'Can the subaltern speak?', in P. Williams and L. Chrisman (eds), *Colonial Discourse and Post-Colonial Theory*. Cambridge: Harvester Wheatsheaf, pp. 66–111.

Turner, L. (2007) '"First world health care at third world prices": Globalization, bioethics and medical tourism', *BioSocieties*, 2, 303–325.

Watts, J. (2004) 'I don't know how it works', 1 December, *The Guardian* (UK), accessed 17 October 2021 at http://www.guardian.co.uk/education/2004/dec/01/highereducation.uk1

Van Voorst, R. (2015) 'Applying the risk society thesis within the context of flood risk and poverty in Jakarta, Indonesia', *Health, Risk & Society*, 17(3–4), 246–262.

Zhang, J.Y. (2012) *The Cosmopolitanization of Science: Stem Cell Governance in China*, Basingstoke: Palgrave Macmillan.

Zhang, J.Y. (2015) 'Cosmopolitan risk community and China's climate governance', *European Journal of Social Theory*, 18(3), 327–342.
Zhang, J.Y. (2018) 'Cosmopolitan risk community in a bowl: A case study of China's good food movement', *Journal of Risk Research*, 21, 68–82.
Zhu, Y. and J. Wu (2006) 'A Chinese doctors' transnational IP struggle', 7 July, Xinhuanet, accessed 17 October 2021 at http://news3.xinhuanet.com/newscenter/2006-07/07/content_4806688.htm
Ziman, J. (1978 [1996]) *Reliable Knowledge: An Exploration of the Grounds for Belief in Science.* Cambridge: Cambridge University Press.

Websites

Cell Transplantation: https://journals.sagepub.com/metrics/cll
International Association of Neurorestoratology: www.ianr.org.cn
Journal of Neurorestoratology: http://jnr.tsinghuajournals.com/EN/2324-2426/home.shtml

15. The political economy of climate vulnerability: searching for common ground in a retrotopian world

David Champagne

INTRODUCTION

The impact of climate hazards has dramatically expanded over the past decades, producing a complex field of injustices. Many scholars describe climate injustice as a function of the uneven exposure to hazards. In the process, the mitigation of climate hazard vulnerability has taken a commanding role in economic and environmental policy. Many predominant climate mitigation and adaptation schemes mobilize reified notions of climate vulnerability—the social construction of abstracted markers of climate vulnerability such as the forecast of global temperatures, of sea level rise, of wildfire risks, and so forth as an objective existing agency (Hulme, 2018). Such forms of climate reductionism, or climatism, mobilize future climate forecast as a deciding factor of public discourse (Hulme, 2018). However, these forecasts often misrepresent actually occurring hazards in local communities and their adaptative capabilities. Coextensively, this approach can seem to prey on the most vulnerable, who will have to bear the greater brunt of climate hazards (Swyngedouw, 2021). Indeed, across the world, unprecedented environmental change creates extreme situations overwhelmingly impacting the poorest (Dawson, 2017). Following such climate forecasts, should the reduction of climate vulnerability be an end in itself? If so, are the poorest condemned to await an adequate climate mitigation often at the whim of the powerful, or to craft one of their own at great risk for their lives? In what follows, I seek to problematize the reduction of climate vulnerability as a self-satisfactory societal project.

I argue that the social construction of climate vulnerability is an inseparable dimension of climate-related injustices. Importantly, the climate vulnerability affecting the poorer populations exposes uneasy challenges when considering what many describe as a collapse of the governing social imagination (Bauman, 2017; Swyngedouw, 2021). Many find that dominant conceptions of governed natures and environments by state, urban, and regional planning or corporate actors are unsustainable as they misrepresent or deny earthly limitations (Harlow et al., 2013). In this, meaning-making processes attached to anthropogenic hazards can seem like little more than a forsaken realm of social regulation (Latour, 2020). Indeed, disruptive hazards largely fall under the umbrella of emergency regulations. They appear as sudden, unexpected events, rather than regularly occurring environmental incidents (Collier and Lakoff, 2014). In addition, public discourses overwhelmingly associate climate change with an apocalyptic imaginary (Swyngedouw, 2010, 2021). Climate vulnerability is then a sign of a universal and terminal threat to human societies. Furthermore, according to Erik Swyngedouw (2010, 2021), the growing consensus around climate mitigation and adaptation involves a widespread depoliticization, supported by technocratic management and collaborative consensus-making.

This conundrum suggests an apocalypse without end that mobilizes fear to justify climate mitigation efforts (Swyngedouw, 2010:218–220).

In this chapter, I discuss Latour's (2017) ideas about the loss of a shared earth and the challenge of finding a reliable "common ground" in uncertain times. In this, I question how climate vulnerability becomes an object of discourse. I first contextualize the meaning of climate vulnerability within the contemporary representations of the environment as discussed by Bauman (2017) and Latour (2017). Second, I promote the relevance of cultural political economy to enlighten meaning-making processes surrounding climate hazards. I follow scholarly works that elicit the impact of culture onto governance processes (Jessop and Oosterlynck, 2008; Jessop and Sum, 2016). Using such a perspective, I emphasize climate vulnerability through the lens of a stabilized regime of expectations (Jessop, 2010, 2012, 2014). Third, and lastly, I elaborate on the importance of social classes for the cultural production surrounding anthropogenic climate events. In this, I hope to highlight how climate injustices are also about who can maintain control over the predominant social imaginary of climate change. As I argue here, this dimension is essential to understand contemporary injustices.

SEARCHING FOR THE IMAGINATION OF CLIMATE HAZARDS

Contemporary societies are no doubt in desperate need of a place to "land". In a recent book, Latour (2017) heralds the loss of a shared planet as a frame of reference in public discourse. He argues that centuries of capitalist exploitation have inexorably lost the notion of a common land. But Latour is not the only one to question the state of the predominant social imaginary. In a parallel discussion, the late Zygmunt Bauman (2017) claimed that contemporary politics tends to be trapped within a nostalgic horizon. Thomas More's vision of a utopia, a place, a sovereign state, city, polis, or topos, where an ideal state of progress, wellbeing, and freedom could be achieved, supersedes today's retrotopia: places enacting privatized and individualized ideas of progress and wellbeing (Bauman, 2017). These locations rest on visions of places of the past—even if still mobilizing hopes of security and freedom as in More's utopia (Bauman, 2017:4–6). If retrotopia is as widespread as Bauman suggests, many of today's most potent political projects can only be based onto "retrotopian" parameters, reenacting built environments of the past such as those of the Thirty Glorious Years.

From this standpoint, climate vulnerability, although essential for climate mitigation and emergency response, appears as the sign of a flawed yet stubborn social imaginary of nature (Malm, 2018). It is also a social imaginary that enables climate vulnerability in its current sociocultural form. It corresponds to the narrative universe of scientific, media, or otherwise public discourses surrounding climate vulnerability. A social imaginary is a shared symbolic condition of possibility for individual and collective action (Angelo, 2015; Löw, 2013). On the one hand, climate vulnerability exists in part as a result of the inability of predominant culture to find common ground on a climate-ridden planet. On the other, it is coextensive of the use of past landmarks as the template for uncertain futures, which, in turn, can favor a withdrawal into one's own preexisting social and environmental privileges (Bauman, 2017:118–123).

Reading the late Zygmunt Bauman (2017), it does not seem a stretch under present circumstances to claim that the quest of reducing climate vulnerability often takes place in a retrotopian worldview. Certainly, vulnerability to climate hazards is a specific kind of risk in Beck's (1989) sociology: "a systematic way of dealing with hazards and insecurities induced by modernization itself. Risk, as opposed to older dangers, are consequences which relate to the threatening force of modernization and to its globalization of doubt" (21). At the end of the spectrum, "disasters" refer to hazards of a particularly disruptive scope (Arcaya et al., 2020:673). A common notion of hazards in sociology refers to an "ongoing environmental risk that has the potential to become a disaster" (Arcaya et al., 2020:673). Following a distributive view of climate injustice, individuals face "the probability of suffering the negative effects of hazards and disasters and the likelihood that some groups will be less able than others to navigate the recovery process successfully" (Arcaya et al., 2020:673). However, "risk", "hazards", and "vulnerability" are tied to the composite layering of scientific, expertise-based, political, and community-based assessments (Bankoff, 2003; Dawson, 2017). Thus, these notions exist amidst specific social imaginaries, unevenly appropriated by local communities.

From a retrotopian standpoint, the mitigation of climate vulnerability appears at the advantage of privileged individuals and communities. After all, although essential for scientific and public intervention purposes, the notions of climate hazards and vulnerability are in part the offspring of a legacy of colonialism and global capitalism (Bankoff, 2003; Bankoff et al., 2012; Ford et al., 2018). At first, the notion of hazard became a reified category of domination through a historical process of making the world unsafe, especially in the colonies. It naturalizes onto the oppressed the dangers that the West exported onto them (Bankoff, 2003). Of course, contemporary climate vulnerability is a socio-historical construct possessing various meanings in local contexts (Jessop and Oosterlynck, 2008). But the discursive construction of hazardous environments tends to transform them into scientifically assessed danger zones or ecologies of fear nonetheless (Davis, 1998; Ross, 2011; Swyngedouw, 2010:217). The present state of climate racism and climate apartheid—a governance regime that abandons the world's poorest to their endangerment or their bare survival (Harlan et al. 2015:146)—suggests that we have passed beyond risk and entered a world-system-governed destruction where First World elites have the upper hand (Nixon, 2013).

One could argue that the environments of the climate-privileged embody a privatized retrotopia (Bauman, 2017; Harlow et al., 2013). Such environments largely correspond to those of the Global North, who will suffer less from climate hazards and who can benefit from "sustainable" lifestyles. Indeed, evidence from various scholarly traditions points to a structure of injustice that does not ultimately vanquish climate injustices for good. The production of privatized sustainability-labeled environments and social practices conceal many equity issues (Agyeman and Evans, 2004; Champagne, 2020). Such "sustainable" practices enact a sense of moral acceptability and of environmental empowerment for the privileged (Huddart Kennedy and Givens, 2019; Pelling, 2003; Pelling and Garschagen, 2019; United Nations, 2019; Wachsmuth et al., 2016). The overall response to climate vulnerability and disasters tends to be largely at the advantage of the privileged.

The urgent need for a viable relationship with a rapidly changing environment is undisputable to avoid the more extreme specter of climate apartheid (Dawson, 2017; Pelling and Garschagen, 2019; United Nations, 2019; Wachsmuth et al., 2016). Assessments of climate vulnerability are an important tool in this sense, but from the standpoint of the ruling social imaginary, climate vulnerability is arguably integral to what Bauman (2017) referred to as retrotopia. Keeping this in mind, although essential in capturing climate injustice (Curran, 2018), a "distributive" definition of climate justice—focusing on the uneven distribution of social, economic, cultural resources—looks incomplete. Why? Because it dispenses with "structural or systemic phenomena which exclude[s] people from participating in determining their actions or the conditions of their actions" (Young, 1990:53). Therefore, a crucial dimension of climate-related injustices is how governing bodies and local communities elaborate meaning-making responses about disasters (Auyero and Swistun, 2009; Bankoff, 2003; Bankoff et al., 2012; Erikson, 1994; Piper and Szabo-Jones, 2015). Unless we document these processes, our understanding of climate injustice remains partial.

CLIMATE VULNERABILITY IN A RETROTOPIAN WORLD

In a recent discussion on the governance of the COVID pandemic, Latour (2020) suggested there exists no equivalent to what we conventionally associate with a biopolitics when it comes to environmental or climate hazards. Biopolitics refers to an administration possessing the sole legitimate right and authority to rule over life and wellbeing. The state apparatus takes charge of the investigation, control, domination, and discipline of life. It endeavors to transform nature into "legible" ontologies (Scott, 1998:11–18). In contrast, the ecological crisis is a new terrain of biopolitics (Collier and Lakoff, 2014). Despite arguably not constituting a biopolitics in the more conventional sense, urban sustainability governance is undoubtedly a form of politics of climate change (Bulkeley, 2013; Champagne, 2020; Hughes, 2019; Vanolo, 2014; Vojnovic, 2014). Although variegated and evolving, a conjuncture of social actors produces a stabilized cultural understanding of environmental hazards across the population (Jessop, 2010).

How can we integrate climate hazards in the governing social imagination? Although Latour (1991, 2017) delivers thought-provoking insights in that direction, the integration of those many hazards into an integrated view of the earth is not his cardinal focus. With his notion of the "terrestrial", Latour (2017) promotes an epistemological space where he hopes to ground a sustainable relation with nature. This space would surpass the nature–society binary, integrating human and non-human natural agencies altogether. But what of climate hazards? Climate change increasingly populates environments with unforeseen, incremental, and irreversible hazards. We need not adapt to a fixed state of the terrestrial, but rather to an environment that is progressively discovered and evolving.

Coalitions of institutions, communities, and individuals must manage this conundrum. In this, they display an uneven ability to mobilize scientific, emergency, or state knowledge (Beck, 1989). Despite the promise of a perspective more in line with what Latour calls the "terrestrial", the global trajectory of climate mitigation and adaptation seems to support a retrotopian adaptation to climate change (Bauman, 2017; Swyngedouw, 2021). The "terrestrial" is a political agent comprising the earth and all of its living beings as acting agencies. Human, non-human natures, and hybrids are all part of a renewed parliamentary constitution, a Parliament of Things (Latour, 1991:142–144, 2017:49–52). Considerable hurdles nonetheless hinder this somewhat idyllic vision. Latour argues that governing elites are developing a "planet" of their own—in the epistemological and in the cultural acceptation of the word—by transforming hegemonic terms for their own purposes. These notions include the earth, soil, planet, environment, and related terms of state regulations: the public, justice, equitable, truth, democratic, and so forth (Latour, 2017:37–38). According to Latour, ruling elites use these terms as a form of environmental injustice directed towards the so-called Third World within the confines of post-WWII consumption society. In this reading, those in power can benefit from mobilizing these terms even though no existing world or land corresponds to what their ideology depicts.

In this situation, how can such a retrotopian social imaginary become a means of injustice? This is where cultural political economy can be insightful. Over the past three decades, numerous scholars have worked towards the integration of the cultural turn into heterodox political economy. Bob Jessop and his collaborators are prominent voices among them (Jessop, 2010, 2012, 2014; Jessop and Oosterlynck, 2008; Jessop and Sum, 2016). Cultural political economists analyze the forces implicated in the social construction of hegemony, how semiotic and extra-semiotic elements are interdependent and co-evolve in the making of a hegemony. In sum, it is a work of denaturalizing political economic imaginaries using critical discourse analysis (Jessop, 2010:336–337). Cultural political economy provides a heuristic vocabulary tied to the political economy of the environment: the control over the means of producing and regulating the social and environmental livelihood of communities (Rudel et al., 2011:222). This encourages scholars to link a layperson's vernacular classifications of climate hazards to those promoted by governing bodies. Many perspectives do not particularly uncover the meaning of climate vulnerability in the worldviews of communities (Ford et al., 2018). As Jessop puts it, it involves "semiotic systems that frame individual subjects' lived experience of an inordinately complex world and/or inform collective calculation about that world" (Jessop, 2010:344). In order to link cultural production to political–economic processes it seems relevant to document emerging patterns of meaning surrounding climate hazards. This semantic production is part of a stabilized regime of meaning implicating conflicts and uneven voices (Jessop and Oosterlynck, 2008; Löw, 2013).

This underlines a struggle over governance and scientific notions related to climate risks (Latour, 2017:37–38). Elite groups' agencies, media, firms, industries, develop an alternative reality-denying worldview with alternative "facts", departing from all forms of rationality (Latour, 2017:38). Follow Latour's essay, the legitimization of alternative realities encourages each and every one to undermine the opinion of the other, while simultaneously one's own opinion becomes all the more partial. The denialist ideology puts itself outside of worldly constraints. It becomes an instrument for the destruction of what it alienates us from; the earth, the soil, nature, the environment (Latour, 2017:58).

Throughout this cultural context, climate vulnerability takes different discursive forms, many of which do not always recognize the anthropogenic dimension of climate change (Cutter et al., 2003; Cutter and Emrich, 2006; Tierney, 2019). Understood within Latour's (2017) fourfold typology of how governing bodies envision nature, state dealings with climate vulnerability often privilege market-based or technological solutions. The four attractors of Latour's typology include the globalist economic imperative, with its modernist imperatives in favor of globalized economic growth and technological solutions to structural problems; the localist imperatives with its anti-modernist, degrowth, and anti-globalization focus; the out-of-this-world perspective, with its denialist stance towards nature; or lastly the terrestrial, that is to say, a rediscovery and tentative reinscription of the agency of the earth into predominant ways of dealing with nature (Latour 2017:60). If we identify with progress and the global, we identify with an unviable, unsustainable worldview. If we identify with the local, we identify with the backward, the old, the passé, until its disintegration by the forces of modernization.

It may seem unlikely that capitalist or state governing bodies would adopt a "terrestrial" view of nature and climate hazards, insofar as this usually appears contrary to the requirements of capital accumulation (Latour, 2017:68; Molotch, 1976; Moore, 2015). Still, the potential remains to integrate climate hazards as a broader target of politics rather than as an object of emergency regulations. After all, state agencies work to make nature and environments legible, easily administered, and subjected to discipline and control (Scott 1998:54–55). If modern institutions and expertise have tamed human and non-human natures and individuals, managing hazards and risks is also integral to the normal forms of government (Collier and Lakoff, 2014).

In any case, Latour's fourfold typology elicits the ways in which institutions and individuals instrumentalize nature and hazards as objects of injustices (Clapp and Dauvergne, 2005; Jessop, 2010). Between these worldviews, knowledge and political claims between governments, types of expertise and of localities produce uneven climate injustices (Swyngedouw, 2021). As climate events become the new normal, it remains to be seen how dominant cultural understandings of nature can integrate hazards as well.

STABILIZING CLIMATES THROUGH SOCIAL CLASSES

In contrast to a focus on the distributive outcomes of climate vulnerability, I emphasize that retrotopia is a notable cultural force of climate injustice. In other words, a privileged experience of climate vulnerability is not only encapsulated by one's ability to enjoy a climate hazard-free environment. Individuals and communities' wherewithal to appropriate a retrotopian worldview is also a phenomenon that merits attention in its own right.

Throughout the stabilization of this "apocalypse forever" (Swyngedouw, 2010, 2021) as a justification for capital accumulation (Jessop and Oosterlynck, 2008), scholars suggest that the perception of climate change is a function of social class differences. However, this claim calls for additional scrutiny. For one, if social classes are still differentiators of climate vulnerability and perception (Curran, 2018), it is also essential to adopt an intersectional conception of injustice able to encompass gender, race, environments, and more, as multiple forms of oppression that traverse social classes and often beyond (Collins, 2000:18; Harlan et al., 2015; Krange et al., 2019). Furthermore, it is in part as a response to state disinvestment from climate affairs that local communities and governance bodies are encouraged to produce climate solutions (Swyngedouw, 2010). As Boltanski and Chiapello (2005) discuss, neoliberal times bear the mark of public sector downsizing and are a key ingredient to the making of "projective" cities. In such cities, individuals, local communities, and municipal bodies are called forth to make and support the city with their own innovative projects. The prevailing economic development is predicated upon an imperative for self-responsibilization (Brenner et al., 2010:334). In light of this, climate mitigation appears as a performative activity in neoliberal times.

That said, in capturing how the mitigation of climate vulnerability creates additional injustices, a recurring argument is that risk amplifies the differentiation of class positions (Beck, 1989:36; Curran, 2018). With growing climate risks, inequalities of income and wealth would then weigh greater onto an individual's life chances (Curran 2013, 45). This statement is true of climate hazards for the greater part. In the sociological literature, those enjoying a wealthier lifestyle do not typically live in the same environment, including natural and social amenities, social services, and infrastructures, as the poorer (Pellow, 2002; Taylor, 2009). Broadly speaking, social scientists define social class as a permeable hierarchy of statuses, occupations, practices, and symbols, and the socially recognized possession of wealth including "consumer goods, incomes, educational opportunities, property" (Beck, 1989:26). A socio-economic strata tends to correlate to specific experiences and discourses about environmental privilege and hazards (Howell and Elliott, 2019).

But then, if research on environmental capital (Huddart Kennedy and Givens, 2019) and risk class (Curran, 2018) suggests that social classes encourage individuals to maximize their environmental privileges, they marginally integrate the meaning-making processes surrounding climate hazards, although this is a growing field of research. Environmental sociologists suggest that environmental concern—"about environmental problems and support for environmental protection" (Dunlap and York, 2008:533)—depends more on cultural capital than on economic capital. Even poorer and richer populations can express discursive commonalities, such as that of eco-powerlessness versus eco-habitus towards climate issues (Carfagna et al., 2014; Huddart Kennedy and Givens, 2019). One's "environmental capital" (Huddard-Kennedy and Givens, 2019) defines one's differentiated status based on environmental concerns in consumption. High status comes to be equated with being "green", "sustainable", and/or "ecological". One's eco-habitus is a system of embodied dispositions defining the association between high cultural capital and the consumption of sustainability-labeled products and lifestyles (Carfagna et al., 2014; Huddart Kennedy and Givens, 2019). Still, if this environmental capital is essentially tailored to consumption practices, it is nonetheless related to climate vulnerability as a key justification. This dimension, I would argue, calls for greater scholarly attention.

Certainly, an integrated hierarchy of cultural fields of practices can solidify a privileged experience of climate vulnerability within the realm of consumption and beyond. Privileges pertaining to one's physical environment are also coextensive of the cultural productions that communities engage in as they encounter climate disasters (Dawson 2017; Erikson, 1994; Krüger et al., 2015; Pelling, 2003). Furthermore, in the study of climate risks, one can expect that individuals have a varied risk position as a function of the uneven knowledge they possess about climate risk (Beck, 1989). In Bourdieu's classic rendition, dominant classes tend to hold the monopoly over the legitimate means of classifying people, environments, non-human natures, and so forth, monopolizing the more legitimate cultural practices from which many others are excluded (Bourdieu, 1984, 254, 291, 452). Taking on this broad hypothesis, I have discussed here whether one's ability to enjoy a climate hazard-free environment and to sustain a retrotopian worldview can entail a privileged experience of climate vulnerability.

CONCLUSION

In this chapter, I have questioned how a reified notion of climate vulnerability risks concealing key dimensions of today's climate injustices (Hulme, 2018). I discussed dilemmas pertaining to the cultural political economy of climate vulnerability in the context of the alleged collapse of the predominant social imagination (Bauman, 2017). This collapse appears under the label of the loss of a shared planet as a frame of reference (Latour, 2017), the rise of retrotopia (Bauman, 2017), and an apocalyptic imaginary of climate change in dominant discourse (Swyngedouw, 2010). As Swyngedouw (2010) argued, an apocalyptic imaginary forms the background of the prevailing rhetoric of climate change. However, contrary to traditional apocalyptic representations that could still bolster hopes for redemption, the environmental apocalypse is devoid of any affinity with good or evil (Swyngedouw, 2010:218–219). Although I engaged with broad cultural phenomena in this chapter, we must use concepts such as climate vulnerability and social imaginary with great caution. In no way do they replace the local, situated experiences of individuals (Smith, 1990:34).

This is why I promoted the role of culture in governance processes to question whether retrotopia became a prevailing perspective upon which politicians, policy experts, think tanks, and planners produce climate mitigation and adaptation strategies. I followed Bob Jessop's (2010) cultural political economy and discussed climate vulnerability as a key target of the post-2008 economic crisis recovery. In a context where considerable civic and scholarly work focuses on, and indeed often favors, greater climate mitigation and adaptation as a response to growing vulnerability, I encouraged an investigation of their underlying meaning-making processes spanning from local communities to governing bodies. Communities can develop a distinct, complex, and heterogenous culture about climate hazards throughout their own views, discourses, representations, and practices. This perspective aims to decipher conflict, solidarity, and resistance about concepts such as climate hazard vulnerability. Such a perspective appears essential to gain access to the local experiences of injustice. Vulnerability to climate hazards is not only an intricate component of inhabiting contemporary environments; it is also fashioned through prevailing cultural worldviews. Broadly speaking, I argued for the necessity to free ourselves from a retrotopian worldview if we are to find common ground about today's ever-growing climate vulnerability.

REFERENCES

Agyeman, J. and B. Evans (2004), "'Just sustainability': the emerging discourse of environmental justice in Britain?", *The Geographical Journal*, 170(2), 155–164.
Angelo, H. (2015), "How Green Became Good: Urban Greening as Social Improvement in Germany's Ruhr Valley", PhD Dissertation, New York University, September.
Arcaya, M., E.J. Raker, and M.C. Waters (2020), "The social consequences of disasters: individual and community change", *Annual Review of Sociology*, 46, 671–91.
Auyero, J. and D.A. Swistun (2009), *Flammable: Environmental Suffering in an Argentine Shantytown*, Oxford, UK: Oxford University Press.
Bauman, Z. (2017), *Retrotopia*, Cambridge, UK: Polity Press.
Beck, U. (1989), *Risk Society*, London, UK: Sage.
Beck, U. (2010), "Climate for change, or how to create a green modernity?", *Theory, Culture and Society*, 27(2–3), 254–266.
Beck, U. (2013), "Why 'class' is too soft a category to capture the explosiveness of social inequality at the beginning of the 21st century", *British Journal of Sociology*, 64(1), 63–74.
Bankoff, G. (2003), *Cultures of Disaster: Society and Natural Hazard in the Philippines*, London, UK: Routledge.
Bankoff, G., U. Lübken, and J. Sand (eds) (2012), *Flammable Cities: Urban Conflagration and the Making of the Modern World*, Madison, WI, USA: University of Wisconsin Press.
Boltanski, L. and E. Chiapello (2005), *The New Spirit of Capitalism*, London, UK: Verso.
Bourdieu, P. (1984), *Distinction*, Cambridge, MA, USA: Harvard University Press.
Brenner, N., J. Peck and N. Theodore (2010), "After neoliberalization?", *Globalizations*, 7(3), 327–345.
Bulkeley, H. (2013), *Cities and Climate Change*, New York, NY, USA: Routledge.
Carfagna, L.B., E.A. Dubois, C. Fitzmaurice, M.Y. Ouimette, J.B. Schor, M. Willis, and T. Laidley (2014), "An emerging eco-habitus: the reconfiguration of high cultural capital practices among ethical consumers", *Journal of Consumer Culture*, 14(2), 158–178.
Champagne, D. (2020), "Urban sustainability policies in neoliberal Canada: room for social equity?", *Current Sociology*, 68(6), 761–779.
Clapp, J. and P. Dauvergne (2005), *Paths to a Green World*, Cambridge, MA, USA: MIT Press.

Collier, S. and A. Lakoff (2014), "Vital systems security: reflexive biopolitics and the government of emergency", *Theory, Culture and Society*, 32(2), 19–51.

Collins, P.H (2000), *Black Feminist Thought*, New York, NY, USA and London, UK: Routledge.

Curran, D. (2013), "Risk society and the distribution of bads: theorizing class in the risk society", *The British Journal of Sociology*, 64(1), 44–62.

Curran, D. (2018), "Environmental justice meets risk-class: the relational distribution of environmental bads", *Antipode*, 50(2), 298–318.

Cutter, S.L. and C.T. Emrich (2006) "Moral hazard, social catastrophe: the changing face of vulnerability along the hurricane coasts", *The Annals of the American Academy of Political and Social Science*, 604(1), 102–112.

Cutter, S.L., B.J. Boruff, and S.W. Lynn (2003), "Social vulnerability to environmental hazards", *Social Science Quarterly*, 84(2), 242–261.

Davis, M. (1998), *Ecologies of Fear*, New York, NY, USA: Metropolitan Books.

Dawson, A. (2017), *Extreme Cities*, London, UK: Verso.

Dunlap, R.E. and R. York (2008), "The globalization of environmental concern and the limits of the postmaterialist values explanation: evidence from four multinational surveys", *The Sociological Quarterly*, 49(3), 529–563.

Erikson, K. (1994), *A New Species of Trouble: The Human Experience of Modern Disasters*, New York, NY, USA and London, UK: W. W. Norton & Company.

Ford, J.D., T. Pearce, G. McDowell, L. Berrang-Ford, J.S. Sayles, and E. Belfer (2018), "Vulnerability and its discontents: the past, present, and future of climate change vulnerability research", *Climatic Change*, 151, 189–203.

Harlan, S.L., D.N. Pellow, J.T. Roberts, S.E. Bell, W.G. Holt William, and J. Nagel (2015), "Climate Justice and Inequality", in Dunlap Riley and Brulle Robert (eds), *Climate Change and Society: Sociological Perspectives*, Oxford, UK: Oxford University Press, pp. 127–163.

Harlow, J., A. Golub, and B. Allenby (2013), "A review of utopian themes in sustainable development discourse", *Sustainable Development*, 21, 270–280.

Howell, J. and J.E. Elliott (2019), "Damages done: the longitudinal impacts of natural hazards on wealth inequality in the United States", *Social Problems*, 66, 448–467.

Huddart Kennedy, E. and J.E. Givens (2019), "Eco-habitus or eco-powerlessness? Examining environmental concern across social class", *Sociological Perspectives*, 62(5), 1–22.

Hughes, S. (2019), *Repowering Cities Governing Climate Change Mitigation in New York City, Los Angeles, and Toronto*, Ithaca, NY, USA: Cornell University Press.

Hulme, M. (2018), "Climatism and the reification of global temperature", mikehulme.org, 24 September, accessed May 2, 2021 at https://mikehulme.org/climatism-and-the-reification-of-global-temperature/.

Jessop, B. (2010), "Cultural political economy and critical policy studies", *Critical Policy Studies*, 3(3–4), 336–356.

Jessop, B. (2012), "Economic and ecological crises: green new deals and no-growth economies", *Development*, 55(1), 17–24.

Jessop, B. (2014), "A specter is haunting Europe: a neoliberal phantasmagoria", *Critical Policy Studies*, 8(3), 352–355.

Jessop, B. and S. Oosterlynck (2008), "Cultural political economy: on making the cultural turn without falling into soft economic sociology", *Geoforum*, 39, 1155–1169.

Jessop, B. and N.G. Sum (2016), "What is critical?", *Critical Policy Studies*, 10(1), 105–109.

Krange, O., B.P. Kaltenborn, and M. Hultman (2019), "Cool dudes in Norway: climate change denial among conservative Norwegian men", *Environmental Sociology*, 5(1), 1–11.

Krüger, F., G. Bankoff, T. Cannon, B. Orlowski and E.L. Schipper (eds) (2015), *Cultures and Disasters: Understanding Cultural Framings in Disaster Risk Reduction*, London, UK: Routledge.

Latour, B. (1991), *We Have Never Been Modern*, Cambridge, MA, USA: Harvard University Press.

Latour, B. (2017), *Down to Earth*, London, UK: Polity Press.

Latour, B. (2020), "Le surplus de subsistance: quel état peut imposer des 'gestes barrières' aux catastrophes écologiques?" *Esprit.presse.fr*, July/August, accessed June 1st 2020 at https://esprit.presse.fr/actualites/bruno-latour/le-surplus-de-subsistance-42765.

Löw, M. (2013), "The city as experiential space: the production of shared meaning", *International Journal of Urban and Regional Research*, 37(3), 894–908.

Malm, Andreas (2018), *The Progress of This Storm: Nature and Society in a Warming World*, London, UK: Verso.

Molotch, H. (1976), "The city as a growth machine: toward a political economy of place", *American Journal of Sociology*, 82(2), 309–332.

Moore, J.W. (2015), *Capitalism in the Web of Life*, New York, NY, USA: Verso.

Nixon, R. (2013), *Slow Violence and the Environmentalism of the Poor*, Cambridge, MA, USA: Harvard University Press.

Pelling, M. (2003), *The Vulnerability of Cities: Natural Disasters and Social Resilience*. London, UK: Earthscan Publications.

Pelling, M. and M. Garschagen (2019), "Put equity first in climate adaptation", *Nature*, 569(7756), 327–329.

Pellow, D.N.b (2002), *Garbage Wars: The Struggle for Environmental Justice in Chicago*, Cambridge, MA, USA: MIT Press.

Piper, L. and L. Szabo-Jones (eds) (2015), *Sustaining the West: Cultural Responses to Canadian Environments*, Waterloo, ON, Canada: Wilfrid Laurier University Press.

Ross, A. (2011), *Bird on Fire*, Oxford, UK and New York, NY, USA: Oxford University Press.

Rudel, T.K., R.J. Timmons, and J. Carmin (2011), "Political economy of the environment", *Annual Review of Sociology*, 37, 221–38.

Scott, J.C. (1998), *Seeing Like a State: How Certain Schemes to Improve the Human Condition Have Failed*, New Haven, CT, USA: Yale University Press.

Smith, D.E. (1990), *The Conceptual Practices of Power*, Toronto, ON, Canada: University of Toronto Press.

Swyngedouw, E. (2010), "Apocalypse forever? Post-political populism and the specter of climate change", *Theory, Culture & Society*, 27(2–3), 213–232.

Swyngedouw, E. (2021), "'The apocalypse is disappointing': the depoliticized deadlock of the climate change consensus", in Luigi Pellizzoni, Emanuele Leonardi, and Viviana Asara (eds), *Handbook of Critical Environmental Politics*, Cheltenham, UK and Northampton, MA, USA: Edward Elgar Publishing (forthcoming), available at: https://www.researchgate.net/publication/347559594_The _apocalypse_is_disappointing_The_Depoliticized_Deadlock_of_the_Climate_Change_Consensus (accessed February 23, 2021).

Taylor, D.E. (2009), *The Environment and the People in American Cities, 1600s–1900s: Disorder, Inequality and Social Change*, Durham, NC, USA: Duke University Press.

Tierney, K. (2019), *Disasters: A Sociological Perspective*, Cambridge, UK: Polity Press.

United Nations (2019), "World faces 'climate apartheid' risk, 120 more million in poverty: UN expert", *News.un.org*, 19 June, accessed June 30, 2020 at https://news.un.org/en/story/2019/06/1041261.

Vanolo, A. (2014), "Smartmentality: the city as disciplinary strategy", *Urban Studies*, 51(5), 883–898.

Vojnovic, I. (2014), "Urban sustainability: research, politics, policy and practice", *Cities*, 41, S30–S44.

Wachsmuth, D., D. Cohen, and H. Angelo (2016), "Expand the frontiers of urban sustainability", *Nature*, 536(7617), 391–393.

Young, I.M. (1990), *Justice and the Politics of Difference*, Princeton, NJ, USA: Princeton University Press.

Index

Printed and bound by CPI Group (UK) Ltd, Croydon, CR0 4YY

16/04/2025

14658396-0001